Intoxicating Pleasures

CALIFORNIA STUDIES IN FOOD AND CULTURE
Darra Goldstein, Editor

Intoxicating Pleasures

The Reinvention of Wine, Beer, and
Whiskey after Prohibition

Lisa Jacobson

UNIVERSITY OF CALIFORNIA PRESS

The publisher and the University of California Press Foundation gratefully acknowledge the generous support of the Peter Booth Wiley Endowment Fund in History.

University of California Press
Oakland, California

© 2024 by Lisa Jacobson

Library of Congress Cataloging-in-Publication Data

Names: Jacobson, Lisa, author.
Title: Intoxicating pleasures : the reinvention of wine, beer, and whiskey after prohibition / Lisa Jacobson.
Other titles: California studies in food and culture ; 83.
Description: Oakland, California : University of California Press, [2024] | Series: California studies in food and culture ; 83 | Includes bibliographical references and index.
Identifiers: LCCN 2024008383 | ISBN 9780520401099 (hardback) | ISBN 9780520401105 (paperback) | ISBN 9780520401112 (ebook)
Subjects: LCSH: Alcoholic beverages—Social aspects—United States. | Alcoholic beverage industry—Social aspects—United States. | Drinking of alcoholic beverages—United States. | Prohibition—United States—History.
Classification: LCC HD9355 .J35 2024 | DDC 394.1/3097309043—dc23/eng/20240613
LC record available at https://lccn.loc.gov/2024008383

33 32 31 30 29 28 27 26 25 24
10 9 8 7 6 5 4 3 2 1

For John and Sam

Contents

List of Illustrations   ix
Acknowledgments   xi

Introduction   1

PART ONE. CHARTING ALCOHOL'S PATH TO REDEMPTION

1 The Potent Politics of Weak Brews   15
2 A New Deal for Alcohol?   41
3 Fermented Beverages and the Gospel of Moderation   73
4 Spiritous Beverages and the Muddled Meanings of Moderation   105

PART TWO. THE POLITICS OF PLEASURE

5 Beer Goes to War   141
6 Whiskey, Weapons, and the Wartime State   171
7 Wine and Culinary Innovation on the Kitchen Front   201
8 Rank Privilege: The Politics of Intoxicating Pleasures in
   the US Military   236

Epilogue: The Power and Limits of Reinvention   274

Abbreviations   285
Notes   287
Bibliography   339
Index   367

Illustrations

1. Parade marchers demand "Beer for Taxation," New York City, March, 14, 1932 / *16*
2. Beer delivery in Cleveland, Ohio, April 6, 1933 / *38*
3. Interior of state-run liquor store in Welch, West Virginia, c. 1940s / *65*
4. Cartoon distributed by Renault & Sons, East Coast bottlers of California wines, 1937 / *87*
5. Anti-prohibition trade card distributed by a Detroit brewer, 1883 / *100*
6. Advertisement from Seagram's moderation campaign, 1937 / *114*
7. Seagram's Crown Blended Whiskies magazine advertisement, 1937 / *124*
8. Calvert's "Special Reserve" Blended Whiskey advertisement, 1937 / *127*
9. Calvert Blended Whiskey magazine advertisement, 1940 / *129*
10. Brewing Industry Foundation magazine advertisement, 1944 / *142*
11. Brewing Industry Foundation magazine advertisement, 1943 / *152*
12. Brewing Industry Foundation magazine advertisement, 1945 / *157*
13. "Brewing Is an Essential Food Industry," *Modern Brewery Age*, April 1942 / *163*

14. "Brewers' Yeast in Industrial Nutrition," *Modern Brewery Age,* September 1942 / *165*
15. Macy's Department Store, Manhattan, New York, c. 1942 / *172*
16. Old St. Croix Rum magazine advertisement, 1943 / *176*
17. "A Cocktail for the Axis," illustration from *Volunteer for Victory: The Story of How a Great Industry Enlisted for War,* 1943 / *189*
18. G & W Five Star Whiskey magazine advertisement, *Wine and Liquor Retailer,* 1943 / *193*
19. Wine Advisory Board magazine advertisement, 1939 / *210*
20. Wine Advisory Board magazine advertisement, 1940 / *211*
21. Wine Advisory Board magazine advertisement, 1943 / *222*
22. US Navy Seabees drink 3.2 percent beer at a rest camp in the South Pacific / *237*
23. Brewing Industry Foundation magazine advertisement, 1944 / *240*
24. Sicilian policeman offers a jug of wine to a US infantryman, 1943 / *248*
25. Bill Mauldin cartoon, *Stars and Stripes* (Mediterranean edition), February 22, 1944 / *256*
26. Bill Mauldin cartoon, *Stars and Stripes* (Mediterranean edition), January 11, 1944 / *257*
27. Wine cartoon by Michael Berry, *Collier's,* 1944 / *270*
28. Men at a US naval base in Manila with four beer cans each, August 15, 1945 / *271*

Acknowledgments

In the years that I have worked on *Intoxicating Pleasures*—more years than I care to admit—I have accumulated many debts to colleagues, friends, and family who contributed to the book's creation. In hindsight, the tiniest seeds of the book were sown in the late 1980s—before I started graduate school at UCLA and nearly two decades before I began researching this book in earnest. I likely would have never come to study alcohol's history had it not been for Ruth Teiser, a writer and oral historian who interviewed dozens of California winemakers and wine advocates for the Regional Oral History Office at UC Berkeley's Bancroft Library. As her student and collaborator, I learned from a master of the oral history craft and acquired an enduring curiosity about the ways businesses spur social change, interpret cultural trends (rightly and wrongly), and cultivate distinctive identities to accrue political advantage.

Like all authors, I owe some of my deepest intellectual debts to the scholars whose names line the footnotes of this book and whose ideas and critical insights helped frame my questions and arguments. My foray into the interdisciplinary world of food studies was enriched by my participation in the University of California's Multicampus Research Program on Food and the Body, led by Julie Guthman, Melissa Caldwell, Charlotte Biltekoff, Carolyn de la Peña, and Erika Rappaport. On the long car rides to the Food and the Body workshops, Erika and I enjoyed numerous enlightening and entertaining conversations about food and food history, politics, and family. Her feedback on my research has been invaluable and our most significant collaboration—developing a Food in World History course at UCSB—has also shaped this book.

This book has benefitted enormously from the astute observations and insightful comments of several UCSB colleagues who read chapter drafts workshopped at the Gender and Sexualities Colloquium and the History and Political Economy Colloquium. Laura Kalman deserves special thanks for her careful reading of several whiskey chapters and her enthusiastic support. When I thought I was about three-quarters of the way finished—and somewhat appalled by the mounting page count—Sherene Seikaly convinced me that I was trying to write two books at once. Although my husband, John Majewski, had been telling me something similar for years, Sherene's advice came at a point when I could better appreciate that World War II provided a satisfying conclusion to a narrative. Serving as a guest discussant in graduate seminars led by Alice O'Connor and Salim Yaqub helped me clarify key ideas. The Business History Conference has been an important home for presenting work in progress and I owe special thanks to many who have commented on papers, including Mark Wilson, Patrick Fridenson, Tracey Deutsch, Shane Hamilton, Teresa da Silva Lopes, Traci Parks, K. Austin Kerr, and Alfred Reckendrees. The Society for the History of Alcohol and Drugs has provided an engaged community of scholars and I am especially grateful for the comments I have received from David Herzberg, Dan Malleck, and Scott Martin. I have also received insightful feedback from James Lapsley, Krishnendu Ray, Jeffrey Charles, Steven Elliott, and the terrific audience at the Society for Military Historians. Over the years my work has been enriched by conversations with Pamela Laird, Phil Scranton, Ken Lipartito, Roger Horowitz, Amy Bentley, Regina Blaszczyk, and Ken Mouré. I would also like to thank Megan Elias, Stephan Miescher, and France Winddance Twine for their enthusiastic support of this project.

Several UCSB graduate students also made substantive contributions to the book. Nicole de Silva and Susan Falck offered insightful comments on an early chapter draft. Sarah Dunne was remarkably resourceful in identifying primary sources and highlighting relevant passages from memoirs and military newspapers. Brian Griffith, who studies the Italian wine industry, generously shared and translated useful primary sources that he unearthed during his archival research. Stephanie and Mark Seketa helped me acquire a deeper grasp of the distinctive sensory appeals of bourbons and blended whiskeys by leading me through a tasting of classic brands. Makoto Hunter took great care in preparing the bibliography, correcting and shortening footnotes, and reviewing the entire manuscript for clarity and consistency.

My research was facilitated by funding from UCSB's Interdisciplinary Humanities Center, a Regents Humanities Faculty Fellowship, the Hagley Museum and Library, and the UC Humanities Network and Mellon Foundation's Changing Conceptions of Work grant. I am grateful for the assistance of several librarians and archivists at the New York Public Library, the John W. Hartman Center for Sales, Advertising, and Market History at Duke University, the Franklin Delano Roosevelt Presidential Library, the National Archives, and the Library of Congress. Special thanks go to Lynn Catanese and Jon Williams at the Hagley Library; Gina Nichols of the Port Hueneme Navy Seabees Museum, who helped me locate the original copy of a key photograph; Tom McAnear at the National Archives in College Park for helping me track down missing citation data; and Kenley Brinton at Fantagraphics Books, Julia Masnik at Watkins/Loomis, and Emma Halm at the Billy Ireland Cartoon Library and Museum, who provided key leads that helped me to identify copyright holders.

One of the joys and hazards of doing research on twentieth-century topics is the abundance of archival and published primary source material. I benefited from the invaluable research assistance of several graduate and undergraduate students who tracked down sources, perused magazine ads, identified key passages in newspapers, memoirs, and community studies, and made scans and photocopies. Many thanks to Allison Fischer, Benjamin Schwartz, Samuel Majewski, Brittany Bounds, Andrea Thabet, and Sasha Coles for their help in these regards.

This book has also benefited from the astute editors and peer reviewers of three academic journals in which portions of this work have previously appeared. Chapter 3 reprints portions of "Will It Be Wine or Cocktails? The Quest to Build a Mass Market for California Wine after Prohibition," *Enterprise and Society* 18 (June 2017): 360–399. Some sections of chapter 4 appeared in "Navigating the Boundaries of Respectability and Desire: Seagram's Advertising and the Meanings of Moderation after Repeal," *The Social History of Alcohol and Drugs: An Interdisciplinary Journal* 26 (Summer 2012): 122–146. Much of chapter 5 originally appeared as the article "Beer Goes to War: The Politics of Beer Promotion and Production in the Second World War," *Food, Culture and Society* 12 (September 2009), 275–312.

Finally, this book would never have crossed the finish line without the thoughtful comments of peer reviewers for the University of

California Press and the help of Nora Becker, Niels Hooper, Darra Goldstein, Lynda Crawford, Jessica Moll, and the production team at the press. The anonymous reviewers helped me see where I could profitably trim the book to improve the pacing and sharpen the arguments. I am especially grateful to Pamela Pennock and Vicki Howard for their generous comments, helpful suggestions, and astute readings of the manuscript. Nora Becker promptly answered dozens of questions about securing copyright permissions and graciously nudged me (as needed) to keep me on track. Niels Hooper offered encouraging words and helped me to prioritize the most essential revisions. Special thanks to Michelle Black for designing an alluring book cover.

I am grateful for the love and encouragement of my family and the many conversations we have enjoyed over glasses of wine and bourbon-infused desserts. My sisters, Melanie and Karen Jacobson, my brothers-in-law, Jim Pearson and Jerry Schwartz, and my nephews Aarron and Benjamin Schwartz periodically inquired about the book but also intuited when not to ask. My parents, Vivienne and Charles Jacobson, died before they could see the book in print, and I am thankful to both for passing down their love of good food, good wine, and the pleasures of the palate. My wine connoisseur father, who particularly enjoyed quirky tales from the archives, first learned about wine in a course offered to UC San Francisco medical students—a course that by virtue of its regular place in the curriculum furthered the process of wine's cultural reinvention.

My deepest gratitude goes to my husband, John Majewski, who helped me in countless ways, from critiquing drafts and listening to half-formed ideas to keeping Maverick, our beloved German Shepherd, entertained when I was immersed in writing—though at times Maverick's persistent attempts to liberate me from the keyboard was just what I needed. My most trusted reader, John was always the first to see a completed draft and the first to help me sharpen my argument and tighten my prose. He was always game for combining vacations with writing retreats, and his enthusiasm for the project kept me going. My son Sam grew up with this project and cheered me on in the book's final stages of completion. It is to John and Sam that I dedicate this book.

Introduction

History is replete with instances of troublesome commodities that have undergone dramatic cultural reinventions. The changing public image of alcoholic beverages is a prime example. After the industrial revolution, many societies that had once regarded wine and beer as aides to health, wellness, and sociability came to view them instead as propagators of moral corruption and social ills. By the late nineteenth and early twentieth centuries, prohibitionists had so successfully villainized alcohol in all its forms that many used the same moniker—Demon Rum—to refer to wine, beer, and spirits, despite their varied potencies and uses. Cocaine followed a similar downward reputational spiral. Initially embraced in the 1890s as a "medical marvel," cocaine achieved mass popularity as the not-so-secret ingredient that refreshed and energized drinkers of Coca-Cola (until the firm substituted caffeine for cocaine in 1903). Cocaine's halo quickly faded, however, as its use spread from physicians' white, middle-class patients to Southern Black dockworkers, factory hands, and prostitutes in the urban underworld. Within a span of two decades, cocaine's journey from "medical marvel" to "social menace" was complete.[1]

We know much about the complex processes that transformed widely accepted psychoactive substances into demons or heavily regulated outcasts. Growing awareness of their social harms, their incompatibility with industrial efficiency and mechanization, and their increasing use by disliked or "deviant" groups sparked international crusades to ban or strictly regulate their use. Although ridiculed by their critics as puritanical killjoys, many anti-alcohol crusaders cast their mission as righteous and progressive. They sought to protect women and children from abusive men who squandered the family's meager income at the saloon. They aimed to defeat the "liquor traffickers" who preyed on the oppressed and held politicians captive to their interests. They railed against profit-maximizing saloonkeepers who indulged excessive drinking and permitted prostitution and gambling on their premises. In the United States, white, middle-class Baptists and Methodists formed the core of the anti-alcohol movement and women served as its foot soldiers. But the prohibitionist cause also attracted support from African Americans, Native Americans, and some working-class groups. The diverse coalition that helped to ratify the Eighteenth Amendment banning alcohol included critics of predatory capitalism as well as anti-democratic, Christian nationalists who sought to impose their morality on an increasingly diverse populace.[2] The masterful propagandists among them created powerful narratives that the alcoholic beverage industry would endeavor to counter long after disenchantment with national Prohibition had set in.

Intoxicating Pleasures tells the story of how wine, beer, and whiskey shed their stigmatized pasts and became emblems of the American good life by the middle decades of the twentieth century. Alcohol's path to mainstream respectability was not as smooth as historians and popular culture have led us to believe.[3] In the most conventional telling, Prohibition's downfall signaled alcohol's decisive victory in a decades-long culture war that pitted pluralistic values and permissive social norms against outdated Victorian moralities and ineffective methods of social control. This, in essence, was the story that the cultural moderns of the 1920s told about themselves.[4] During the ostensibly dry decade of the 1920s, a "revolution in morals and manners" loosened middle-class sexual restraints, expanded new gender freedoms, and fueled the widespread social nullification of Prohibition in major metropoles and smaller cities. Women who had once shunned drinking in public now drank alongside men in nightclubs and speakeasies.[5] More rebellious still were the drinking men and women who pursued same-sex desires in gay and lesbian bars or transgressed the sexual color line in racially integrated "Black and Tan" clubs.[6] Drinking in private, while still legal, also acquired greater social cachet. As Frederick Lewis Allen, one of Prohibition's earliest chroniclers, recounted, no "fashionable dinner party" was complete without the obligatory service of "contraband cocktails."[7]

These social and cultural transformations, as the conventional story goes, paved the way for alcohol's rapid normalization after repeal. In historian John Burnham's exaggerated account, alcoholic beverage producers may have imagined themselves as an embattled industry, but they pulled all the strings. The industry's economic resources and media savvy and the government's dependence on alcohol revenues propelled "the alcoholic-beverage business to sudden respectability."[8] Another historian, noting the ubiquity of alcohol advertising and Hollywood's glamorous portrayal of drinking, characterized the acceptance of alcohol in "mainstream middle-class American culture" as "almost effortless."[9] The images of Prohibition-defying revelers that dominate TV and movie screens to this day helped to solidify the common assumption that alcohol's post-repeal normalization was all but assured.[10]

The conventional narrative also perpetuated the myth that Prohibition's demise successfully ushered alcohol off the political stage. Once the Twenty-First Amendment rescinding Prohibition returned alcohol regulation to the states, the story goes, the federal government washed its hands of the alcohol question to focus on the weightier political matters of the Great Depression, the rise of fascism abroad, and World War II.[11] Determined to protect robust liquor revenues and avoid "reviving the wet-dry wars," the federal government did its best to keep the alcohol question at bay.[12] Others contend that the ascendancy of the "alcoholism as disease" paradigm further diminished alcohol's potency as a political issue by shifting blame for problem drinking from a predatory industry or sinful society to psychologically damaged individuals.[13] Even historians who highlight Prohibition's enduring imprint on the state and the penal system contend that repeal brought the decades-long War on Alcohol to a conclusive end. In Lisa McGirr's masterful account, the surveillance state that Prohibition created persisted, but it quickly shifted its gaze from alcohol to ostensibly more nefarious drugs.[14]

Instead of viewing repeal as the culmination of a century-long battle over alcohol, *Intoxicating Pleasures* positions repeal as the opening chapter of a new set of cultural and political contestations over the place of pleasure in modern American life. Beginning with the campaign to repeal Prohibition, this study examines how alcoholic beverage producers, industry trade associations, and self-styled drinking reformers reframed the moral parameters of debate by asking not how societies should eradicate vice but rather how they could most effectively regulate and accommodate intoxicating pleasures. It adds to ongoing conversations about how communities endow commodities with new symbolic meanings, how food and drink become emblems of national and group identities, and how different societies come to embrace previously stigmatized and foreign commodities as their own.[15] Alcohol's cultural reinvention occurred against the backdrop of the Great Depression and World War II—two major global crises that profoundly shaped alcohol's path to redemption and respectability. Rather than seeking to depoliticize alcohol, trade associations, mass marketers, and a host of other intermediaries connected wine, beer, and whiskey to economic recovery, national identity, and wartime food crusades. In so doing, they put new visions of pleasure at the center of broader debates about the rights and obligations of citizens and the proper boundaries of state power.

Intoxicating Pleasures also revises conventional narratives that position liberalism and pluralistic values as the clear-cut victors in the culture wars that ended Prohibition and catapulted the alcoholic-beverage industry to "sudden respectability."[16] Alcohol's journey to respectability was neither sudden nor assured. The federalized system of liquor control, which returned responsibility for alcohol regulation to the states, left one in six Americans living in states or counties that prohibited alcohol.[17] Only four states—Arizona, California, Indiana, Wyoming—and the District of Columbia permitted "the maximum wetness," allowing sale by the drink for consumption on premises and sale by the bottle (or case) for consumption off premises. In many states where "damps" and "drys" exerted significant influence, the new alcoholic beverages controls continued to treat alcohol as morally suspect and gave alcohol enforcement agencies broad authority to police transgressive behavior unconnected to public drunkenness. Even the cultural moderns who rejected Prohibition endorsed new (and sometimes more subtle) modes of disciplining consumer appetites and bodily desires.[18] "Rather than initiating a new era of laissez-faire tolerance in urban life," historian George Chauncey has argued, "Repeal inaugurated a more pervasive and more effective regime of surveillance and control."[19] The working-class men who ordered up a round, the women who took their place at the bar (or heaven forbid, behind the bar), the gay men and lesbians who gathered in neighborhood bars, and the tavernkeepers who screened their interiors from public view all remained fraught symbols of alcohol's potential to unleash social and sexual chaos.

The conventional interpretation of alcohol's quick and decisive victory in the culture wars is also flawed because it disconnects alcohol's cultural reinvention from narratives of reform.[20] The impulse to reform

American drinking habits not only drove the crusade to repeal Prohibition, but it also survived its downfall.[21] A wide variety of groups—from brewers and vintners to New Deal policymakers, government regulators, and food and drink columnists—welcomed alcohol as an adjunct to the good life but rejected a return to the saloon and the unbridled drinking freedoms of the Jazz Age. Although the new self-styled drinking reformers envisioned a larger role for alcohol in American leisure, they carefully cast themselves as third way between the old cultures of wet indulgence and dry abstention. They shunned Prohibition as an ineffective and overly intrusive state intervention, but they sanctioned subtler forms of consumer surveillance, maintained by the force of social pressure, the regulatory state, or the civilizing presence of women drinkers. They hoped that imposing greater restrictions and higher taxes on spirits would wean Americans from their liquor-loving ways and transform the United States into a republic of temperate wine and beer drinkers. They looked less to the nation's past for models than to the French and Italian customs of drinking wine with meals and the family-friendly beer gardens of Germany. At the same time, they endeavored to Americanize moderate drinking by associating alcohol with whiteness and class respectability.

Telling the story of alcohol's cultural reinvention requires a large cast of characters. Winemakers, brewers, and distillers developed different strategies to elevate alcohol's respectability and expand its mass market appeal. Trade association directors and the experts they hired to craft advertising and public relations campaigns sometimes worked as hard to win over their clients as they did to win over new consumers. Restaurateurs, alcohol retailers, and tavernkeepers did their part to amplify industry messaging, but these allied trades could also undermine the carefully cultivated public image that trade associations sought to promote. An even broader array of tastemakers—from cookbook authors and home economists to magazine columnists, novelists, and writers of drinking guidebooks—sought to teach Americans how to incorporate alcohol into domestic hospitality and gracious living. Some home economists found their way into the alcoholic beverage industry's employ, while other tastemakers incorporated publicity material supplied by trade associations into their cookbooks, novels, and magazine columns. By no means did such broad coordination guarantee success. Some campaigns backfired or fell flat. Trade associations struggled to maintain unity among their own ranks when the pursuit of moral redemption appeared to undercut the pursuit of profits.

The vast alcohol publicity machine would not have labored so incessantly if the older stigmas that clung to wine, beer, and whiskey had easily melted away.[22] New mythologies about intoxicating beverages had to be created and mobilized to counter the old mythologies that had justified their prohibition. Beer and whiskey had to be redeemed from the disrepute of the saloon. Wine had to be rescued from its foreign associations with both immigrant drinking traditions and elite connoisseurship. Trade barriers that barred liquor from restaurant menus and kept wine and beer off grocery shelves had to be dismantled. And none of these obstacles could be removed without winning women to the industry's side.

Much as women were key to alcohol's downfall, they were also key to its resurrection and cultural reinvention. Although women on the whole consumed less alcohol than men, women represented both the biggest new market opportunity and the biggest peril to market expansion. As the former foot soldiers of the prohibition crusade and as voters who could swing local option elections, women could either stymie or advance alcohol's mass market success. In many cases, women also decided how much and what kind of alcohol entered the home. American brewers and vintners waged an aggressive campaign to secure women's confidence and consumer patronage. Advertisers, recipe writers, and the new doyennes of drinking etiquette presented wine and beer as an essential element of domestic hospitality. Some even heralded women as the new guardians of the pleasure revolution who would safeguard drinking in moderation. Whiskey makers, by contrast, observed a self-imposed ban on representing women in liquor ads until 1958 to preempt prohibitionist attacks and bolster their claims to respectability.[23] In the near term, whiskey makers likely gained more in goodwill than they lost in potential revenue, owing to whiskey's longstanding reputation as a man's drink and the liquor store's reputation as a masculine domain.[24]

Intoxicating Pleasures narrates the story of alcohol's cultural reinvention in two parts. The first part examines efforts to reconstruct the industry and fashion new cultures of drinking during the Great Depression and the second part analyzes how World War II transformed alcohol into an emblem of the American good life. Wine, beer, and whiskey each entered the post-repeal era with distinct cultural and political biographies that their chief promoters revised and adapted to build mass markets and curry regulatory favor. In Part I we see how brewers, vintners, distillers, and their allies sketched the outlines of three distinctive cultures of drink that shaped alcohol policymaking and middle-class

American leisure for decades to come. With varying degrees of success and conviction, vintners, brewers, and distillers preached their own variants of the gospel of moderation, each aiming to establish the moral superiority of their commodity to the "harder" alternatives. Brewers and vintners, who had long cast wine and beer as the beverages of "true temperance," secured lower excise taxes by associating their products with wholesome conviviality and heterosocial leisure and, when necessary, by scapegoating whiskey as the cause of problem drinking. Although whiskey's greater alcoholic potency made it a convenient target for brewers and winemakers, whiskey's defenders refused to surrender the banner of moderation.

During the Great Depression, the industry ran headlong into a hard reality: promoting drinking in good taste offered no guarantee that wine, whiskey, and beer would, in fact, taste good. Bland beers, sour-tasting wines, and underaged, headache-inducing whiskeys all sparked consumer disappointment. By necessity, alcohol's cultural reinvention also hinged on the industry's success in reeducating consumers' sensory perceptions of taste and intoxication. California winemakers exhorted consumers to describe table wines as "dry" rather than "sour" and to refer to sweet, higher alcohol wine as "dessert wine" rather than "fortified wine"—a pejorative that primed consumer expectations for an intoxicating kick. Distillers assured consumers that they would be spared the pain of hangovers and the embarrassment of drunkenness if they simply learned to choose the right brand of whiskey and savor its quality. Beer's blandness became its own selling point, reassuring consumers that beer was unlikely to promote drunkenness.[25] Marketers, in essence, promised consumers that alcohol would be gentle on the senses: pleasing (or pleasing enough) to the palate and capable of producing a mild euphoria.

Reeducating consumers' sensory perceptions advanced the alcoholic beverage industry's larger quest to transform drinking from a transgressive vice into an ordinary pleasure. Drinking guidebooks, magazine advertisements, and publicity materials gently goaded consumers to moderate their Prohibition-era excesses and observe the etiquette (and imperative) of responsible drinking. The repeated injunctions to sip, savor, and avoid one too many enabled alcohol firms to proclaim their commitment to corporate social responsibility while shifting actual responsibility for drunkenness to the individual. At the same time, the industry assured consumers that drinking alcohol in the right sensory environments with the right mindset would make self-discipline easier to achieve and intoxication easier to manage. By depicting the enjoyment of wine, beer, and spirits in fashionable restaurants, respectable middle-class homes, and wholesome recreational venues, magazine ads presented an alluring and reassuring vision of consumers casting off sensorial restraints without succumbing to the sensory excesses of the boisterous masculine saloon and the Prohibition-era speakeasy. The pleasure revolution that alcohol promoters envisioned—one that was sensuous yet controlled—reconciled the modern "desire to transcend regulated minds, bodies, and environments" with the competing modern "desire for sensory order."[26]

In separate chapters on beer, whiskey, wine, and alcohol provisioning in the military, Part II demonstrates why World War II proved to be a more transformative moment in alcohol's cultural reinvention than Repeal. The war gave business, consumers, military personnel, and organized drys new opportunities to make claims on the state. Emboldened by memories of their previous victory in World War I, when wartime exigencies had swept national prohibition into law, drys saw the return of total war and food conservation as a tantalizing opportunity to revive prohibition. Protestant churches and the Woman's Christian Temperance Union swamped Congress with petitions demanding bans on the use of grains in alcohol production and the sale of alcohol in military training camps. The leading dry organizations wanted to create 10-mile "moral zones" surrounding the training camps with the aim of depleting some of the nation's wettest cities—San Francisco, New Orleans, Los Angeles, New York, and Chicago—of their liquor and their sex workers. Although alcohol bans never won Congressional approval, Protestant petitions forced continuous votes on such measures throughout the war.

Brewers, vintners, and distillers had also absorbed lessons from the previous global war. Having underestimated their prohibitionist foes in the past, they launched massive public relations and advertising campaigns to cement alcohol's place in national mythologies of the American good life. The alcoholic beverage industry was hardly alone in using the war to burnish their reputation. Media propaganda produced by other firms and major business associations credited private enterprise for engineering the production miracle that would win the war.[27] In that same vein, the distillers publicized their patriotic production of industrial alcohol, a crucial ingredient for making smokeless gunpowder and synthetic rubber. Business also helped the wartime state to manage civilian and military morale, a task that grew in importance as the federal government expanded the obligations of citizenship to include observing price controls and food rationing guidelines, growing victory gardens, purchasing war bonds, and—a first for many ordinary Americans—paying income taxes. To make these obligations more palatable, corporate advertisers and government propaganda melded appeals to patriotic duty and sacrifice with assurances that consumer plenty would return in peacetime.[28] Instead of holding out the promise of deferred abundance, brewers and vintners offered consumers more tangible and immediate rewards. Wine and beer, advertising promised, could cheer war-weary civilians and fortify their resolve to defend cherished freedoms. Such claims netted alcohol producers real-world dividends. In recognition of the brewers' production of low-alcohol beer for the military and beer's contributions to home front morale, the government classified brewing as an "essential" wartime industry, a designation that gave brewers access to scarce resources.

Wartime food shortages and food controls also made the war a transformative moment in alcohol's cultural reinvention. Trade associations and tastemakers seized the opportunity to reimagine alcohol's relationship to food. Alcohol promoters did not seek to define wine and beer as food per se. Advertising that overtly did so, in fact, violated Federal Alcohol Administration regulations. Rather they sought to elevate the pleasures of drinking wine and beer to roughly the same moral plane as the pleasures of eating other foods. In short, they sought to bridge the food-drug divide. The cultural gulf between food and drugs had not always been deep. "For most of human history," sociologist Craig Reinarman writes, "alcoholic beverages, psychoactive plants, and medicines were understood as forms of food." The divide between food and drugs began to grow in the eighteenth and nineteenth centuries, when the mass production of gin, rum, and whiskey expanded the availability of these more potent spirits and increased the prevalence of drunkenness and crime. The widening use of coffee and tea as stimulants that enhanced productivity and attentiveness—prized virtues in the new age of mechanization and industrial efficiency—further weakened alcohol's footing in the realm of food. In countries with strong temperance movements, policymakers and reformers exiled distilled spirits—along with beer and wine—from the category of food and reclassified them as drugs that merited strict regulation.[29] This new taxonomy was slower to take hold in beer- and wine-drinking countries. Central Europeans continued to view beer as "liquid bread," while the French and Italians continued to view wine as a salubrious food.[30]

During World War II, American promoters of wine and beer found new ways to straddle the food-drug divide and align their marketing goals with the aims of the wartime state. Brewers, vintners, and distillers had long touted their contribution to the agricultural economy as buyers of grapes and grains. California's winemakers even recast themselves as "wine growers" to imbue themselves with agrarian virtue and secure the state Department of Agriculture's aid in launching a collective advertising campaign.[31] The introduction of food rationing and food conservation paved the way for deeper encroachments on the food-drug divide. Trade associations and cookbook authors capitalized on wartime food controls to promote wine as a mood-enhancing mealtime beverage and the secret ingredient that could tenderize cheap meats, turn low-ration-point organ meats into company fare, and ease compliance with meat and sugar rationing. Brewers aligned beer with the nation's "Food Fights for Freedom" campaign by promoting brewers' yeast, a byproduct of brewing, as a rich source of vitamin B complex that could enrich soldiers' rations and boost defense workers' productivity.

Despite alcohol's centrality to wartime foodscapes, alcohol has, for the most part, been sidelined from narratives that examine how wartime states managed food shortages on the home front and how they provisioned soldiers on the battlefront.[32] Bringing alcohol into these narratives enables us to think more deeply about how wartime scarcities politicized pleasure and shaped perceptions of deprivation. On both the home front and the battlefront, scarcity enhanced whiskey's status as a prized commodity. Much like the shortages of meat, another highly coveted food, shortages of whiskey threatened morale and compliance with price controls.[33] By 1943, whiskey bootlegging rings, liquor hijackings, and under-the-counter liquor sales—conditions reminiscent of Prohibition—had attracted so much press attention that officials at the Treasury Department and the Office of Price Administration debated whether the state should intervene to protect access to a nonessential luxury. Eventually officials bowed to lobbying pressure and granted the distillers three furloughs from war production to replenish their dwindling whiskey stocks—a reprieve many other industries were denied. The decision to grant the "liquor holidays," as they were dubbed in the press, reveals much about the pragmatism and cultural sensibilities of the New Deal wartime state. Secured in part through a defense of the consumer's "right to decent whiskey," the liquor holidays reflected the turn to a more rights-oriented liberalism that increasingly prioritized freedom of consumer choice over freedom from want in the postwar period.³⁴ They also protected what President Franklin Delano Roosevelt and Treasury Secretary Henry Morgenthau regarded as one of the New Deal's signature achievements: the repeal of Prohibition and the destruction of bootlegging rings in the mid-1930s. As Morgenthau understood it, intoxicating pleasures, properly controlled, did more than simply bolster civilian morale—they also bolstered confidence in the New Deal state.

Conflicts over unequal access to alcohol in army training camps and on the battlefront also had significant political repercussions. World War II was the first twentieth-century war in which the US military designated 3.2 percent beer as an essential provision for the troops. While enlisted men could purchase limited quantities of weak beer from Army Post Exchanges, officers could enjoy cocktails, wine, and beer in the mess, plus a monthly ration of whiskey, scotch, gin, and brandy. Enforcement of the color line in the segregated military ensured that both Black officers and Black enlisted men had less access to alcohol when they entered their segregated PX and officers' mess. Their attempts to patronize local bars and restaurants at home and abroad often elicited violent resistance from white enlisted men and punitive measures from the higher command. The military's inequitable provisioning for pleasure indelibly shaped how servicemen fought in the war and remembered the war. It also galvanized Black struggles for equality during and after the war.

As these wartime episodes reveal, alcohol had become such an expected feature of the good life and such a potent marker of belonging that intoxicating pleasures could not help but seep into broader public debates over the rights and obligations of citizenship and the proper boundaries of state power. Alcohol commanded the attention of the wartime state because shortages of highly desired intoxicants exacerbated public discontent with price control violations, food shortages, and racial segregation inside and outside the military. These conflicts compelled the federal government to consider whether it should intervene to stabilize markets in nonessential luxuries like whiskey and whether alcohol's contributions to morale management warranted classifying brewing as an essential wartime industry. Black military officers and enlisted men of all races came to view access to intoxicating beverages as an entitlement of citizenship and military service—not just for white officers, but across the spectrum of race and rank.

The repeal of Prohibition had not buried the alcohol question once and for good. Instead alcohol continued to court controversy and federal attention because pleasure had become so central to how citizen-consumers articulated their rights and measured their belonging. Assuring access to intoxicating pleasures—but not necessarily their affordability—had also become central to how the New Deal state imagined a robust capitalist political economy. The profound wartime shifts in alcohol's political fortunes were not the doing of the alcoholic beverage industry alone. A broad network of trade associations, food and drink columnists, cookbook authors, New Deal planners, and other tastemakers laid the cultural groundwork for alcohol's reinvention as an emblem of the American good life. World War II sealed the deal.

PART ONE

Charting Alcohol's Path to Redemption

1

The Potent Politics of Weak Brews

On May 14, 1932, amid rising unemployment rates and a deepening depression, Mayor Jimmy Walker led more than 150,000 of his fellow New Yorkers in an eleven-hour march to demand that Congress relegalize beer. The flamboyant, two-term liberal Democratic mayor—known to many as a nightclub regular and a lax enforcer of Prohibition—would soon be forced from office on corruption charges, but on this grand occasion Jimmy Walker reveled in the city's massive turnout to bring back beer. As the marchers made their way down Fifth Avenue and around Central Park, crushing the pretzels strewn in their path, the city reverberated with shouts of "We Want Beer!"—a slogan that had become a popular political chant at labor union conventions and veterans' association gatherings. Men and women from all walks of life, including onlookers numbering in the hundreds of thousands, joined the massive beer demonstration. Labor unions, veterans' associations, German Americans, Italian Americans, and African Americans—the multiethnic and multiracial working-class core of the growing anti-Prohibitionist coalition—all sent large delegations. Automobile executive Walter Chrysler and financier E. F. Hutton, who headed a contingent of several dozen "leaders of industry," marched under the banner "End the Business Stagnation with Beer Taxation," hopeful that the return of regressive beer taxes would also relieve their income tax burden. Other groups demanded "Beer for Taxation," too—cleverly redefining a consumer demand as a kind of patriotic sacrifice (see Figure 1).

FIGURE 1. Parade marchers demand "Beer for Taxation," New York City, March, 14, 1932. Scherl/Süddeutsche Zeitung Photo via Alamy.

The announcer who narrated a newsreel documenting the beer parade echoed the conservative framing of the parade's organizers: "It's not that the marchers want beer as beer," he said, but "beer for taxation."[1]

The parade's festive atmosphere did not fully square with the newsreel announcer's conservative spin. Bands played old drinking songs, onlookers cheered from the sidelines, and the choruses of Broadway shows joined the procession. Several men—and a few women—marched with tin buckets in hand, perhaps referencing the empty dinner pails that would be filled when beer and jobs returned.[2] More likely, parade marchers and spectators recognized the tin pails as a defiant homage to the growler, the half-gallon bucket that working-class saloons once filled for a dime. Although the prospect of beer's return meant different things to different marchers, all concurred on one crucial claim: If Congress amended national Prohibition to bring back beer, Congress could generate new jobs, stimulate business, and balance the budget with new beer taxes. New York's "Great Beer Demonstration," as it came to be known, was just one of several beer parades staged in cities across the nation that day. It was also likely the only occasion in US history when Americans took to the streets to demand that Congress raise their taxes. Though none of the other parades matched New York's in size or its eleven-hour duration, organizers hoped the coordinated nationwide effort would build support for repealing the Eighteenth Amendment or—at the very least—compel Congress to modify the Volstead Act, the legislation that implemented national Prohibition.

At the time, the chances of repealing Prohibition outright still seemed distant. At least three-quarters of the states would have to ratify the Twenty-First Amendment, and some anti-prohibitionists feared that a determined block of thirteen states, mostly Southern, had "it in their hands to prevent" repeal "and defy the wills of some 75 to 95 per cent of the people of this country."[3] Still convinced of Prohibition's assured longevity, Texas Senator Morris Sheppard, who helped write the Eighteenth Amendment, famously boasted in 1930, "There's as much chance of repealing the Eighteenth Amendment as there is for a hummingbird to fly to Mars with the Washington Monument tied to its tail."[4] Given these uncertain prospects, many anti-prohibitionists, in the interim, set their sights on amending the Volstead Act to bring back low-alcohol beers and light wines. Some viewed this modified form of Prohibition as a worthy end in itself.

Congress took notice. In 1932 and 1933, the House of Representatives and the Senate held three sets of hearings on proposals to amend the Volstead Act. Proponents of modification took aim at what many considered the most egregious provision of the Volstead Act: a breathtakingly restrictive definition of "intoxicating" that banned the manufacture, sale, and transportation of any beverage containing more than 0.5 percent alcohol by volume. This threshold made the United States far more restrictive than other countries and provinces that experimented with prohibition in the 1920s. The Mexican state of Yucatán permitted beverages with up to 5 percent alcohol, while Quebec, Norway, and Belgium banned only spirits but not beer and wine.[5] Although there was a legal basis for the 0.5% standard—federal and state liquor laws used that marker to assess taxes on wine, beer, and spirits—the low percentage invited deserved ridicule. As Senator Hiram Bingham of Connecticut observed, "Old-fashioned ginger ale frequently contained three-fourths of 1 per cent" and buttermilk—widely embraced as a temperance drink—"frequently contains more than one-half of 1 per cent."[6] To restore beer and light wines, legislators had to come up with a new definition of intoxication—one capacious enough to permit low-alcohol beers and table wines, but reasonable enough to still comply with the Eighteenth Amendment.

Scientists, alcohol producers, and wet activists used the hearings to demarcate new boundaries between respectable pleasure-seeking and dangerous overindulgence. Most significantly, they articulated a defense of pleasure that affirmed alcohol's place in modern American life while rejecting the old excesses of the saloon and the new excesses of Jazz Age cocktail culture. Although the testimony addressed a range of topics, the hearings raised particularly meaty questions about the political economy of psychoactive pleasures. How could the state both regulate and accommodate the recreational use of euphoric substances?[7] What kinds of alcohol-induced euphoria could responsible citizens enjoy without compromising productivity? What kinds of regulatory limits on intoxicating beverages could garner broad acceptance in a pluralistic society?

The intervention of new kinds of scientific experts in these debates lent the appearance of objectivity and the weight of scientific moral authority to claims that brewers and vintners had long made about the safety and mild potency of beer and wine. As star witnesses at the hearings, physiologists and industrial toxicologists established new quantitative measures of risk that enabled brewers to associate beer with bodily health, personal well-being, and worthy uses of leisure. Although vintners failed to persuade Congress that wine containing 10 to 12 percent alcohol by weight was nonintoxicating, the Beer and Wine Revenue Act, passed in March 1933, officially recognized 3.2 percent beer by weight as the standard by which alcoholic beverages could be judged nonintoxicating. Henceforth the number 3.2 became enshrined as the mark of alcoholic innocence in the US military and the liquor control regulations of virtually every state, including the states that continued to ban all other forms of alcohol after Prohibition. How that came to pass is the story that follows.

ORGANIZING AGAINST PROHIBITION: A NEW POLITICAL COALITION TAKES SHAPE

During the 1920s, a broad swath of Americans, from ardent wets to disillusioned drys, came to view Prohibition as an ineffective, even counterproductive, way to reform American drinking habits. Opposition hardened into utter contempt among the working-class Black Americans and working-class ethnic Americans who bore the brunt of Prohibition's selective enforcement.[8] While most opponents of Prohibition expressed their disdain for the law simply by ignoring it, some formed and joined organizations to press for change. Even though repealing a constitutional amendment seemed a remote possibility, some opposition groups refused to accept any measure short of full-scale repeal. Other organizations endorsed the compromise of modifying the Volstead Act to permit beer and light wines either as an interim measure or an end in itself.[9] Even before Prohibition became law, the Association Against the Prohibition Amendment (AAPA), formed in 1918, had adopted the slogan "Beers and Light Wines NOW, but no Saloons EVER" in hopes of forestalling the Eighteenth Amendment's ratification. The sentiment behind the slogan continued to rally Prohibition's opponents throughout the 1920s and early 1930s.

By 1923, moderation leagues had formed in New York, Ohio, Minnesota, and Pennsylvania to advance modification at the state and national levels.[10] Early polling registered solid support for their cause. A 1922 *Literary Digest* survey of nine hundred thousand subscribers found that a plurality (40.8 percent) favored modifying the Volstead Act to permit light wines and beer; 20.6 percent favored outright repeal; and 38.6 percent favored enforcement of existing laws. Support for modification was especially high (62 percent) among factory workers, who denounced Prohibition as class legislation that deprived workers of their beer while allowing the wealthy and the well-connected to continue imbibing stronger intoxicants.[11] Because the Eighteenth Amendment banned the production, transportation, and sale of alcohol but not its consumption, elites could gradually draw down the liquors and wines stored in their vast cellars—or pay exorbitant sums for quality liquor smuggled from distant ports. The working class, on the other hand, had to forgo such pleasures or risk injury and ill health by consuming the bootlegger's adulterated and often toxic supply.[12] As a Slovak priest living in Chicago lamented, Prohibition's biggest sin was that it gave "the good stuff to the sewer and the bad stuff to the people."[13]

The two organizations with the longest record of opposing Prohibition—the American Federation of Labor (AFL) and the big-business dominated AAPA—made for strange political bedfellows. Under the stewardship of Samuel Gompers, who had long championed 2.75 percent beer as the working-man's due, the AFL renewed its call for modification each year, beginning in 1922.[14] The wealthy industrialists who poured their considerable financial resources into the AAPA's lobbying efforts included such business luminaries as Pierre du Pont, the chairman of General Motors and the DuPont Company, and his brothers Lammot and Irénée du Pont; publisher Charles Scribner; real estate mogul Vincent Astor; and department store magnate Marshall Field.[15] Like the AFL and other labor leaders, the AAPA denounced Prohibition's violation of personal liberties and its attempt to legislate private morality. Pierre du Pont, who enjoyed drinking wine and spirits in moderation, even expressed sympathy for labor's critique of Prohibition's "heavy-handed paternalism."[16] The AAPA's elite membership, however, also had a vested economic interest in seeking repeal. Once alcohol returned, they argued, the restored excise taxes on alcohol would generate enough revenues to greatly reduce—or perhaps even eliminate—the personal income and corporate taxes that many wealthy industrialists viewed as another unjust government intrusion on their liberty and property rights.[17]

Women's organizations took longer to gain mass support for the anti-Prohibition crusade, but their conservative framing of the cause ultimately proved the most fruitful and influential. Women's groups that centered personal liberty appeals, such as the short-lived Molly Pitcher Clubs, named after the Revolutionary War heroine, failed to gain much traction.[18] The Women's Organization for National Prohibition Reform (WONPR), on the other hand, attracted 1.5 million women who signed onto the group's call for the restoration of "true temperance." Founded in 1929 by Pauline Morton Sabin, heir to the Morton Salt company fortune and a Republican Party fundraiser, the group attracted women with diverse class backgrounds, ethnic identities, and partisan affiliations, including many disillusioned former prohibitionists. The WONPR owed some of its success to timing. By 1929, many more Americans had come to believe that Prohibition's negative consequences far outweighed its benefits. As stock prices plummeted and unemployment soared, the idea of ending Prohibition to save the economy also grew more alluring.

The WONPR's shrewd use of the home protection rhetoric that prohibitionists had perfected also contributed to its broad appeal. Emphasizing Prohibition's moral threat to the American home and children's welfare, the WONPR asserted that Prohibition had corrupted youth by glamorizing drinking and breeding disrespect for the law. Although the WONPR acknowledged that Prohibition violated "constitutional guarantees of individual rights," the group "studiously avoided any implication that drinking was one of those rights." The WONPR stressed that prohibition had hindered the cultivation of temperate habits but remained deliberately vague about what precisely "true temperance" would look like.[19] As we will see, brewers, vintners, and wet-aligned scientists lacked any such reticence. They used their testimony at the 1932–33 congressional hearings to firmly anchor the concept of "true temperance" in the realm of pleasure.

THE INDUSTRY TAKES THE STAND

Congress first took up the modification question in 1924 and nearly every year between 1925 and 1933 Congressman Adolph Sabath, a Jewish immigrant representing Chicago, introduced bills to allow wine and beer under the Volstead Act.[20] For most of the 1920s, supporters of modification failed to make much headway. Although three states passed modification referendums in 1926, the Republican and Democratic parties refused to endorse modification in their 1924 platforms and Congress rejected modification in 1924 and 1926.[21] The Great Depression and widespread public disenchantment with Prohibition shifted political momentum in beer's favor. Repealers and modificationists argued that bringing back beer and light wines would generate new tax revenues and create hundreds of thousands of jobs for brewery workers, wait staff, bartenders, restaurateurs, coopers, and bottle makers. From there the multiplier effects would expand exponentially. Capital outlays in materials, trucks, advertising, and sales would promote economic growth, railways would see increased traffic, and growers would get higher prices for their grains. In short, the return of legal beer would bring the blessings of economic stimulus to nearly every sector of the economy.[22]

The January 1932 Senate hearings before a subcommittee of the Committee on Manufacturers focused on two bills. Senate Bill 486 defined as intoxicating any beverage containing more than 3.2 percent alcohol by weight (or 4 percent by volume)—a slightly stronger brew than the weak 2.75 percent "war beer" permitted during World War I. President Woodrow Wilson had lowered beer's alcohol content to preserve grain and appease prohibitionists, who were demanding stricter emergency wartime controls on alcohol. Senate Bill 2473, the companion legislation to S. B. 486, addressed concerns that bringing back beer would also bring back the saloon. It prohibited on-premises sales of draught beer and allowed the sale of pint-sized beer bottles only through grocery stores or in restaurants and hotels that served beer with meals.

Although neither bill passed, the prospects of similar bills brightened as campaigning for the congressional and presidential elections went into full swing. At the Democratic National Convention in June 1932, the issue of ending Prohibition and legalizing beer galvanized the delegates like none other. They applauded when keynote speaker Senator Alben Barkley, the Kentuckian who would later become the Senate majority leader and serve as vice president under President Harry S. Truman, talked about government relief for farmers and the unemployed. But the delegates shouted and cheered for twelve minutes straight when Barkley, himself a former dry and the coauthor of the Eighteenth Amendment, declared the Democratic Party's unequivocal support for ending national Prohibition. An even bigger demonstration erupted when Nebraska Senator Gilbert Hitchcock read the plank calling for repeal and the immediate legalization of beer. "For twenty-five minutes," historian Michael Lerner recounts, "the Democratic delegates stomped, cheered, and waved signs . . . while women wets milled about the convention floor, leading the Democrats in song."[23] The landslide Democratic victory in the 1932 elections gave the supporters of repeal and modification the bold mandate they desired. During a special session of Congress in December 1932, Democratic lawmakers introduced two new bills. Though similar to the previous beer bills, the more liberal Collier Bill (H.R. 13812) included a provision to legalize wine and levied a $5/barrel tax on beer, $2.50 lower than the tax proposed in the O'Connor Bill (H.R. 13031).

No issue was more central to the passage of any bill than establishing a definition of intoxication that would legalize low-alcohol beers and light wines without violating the Eighteenth Amendment. Establishing such a definition was a somewhat dicey proposition since the US Supreme Court had already affirmed the legitimacy of the 0.5 percent standard. Supporters of modification were undeterred. Because definitions of intoxication had varied widely at the state level before Prohibition, there were no universally recognized precedents for defining certain beverages as intoxicants. Eleven states with dry laws recognized 0.5 percent alcohol as an intoxicant, but twice as many states allowed juries to decide what constituted intoxication.[24]

The far trickier problem was identifying a "nonintoxicating" alcohol content that did not violate the Eighteenth Amendment but still delivered enough kick to satisfy consumer tastes. What, after all, would be the point of legalizing an overly weak brew, if it failed to stimulate consumer demand? Unless beer provided drinkers some sort of sensory stimulus, beer would fail to supply the economic stimulus modificationists promised. Brewers and their allies thus had to reconcile two seemingly contradictory positions: they had to persuade Congress that a pleasure-giving beer, capable of producing a mild euphoria, still qualified as a nonintoxicating beverage.

Modificationists initially proposed legalizing 2.75 percent beer, the weak brew permitted during World War I, arguing that it would "lessen the desire for strong drinks."[25] August A. Busch, president of Anheuser-Busch, one of the nation's largest beer firms, was not nearly so sanguine. In letters and statements entered into the official record of the hearings, Busch warned that 2.75 percent beer, a beer in "name only," would not satisfy the "masses" who sought the "warmth, satisfaction, and contentment that a mild stimulant like a good, wholesome beer supplies."[26] Busch's preferred strength, a 3.2 percent beer (by weight), was less potent than pre-Prohibition Budweiser, which contained 4 percent alcohol by weight (4.5 to 4.7 percent by volume) and was significantly less potent than the homebrews Americans made and drank during Prohibition, which sometimes climbed as high as 11 percent alcohol owing to the absence of refrigeration controls.[27]

To justify the higher 3.2 percent, brewers crafted new distinctions that sought to separate respectable pleasure-seeking from hedonistic excess. Lawmakers made "a fundamental error," Busch insisted, when they equated stimulation with intoxication.[28] The former produced a mildly euphoric state, rooted in sensual pleasure and fellowship, while the latter engendered anger and negativity. According to Busch, a 3.2 percent beer "will give a warm glow that spreads over you, that stimulates you slightly, makes you feel good and at peace with the world; that makes you want to sing and not to fight; makes you good natured, not ugly." By contrast, "whisky makes a man see red, puts a fighting spirit into him, robs him of his good judgment; in other words, makes him drunk."[29]

As Busch's testimony suggests, persuading Congress to endorse an alcohol content that provided satisfaction without intoxication required skillful play with euphemism. The English language supplied an impressive array of synonyms for intoxication. One could be drunk, inebriated, smashed, loaded, bombed, besotted, lit, tanked, toasted, zozzled, or three sheets to the wind—and that was just for starters. The literary critic Edmund Wilson compiled more than a hundred terms for drunk in his "Lexicon of Prohibition" (1927), well shy of the 225 synonyms that Benjamin Franklin published in "The Drinkers Dictionary" (1737) and the 353 synonyms listed in the *Dictionary of American Slang* (1975).[30] The proponents of modification needed a different vocabulary altogether to describe a benign altered state—something short of drunkenness but beyond sobriety—and here the linguistic well did not run nearly as deep. Busch, for example, alluded to beer's ability to stimulate a "warm glow" and feelings of being "at peace with the world." Ohio Congressman Wilbur White, who advocated legalizing pre-Prohibition strength beers, was equally inventive. When a skeptical congressman asked if White favored 4.5 percent beer because he thought it "would be more palatable, or because it will be, to a degree, intoxicating, and as a result more satisfying," White replied with a wink and a nod: "It would be more palatable and the spiritual effect would doubtlessly be slightly different."[31]

Such arguments, of course, exposed modificationists to ridicule from their prohibitionist opponents. Representative Thomas Blanton of Texas decried the hypocrisy of the bill's supporters for promoting 3.2 percent beer as nonintoxicating when their actions suggested they knew otherwise. "In one breath," Blanton stated, "the Beer Bill now before us provides for a beer asserted to be innocent and non-intoxicating and in the next breath it makes it an offense to sell it to minors, because we are hoping to keep the minors sober."[32] Senator William Borah, a staunch prohibitionist, also scoffed at the notion that proponents of the bill sincerely regarded 3.2 percent beer as nonintoxicating. The defenders of 3.2 percent beer understood all too well that legalized beer would not increase federal revenues unless the beer had some zing: "Does anyone believe the government will collect $150,000,000 in taxes on a nonintoxicating beverage? This is the beer the brewers want."[33]

The wine industry faced a much steeper climb in their quest to persuade Congress that "light wines" were nonintoxicating. The term "light wines," used today more frequently in Europe than the United States, legally applied to table wines with less than 14 percent alcohol.

The term also distinguished such beverages from ports, sherries, and other sweet, fortified wines with an alcohol content of 18 to 21 percent. In calling for the restoration of "light wines and beer," modificationists may have hoped to persuade voters and legislators that "light" and "low alcohol" were interchangeable terms. The political pairing of "light wines and beer" failed to achieve such rhetorical magic, however. The more the hearings got mired in a debate over whether 0.5 percent, 2.75 percent, or 3.2 percent represented the best quantitative measure of intoxication, the less likely it became that Congress would give vintners an easy pass. If brewers and their scientific allies were willing to concede that porters, stouts, and ales containing 6 to 8 percent alcohol were intoxicating, how could vintners possibly defend table wines with 12 to 14 percent alcohol as nonintoxicating?[34]

Since quantitative arguments were a sure loser, wine industry spokesmen instead relied on clever legal interpretations of the Volstead Act and cross-cultural comparisons to affirm wine's virtue as a nonintoxicating article of food and an accoutrement of gracious living. The core of their argument rested on the premise that the manner in which wine was ordinarily consumed—with meals, in moderate amounts, and in a leisurely fashion—made intoxication nearly impossible. Former congressman Judge Marion De Vries, speaking on behalf of the Grape Growers' League of California, cited Dr. Graham Lusk, a professor of physiology at Cornell University's Medical College and an internationally renowned nutritionist, who asserted that the "ordinary, decent" Frenchman drank his daily pint of claret without becoming drunk.[35] Another physiologist, Dr. Yandell Henderson of Yale University, offered similar assessments of the rarity of drunkenness in wine-drinking cultures.[36]

Particularly noteworthy was Dr. Lusk's adoption of the "ordinary, decent" man standard to assess the probability of intoxication. While prohibitionists formulated public policy with the problem drinker in mind, wet sympathizers underscored the normalcy of drinking by making "the ordinary decent" man—one who enjoyed alcohol in moderation—their default drinker. As Judge De Vries put it, Congress should legislate for the "ordinary, decent man" not for "swine" who consume alcohol to excess.[37] Wet sympathizers also stressed that the cultural practices associated with particular beverages often factored more heavily in intoxication than their alcohol content. Henderson, for example, saw no contradiction in defining both 4 percent beer and 8 percent wine (by weight) as nonintoxicating "because the two beverages are drunk under different conditions and in different amounts." A man would likely become intoxicated if he drank "a quart of wine on an empty stomach" and without a meal, but wine, Henderson insisted, was "not drunk that way."[38] Similarly, Edmund A. Rossi, vice president of the Grape Growers League and president of the Italian Swiss Colony winery, testified that light wines were not intoxicating, despite their higher alcohol content than beer, because ordinary drinkers consumed wines with meals. According to Rossi, the French and Italians avoided intoxication because they "never gulp . . . their wines like Americans do their cocktails—they sip them slowly and really enjoy the aroma and bouquet of their wines."[39]

The wine industry presented additional semantic and legal arguments to persuade lawmakers that wine was nonintoxicating. Since the Eighteenth Amendment applied only to alcoholic *beverages*, they argued, Congress could remove wine from Volstead Act regulations by redefining wine as an article of food, especially when consumed with meals. Judge De Vries found legal precedent for reclassifying wine as a food in two previous court cases (*Savage v. Covell, United States v. Sweet Valley Wine Company*) and in the Pure Food and Drugs Act of 1906, which regulated wine as a food.[40] Such arguments stood little chance of gaining traction in a country where, apart from select immigrant communities, few Americans adopted wine as a regular mealtime beverage. De Vries's proposal better represented vintners' fantasies of what wine could become—a regular mealtime beverage—than the reality of how most native-born Americans consumed wine, if they consumed it at all. When he and other drinking reformers imagined alcohol's place in post-Prohibition America, they envisioned an American drinking culture redrawn along European lines.

Section 29, a quirky provision of the Volstead Act that permitted Americans to produce "nonintoxicating cider and fruit juices exclusively for [home] use," gave supporters of modification a stronger, if still problematic, justification for relegalizing wine. Lawmakers had originally included the fermented fruit juice exemption, with prohibitionists' grudging consent, as a concession to grape growers and apple farmers whose livelihoods partly depended on serving markets for homemade wine and hard cider. Italian- and Greek-American communities had long made their own wine for home consumption and apple farmers had long converted their unsold or unsellable apples into cider. Prohibitionists were receptive to farmers' pleas for a wine and cider exemption because they feared losing the loyalty of cider-loving rural voters (a core dry constituency) and they failed to anticipate that Prohibition would turn home winemaking into a booming cottage industry. The precise definition of *nonintoxicating* in Section 29 quickly came into dispute. Did the Volstead Act's 0.5 percent alcohol by volume standard apply as the permissible limit or did *nonintoxicating* mean something else when fruit juice was involved? Wayne Wheeler, the de facto leader of the Anti-Saloon League, acknowledged that the drafters of Section 29 had left "the term *nonintoxicating* undefined" because they recognized that home producers would not be able to precisely measure the alcohol content of their fermented fruit juices. Rather than holding home winemakers to the impossibly strict 0.5 percent standard, the Prohibition Bureau ruled that enforcement agents and juries simply had to determine whether the wine or cider was "nonintoxicating in fact."[41] When given the opportunity, sympathetic juries in wet districts happily acquitted defendants whose homemade beverages vastly exceeded the 0.5 percent standard.[42] Although many prohibitionists protested that lawmakers never intended to permit homemade wine, the Supreme Court upheld the home winemaking provision, arguing that "no human law could prevent fruit juices from fermenting spontaneously."[43] Wine industry allies seized this loophole to argue that winemaking was already impervious to "constitutional attack."[44] Clever legal reasoning aside, such arguments failed to garner much support beyond a few sympathetic lawmakers from California, the largest wine-growing state.

WET SCIENTISTS TO THE RESCUE

The scientific testimony at the hearings gave anti-prohibitionists their best opportunity to build a persuasive case for modification. Although many Congressmen were predisposed to support modification, especially after the sweeping Democratic victories in November 1932, the beer bill was still constitutionally dicey. If any Congressmen felt they needed cover to pass a beer bill while the Eighteenth Amendment remained in effect, reasonably sound scientific testimony could provide it.

The 1932 hearings were not the first time brewers had used scientific testimony in an attempt to exclude low-alcohol beer from Prohibition. In 1919, after the ratification of the Eighteenth Amendment, Jacob Ruppert, the owner of a major New York brewery and the New York Yankees, funded new research on the psychopharmacology of beer to support his federal lawsuit seeking an exemption under the Volstead Act for 2.75 percent beer, the alcohol content permitted during World War I. Reputable, university-affiliated scientists conducted multiple experiments on human subjects to measure the effects of 2.75 percent beer on blood alcohol concentration, mental clarity, and motor skills. Only subjects who suffered substantial physical impairment, such as being unable to walk straight, were judged intoxicated. Although the researchers all concluded that the weak war beer failed to produce symptoms of intoxication, even when subjects drank seven quarts, their studies failed to win brewers their desired exemption.[45] When Congress took up modification again in 1926, brewers chose not to introduce the Ruppert-funded studies because researchers had adopted a more restrictive definition of intoxication that gave drys the upper hand. The new standard defined any substance that compromised optimal bodily efficiency and alertness as an intoxicant.[46]

At the 1932 hearings, supporters of modification presented new scientific testimony that redefined the meaning of intoxication yet again. Their star witness was Yandell Henderson, a professor of applied physiology at Yale University who had taught in the medical school for twenty years. Henderson had made his scientific reputation studying ways to manage industrial chemicals and prevent carbon monoxide poisoning. During World War I Henderson tested gas masks for the Chemical Warfare Service and he later established the carbon monoxide standards for mines, car repair shops, and the Holland Tunnel in New York City. Having already shown how Americans could live safely in the presence of potentially toxic substances, Henderson's earlier research gave him the credibility to assess the hazards alcohol presented and the conditions under which it, too, could be safely consumed.[47] Henderson reoriented the debate by changing the question. Instead of attempting to ascertain the amount of alcohol that impaired optimal bodily efficiency, Henderson asked how could alcohol's potential dangers be managed so that alcohol's pleasurable qualities could be enjoyed?

Henderson treated alcohol as he treated other volatile poisons: as a substance that could be assessed by "its mode and speed of absorption and excretion, and the intensity of its effect."[48] Instead of measuring intoxication by outmoded standards, such as whether a man could still walk straight, Henderson argued that context was everything. In the machine age, the proper measure of intoxication was the "amount which appreciably impairs the ability of a man or woman to drive an automobile" safely. He stressed that a beverage's alcoholic strength was only one determinant of its intoxicating effects. Alcohol consumed with a meal was less intoxicating than alcohol consumed on an empty stomach because the food slowed alcohol's rate of absorption. In addition, while highly concentrated alcohol passed quickly into the bloodstream, dilute alcohol like beer stayed in the stomach longer and got slowly absorbed into the bloodstream as it passed through the intestines.[49]

Henderson classified beer as a relatively harmless substance by contrasting the intoxicating effects of hard liquor and low-alcohol beer and the social and temporal contexts in which drinkers consumed them. Henderson urged lawmakers to regulate spirits more strictly because Americans typically drank their liquor-based cocktails on an empty stomach but they drank their beer and wine "with or after meals."[50] Even a solitary late-afternoon cocktail, consumed on an empty stomach, was too often the culprit behind "serious automobile accidents, just as men are driving home."[51]

The scientific and medical testimony sought to establish moral equivalencies between alcohol and other commonly consumed commodities that some Americans regarded as minor vices. While Henderson conceded that alcohol, like other volatile poisons, carried the potential for harm, he also insisted that under appropriate circumstances alcohol posed no greater risk to Americans' health, safety, and welfare than soda, coffee, and tobacco.[52] Establishing equivalencies between alcohol and other common foods also challenged one of the drys' favorite claims: that Prohibition had made Americans healthier by ridding the country of its most dangerous vice. Dr. Oliver T. Osborne, professor emeritus of therapeutics at Yale's School of Medicine, suggested that the ill-effects of increased soda, coffee, and tobacco consumption proved otherwise. Thanks to sugary soda drinks, cases of diabetes were on the rise. Making matters worse, Americans were turning to tobacco and cigarettes to cope with "excessive nervousness" fueled by their increased caffeine consumption.[53] Dr. Osborne saw tobacco in much the same light as prohibitionists saw wine and beer—as a gateway drug that ineluctably led to more dangerous drug use. Trade unionists joined physicians in condemning the "soda-fountain habit" many Americans had developed after either abandoning alcohol or discovering how well Coca-Cola masked the harshness of bootleg liquor. Although prohibitionists saw themselves as protectors of working-class health, American Federation of Labor vice president Matthew Woll lamented that Prohibition had compelled the working class to substitute harmful soft drinks for the nutritious beer they preferred.[54]

At the hearings scientists and wet activists helped to create a new definition of intoxication that cast notions of risk and harm in relative terms. The attempt to characterize intoxication as a scientific absolute, with definitive measures, was misleading, they argued, because intoxication was also contingent upon a host of other factors. A better assessment of a substance's intoxicating effects also required an assessment of how sensibly drinking practices meshed with the time of day, patterns of work and leisure, related food practices, and the drinker's body mass. As a morning beverage, two cups of coffee were superior to beer, Henderson testified, because caffeine made a man more alert for work, but as an evening drink coffee was inferior to beer because it disrupted sleep. By contrast, the habit of drinking several beers "with and after dinner" was both respectable and worthwhile because it provided the tired and overstressed businessman with a mild "sedative ... to help restore his peace of mind and sociability." Even if the evening beer had a mildly intoxicating effect, Henderson implied, there was little reason for concern, since it would not impair the businessman for the activities "a man ordinarily has to do in the evening."[55] So long as citizens confined beer drinking to the right times and spaces, they could honor demands for discipline at work without sacrificing their need for compensatory pleasure at home.

Prohibitionists trotted out their own army of physicians and scientists to testify that 2.75 percent beers could indeed produce intoxication. Some physicians, in fact, questioned whether anyone would choose beer for any other purpose. As Dr. Richard C. Cabot, a Boston physician, asserted, "men drink beer, not because they are thirsty or because they like the taste particularly, but because they want to produce a certain sensation of exhilaration and forgetfulness."[56] In many instances, white racial anxieties amplified deep suspicions of the pleasures of food and drink. In the view of early twentieth-century elites, historian Helen Zoe Veit writes, "Self-discipline and the dutiful, even easy, eschewal of pleasure were supposedly distinguishing traits of whiteness, while wholehearted joy in the pleasures of food was a characteristic that whites ascribed to nonwhites."[57] Prohibitionists, home economists, and nutrition scientists viewed any hindrance to bodily efficiency and productivity as a blow to virtue and self-mastery and they judged the merits of particular foods and beverages accordingly.[58] The dry-aligned scientists who testified at the hearings measured pulse rates, reaction times, and coordination to reveal the compromised bodily efficiency of their research subjects after consuming a liter of 2.75 percent alcohol.[59]

When wet-allied scientists contested dry scientists' quantitative measures of intoxication, they rejected not only the drys' numbers but also their emphasis on optimal bodily efficiency as the premium measure of virtue. Henderson readily conceded that two quarts of even mild beer in the morning would reduce productivity, but he also insisted that the same amount could not be judged intoxicating when consumed at home after a hard day's work, even if the beer induced mild impairment. Dry-aligned scientists made no such allowances for the different levels of efficiency required of bodies at work and bodies at leisure. In essence, the prohibitionists' normative body was never off the clock, while the moderate drinker's body, in Henderson's view, deserved the evening off to relieve the day's stresses.

TOWARD A NEW MORAL FRAMEWORK FOR ALCOHOL CONTROL

The wet-allied scientists who testified at the Congressional hearings on modification ventured far beyond their expertise on quantitative measures of intoxication. They also joined brewers and vintners in blaming distilled spirits for the nation's drinking problems and in presenting light wines and beer as the antidote to the Prohibition-era cocktail craze. While wine and beer fostered pleasant sociability, they argued, whiskey, rum, and gin encouraged drinkers to abandon all limits of propriety and self-restraint. The larger issue at stake in the modification debates, then, was what kinds of pleasures the regulatory state should accommodate and what kinds of pleasures it should control.

At the hearings several legislators and witnesses depicted the war on alcohol as a violation of personal liberties and the nation's pluralistic values. The AFL's Matthew Woll invoked Samuel Gompers, the previous AFL president, who had warned President Woodrow Wilson in 1917 that government interference with working-class and immigrant customs of drinking beer and wine, particularly with meals, would assault "the cosmopolitan character of a large mass of our people."[60] Representative Mary Norton of New Jersey similarly stressed the folly of imposing Anglo-Saxon visions of moral purity on European immigrants who would never be convinced that drinking beer and wine was sinful.[61] While these critiques of an overly intrusive state undoubtedly resonated with the beer parade marchers who defiantly shouted, "We Want Beer!," most witnesses did not base the case for modification on personal liberty arguments. Instead, they supported beer's relegalization in more conservative terms: as a necessary corrective to the excesses of Prohibition-era cocktail culture. Yandell Henderson, who had taught college students for forty years, offered a damning report of the cocktail party scene on college campuses. In the absence of good beer,

Henderson reported, students indulged in "highly intoxicating" distilled spirits and drunken escapades.[62] Similar stories of fallen youth succumbing to hard liquor during Prohibition became a common refrain at the hearings.[63]

American youth were hardly the only victims of Prohibition-era excesses. The Prohibition-era "cocktail habit," Henderson lamented, also afflicted businessmen who knocked back three or four cocktails in their men's clubs and then attempted to drive home.[64] Even Europeans had noticed that American drinking habits had "changed for the worse" since Prohibition. "Formerly, when Americans went abroad," Henderson testified, "they tried the wine of the country." Now "Americans leave the harmless European beverages alone and go straight to . . . the 'American bar' for cocktails." Heavy drinking became such a prominent feature of upper-middle-class leisure during the 1920s that steamship companies began equipping all their liners with an "American bar."[65]

Forbidden drinking during Prohibition reinforced a longstanding American pattern of binge drinking after periods of abstinence. As social scientists have observed, the increasing segregation of work and leisure in the nineteenth and twentieth centuries encouraged many Americans to engage in dichotomized drinking marked by sober work weeks and drunken weekends. Binge drinkers often viewed alcohol consumption as a "time out," when the normal rules of social behavior and the consequences of violating them were relaxed. Although industrialization and the bureaucratization of work had sharpened the spatial, temporal, and behavioral divides between work and leisure, not all industrial societies adopted dichotomized patterns of drinking and associated alcohol consumption with the "remission of social controls."[66] Scientists, brewers, and vintners underscored this very point at the Congressional hearings. They repeatedly drew sharp contrasts between American drinking patterns and the temperate drinking cultures in France, Germany, and Italy to argue that wine and beer could foster sociability without inviting overindulgence.

Physicians and physiologists were uniquely positioned to make the case for wine and beer over spirits because their European travels (for pleasure and professional development) enabled them to demonstrate how French and German drinking traditions differed from those in the US. Wine-drinking France, Henderson testified, suffered few alcohol problems "until spirits were introduced on a considerable scale."[67] The physicians and scientists who had studied in Europe found Germany's beer gardens especially worthy of emulation. "There is no pleasanter or more harmless way to spend a summer evening," Henderson testified, "than to sit in a Munich beer garden, eat roast goose, listen to a good brass band, and drink a liter or two of the light Munich beer."[68] Senator Bingham cited a letter from an American traveling in Vienna in 1859, who wrote admiringly of German beer gardens, where "even the ladies—rich, refined, intelligent—think nothing of drinking a bottle of beer apiece."[69] Although the presence of women and children in beer gardens dismayed American prohibitionists, German-Americans saw beer gardens as wholesome "extensions of home" and viewed the presence of women and children as "a check to any excesses or improprieties."[70]

The cross-cultural comparisons of European and American drinking patterns had clear policy implications. Yandell Henderson regarded the "cocktail habit" as "a form of drug addiction" and the "worst feature of the alcohol problem ... in civilized society."[71] If lawmakers regulated distilled spirits as narcotic drugs, Henderson argued, Americans could learn to drink more like the French, Germans, and Italians.[72] If colleges encouraged their male and female students to "substitute wine for cocktails" and beer for hard liquor, Henderson testified, they would pursue "clean healthy pleasures" and avoid "serious outside dissipation."[73] Representative William Stafford of Wisconsin was equally sanguine about beer's potential to resurrect more wholesome forms of leisure. If beer returned, bowling teams, Stafford said, would stop using strong liquor and return to their "old practice of using a nonintoxicating ... light beer."[74]

Such testimony was music to brewers' and vintners' ears. Even though wet-allied scientists often used cultural comparisons to frame their defense of wine and beer, their testimony added an aura of scientific objectivity to brewers' and vintners' longstanding claim that wine and beer cultivated temperate habits and whiskey was the troublemaker lawmakers needed to constrain. Echoing Henderson, Edmund Rossi of Italian Swiss Colony told lawmakers that "the majority of our cities would soon learn the difference between the use and abuse of drink" if Congress would only permit Americans to drink light wines and beers instead of strong spirits.[75] Lawmakers could have dismissed such testimony as patently self-interested had brewers and vintners been the only ones to blame spirits for problem drinking. But such claims acquired greater credibility during the early 1930s, thanks to concurring testimony from physicians and physiologists. Prohibition itself also made it easier to pin drinking problems on hard liquor since distilled spirits dominated black market sales of alcoholic beverages. Beer and wine could still be found, but if consumers went to the trouble and expense of buying on the black market, they usually preferred something that packed a bigger punch.[76]

Though still distrusted, brewers gained some credibility as witnesses by standing firm against the return of the saloon. This position put Busch squarely in line with public opinion. Even many Americans who disdained Prohibition conceded that Prohibition had produced one worthy achievement: the destruction of the saloon. Before Prohibition, brewers had distributed most, if not all, of their production through saloons, and the leading brewing trade association had refused distillers' invitation to help them fend off prohibition by pressing for saloon reform. Instead, brewers naively hoped to evade prohibition by blaming whiskey for saloongoers' transgressions. Brewers may not have persuaded anyone but themselves, but they stubbornly stuck to their story: the only drunks who came out of saloons were the patrons who downed whiskey instead of beer.[77] Brewers sang a much different tune at the modification hearings. If brewers were to earn "the respect of the better class of citizens," August Busch acknowledged, they would have to banish "all saloon-like tendencies . . . from beer selling" and make the beer parlor or summer beer garden "as respectable a place as the most refined cafe is now."[78]

Even as the beer bill's chief proponents condemned Prohibition's moral overreach and violation of personal liberties, many of them also sought to advance a subtle moral reform agenda of their own. The bill's bottled beer provisions, which limited where the beer could be sold and who could most easily buy it, offer a case in point. The bill's supporters proposed to render the saloon obsolete by permitting beer's sale only in bottles that could be purchased by the case from grocery stores or with meals in hotel dining rooms and "high grade" restaurants, making it too expensive for buyers with strained budgets.[79] Although such provisions disadvantaged working-class consumers, they significantly advantaged the large national beer firms that could more easily shift their primary mode of distributing beer from the tap to the bottle.[80] Before Prohibition, most regional and local firms had relied entirely on saloons to sell their draught beer; by the late 1930s, many smaller firms that continued to distribute most of their production this way had been driven out of business. By contrast, during Prohibition large national shippers such as Anheuser-Busch, Schlitz, Pabst, and Blatz had used funds from selling off their saloons to expand their fleet of automobiles and trucks and their bottling facilities for nonalcoholic "near beer."[81]

As the head of a national shipping firm with expanded bottling capacity, Busch thus had a vested interest in calling upon brewers to rid beer selling of its "saloon-like tendencies." By advocating the sale of bottled beer in "beer parlors," "beer gardens," and high grade restaurants, the proponents of modification endeavored to free beer from the taint of the saloon and relocate beer drinking to sites where men would likely drink beer in the civilizing presence of women and food.[82] Even using the term "beer parlor" did important cultural work by connecting beer to another powerful symbol of genteel respectability: the home parlor, where families and guests presented their most polished selves.[83]

In many respects, the fantasy of transforming a hard-liquor nation into a beer- and wine-loving nation was the fantasy of immigrants who yearned to win broad respect for their own ethnic drinking traditions. Decades before Prohibition became law, Philadelphia Rabbi Joseph Krauskopf, had urged lawmakers to reject prohibitionism and instead follow the example of Jews who had used wine wisely for thousands of years. In an 1889 sermon, Krauskopf attested that home consumption of alcohol not only kept Jewish men from the saloon, but it "contributed no small share to their . . . domestic purity and happiness."[84] The widespread dissatisfaction with Prohibition created a more receptive audience for such arguments. August Busch and Judge Marion de Vries, both leaders of key industry trade associations, genuinely thought that real reform and economic recovery would follow if lawmakers adopted public policies that privileged beer and wine as the agents of "true temperance."

THE BEER BILL BECOMES LAW

Although Congressional sympathies were clearly aligned with the brewers and their wet allies, the congressional hearings gave prohibitionists equal time to rebut the wet testimony point by point. When brewers and vintners suggested that fermented beverages could wean Americans from whiskey, the "dry" witnesses countered that low alcohol beer would simply stimulate drinkers' appetites for more potent spirits.[85] And when brewers portrayed beer as a convivial family-friendly drink, prohibitionists reiterated their most deeply held conviction: that alcohol destroyed families, victimized women and children, and left poverty and despair in its wake.[86] The dry witnesses also scoffed at the notion that European drinking cultures were worthy of emulation, noting that drunkenness plagued wine-drinking and beer-drinking countries, too.[87]

As proof that beer invariably led drinkers down the slippery slope to wine and hard liquor, Reverend William Sheafe Chase testified that Germany had sacrificed victory in World War I because the beer-loving Germans "could not restrain themselves" when they "fell upon the [French] wine cellars" just as they were about to capture Paris.[88]

Despite the forceful objections of drys, the beer bill coasted to victory on a vote of 316 to 97 in the House and 43 to 36 in the Senate.[89] The odds that a modification bill would finally pass after three previous failed attempts in 1924, 1926, and 1932 had risen substantially when the landslide electoral victory in November 1932 swept President Roosevelt and a huge Democratic congressional majority into office. Not only had the Democratic Party platform included a plank endorsing both modification and repeal, but several of the newly elected Republicans had pledged to add their votes to the wet column.[90] The *New York Evening Journal* had a good sense of the future when it predicted "Waterloos for the Water-Wagon."[91] The odds of swift passage rose even higher when President Roosevelt recommended immediate legalization of beer to meet the government's urgent need for revenues.[92] Dry senators initially resisted, but just enough fell in line when they realized that constituents might resent a nay vote if the absence of beer taxes forced Congress to raise taxes through less desirable means.[93]

On March 22, 1933, less than three weeks into Roosevelt's first term, Congress approved the Cullen-Harrison Act (known informally as the Beer and Wine Revenue Act) and set April 7, 1933 as the date for legal beer's big debut. Coming on the heels of the Emergency Banking Act and the Economy Act, the new law became the third major legislative achievement of the president's first 100 days and "ensured that FDR would remain forever identified with repeal."[94] Envisioned as an economic stimulus, a budget balancer, and a jobs creator, the Beer and Wine Revenue Act, quite literally gave many Americans their first taste of the New Deal. In immeasurable ways, beer's legalization bolstered confidence that the federal government could act decisively to address national problems. Even though African American and ethnic working-class voters deeply resented Prohibition as a discriminatory and unwarranted government intrusion, Prohibition did not diminish their appetite for using federal power to bolster economic security and labor rights.[95] At the same time, the beer bill also portended the federal government's diminished post-Prohibition role in alcohol regulation. The new 3.2 percent standard applied only in states that passed similar legislation, and the bill barred beer shipments to states that continued to ban 3.2 beer. Almost overnight, new kinds of culinary tourism sprung up to circumvent such restrictions. Parched citizens in dry Texas, Oklahoma, and Arkansas could not buy beer locally, but they could board a train to enjoy much-hyped beer excursions to St. Louis, Shreveport, and Lake Charles, Louisiana.[96]

The final legislation gave brewers most of what they wanted short of full-scale repeal, but it rejected the vintners' appeal for an early reprieve from Prohibition. The Beer and Wine Revenue Act raised the definition of intoxicating from 0.5 percent to 3.2 percent by weight (or 4 percent by volume), just slightly above 2.75 percent "war beer." Some winemakers decided to make the best of the new 3.2 percent alcohol limit by marketing bottled wine punches diluted with seltzer. The results disappointed. Congressman John J. O'Connor, a conservative Tammany Hall Democrat, likened the diluted wine's taste to "a prophylactic mouth wash."[97] Although Congress had, in theory, judged 3.2 beer nonintoxicating, the regulations governing its sale varied widely. The most liberal states permitted sales of bottled beer in grocery stores, chain stores, and delicatessens.[98] More restrictive states pointedly kept 3.2 beer out of soda fountains and drug stores, fearing that beer sold there would become a "constant temptation" to minors.[99] In the eyes of state policymakers, beer's innocence did not rest on its low alcohol content alone. It also hinged on the reputability of the venues that sold it and the customers who bought it.

Even the brewing industry cautiously broached the new 3.2 percent limit. Testing conducted by the Anti-Saloon League and public health officials revealed that most beer in New York contained 2.2 to 2.6 percent alcohol—well below the 3.2 percent standard.[100] The brewers' caution was not unwarranted. Many drys greeted beer's return grimly determined to reveal the folly of sanctioning 3.2 percent beer.[101] *Newsweek* reported that prohibitionists in Minneapolis planned to scout bars and taverns for inebriated customers and then "haul them to court to prove that 3.2 is an inebriating percentage."[102] These were not idle threats. As historian Lisa McGirr has shown, in the country's prohibitionist strongholds, volunteer "citizen warriors" drawn from the Woman's Christian Temperance Union, the Anti-Saloon League, and the Ku Klux Klan bolstered the work of overwhelmed Prohibition agents by acting as their eyes and ears. Throughout the 1920s and early 1930s, the religious right's "shadow" army of citizen enforcers conducted raids and door-to-door house searches and even made arrests.[103] A far cry from the temperance women of the previous century who prayed

FIGURE 2. Beer delivery in Cleveland, Ohio, on April 6, 1933, the day before 3.2 percent beer became legal. Everett Collection via Alamy.

outside saloons to encourage righteous behavior, the Prohibition era's citizen warriors preferred strong-arm tactics over moral suasion.[104] In 1933, organized drys remained an intimidating force in Ohio, the state that gave birth to the Anti-Saloon League. Even though Ohio permitted sales of 3.2 beer in grocery stores and at drug store lunch counters, most grocery stores and chain stores opted not to sell the mild beer after dry organizations threatened to boycott them.[105] The success of such threats provided an early glimpse of the headwinds that alcohol producers and purveyors would confront in the new post-repeal era.

CONCLUSION

Most histories of Prohibition acknowledge the Beer Bill as an important steppingstone along the path to full-scale repeal, but they bypass the 1932–33 Congressional debates on modification that preceded the bill's passage. It's easy to understand why. The beer parades and the sweeping Democratic electoral victories in 1932 election made beer's relegalization seem like a foregone conclusion. In skipping past the Congressional hearings, however, historians miss something important. The brewers, winemakers, industrial toxicologists, physicians, and labor leaders who testified at the hearings articulated a defense of pleasure that the most influential anti-prohibitionist organizations had been reluctant to do. If their testimony did not directly shape how policymakers imagined new regulatory frameworks for alcohol control, it likely fortified their commitment to policies already under consideration. As we will see in chapter 2, the Rockefeller Report, which outlined a model for liquor control that many states adopted after repeal, echoed scientists' calls to regulate spirits more strictly than beer and wine.[106]

The hearings also compel us to reconsider how modern science facilitated Prohibition's downfall. Historian Philip Pauly contends that Yandell Henderson's view of the relatively innocuous effects of low-alcohol beers and light wines "prevailed because his perspective on the meaning of alcohol intoxication and the degree of hazard it represented was consistent with the kind of experience that millions of Americans already had with a wide range of volatile poisons."[107] The new ways of calculating thresholds of risk, however, were not the only, or even the most significant, contribution that scientists made to the debate over the meaning and measurement of intoxication. By arguing that alcohol potency alone did not determine intoxication, Henderson and others undercut the basic premise of "pharmacologicalism"—the idea that the underlying chemical properties of psychoactive substances determine their pharmacological effects.[108] They argued instead that the social, spatial, and temporal contexts in which drinkers consumed alcohol also factored into the equation, sometimes muting and sometimes enhancing alcohol's intoxicating effects.

If we locate the modification hearings within a longer historical frame, going back to the late nineteenth- and early twentieth-century battles to forestall Prohibition, we might instead credit science for lending credibility to older anti-prohibitionist arguments and cherished ethnic traditions that regarded beer and wine as the temperate alternatives to hard spirits. Physiologists and physicians could challenge established scientific orthodoxies because they, more so than brewers and vintners, possessed the moral and scientific authority to advance a compelling defense of pleasure. Yandell Henderson's argument that the social and spatial contexts of alcohol consumption also determined alcohol's intoxicating effects was an argument that brewers and vintners had been making all along.

For a variety of reasons, legislators gave brewers and vintners a much more sympathetic hearing in 1932 and 1933 than they had during World War I, when the Eighteenth Amendment was steamrolling its way to ratification. Anti-immigrant prejudice, fueled by the jingoism of war, had stifled vocal opposition to Prohibition.[109] Although such prejudices persisted in the early 1930s, the "claims that immigrants' drinking habits . . . posed a threat to American society had become less convincing." Southern and eastern European immigrants had become "more integrated into American culture" and "no one ethnic, religious, racial, or economic group had a monopoly on illegal alcohol purveyance or consumption."[110] In addition, ethnic food entrepreneurs had gained a stronger foothold in the broader American food marketplace during Prohibition. Home economists and food reformers who had long encouraged Americans to "forgo the pleasures of" an ethnically diverse "food marketplace" increasingly found themselves on the losing end of a national food fight that pitted those who viewed food as a form of pleasure and recreation against those who viewed it merely "as the fuel" to optimize bodily functions.[111]

For many senators and representatives, the need to address soaring unemployment and the demands of their constituents were reason enough to bring back beer. Nevertheless, the testimony of brewers, vintners, and scientists set forth important ideas that continued to reverberate in subsequent policy debates about the state's role in managing the pleasures and perils of intoxicating beverages. The potent politics of weak brews put the state's duty to accommodate pleasure on par with its obligation to regulate vice.

2

A New Deal for Alcohol?

As the Twenty-First Amendment made its way through state legislatures in the final months of 1933, businesses, politicians, and alcohol consumers greeted Prohibition's imminent demise with great expectations. At home, supporters of repeal predicted that a resurrected alcoholic beverage industry would spur economic recovery and solve the farm crisis. Expectations across the Canadian border and across the Atlantic were just as exuberant. *Collier's* reported that Canadian distillers were "withholding [whiskey] from bootleg channels," anticipating "a grand American cleanup on the basis of a short supply and high prices." Some even imagined that Great Britain and France could "square their war debts with exports of Scotch and Irish [whiskey], cognac and champagne."[1] French winemakers, plagued by oversupply, reveled in the possibility that American consumers, with their "supposed capacity for unlimited alcoholic consumption," might rejuvenate "the failing French wine industry."[2]

Meanwhile, in the United States, self-styled drinking reformers feverishly penned drinking guidebooks to instruct Americans how to drink well without drinking too much. Dozens of such books, with titles like *Quiet Drinking* and *Bacchus Behave!: The Lost Art of Polite Drinking*, flooded bookstores and libraries in anticipation of Prohibition's repeal.[3] The zeal for drinking reform even extended to the Roosevelt Administration. In a 1934 address to the Women's National Democratic Club, Rexford Tugwell, the assistant secretary of the Department of Agriculture and a member of President Roosevelt's Brain Trust, urged women to accompany their husbands to "beer gardens and consume the long, slow drinks" that encourage "pleasant conversation." If Democratic clubwomen entertained with wine and beer, Tugwell asserted, they could strike a blow against the "excesses of the bootleg decade."[4]

Repeal was slow to answer the high hopes for revitalized markets and drinking reform. Although many of the new alcoholic beverage controls privileged wine and beer over distilled spirits, drinking reformers made little headway in their quest to transform a liquor-loving nation into a temperate republic of wine and beer drinkers. The Great Depression, the low quality of commercial alcohol, and a chaotic regulatory environment all stymied the development of robust alcohol markets. By the mid-1930s, per capita consumption of wine, beer, and spirits had reached only 60 percent of the highest pre-Prohibition rates.[5] In addition, many Americans who had voted to abandon Prohibition had not yet abandoned their mistrust of the alcoholic beverage industry. In the eyes of many voters, alcohol, as Edward Bernays, the famed public relations counselor, put it, was still "on probation."[6]

Throughout the 1930s, alcoholic beverage producers encountered many obstacles on the road to recovery and redemption. The economic and sensory legacies of Prohibition left brewers, vintners, and distillers befuddled by consumers' changing tastes and ill equipped to meet their expectations for higher quality alcohol. In many states, public mistrust and the lingering influence of drys kept trade associations on the defensive. Rather than settling the alcohol question for good, the end of Prohibition opened new conversations about how business and the state could simultaneously accommodate and discipline consumers' appetites for intoxicating pleasures. Concerns about restricting access to more potent forms of alcohol guided policymaking, but when it came to regulating public drinking, cultural anxieties about alcohol's potential to disrupt hierarchies of race, class, gender, and sexuality left a bigger imprint. Tastemakers and self-styled drinking reformers were not content to entrust repeal's success to state liquor authorities alone. In their eyes, making repeal work would also require women to embrace new roles as the guardians of pleasure.

COMING TO TERMS WITH PROHIBITION'S ECONOMIC LEGACIES

Alcohol's post-repeal debut was a disaster waiting to happen. In the fall of 1933, when only a few more states needed to ratify the Twenty-First

Amendment, hundreds rushed into the wine business, swelling the ranks of California's wineries from 130 to over 800.[7] Profit-seekers ignorant of sound winemaking techniques used poor quality grapes, out-of-date technology, and bacteria-infested cooperage.[8] They then loaded bulk wine destined for eastern markets into unlined metal tank cars, some having previously carried olive oil or petroleum.[9] Some inexperienced vintners bottled grape juice still undergoing fermentation. In time those bottles would explode on store shelves.[10] The wine that did make its way into restaurants and family dining rooms often tasted harsh and sour. Not surprisingly, the reputation of the entire state of California, which produced 90 percent of US wines, came under attack. "If California had been any state but California it might have produced something fine in wines," *Fortune* wrote in its February 1934 feature on the US wine industry. "But California has always done things on a grand scale: it would rather produce the *most* than the *best*."[11]

Much of the whiskey carried by licensed package stores or the new state-controlled monopolies tasted little better than whiskey hot off the still. Initially, given the limited supply of aged whiskey on hand, the best many distillers could deliver was an unpalatable "mélange of green liquor and neutral spirits."[12] One journalist, taking stock of the situation, concluded that "pedigreed whisky is about as common as hens' teeth in this country."[13] Liquor fanciers who had expected repeal to hasten the death of cut whiskey and shoddy blends (mixed with a smidge of whiskey and plenty of additives) instead discovered that the adulterated whiskeys of Prohibition had followed them into the new era. Dr. Shirley Wynne, New York City's Health Commissioner, analyzed twenty-five samples of legal whiskey sold in the city and "found that twelve low-priced brands were composed of 'less whisky than any self-respecting bootlegger would put in a blend, together with alcohol, rye flavoring, coloring matter, and water.'"[14]

One group clearly benefitted from the bad commercial wine and whiskey that flooded the market: bootleggers who could supply untaxed alcohol (of similar or better quality) at a much lower price. Journalist Edward Angly noted that experienced and well-capitalized illicit distillers were producing product "as pure and pleasurable as most of the liquor coming ... from the approved plants in Illinois, Indiana, Kentucky, Maryland, and Pennsylvania."[15] Troubled by the bootleggers' price advantage, the Federal Alcohol Control Administration (FACA) allowed 20 million additional gallons of Canadian whiskey to pass into the United States to boost the supply of legal whiskey and lower prices.[16]

In the meantime, American whiskey distillers developed shortcuts to speed the process of aging and produce the closest approximation of four-year-old whiskey that chemists could achieve. Chemists experimented with raising warehouse temperatures twenty to thirty degrees, agitating the barrels to increase whiskey's contact with the staves, adding charred chips, and artificially stimulating oxidation—anything that would take the newness out of whiskey and eliminate undesirable elements.[17] Others tried exposing whiskey to ultraviolet light and passing an electric current through it.[18]

Consumers were not easily fooled. In the first few months of repeal, pent-up demand guaranteed brisk alcohol sales no matter what the industry put on the market. Demand slackened, however, after the initial flurry of buying, in no small part because commercial grade alcohol was so poor. Americans drank 65 million gallons of whiskey annually before Prohibition and less than half that much in 1934, the first year of repeal. Regulators, FACA officials, and distillers suspected that purchases of bootleg whiskey accounted for much of that lost volume.[19] Many consumers during the Depression simply had no money to spare for alcohol of dubious quality. Chaotic depression-era markets eventually drove many newcomers out of business, but they had put enough bad stuff on the market to strain consumer trust. Infuriated wine industry spokesmen blamed disappointing consumer demand on out-of-state bottlers and other "get-rich-quick" schemers who blended California bulk wines with raisins, extracts, water, sugar, and other adulterants.[20]

Prohibition also deserved blame for the low quality of wine. Only a few trained winemakers had made sacramental wines during Prohibition and the resultant loss of winemaking expertise and deterioration of production facilities hampered the industry's post-repeal reconstruction. Maynard Amerine, the UC Davis enologist who guided the industry's recovery, recalled the dire situation: "By and large, the industry had no laboratories, they had poor equipment, they had poor grapes, they were undercapitalized and they didn't have enough ... trained winemakers."[21] Ernest Gallo candidly acknowledged that "neither myself nor my brother knew anything about winemaking" beyond what they had gleaned from two winemaking pamphlets unearthed in the Modesto Library. "We were aware ... that when my father made wine at home during Prohibition, the wine started out being sweet soon after it was made in November or December, and gradually became sour, so that in July it was very sour." Determined to get their wine to market before it soured, they shipped their first batch in December 1933 over the stern objections of veteran Napa Valley winemakers who warned that the wine was "still in the process of fermentation" and would "blow the ends out of those barrels." Gallo ignored their advice and sold the first year's entire output in bulk, knowing that the wine would carry the bottler's name and not their own.[22]

The brewing and distilling industries recovered more quickly from Prohibition because many large firms had adapted their equipment to nonalcoholic enterprises and could easily readapt that equipment when alcoholic beverage production again became legal. To produce the nonalcoholic "near beers" or "cereal beverages" sold during Prohibition, breweries still had to brew the beer before de-alcoholizing it. They could also sell yeast cakes and livestock feed yielded from the brewing process. Although breweries had to reconfigure their machinery to produce malt syrup, soda drinks, cheese, ice cream, and cider vinegar, these sidelines helped breweries preserve their brand names and their distribution networks. The Volstead Act's exemption for medicinal whiskey also kept a small number of distillers in business. The federal government licensed six distillers to sell their pre-Prohibitions stocks of 100-proof bonded spirits to pharmacies, doctors, and dentists. When those stocks ran low in 1928, the government allowed them to manufacture 3 million gallons of whiskey collectively. As a result, the lucky six—Schenley, National Distillers, Glenmore, Brown-Forman, Frankfort, and Stitzel—entered the repeal era with stocks of aged whiskey on hand and a leg up on the competition.[23] Other distillers kept their machinery humming by producing industrial alcohol, a key ingredient in the manufacture of toiletries, shoe polish, and other consumer goods.

The Volstead Act's curious provision permitting homemade "nonintoxicating cider and fruit juices" also undermined wine quality after repeal. The fermented fruit juice clause in Section 29 of the Volstead Act dramatically changed the types of grapes that California growers planted and cultivated for the home winemaking market. In Chicago, New York, Boston, Philadelphia—cities with large populations of wine-drinking immigrants—home winemakers favored the fat, thick-skinned shipping grapes like Alicante Bouschet and table and raisin grapes like Muscat and Malaga, which produced sweeter wines. Many buyers passed over the best wine grapes, which often appeared scroungy after the long transcontinental rail journey. Carignane and Zinfandel (both red wine grapes) sometimes found their way into buyers' trucks, but the grape that won home winemakers' hearts and soon took over large swaths of California's San Joaquin Valley and Livermore Valley was the

Alicante Bouschet. The hardy Alicantes not only shipped well, but, as Daniel Okrent has written, their "uncommonly dark red flesh produced something that not only looked like decent wine but managed to maintain that deception after two or three pressings, or god knows how many dilutions." The Alicante was so rich in color that some winemakers who added sugar and water to the mass remaining after the first pressing could get 600–700 gallons of red wine from a single ton of Alicantes—significantly more than the 150 gallons that ordinary winemaking methods produced. Such robust yields explain why many Italian home winemakers willingly paid up to one dollar more for a box of Alicante over other varietals.[24] Some may have also judged the diluted Alicante wine superior to the *vinelli* that Italian peasants made by adding water to the leftover sediments and grape skins. In the Old Country peasants could not afford undiluted wine.[25]

The fermented fruit juice exemption set off a frenzy of vineyard planting in California and across the nation that degraded the quality of wine for decades after Prohibition's demise. When the shipping grapes and table and raisin grapes favored by East Coast buyers began fetching outrageously high prices, growers dedicated the new acreage to inferior table and raisin grapes. They resisted calls to replant superior wine grapes after Prohibition because wine grapes yielded less fruit per acre and cost more to cultivate.[26] Throughout the 1930s, roughly equal portions of wine grapes and table and raisin grapes landed in the crushers, assuring, at best, a mediocre wine.[27]

The alcoholic beverage industry struggled to shake off another troubling legacy of Prohibition: the stigma of black market enterprise. After repeal, many Americans still regarded the legal alcoholic beverage industry as an unsavory business run by unsavory characters. Alfred Fromm, a German-Jewish wine importer who counted numerous Hollywood movie stars among his wealthy patrons, learned quickly that wine selling in the United States was not the "highly respected" business it had been in Europe. William Randolph Hearst, one of Fromm's first calls after he immigrated to the United States, ran a background check on Fromm before even consenting to an appointment. Although he eventually secured a $5,000 order from the publishing magnate, Fromm was stunned "that someone could think I might be a gangster or bootlegger."[28]

Popular ways of talking about alcoholic beverage producers as "merchants of booze" and "alcohol traffickers"—a vernacular that tied the industry to drug pushers and the underworld—reinforced the industry's unsavory image. Several key industry players had actually made their fortunes and honed their merchandising savvy running bootleg operations during Prohibition. Seagram's Samuel Bronfman sold whiskey to American bootleggers who took liquor across the Canadian border into Montana, North Dakota, and Minnesota. The Bronfman brothers coordinated smuggling into California from a post in British Columbia and they established other posts in Nassau, Havana, and Belize to move liquor into Florida and various Gulf Coast ports. Hiram Walker's Harry Hatch smuggled Canadian liquor across Lake Erie into Detroit and Buffalo. Schenley's Lewis Rosenstiel maintained a thoroughly legitimate business selling medicinal whiskey during Prohibition, but he too imported liquor from Canada and Bermuda during Prohibition. Other bootleggers formed legal alcohol distribution companies. Abner Zwillman and his bootlegging partners formed Browne Vintners, which distributed alcohol in the New York region, while John Torrio helped establish Prendergast and Davies.[29]

Bootlegging's continued existence after repeal compounded the industry's troubles. The relatively low excise taxes on beer and the high cost of proper refrigeration equipment made it difficult for bootleggers to compete with brewers on both price and quality.[30] Moonshiners and home winemakers, however, continued to churn out product. A comprehensive consumer survey of New York City residents by the *New York World-Telegram* in 1934 found that more than a quarter of the city's poor were still fermenting and distilling their own.[31] While a good deal of homemade wine found its way to the family dinner table—a practice that was still legal—a portion made its way into bootleg channels. Most bootleggers trafficked in spirits, selling their supply to licensed dealers, who poured the illicit liquor into empty trademarked bottles or counterfeit bottles adorned with fake whiskey labels and revenue stamps.[32] Consumers who purchased the counterfeit liquor either could not tell the difference or, as one journalist speculated, simply did not "care what they drink as long as it packs a wallop."[33] FACA Director Joseph Choate estimated that the government was collecting revenue on only half of the spirits consumed.[34] Vintners and distillers complained that high excise taxes and excessive regulation had forced consumers to seek alternative suppliers. "What clerk working for thirty dollars a week," one journalist wondered, "will spend a day's pay for a quart of legal rye when he can go around the corner and get a gallon of bootleg for the same money?"[35] Making matters worse, many states prohibited sales of bulk wine directly from barrels, eliminating the most affordable wine option for "folks of modest means."³⁶ Vintners and distillers were surely correct that high prices had deflated consumer demand, but they had yet to grasp the possibility that their products also failed to suit consumers' fancy.

COMING TO TERMS WITH PROHIBITION'S SENSORY LEGACIES

One of Prohibition's most significant legacies was its impact on consumer's drinking practices and sensory perceptions of taste. After repeal, alcohol producers quickly discovered that they were operating in a new and somewhat unfamiliar sensory environment. Dry table wines and hoppy beers had sold well before Prohibition, but they now struggled to find a broad market. A new generation of drinkers who had never sampled alcohol had yet to acquire a taste for it, while Americans who had imbibed illicit potables now exhibited an affinity for alcohol that packed a punch. Conditioned by the expanding market for soft drinks and processed foods, American palates increasingly favored the sweet and the bland.³⁷ During the 1920s, coffee, orange and grape juice, carbonated soft drinks, and milk all surged in popularity. Backed by multimillion-dollar advertising campaigns, food companies helped to make drinking OJ for breakfast and soda for an afternoon pick-me-up a daily habit for millions of Americans.³⁸ Sales of orange juice and soda also boomed because consumers adopted them as mixers to mask the unpleasant taste of bootleg alcohol.³⁹ Promoted as "The Drink That Cheers But Does Not Inebriate," Coca-Cola provided the perfect fizzy cover for the bathtub gin that did inebriate.

During Prohibition, the greater availability of homemade wine and the greater desirability of spirits transformed established drinking patterns. According to the estimates of one economist, by the late 1920s beer drinking had plunged by 70 percent from its peak in 1914, while the use of spirits had risen by 10 percent and the use of wine had increased by 65 percent.⁴⁰ These new drinking practices affirmed the "iron law of prohibition," which holds that government prohibitions drive out the milder forms of banned substances and boost the consumption of stronger (and potentially more dangerous) substances.⁴¹ Beer fared more poorly than wine and spirits because its bulkiness made beer difficult to hide and risky to smuggle. Beer's lower alcohol content also made it less lucrative for black market dealers. Consumers largely rejected the de-alcoholized "near beer" that brewers promoted as a "cereal beverage" but branded with suggestive-sounding names like

Pivo (the Bohemian word for beer), Bevo, and Nearo to signal their beer-based origin. Although the initial sales looked promising—in 1921 Americans drank 300 million gallons of de-alcoholized beer—sales nosedived when the fake beers failed to attract repeat buyers and consumers turned to more potent alternatives. By 1932, breweries sold a meager 85.7 million gallons of near beer—and much of that was likely destined for consumption as "needle beer," a potent drink that consumers and speakeasy proprietors created by injecting ethyl alcohol into the bottle. Anheuser-Busch, Pabst, Schlitz, Miller, and other breweries saw much better returns from their malt syrup and yeast—each sold separately as baking goods but marketed under the famous beer trademarks and combined at home to remarkably good effect.[42]

None of these commercial beer substitutes took off like homemade wine or moonshine. Before Prohibition, making wine from California grapes had become such a well-established annual tradition in New York's Little Italies that many families outfitted their basements with presses, barrels, and bottling equipment. During Prohibition what had once been a "domestic routine" became a "commercial livelihood" when many residents in the ethnic districts of American cities took advantage of a quirky provision in the prohibition law that permitted the production of "nonintoxicating cider and fruit juices."[43] Appearing in Section 29 of the Volstead Act, the fermented fruit juice exemption fueled wine's wild rise from the 55 million gallons produced commercially in 1919 to an estimated 111 million gallons produced annually in American homes between 1922 and 1929.[44] Subsequent regulations established that male heads of household could produce 200 gallons of fermented fruit juice a year *exclusively* for home use—a volume roughly equivalent to three bottles a day. Not surprisingly, much of the surplus production found its way into bootleg channels.[45] In Greenwich Village, home to a large Italian American community, "every Italian barber, bootblack, cigar store, and grocer," Caroline Ware reported, sold bootleg wine. Greenwich Village's Italian restaurants—a popular stop for nightclubbing Uptowners—served up more of the surplus wine with their spaghetti and veal parmigiani. As one former flapper, Katherine Young, recalled, "The wine was raw and strong and everyone loosened up quickly and got drunk easily."[46]

When prohibitionists grudgingly consented to the fermented fruit juice exemption, few of them anticipated the scale of home-winemaking operations that would emerge in the ethnic districts of major US cities. The voluminous production hardly surprised Italian American vintners.

"In the old country," California vintner Horace Lanza recalled, "the ordinary Italian . . . made his wine. He didn't buy wine."[47] Responses to the ambiguous legality of home winemaking varied sharply. In Williamson, a county in southern Illinois, Ku Klux Klan vigilantes, spurred by ethnic hatred, invaded the homes of immigrant Italian mineworkers and terrorized their families. When the Klansmen found wine, they bloodied the men and dragged them off to jail.[48] By contrast, in regions where disdain for Prohibition was high, sympathetic wet juries refused to convict home winemakers and enforcement officials looked the other way.[49] The volume of home winemaking was so high that San Francisco's trash collectors delivered demijohns filled with red wine and picked up the empties as part of their regular service.[50] In wet cities, few home winemakers even bothered to conceal their semi-licit activities. A *New York Times* reporter touring San Francisco's Italian neighborhoods sighted numerous wine presses drying in front yards.[51] The red-stained street gutters and grape-stained hands of women grocery store workers in New York city's Italian enclaves were certain giveaways that fall winemaking was underway.[52]

Vineyardists in California, New York, and Ohio broadened the base of wine-curious consumers by developing new products that made home winemaking easier for the uninitiated. Their cunning marketing schemes took care to preserve the illusion of homemade wine's legal innocence. Caligrapo's grape concentrate, packed in a five-gallon tin can, instructed the consumer to add three cans of water but warned against putting the diluted concentrate "in a warm place because it will ferment and that is against the law."[53] Other companies sold juice kegs and wine bricks with "a yeast pill to start fermentation and a printed warning not to use it 'because if you do, this will turn into wine.'" The makers of the Vino Sano Grape Brick brand could not have winked more conspicuously when they instructed consumers to add 1/10 percent of benzoate of soda to prevent fermentation.[54] Working-class consumers with long-established wine drinking traditions favored fresh grapes and the less expensive wine bricks, while doctors, dentists, lawyers, engineers, and stockbrokers favored the home-delivered reconstituted concentrate, priced at a hefty fifteen dollars for a five-gallon keg. The George Lonz Winery, which sold kegs of juice from grapes grown on the Lake Erie islands, established a diverse customer base of Germans in Ohio (wine drinkers by tradition), ordinary working people in Detroit, salaried professionals, and the presidents of Columbia Motors and the Ohio Bell Telephone Company.[55]

The vineyardists' most audacious and legally dubious marketing scheme was Vine-Glo, a grape concentrate available in eight varieties—Port, Virginia Dare (a scuppernong wine), Muscatel, Tokay, Sauterne, Riesling, Claret, Burgundy—and delivered directly to the buyer's home. The product was the brainchild of New York winemaker Captain Paul Garrett, who produced Virginia Dare, the nation's most popular pre-Prohibition wine. In 1929, Garrett, together with California vineyardist Donald D. Conn, organized the largest surviving California wineries and his New York wineries into a giant cooperative called Fruit Industries, Inc. Pledging to relieve California's grape surplus, Fruit Industries secured millions in loans from the Federal Farm Board, which President Herbert Hoover had created to stabilize agricultural commodity markets. In no small irony, Fruit Industries also managed to hire Mabel Walker Willebrandt, the former assistant US attorney general responsible for Prohibition enforcement, to vouch for the legality of their enterprise. Assured by magazine ads that Vine-Glo was "legal in your own home," consumers bought a million gallons in 1929–30. Conn expected to double sales the following year, but President Hoover, under pressure from drys, withdrew his support and ordered Fruit Industries to stop further production.[56]

Although the Volstead Act's fermented fruit juice exemption boosted wine's popularity, the practice of home winemaking and the entry of highly sweet sacramental wine into bootleg channels created several long-term headaches for the resurrected wine industry. Most significantly, Prohibition accustomed American consumers to wines that often had more residual sugar and alcohol (18 to 20 percent by volume) than table wine, and these tastes proved remarkably resistant to change. Prohibition-era home winemakers encouraged the trend away from table wines by adding sugar during fermentation to boost potency, sweetness and volume. Sweet wines like Angelica, Muscat, and Tokay—all fortified to 18 percent alcohol—also dominated the sacramental wine market, which, thanks to weak oversight, stretched well beyond the perimeters of Catholic churches and Jewish synagogues.[57] Prohibition-era scarcity also saddled wine with negative associations. Popularly derided as "basement rotgut," "red ink," and "dago red," the raw, strong, and inebriating wine that flowed into the black market became inextricably linked in public memory with bootleggers, immigrants, and skid row derelicts. Marketing experts viewed wine as a particularly tough sell for the younger drinkers who had consumed large quantities of bootleg "red ink"—"not by choice but because it was cheap." Assuming the quality of bootleg wine to be typical wine, the younger generation "would not think of buying wine," H. F. Stoll Jr. predicted, "now that legal beer and hard liquor [could] be bought."[58]

Prohibition also dealt a huge blow to the tradition of dining with wine. Although some cosmopolitans who ventured into any Little Italy during Prohibition in search of "booze" developed a fondness for spaghetti and the red wine that Italian restaurants surreptitiously served in coffee cups, many of the higher-echelon restaurants either shuttered their doors or limped along in the absence of alcohol revenues.[59] Prohibition further eroded wine's place in the middle-class home "by making cooking with wine taboo in public and expensive in private." "The recipes for French dishes which survived in middle-class cookbooks," historian Harvey Levenstein has written, "became charades of their former selves: wineless 'Chicken Bordelaise,' and Chicken Marengo which was merely chicken in tomato sauce."[60] Jessica McLachlin, a staff writer for the Wine Institute, lamented in 1934 that a "lost generation" had "forgotten the delights of dining with wine."[61]

After repeal, brewers also struggled initially to adapt to changing consumer tastes. Although Americans had long preferred blander lagers, consumers pushed brewers to make them blander still after Prohibition. Finding the early beers too hoppy and too heavy, consumers rejected the beers that seasoned brewmasters had created using the old formulas and brewing methods. Beer's share of the market fell from 63 percent of all alcoholic beverages sold in 1915 to 47 percent in 1935. Sales began to pick up when brewers reduced the hops and malt enough to produce a less full-bodied and less-filling beer.[62] Although spirits claimed a larger share of the alcoholic beverage market after Prohibition than it had before, gin and blended whiskey (a mix of aged whiskey and neutral grain spirits) both entered the repeal era with diminished reputations. Gin became the go-to staple of "industrial-scale bootleggers" because it was easily flavored with juniper oil and "a dash of glycerin" and it required no more aging, one writer observed, than the "time it takes to get from the bathroom where it is made to the front porch where the cocktail [party] is in progress."[63] After repeal, gin continued to be readily available and more accessibly priced, but lingering memories of bathtub gin and the sensory punishment of consuming the adulterated "mixtures of bootleggers" caused many consumers to distrust commercial gin and blended whiskeys.[64]

Despite Prohibition's success in reducing aggregate demand, it also reinforced the allure of whiskey and cocktails, heightened the appeal of fortified wines, and reduced the consumption of the lower-alcohol alternatives. A new breed of drinking reformers aimed to reverse those trends.

WOMEN DRINKERS AND THE UTOPIAN POSSIBILITIES OF DRINKING REFORM

A wide variety of self-styled drinking reformers—including New Deal administrators, drinking etiquette counselors, restaurateurs, and alcohol trade associations—saw repeal as a moment that unleashed utopian possibilities. Arriving at a time when many Americans sought to reform capitalism and redress the maldistribution of wealth, repeal opened the door to reforming American drinking practices as well as the political economy that underpinned particular cultures of drink. Some reformers operating both within and outside the alcoholic beverage industry hoped to transform the United States into a republic of temperate wine and beer drinkers. If used properly, beer and wine, they argued, could serve as antidotes to the over-mechanization of work and play and to the cultural excesses of the Jazz Age. Winemaker Paul Garrett and the American Temperance-Wine League, a Virginia-based advocacy group, even imagined that a nation planted in vines tended by yeoman farmers, could solve the problem of mass unemployment and create a self-sustaining economy.[65] Such utopian fantasies of economic and cultural revitalization seeped into the Roosevelt Administration as well. Shortly after leaving his post as director of the Federal Alcohol Control Administration, Joseph Choate published a lengthy piece in the *New York Times* touting wine as the solution to the nation's farm and drink problems. If every American put down their liquor glass and instead drank "four glasses of wine a week"—roughly half the volume consumed by the French and Italians according to Choate's calculations—temperate habits would take hold, unemployment would fall, and farmers in sectors plagued by overproduction could develop new livelihoods cultivating grapes.[66]

Although the new drinking reformers envisioned a larger role for alcohol in American leisure, they carefully cast themselves as third way between the old cultures of wet indulgence and dry abstention. They welcomed alcohol as an adjunct to the good life but rejected a return to the saloon and unbridled drinking freedom. They shunned Prohibition as an overly intrusive and ineffective state intervention, but they also sanctioned subtler forms of consumer surveillance, whether exercised by the regulatory state or by the force of social pressure and the civilizing presence of women drinkers.

Several drinking reformers imagined that women would assume a central role in the new drinking order as the guardians of moderation. The idea had precedent—in middle-class culture women had long served as arbiters of good taste and respectability—but it also encountered a good deal of skepticism. Both before and during Prohibition, popular representations of women as drinkers and anti-drink crusaders had frequently depicted women in an unflattering light. In cartoons, cultural commentaries, and films, women were either cast as axe-wielding fanatics—the puritanical enemies of drink—or as inept and inexperienced drinkers who routinely overstepped their limits. The caricatures at both extremes perpetuated a myth that the women's temperance movement had helped to create: the myth that respectable women never drank. Women temperance activists had so thoroughly succeeded in painting men as the problem drinkers in need of reform that they effectively erased women's drinking from public memory. The reality of women's drinking was quite different. In the late nineteenth and early twentieth centuries, long before Prohibition turned women's drinking into a fashionable rebellion, working-class and immigrant women entered saloons through the ladies' side entrance to enjoy a beer with their free lunch in the backrooms or to purchase a growler of beer to enjoy with the family dinner or with other tenement wives.[67] The respectable middle-class and upper-class hostess usually had some knowledge of wines and liqueurs. She often kept a decanter of wine on the sideboard for visitors (or herself), and at formal dinner parties, she usually served different types of wine and offered guests more than one glass.[68]

Because the Volstead Act had banned only public drinking but not private consumption, alcohol continued to play an important role in domestic sociability during Prohibition. Women's apparent enjoyment of cocktails at the parties they attended and hosted excited much public commentary. Even as Prohibition exploded the myth that respectable white, middle-class matrons never drank, it gave birth to a new caricature: the "lit lady" who repeatedly misjudged alcohol's intoxicating power. Although drinking by itself no longer imperiled a woman's reputation, critics worried that women's proclivity to overstep their limits deprived their children of a good example and stripped motherhood of its moral force. Far from viewing women as exemplars of responsible drinking, Eudora Richardson urged husbands to monitor their wives' drinking at parties. Make sure that her "drinks are mild," Richardson counseled, "and that her glass is not too frequently refilled."[69]

Despite such doubts about women's capacity to judge their limits, other drinking reformers invested high hopes in women's ability to foster and safeguard a new culture of moderate drinking. Rexford Tugwell, the Roosevelt Administration's new assistant secretary of agriculture, entrusted women with precisely that mission when he addressed a gathering of the Women's National Democratic Club in February 1934. Having learned to enjoy wine in Europe, where he had lived for a time after World War I, Tugwell encouraged the Democratic clubwomen to serve wine with meals—preferably American wine—and to accompany their husbands to beer gardens. Although Democratic women were more likely to identify as "wet" than their Republican counterparts, the bipartisan Women's Organization for National Prohibition Reform included former prohibitionists who still held moral qualms about drinking.[70] This may explain why Tugwell warned women that if they snubbed legalized alcohol altogether, they would likely "drive back their men to the bar-room and the short stiff drinks." If women instead used wine "as a mild social stimulant, together with good food, good talk and good company," Tugwell argued, women could reform American drinking habits and encourage the pursuit of higher pleasures.[71]

Portions of Tugwell's address—particularly his critique of the "excesses of the bootleg decade" and the Jazz Age—were fraught with racial subtext. When "either bathtub gin or three-weeks whiskey is substituted for [wine]," Tugwell told the Democratic clubwomen, "the result is best characterized by the associations we have with the word 'jazz.'" For Tugwell, jazz evoked "the hectic type of existence" mirrored in jazz rhythms and the licentiousness and reckless drinking that flourished in speakeasies.[72] Cultural critics and political commentators continually returned to F. Scott Fitzgerald's metaphor of the "Jazz Age," because jazz so effectively symbolized both the promises and the perils of the decade's profound cultural transformations. At the forefront of those transformations was the cultural triumph of African American–created jazz, an improvisational art form that for many African Americans, historian Gerald Early remarked, represented "liberation, freedom of the spirit," and "democratic possibilities" not yet realized.[73] As historian Joel Dinerstein has written, jazz created a "secular space" in which Black Americans could "reclaim their bodies from the boss and 'the Man'" and "assert their 'somebodiness' in a world that daily denied it."[74]

For many white people, jazz represented a different kind of liberation: an escape from the restrictive social conventions, repressive sexual norms, and bureaucratic routine that governed their daily lives. Thousands of white middle-class thrill-seekers ventured into the racially mixed nightclubs of Harlem, Chicago's South Side, and Culver City (just outside of Los Angeles) to partake in the libidinous pleasures and illicit liquor that magazine articles and tourist guidebooks hyped as essential highlights of any good "slumming" excursion. More often than not, rather than "bridging racial differences," such expeditions into Black neighborhoods reinforced "a sense of white superiority" as white "slummers" contrasted "their own increasingly public sexual behavior . . . with the spectacle of cross-racial and black sexuality presented in local black and tans."[75] The very things that made jazz so appealing to some—its associations with sexual freedom, racial progress, and the flouting of Prohibition—made jazz profoundly threatening to others.[76] When Tugwell expressed his hope that a new era of responsible drinking would "clamp down on these lusty juvenilia and . . . substitute a tradition of greater maturity," his evocative phrasing likely called to his listeners' minds the deeply entangled associations of jazz with sexual permissiveness, interracial mixing, and overindulgent drinking.[77]

Tugwell tasked women with elevating leisure and safeguarding responsible drinking because he saw heterosociability itself as a moderating influence. Beer gardens, open-air cafes, and wine-halls earned Tugwell's praise as places where "decent men and women can drink quietly . . . under the eyes of their neighbors and . . . exert on each other the discipline of each other's presence."[78] As Tugwell saw it, heterosociability provided its own form of moral regulation, joining discipline and pleasure in ways that the exclusively masculine saloon never could. Tugwell's assumption that drinking in beer gardens and open-air cafes would take place "under the eyes of their neighbors" intimated that drinking in racially homogeneous settings, among neighbors, might also exert a disciplining effect. Once drinking was stripped of its thrilling secrecy and removed from the illicit mixed-race settings that magnified its allure, Tugwell implied, drinking could once again be done in moderation.

Even as Tugwell saw some degree of social surveillance as an essential component of drinking reform, he also warned against moral overreach by the state. In a piece for his recurring newspaper column "Design for Government," Tugwell wrote, "If we begin by telling people they can only drink sitting down and not standing up; if we restrict hours of sale arbitrarily, or sell only in packages, we shall have only minor and more irritating forms of the prohibition we are all so glad to escape from now." The better solution to the problem of excessive drinking, Tugwell argued, was to replace the "grimy corner saloon" with "public beer gardens and wine-halls on the Viennese model."[79]

In calling for such alternatives, Tugwell joined a broader public conversation about how Americans used their spare time amid rising unemployment and what the state might do to encourage worthy uses of leisure.[80] Like Tugwell, the economist Stuart Chase, another member of FDR's Brain Trust, believed that modern commercial recreation no longer provided a counterweight to the mechanized workplace. "Play is the flywheel of life," Chase wrote in *Men and Machines* (1935), "and America ... does not know how to play. It can only step on throttles, insert coins in metal slots, ... [and] rush headlong down roller coasters."[81] Like Tugwell and Chase, many other intellectuals in the early 1930s sensed that mechanization and the faster tempo of modern life had brought on something of a "spiritual" crisis. Bombarded with an increasing array of sensory inputs—from the barrage of new information to the cacophonous sounds of whirring machines and clanging trolleys—Americans, commentators observed, had adapted to a sped-up existence but had also forgotten to enjoy the pleasures that restored the mind and spirit.[82] In his talk to the Democratic clubwomen, Tugwell proposed that a "calmer" wine- and beer-centered leisure would slow the tempo and foster enjoyment of "the good things of the spirits: reflection, philosophy, conversation and leisure."[83] Once freed from the "tension"-producing "emphasis [on] motion, speed and ... hectic entertainment," city dwellers, Tugwell wrote in his column, would then discover "what the Germans call gemutluchkeit, a kind of fellow feeling and kindliness of spirit."[84] Both Tugwell and Chase shared some of the sensibilities of Jane Addams and other Progressive Era reformers who had championed city-built playgrounds and community recreation centers as wholesome, edifying alternatives to the cheap thrills of mechanical amusement park rides, penny arcades, and movie theaters.[85] Americans could reclaim their cities and their leisure, Addams and Tugwell both suggested, if they substituted enlightening and restorative alternatives for empty pleasures. (Of course, Jane Addams, as a Woman's Christian Temperance Union member and a supporter of Prohibition, would have likely disapproved of Tugwell's call to replace saloons with beer gardens and wine-halls.)

Tugwell's address to the Democratic clubwomen ignited a firestorm of protest from drys outraged by his call for women to oversee a new era of responsible drinking. Methodist parishioners were still demanding Tugwell's dismissal two months after he delivered his address. A chagrined Tugwell wrote Eleanor Roosevelt to apologize for drawing her into the controversy by suggesting that women follow her example of serving wine with dinner.[86] In reply, Eleanor lauded Tugwell's courage after teasing him for "think[ing] that the Methodists would not expire over the [talk's] title of 'Wine, Women and the New Deal' . . . Your sense of humor does lead you into traps I am afraid!"[87] Although the Roosevelt Administration did not comment officially on Tugwell's address, not long after the furor had subsided the White House announced that it would be serving light wines at State dinners.[88] In a bow to moderation, Eleanor Roosevelt made a point to serve only two "light American wines" with dinner—one red and one white—instead of the customary four-to-six dinner wines served at the Woodrow Wilson Administration's State dinners.[89] Eleanor's patriotic gesture won the gratitude of many American winemakers. In a letter to the President, Paul Garrett pledged, "My next vote goes to Mrs. Eleanor Roosevelt as Commander-in-Chief."[90]

The title of Tugwell's talk "Wine, Women, and the New Deal"—a deliberate play on the common phrase "wine, women, and song"—conveyed Tugwell's conviction that women's contributions to drinking reform would also advance the New Deal's larger cultural and even spiritual aims. In his address, Tugwell explicitly linked the enjoyment of wine and beer to the New Deal's ambition "to make possible a more abundant life for the American people."[91] President Roosevelt himself had spoken about the government's aim to secure the "abundant life" for every American in an address to the Federal Council of Churches of Christ, delivered the day after he signed the Twenty-First Amendment into law. The vaguely defined "abundant life" hinted at material well-being and security, but Tugwell's call for temperate drinking suggested that the abundant life fulfilled more than just material needs. The abundant life also enabled citizens to seek fulfillment through the pleasures of "reflection, philosophy, conversation and leisure"—pleasures that in Tugwell's view went hand-in-hand with the enjoyment of wine and beer.[92]

Other self-styled drinking reformers who shared Tugwell's conviction that women could promote a new culture of moderate drinking eagerly turned their new cause into a business opportunity. In 1933 and 1934 publishers churned out dozens of drinking guidebooks that instructed readers on the proper etiquette of serving different types of alcoholic beverages. Addressed primarily to middle-class women uncertain of alcohol's place in domesticity, the guidebooks encouraged readers to assure repeal's success by enforcing moderation as the new social norm. Full of snob appeals, the drinking manuals amplified women's importance as the guardians of temperate pleasure-seeking by transforming drinking from a simple pleasure into a complicated ritual of gentility, fraught with potential for "grievous error."[93] Perhaps no drinking etiquette manual better reflected the post-Prohibition zeal for reforming drinking behavior than *Bacchus Behave! The Lost Art of Polite Drinking*. Marketed with testimonials from Hollywood celebrities on its jacket, the drinking primer was written by Alma Whitaker, a popular columnist and feature writer for the *Los Angeles Times*.[94] Like Tugwell, Whitaker called upon women to guard against excess, but her vision of the good life made no pretense of inclusiveness. By arming women with the new "rules for righteous behavior," Whitaker empowered women to confidently enforce the "gentlemanly" drinking customs that Americans had forgotten (or never learned). As the self-appointed "Emily Post" of "refined drinking," Whitaker informed readers that respectable hostesses could no longer tolerate drunkenness or serve guests the "friendship-testing home-brews" that passed for good hospitality during Prohibition. Instead of humoring the drunk, hostesses "must see to it that vulgar excess becomes taboo."[95]

In Whitaker's eyes, the respectable hostess not only monitored her guests' alcohol intake, but she also faithfully observed "the sacred ritual of serving the right beverages with the right courses at the right time," and in quantities that cheered but did not inebriate. Nowhere was this ritual more important than in serving wines. "To misuse or misplace [fine wines] on your menu," Whitaker warned, "is as crass a *faux pas* as using 'ain't' and 'we done' in polite conversation."[96] Even the "wines of the masses"—"the *vin ordinaire* of France, the Chianti of Italy, the dago-red of California," Whitaker insisted, deserved "due regard for the niceties of social procedure."[97] Such advice sharpened hierarchies of race and class by removing wine knowledge from the realm of ethnic customs and relocating it to the realm of white genteel respectability.

The notion that women were ideally suited to promote the pleasures of moderation drew fire from all sides. While drys zealously guarded women's moral authority as opponents of alcohol, misogynistic wets scoffed at the notion that women might acquire a connoisseur's knowledge of "superior nectars"—a role that, in their view, properly belonged to middle- and upper-class white men. Based on his observations of women's drinking during Prohibition, Gilbert Seldes, a theater and film critic, concluded that women lacked the "technical skill and social grace" to civilize American drinking. Seldes cited women's passion for "drinks slightly sickening in flavor ... and viscous with whipped cream" as but one of their many affronts to dignified drinking.[98] The elite men who formed and joined the new gourmet dining societies also viewed connoisseurship and epicurean adventure as exclusively white, masculine domains. By the mid-1930s, the international Wine and Food Society had sprouted chapters in six US cities: San Francisco, Los Angeles, New York, New Orleans, Chicago, and Boston. None offered membership to women or non-whites. The expense of joining the clubs, their formal dress codes, and members' close ties to private men's clubs limited membership to an exclusive group of white, upper-class men.[99] Such elites were as determined to preserve the homosocial world of male drinking as reformers like Tugwell and Whitaker were determined to dismantle it in the service of promoting moderation.

TOWARD LIQUOR CONTROL

The paternalistic impulse to guide and limit consumer choice did not die with Prohibition. Far from representing the triumph of more permissive norms, many of the new liquor control laws attempted to broker a compromise between wet, damp, and dry opinion.[100] When lawmakers drafted the Twenty-First Amendment, they made state and municipal governments responsible for regulating alcoholic beverages, believing that the only enforceable alcohol regulations were those the local community would accept.[101] The end result was a crazy patchwork quilt of regulations that tightened the state's grip on alcohol buying and selling in some locales and loosened it in others. A few states initially opted to remain entirely dry. Kansas waited out a depression and a world war before ending statewide prohibition in 1948. Oklahoma did so in 1959, and Mississippi followed suit in 1966. Other states legalized only "nonintoxicating" 3.2 percent beer and banned all other alcoholic beverages, including stronger beers. Many others permitted sales of wine and beer but not liquor. At the time of repeal, the laws governing liquor sales in most states reverted to the status quo ante of 1910, when many states and counties had already adopted prohibition.

Most state constitutions underscored the tentativeness of alcohol's victory by permitting voters to change their county's legal status from wet to dry or from dry to wet in annual or biennial elections. Local option elections also allowed voters to decide whether to permit alcohol sales on Sundays, allow grocery stores to sell beer and wine, or sanction on-premises sales of liquor by the drink. California was among the few states to ban local option ordinances out of a well-placed fear that the coexistence of dry and wet counties would merely encourage bootlegging and smuggling across borders.[102] Local option was not a new concept to voters who had come of age before 1920. The Anti-Saloon League had turned large swaths of the country dry by gradually accumulating wins in local option elections.[103] After repeal, state and local option elections allowed alcohol prohibition to endure on a smaller scale.[104] In 1938, one in six Americans resided in either a dry state or a dry municipality created by local option.[105] Prohibition continued to thrive in regions dominated by evangelical Protestants. In Kentucky—home to both the nation's bourbon industry and a large population of evangelicals—the dry counties outnumbered the wet counties (and still do!).[106]

The extent of a state's wetness largely hinged on how a state decided to regulate the sale of distilled spirits. Wet states fell into two broad categories: the control states (also called monopoly states) and the license states (also called open states). The license states permitted privately licensed retailers to sell alcoholic beverages and they established state liquor authorities (and sometimes additional local alcoholic beverage control boards) to approve, reject, or revoke applicants for licenses. To prevent former bootleggers from entering the lawful trade, alcohol control boards conducted criminal background checks and checked character references. The license states also guarded against corruption by operating under a three-tier distribution system, in which producers sold their wares to wholesalers, who in turn sold to retailers. Ensuring strict separation between manufacturers, wholesalers, and retailers, the three-tier model aimed to prevent any brewery from acquiring the kind of monopoly control that brewery-owned saloons had achieved before Prohibition.[107]

In most of the control states, state-run liquor stores (known as "package stores" in the lingo of the trade) served as the exclusive wholesaler and retailer of distilled spirits, wines, and beers above 3.2 percent alcohol. A few control states departed slightly from this model by allowing privately licensed retailers to sell table wine and all types of beer while retaining state control over more potent alcoholic beverages, including wines above 12 to 14 percent alcohol. Provisions for on-premises sales of alcohol in restaurants, clubs, hotels, and other venues varied widely in the control states. Some prohibited on-premises consumption of any alcoholic beverage except 3.2 beer, but most developed a hybrid system that gave the state stores a public monopoly on package sales but allowed privately licensed restaurants and hotels to handle on-premises sales.[108] Only four states—Arizona, California, Indiana, Wyoming—and the District of Columbia permitted "the maximum wetness," allowing sale by the drink for consumption on premises and sale by the bottle (or case) for consumption off premises. These wettest of the wet were also committed to staying wet, as none made provisions for local option elections.[109]

In theory, this decentralized approach allowed states to construct alcoholic beverage controls that were more responsive to local conditions, community standards, and the popular will. Alcohol policymaking quickly coalesced around a few key principles. Most policymakers agreed that the new regulatory apparatus should encourage moderation, privilege fermented beverages over distilled spirits, and eliminate all residues of the saloon. The campaign to repeal Prohibition had already galvanized public support for such principles, but the single most influential alcohol policy document—the Rockefeller Report—originated among elites with strong misgivings about the alcoholic beverage industry. John D. Rockefeller Jr., once a diehard supporter of the Eighteenth Amendment, commissioned Raymond Fosdick, a trusted advisor and an attorney with expertise on American police systems, and Albert Scott, an engineer and member of Alcoholics Anonymous, to study alcohol regulation in Canada and Europe and create a new template for alcoholic beverage controls in the United States. Fosdick and Scott released their findings to the press in the fall of 1933 and published them in the book *Toward Liquor Control*.

Noting that light wine and beer did not constitute a serious problem in other countries, Fosdick and Scott—and Rockefeller himself—hoped that broader access to beer and table wines would eventually wean Americans from distilled spirits.[110] Many of their recommendations followed what physiology professor Yandell Henderson, the star scientific witness at the congressional hearings to legalize beer and light wines, called the "principle of dilution"—the idea that the state should restrict access to the most concentrated forms of alcohol and make the milder forms cheaper and easier to buy. The federal government embraced the principle of dilution when it levied higher taxes on spirits and fortified wines than it did on table wines and beers. So, too, did state governments when they permitted restaurants and hotels to sell wine and beer by the glass but not spirits, as the Rockefeller Report advised. In other locales, shoppers could find beer in delis and grocery stores—another Rockefeller Report recommendation—and they might even find wine, but they almost certainly failed to locate a bottle of whiskey or rum.[111]

Fosdick and Scott's most significant conclusion echoed a longstanding prohibitionist critique: no workable solution to the liquor problem could be achieved without eliminating the profit motive from liquor sales. Convinced that private dealers would invariably pressure customers to buy more than they needed or could afford, they backed the creation of state-run monopoly stores modeled after the state-controlled systems in Canada, Sweden, Finland, and Norway. Unencumbered by the need to maximize revenues, state-run monopolies could limit advertising, hours of operation, and the number of stores, allowing them to meet a "minimum, unstimulated demand" for distilled spirits without forfeiting control to bootleggers.[112]

In one crucial respect, the post-Prohibition alcohol policies of the United States were the most liberal of all the nations that had adopted and then abandoned alcohol prohibition in the early twentieth century: only the United States rejected government ownership of alcohol's manufacture and distribution.[113] American prohibitionists had hoped to create a system "as far-reaching as the post office" in which bottles would come with warning labels that characterized alcohol as "a poison, a narcotic, and a habit-forming drug" and government-run liquor stores would hang posters that illustrated alcohol's deleterious effects on the body.[114] Even Rexford Tugwell, an avowed wet predisposed to central planning, briefly flirted with instituting a federal monopoly on liquor sales and manufacture in the interest of protecting liquor quality and public health.[115] The federal monopoly idea faded quickly once the Twenty-First Amendment returned alcohol regulation to the states, but its appeal across the wet, dry, and damp spectrum signaled that alcoholic beverage producers would not be welcomed back with open arms.[116]

The rejection of a federal monopoly, however, hardly made the repeal of US Prohibition a libertarian victory for individual liberties against an intrusive state. In many states alcohol controls instituted new forms of surveillance that regulated personal drinking habits more effectively than Prohibition had.[117] Even the ostensibly more liberal "open states" that sold alcohol through licensed retailers kept a tight watch over individual drinkers. Wisconsin not only reinstated its dramshop laws, which enabled a wife or relative to forbid barkeepers from selling alcohol to problem drinkers, but it also extended the same authority to the mayor and the police chief.[118] In other open states, liquor stores became extensions of the state's surveillance apparatus. New Mexico required drinkers to become licensed and liquor stores to keep records of consumers' purchases.[119] Such liquor permit systems were similar to the "vast bureaucracy of administrative surveillance" that the Liquor Control Board of Ontario (LCBO) in Canada had created. The LCBO recorded the date and type of liquor purchased by each permit holder and urged store managers to intervene if they thought a patron was buying too much or spending beyond their means.[120] The mere act of retaining such purchase records encouraged permit holders to internalize self-control and moderate their drinking.[121]

The monopoly states exercised far-reaching oversight over drinking habits. Vermont compelled people who committed a crime while intoxicated "to sign a teetotaler's pledge for a fixed period" and the state withheld their wages until the pledge was fulfilled. Following Canada's lead, Montana, a state that had served as an entry point for smuggled Canadian whiskey during Prohibition, attempted to "limit the scope of alcohol-soaked male social gatherings" by permitting only a certain amount of liquor to be present within a given household.[122] Although nearly impossible to enforce, Montana's law stipulated that spirits could be consumed only in the home of the purchaser, presumably with the goal of containing the size and raucousness of social gatherings. Hypothetically, should the host run out of spirits, no guest could "replenish the supply through his own permit, unless the whole party . . . moved to his house."[123] Monopoly states also attempted to curb alcohol consumption by locating their state-run stores ten to thirty miles apart and banning the use of billboards, exterior signs, or loudspeakers to advertise their wares and their location.[124] Convinced that such ploys would backfire, one critic noted, "few citizens are going to drive 20 miles for expensive legal liquor when bootleggers will deliver their product to the door—at a more attractive price."[125] Once inside the state store, shoppers encountered an intentionally uninviting space, with bottles of wine and spirits housed behind the counter, no point of sales material or advertising in sight, and unfriendly clerks instructed merely to process transactions, not dispense helpful advice (see Figure 3).[126] The absence of merchandising in a consumer culture suffused with it sent a powerful message: that consumers' appetites for alcohol, while no longer forbidden, still lacked respectability.

In both the open and monopoly states, policymakers sought to banish all the old customs that kept alcohol flowing: the free lunch, easy credit, and the tradition of treating companions to rounds of drinks. Prohibitionists especially despised the custom of treating for inducing men to waste money and overindulge. When one man treated friends to a round of drinks, reciprocity demanded that each friend respond in

FIGURE 3. Interior of state-run liquor store in Welch, West Virginia, c. 1940s. Alpha Stock via Alamy.

kind, perpetuating a seemingly endless round of rounds.[127] Some efforts to banish saloon culture were modest. Delaware merely advised tavernkeepers and hotel managers to discourage treating.[128] Other wet states eliminated the bar (and with it the custom of treating) by allowing only restaurants and hotels to sell alcohol by the drink.[129] The District of Columbia, the wettest of the wet cities, prohibited the sale of liquor on credit. Other states attempted to seal the saloon's demise by instituting new food rules. In Iowa, Maryland, and Ohio, proprietors could still offer free pretzels, cheese, and popcorn—all sufficiently salty to stimulate drinking, but insufficiently alluring or caloric, in legislators' eyes, to count as a free lunch. Other states required establishments to serve meals with alcohol to ensure that customers did not drink on an empty stomach.[130]

Compliance with the new alcoholic beverage controls demanded attention to zoning laws and the finer details of tavern design and décor. Most cities set closing hours between 2 a.m. and 4 a.m. and prohibited liquor-selling establishments within several hundred feet of churches and schools. Some municipalities limited the number of cabarets and taverns to one for every one thousand residents.[131] Other measures eliminated the use of curtained doors and glazed windows that had enabled saloons and speakeasies to conceal clandestine activities and illicit enterprises, such as prostitution and gambling.[132] Curtainless windows and well-lit interiors, lawmakers presumed, would invite just enough social surveillance to keep proprietors on the up and up and customers on their best behavior.[133] Some purely cosmetic attempts to prevent the return of the saloon (like California's ban on signage bearing the words *cocktail lounge* and *cocktail bar*) drew open ridicule. In his extended rant in the *American Mercury*, H. L. Mencken's staunchly anti-prohibitionist journal, Anthony Turano accused lawmakers of trying to "exorcise" the saloon "through an elaborate series of rhetorical incantations," as if merely substituting the euphemistic word *tavern* would endow an establishment with greater respectability.[134] Some California drinking establishments mocked the new euphemisms by naming their beer gardens "Bee Gardens" and their taverns "Caverns."[135]

These superficial attempts to banish the saloon paled in comparison to Canada's stringent alcohol controls. Until 1954, beer parlours were the only drinking establishments permitted in British Columbia and Ontario. Located mostly in lower-end hotels that served loggers, dockers, and railway workers, beer parlours "regulated class, gender and sexuality, and race" as much as they regulated alcohol consumption.[136] The starkly furnished beer parlours "were purposely . . . unattractive . . . to discourage patrons from lingering" and "remind [them] . . . that they were engaged in a somewhat disreputable activity."[137] Separate men-only and "ladies and escorts" sections attempted to quiet temperance activists who feared that women's presence would invite sexual impropriety.[138] Although generally more inviting spaces, American bars instituted similar paternalistic restrictions on women's drinking. In Massachusetts, restaurants and hotels could serve alcohol to women seated at a table but not to women standing at the bar.[139] Such bans may have reflected the assumption that women could not handle their liquor without food in their bellies, but they also sought to discourage the practice of hiring women hostesses—or B-girls as they came to be known—to "mingle with [male] patrons" and entice them to buy more drinks.[140]

The creation of gendered zones for alcohol service—tables for women, barstools for men—also aimed to preserve the bar as an exclusively male social space, despite evidence that women drinkers increased bar profits. Some men refused to patronize establishments that permitted women at the bar because they wanted to reclaim the bar as a homosocial space "where their dominance was uncontested."¹⁴¹ Others resisted joint drinking between men and women precisely because they recognized heterosociability as a constraining force.

When it came to regulating public drinking, cultural anxieties about alcohol's potential to disrupt hierarchies of race, class, gender, and sexuality left a bigger imprint on alcohol policies than Yandell Henderson's principle of dilution did. Across the board, it was marginalized groups who faced the most intensive surveillance and were subjected first to new modes of control.¹⁴² The working-class men who ordered up a round, the women who took their place at the bar (or heaven forbid, behind the bar), the gay men and lesbians who gathered in neighborhood bars, and the tavernkeepers who screened their interiors from public view all became fraught symbols of alcohol's potential to unleash social and sexual chaos. When states empowered liquor enforcement agencies to revoke the licenses of disorderly drinking establishments, many agents interpreted this as an invitation to police other kinds of behavior—besides drunkenness—that they found objectionable. Aware that state liquor agents could revoke licenses based merely on the appearance of patrons, New York bars and nightclubs trained bouncers and doormen to turn away customers who donned attire that marked them as sexual nonconformists.¹⁴³ As historian George Chauncey has documented, the State Liquor Authority in New York maintained that the mere "presence of lesbians or gay men, prostitutes, gamblers, or other 'undesirables' . . . made an establishment disorderly." Over a period of twenty-five years, it closed popular queer nightspots and "literally hundreds of bars that welcomed, tolerated, or simply failed to notice the patronage of gay men or lesbians." In very real ways, the new alcoholic beverage controls gave enforcement agencies a pretext to regulate social conduct with only a passing connection to containing public drunkenness. "Rather than initiating a new era of laissez-faire tolerance in urban life," Chauncey has argued, "Repeal inaugurated a more pervasive and more effective regime of surveillance and control."¹⁴⁴

CONSUMER BACKLASH AND THE CRISIS OF PUBLIC TRUST

On the first anniversary of repeal, H. L. Mencken, the staunch opponent of all things puritanical, offered a sunny assessment of repeal's salutary effects. By "depriving drinking of its exhilarating naughtiness," Mencken wrote, repeal had made drinking "as banal an act as having one's shoes shined" and had lowered demand "to parity with the actual [moderate] national appetite."[145] By the second and third anniversaries of repeal, sunny assessments were harder to find. Commentators of the wet, damp, and dry persuasion had begun to doubt the industry's capacity for reform and the state's capacity to stabilize markets and judiciously regulate the alcohol trade. Voters registered their disappointment directly at the polls. Between 1934 and 1938, drys won fifty-five hundred out of seven thousand contests in local option elections. Although drys claimed most of their wins in municipalities that had been dry before Prohibition, editorials in *Tap and Tavern* repeatedly warned of the coming "local option deluge" and "a powerful drive to wipe out repeal."[146]

Discontent with repeal pushed in all directions. Diehard wets decried an overzealous regulatory state and the sheer folly of "making angels by legal enactment." In his investigation of state liquor statutes, Anthony Turano, a wet commentator, saw either the imprint of prohibitionists or the naïve hope of drinking reformers that sumptuary legislation would "denationaliz[e]" the "schnapps-loving American ... into a French wineskin or a Bavarian beer-tank." Even in wet states where prohibitionists exercised little political influence, Turano wrote, legislators treated alcohol as belonging to "the bastard category of things legally allowed but morally reprehensible."[147] By contrast, damps and drys feared that lax enforcement and irresponsible tavernkeepers were resurrecting the saloon. Some resented tavernkeepers who served more drinks than food and obstructed clear views of the interior.[148] Others warned of brewers' attempts to revive the now forbidden tied-house saloon—an arrangement whereby saloonkeepers pledged to exclusively sell a brewery's brand in return for the brewery's sponsorship.[149] Even the wet-aligned Joseph Choate, the "liquor czar" who headed the Federal Alcohol Control Administration, rebuked the brewing industry's giveaways of furnishings, equipment, and electric signs to advertise their brands.[150]

The alcoholic beverage industry's growing visibility also contributed to the fall in public trust. According to the Department of Commerce's 1935 census of business, the United States had sprouted 97,852 new drinking places and 12,063 beer and liquor stores. Not including restaurants and department stores (both major retailers of alcohol), alcohol retailers outnumbered candy shops by nearly two to one (109,915 to 55,132) and could have easily rivaled the number of filling stations (196,649) had alcohol-selling restaurants and department stores been factored in.[151] Alcohol's enlarged retailing presence prompted *Christian Century*, a longtime supporter of Prohibition, to condemn the industry for turning "every drugstore and grocery into a liquor store, and nearly every newspaper and magazine into an advertising medium."[152] Drinking's return as a reputable feature of urban nightlife and its augmented presence in Hollywood films compounded the frustration of damps and drys.[153] Drinking and drunkenness had never looked as glamorous as it did in *The Thin Man* (1934), a wildly popular film based on a detective novel by Dashiell Hammett. Even after downing multiple martinis and whiskey highballs, Nick Charles, a retired detective, and his slightly less bibulous wife Nora maintained their flirtatious banter and crime-solving savvy.[154]

The three leading trade associations—the United States Brewers Association (USBA), the Wine Institute, and the Distilled Spirits Institute—recognized the stirrings of a consumer backlash but they struggled to convince their members and the broader trade to change course and embrace collective action. "Too many of our people, especially among the wholesalers and retailers, think that any restrictive law was made to be broken," a liquor executive confessed. "And when you try to frighten them by shaking prohibition in their faces, some of them answer, 'What the hell do we care? We used to make more money that way!'"[155]

In 1936, the USBA hired Edward Bernays, the nation's leading authority on public relations, to diagnose the brewing industry's troubles and develop a public relations campaign to rehabilitate its image. The nephew of Sigmund Freud, Bernays shared his uncle's penchant for probing the instincts and emotions that drive individual behavior—a skill Bernays mobilized to shape and manipulate public opinion. Early in his career, Bernays cultivated his talent as a publicist through his work as a theatrical press agent for Sergei Diaghilev's Ballet Russe, the Polish ballet dancer Vaslav Nijinsky, and the Italian operatic tenor Enrico Caruso. During World War I, Bernays plied his trade as a propagandist for the U.S. Committee on Public Information, the agency that promoted World War I as the war that would "Make the World Safe for Democracy." The "astounding success" of the CPI's wartime propaganda both at home and abroad, Bernays wrote, "opened [his] eyes . . . to the possibilities of regimenting the public mind."[156] Soon thereafter, Bernays jettisoned the title *press agent* for a more "exalted" one: "counsel on public relations."[157] His clients hired him to sell a product or service or improve their corporate image, but he worked his magic, historian Larry Tye writes, by selling "whole new ways of behaving, which . . . redefined the very texture of American life." By the time Bernays had signed on as the USBA's public relations counselor, his campaigns had made bacon and eggs the all-American breakfast and taught women to protect their figures by reaching for a cigarette instead of a sweet.[158] If he could do that for American Tobacco and the bacon producer Beechnut Packing Company, the USBA had reason to hope he could cement beer's place in American leisure and domesticity.

Bernays set out first to ascertain the nature of the brewers' public relations problem. Rather than surveying a broad spectrum of public opinion, Bernays focused on trusted "group leaders," believing that "if you can influence the leaders, either with or without their conscious cooperation, you automatically influence the group which they sway."[159] Bernays surveyed four thousand middle- and upper-middle-class opinion leaders who Bernays thought would most likely promote "laws inimical to the brewing interests." Although his sample included wet-sympathizing labor leaders and clergy, Bernays also surveyed people who viewed beer and liquor as equally harmful: farm representatives, presidents of women's clubs, contributors to Protestant religious journals, and evangelical clergy. The opinion leaders who mattered the most, in Bernays's view, were the persuadable skeptics who would be the brewers' ultimate targets. These included influential writers and editors of newspapers, educators, corporate executives, former political office holders, sociologists and welfare workers, lawyers, prominent career women, and the heads of racial organizations, civic groups, chambers of commerce, and trade associations. Four hundred of the four thousand group leaders Bernays contacted responded to his queries. They shared their views of how states regulated wine, beer, and spirits and how the industry advertised them. They also answered questions about how well their state liquor laws worked and what could improve the alcohol situation.[160]

Bernays's findings thus represented a narrow segment of the American public, skewing heavily to the better educated, the managerial elite, and the reform-minded upper-middle class. His elitist assumptions about the social influence of group leaders mirrored his grandiose conception of his own profession. Public relations experts, Bernays wrote, were the hidden persuaders "who pull the wires which control the public mind . . . and contrive new ways to bind and guide the world."[161] Bernays admitted that a broader sample might have revealed greater indifference to the alcohol question, but he stuck by his maxim: because the voters who favor and oppose an issue are usually evenly divided, what matters most is persuading the undecided 20 percent in the middle.[162] The political dynamics of local option elections affirmed that axiom. In places where neither partisan wets nor partisan drys commanded overwhelming majorities, swing votes determined the outcome. From the get-go then, Bernays's public relations campaign aimed not to win over the masses but to shore up brewers' support among middle-class arbiters of respectability and social responsibility.

Bernays's findings suggested that brewers and prohibitionists both had fertile ground to till.[163] Although Bernays found broad support for regulating spirits more heavily than beer and light wines, most respondents (59 percent) doubted that liquor-loving Anglo-Americans would change their ways.[164] Several respondents identified hard drinking as a deeply ingrained Anglo-American trait. As a North Carolinian clergyman observed, the average drinker desired neither "the taste of wine nor the sociability of beer . . . so much as the quick, stimulating effect of hard liquor."[165] At the same time, however, Bernays also determined that neither the brewers nor the vintners had tested the cultural power of their moderation claims. Only 23 percent of Bernays's respondents reported encountering any post-repeal "agitation" promoting light wines and beers as agents of temperance.[166]

Bernays's survey also documented anxieties about alcohol's potential to corrupt family values and disrupt the existing sexual and racial order. A sizeable majority of Bernays's respondents (61 percent) objected to advertising's use of women and children to sell hard liquor and feared that its glamorization of drinking would lead children and youth astray.[167] Distressed by the increased presence of women in drinking establishments, some respondents found the modern beer tavern little better than the prostitution-ridden saloons of yesteryear. Dayton E. Heckman, a political science professor at the University of Omaha in Nebraska, feared for the reputations of young women bartenders who worked "until late hours shoving out schooners of beer" and the "dime-a-drink" girls who used Omaha's taverns to "solicit not only free drinks, but patrons for their avocation." Even when women were not physically present, Heckman observed, their pictorial representation on the decorative beer calendars that adorned tavern walls created a licentious atmosphere. In one of Omaha's "negro saloons," a scandalized Heckman found a picture of the boxer Joe Louis, "clad in the scanty garments of his profession," hanging next to a beer calendar featuring "a white woman wearing even fewer clothes." The mere possibility of interracial intimacy aroused by the juxtaposition of such images, Heckman warned, could "inflam[e] public opinion against the liquor traffic" in "regions where racial prejudice is fairly strong."[168]

As Heckman's commentary suggested, distrust of the alcoholic beverage industry was as easy to arouse as it was difficult to shake off. The political science professor reminded Bernays that prohibitionists had won converts to their cause by telling southern white voters that the images of nude white women on whiskey labels incited Black men to rape white women.[169] Heckman's reading of history and political motivation was correct. In the first decade of the twentieth century, representations of the drunken Black man as a "dangerous menace" and a "black brute" intent on raping white women circulated widely in southern newspapers and Thomas Dixon's novel *The Clansman*, the primary source for D.W. Griffith's *The Birth of a Nation*. Liquor marketing further inflamed prohibitionists. Consider the audaciously named Black Cock Vigor Gin, a pre-Prohibition brand whose label featured a black rooster and a white woman draped in a diaphanous gown. If the brand name alone failed to signal the gin's effectiveness as a male impotence cure, the advertising copy surely did. While some ads subtly promoted the gin to men of all races as a remedy for "kidney, bladder, and urinary troubles," the verses on the back of a trade card, as reflected in this couplet, were much blunter: "Vim and vigor it imparts and maintains, Gets up the steam in the sinews and veins." White southerners were already inclined to view distilling as a predatory industry, but the Jewish heritage of Black Cock gin's manufacturers, Lee Levy and Adolph Asher, and the Jewish ownership of saloons that catered to Black patrons in southern cities, historian Marni Davis has shown, fed into anti-Semitic tropes that cast Jewish entrepreneurs as unscrupulous businessmen who "would betray white concerns" about the threat Black men posed to white women's sexual purity.[170]

Bernays's findings presented a cautionary tale. Public memories of vice-ridden saloons and industry corruption ran deep. If certain tavern conditions persisted, some respondents warned, damps and drys might remobilize the racial and nativist anxieties that had fueled the prohibition crusade. The growing number of dry local option victories between 1934 and 1938—fifty-five hundred dry wins out of seven thousand contests—seemed to bear out that prediction. Public relations experts and trade association leaders recognized that the industry's legitimacy was probationary, but they had yet to convince enough producers to embrace collective action and chart a new course. How they did so is the subject of the next two chapters.

3

Fermented Beverages and the Gospel of Moderation

During the Great Depression, tastemakers had to straddle a fine line in stressing alcohol's respectability. If they overplayed their hand, they might invite the open ridicule that screwball comedies like *My Man Godfrey* (1936) and *The Devil and Miss Jones* (1941) regularly visited upon out-of-touch high society elites. Journalists particularly delighted in lampooning the peculiar excesses of wine aficionados and the lavish multicourse dinners served at gatherings of the Wine and Food Society.[1] Assigned to cover a wine-and-cheese tasting at the Walfdorf-Astoria, one snide *New York Times* reporter mocked an "enraptured woman," who marveled at the "subtle" aromas and flavors of the limburger she nibbled. "To the vulgar sense of smell," the journalist observed, "this particular delicacy was about as subtle as a pile driver, but the gourmets nodded with ponderous gravity. The reporter sought far corners of the great chamber."[2]

Tastemakers and trade associations understood that the industry could not rebuild mass markets without cultivating respectability. Yet, as the Waldorf-Astoria's wine-and-cheese tasting suggested, the quest for respectability might easily alienate potential consumers if marketing appeals became mired in class snobbery or smacked of inauthenticity and insincerity. The marks against wine, whiskey, and beer were clear enough. If the alcoholic beverage industries wanted to make alcohol an emblem of white, middle-class respectability, they needed to redeem beer from the disrepute of the saloon, reclaim whiskey from the boozers, and rescue wine from both its highbrow mystique and its déclassé reputation.

Alcohol promoters found their answer in the gospel of moderation. A cultural discourse with deep historical roots and global reach, the gospel of moderation promoted wine and beer (and sometimes the right kind of spirits) as the civilizing antidotes to drunkenness and overindulgence. In mass marketers' hands, moderation was a pliable concept, concerned less with identifying quantifiable measures of intoxication than with linking alcohol's respectability to middle-class conceptions of modern gender roles, worthy leisure, and breadwinning success. The gospel of moderation became the vehicle through which the industry attempted to reeducate public tastes and teach Americans the etiquette (and imperative) of responsible drinking. Vintners, brewers, and distillers preached their own variant of the gospel with varying degrees of success and conviction, and often with the aim of establishing the moral superiority of their commodity to the "harder" alternatives. In so doing, they sketched the outlines of three distinctive cultures of drink that would shape alcohol policymaking and middle-class American leisure for decades to come.

Moderation proved an alluring slogan but a surprisingly tough sell. Public relations experts, marketing authorities, and veterans of the pre-Prohibition alcoholic beverage industry often found themselves preaching the gospel of moderation to an uninterested and skeptical crowd. Key players within each sector of the alcoholic beverage industry remained unconvinced that appeals to respectability would broaden markets. Others registered little concern that aggressive, boundary-pushing salesmanship might damage the industry's public reputation. Skeptics also abounded among the many consumers who preferred alcohol that packed a punch, and among the damps and drys who questioned the industry's sincerity. Yet, by the end of the decade, the gospel of moderation's rhetorical magic had secured regulatory concessions and launched wine, beer, and whiskey on the path to legitimacy. This chapter examines how the makers of fermented beverages sought to reclaim the mantle of moderation. The next tackles how the makers of spiritous beverages attempted to do the same.

CALIFORNIA WINE GROWERS AND THE GOSPEL OF WINE

Thomas Jefferson, the nation's second slaveholding president and the chief author of the Declaration of Independence, was perhaps the most famous American exponent of the gospel of moderation. In 1787, Jefferson declared, "No nation is drunken where wine is cheap; and none sober where the dearness of wine substitutes ardent spirits as the common beverage." The Jeffersonian vision of a temperate wine-drinking nation neatly encapsulated what Leon Adams, an investigative-journalist-turned-wine promoter, hoped the Wine Institute, the trade association representing California's vintners, could accomplish for wine. As the Wine Institute's public relations director, Adams became an enthusiastic propagandist for what he called the "gospel of wine": the idea that wine was "the beverage of temperate, civilized dining" and the secret to weaning Americans from the corrupting influences of whiskey and gin. Throughout the 1930s, vintners and wine promoters preached the gospel of wine to legislators, industry regulators, reluctant consumers, and—as a measure of how far they had to go—to members of their own trade. They continually repackaged the gospel in subtle ways, depending on their target audience.

Long before the gospel of wine fell into the hands of post-repeal marketing and public relations experts, however, it had already undergone several reconfigurations. It originated in the eighteenth century as an Anglo-American discourse but had evolved by the turn of the twentieth century into a Mediterranean-inflected critique of American excess and a celebration of immigrant drinkways. All variations of the gospel shared the conviction that fermented beverages spared their drinkers from the ravages of distilled spirits and fostered bodily and spiritual well-being. The distinguished physician and temperance advocate Dr. Benjamin Rush, a contemporary of Jefferson, crafted a "Moral and Physical Thermometer" to measure the effects of different alcoholic beverages on the human body. Highlighting the relative benevolence of wine and other fermented beverages, Rush located distilled spirits in the hazardous zone near the bottom of his thermometer, where disease and vice prevailed. He placed wine, cider, and beer in the middle—just below purified water—because fermented beverages provided strength, nourishment, and good cheer when consumed with meals and in moderation.[3]

Many temperance societies initially shared Rush's views, but by the mid-nineteenth century, temperance activists increasingly favored outright prohibition. Nicholas Longworth, a multimillionaire real-estate speculator and a winemaker with extensive vineyards in the Ohio River Valley, attempted to inoculate wine against prohibitionist attack by championing its naturalness and purity. He asserted that wine only became dangerous when distilling technologies (which included the addition of sweeteners and fortifying materials) compromised wine's "natural" fermentation and boosted its potency. Longworth's emphasis on the purity of "naturally fermented" table wine addressed widespread concerns that merchants routinely adulterated and fortified expensive foreign wines with cheap whiskey and other spirits. "Watering down, fortification and other adulterations were so common," historian Erica Hannickel explains, "that Americans recorded drinking five times as much Madeira as was reported imported into the country."[4]

Winemakers and wine sellers also found useful political allies among horticulturalists, who talked about wine in the same breath as they talked about the fruits Americans grew in their gardens. In an 1867 speech to the American Pomological Society, Marshall Wilder, the society's president, touted the positive "moral and social influences" of all forms of fruit cultivation, but especially winemaking. In Wilder's eyes, wine bestowed the blessings of the garden and civilized living, while distilled spirits cursed families with the "ravages of intemperance."[5]

By the early twentieth century, as the crusade for prohibition was gaining momentum, Italian American winemakers had become wine's most vocal and persistent defenders. Lacking the racial shield of whiteness that previous defenders of wine enjoyed, Italian American winemakers embraced the temperance movement's critiques of American drinking excesses and forthrightly defended their own ethnic wine-drinking traditions. Andrea Sbarboro promoted his version of the gospel of wine in public addresses before trade groups and in his sixty-seven-page treatise *The Fight for True Temperance*, published in 1908. Sbarboro had immigrated to the United States as a young boy from a village in Liguria, the coastal region of northwest Italy. He eventually settled in San Francisco, where he became a successful merchant and banker. In 1881, with financial backing from his fellow northern Italian businessmen, Sbarboro bought fifteen thousand acres of land in Sonoma County. He "renamed the site Asti in honor of the Piedmontese town famous for its wine," and hired Piedmontese immigrant laborers to tend the vineyards. By the end of the century, under the subsequent direction of fellow Piedmontese immigrant Pietro Carlo Rossi, "Italian Swiss Colony had become the largest winery in California in terms of vineyard acreage, production capacity, distribution network, and market reach." Beyond California, the winery mostly catered to urban immigrant markets on the East Coast, leaving the increasingly immigrant-dominated wine business vulnerable to nativist and prohibitionist attacks.[6]

Sbarboro attempted to disarm prohibitionists by coopting their language of moral reform. In a 1906 address to the California Fruit Growers' Convention, Sbarboro condemned "the evil of intemperance" for causing more crime and misery than any other social ill that afflicted the United States. On the critical question of *how* to remedy "the evil of intemperance," Sbarboro and the prohibitionists sharply diverged. Sbarboro argued that temperance societies had "wasted millions of dollars and much valuable time" pursuing prohibition, when the wiser course would have been to encourage Americans to adopt the culinary customs of France, Italy, and Spain, where "every man, woman and child" drank wine in moderation with their meals. In those countries, Sbarboro told the convention, "intoxication is almost unknown, whilst in countries like Russia, Holland, England, Scotland, Ireland and our own United States . . . drunkenness exists to an alarming extent." So long as wine was affordably priced, costing Americans little more than "their tea or coffee," Americans of "all classes" would come to find the French and Mediterranean customs of drinking wine with meals more alluring than the saloon.[7]

Sbarboro's gospel of wine upheld the superiority of "true temperance" over "total abstinence." The ideal of "true temperance" recognized the human need for "some kind of healthy stimulant" and decried prohibition as an inducement to "secret guzzling, hypocrisy, and perjury."[8] Sbarboro might have achieved more for wine's cause had he simply defended pleasures enjoyed in moderation, but Sbarboro had bolder policy prescriptions in mind. He shocked the Women's Christian Temperance delegation attending Congressional hearings on a proposed bill to ban alcohol shipments from wet to dry states "when he claimed that dispensing a bit of wine at lunch to preschool children would make them immune to alcoholism for the rest of their lives"[9] Sbarboro's solution for rehabilitating drunkards likely raised eyebrows as well. Instead of jailing convicted drunks for the standard twenty-four hours, Sbarboro proposed sentencing them to thirty days of road repair or street cleaning work and serving them a glass of wine with lunch and dinner for each day of their jailhouse stay. By the end of the month, Sbarboro predicted, "more than half of the prisoners will" have acquired the wholesome custom of drinking light wines with meals. Recidivists could be sentenced to an additional thirty-day wine-with-meals rehabilitation regime.[10]

Sbarboro's confidence in wine's efficacy as a civilizing tool was, for his time, less outlandish than many prohibitionists likely supposed. In the late nineteenth century, British imperialists worked to establish colonial wine industries in Australia and South Africa, not because they expected to reap great profits but because they hoped that wine would transplant Western civilization to their newly acquired territories and transform colonial populations into healthy, moral, and sober imperial subjects.[11] Sbarboro hoped that Americans, once impressed with the global impact of wine's civilizing effects, would become converts to the gospel of wine. To that end, Sbarboro published forty pages of wine-friendly testimonials from clergy, army generals, physicians, and American ambassadors in wine-drinking countries.[12] Letters from nearly a dozen American consuls based in France, Spain, Italy, Germany, and Algeria affirmed the rarity of drunkenness, even though citizens of all social classes (and ages) regularly enjoyed wine with meals. The American ambassador to Florence underscored wine's innocence by noting that Florentines even packed a small flask of wine in their children's lunch basket.[13] Such testimonials also gave wine's defenders the opportunity to contrast the wholesomeness of European wine drinking cultures with the debauched atmosphere of the American saloon. In Sicily, Consul William Henry Bishop wrote, "the usual place where drinks are publicly sold is most often a pasticceria, cake-shop, or a pleasant cafe, which . . . ladies and children may freely enter. There . . . is no concealment of the interior . . ., for nothing takes place there requiring concealment."[14]

Despite such glowing testimonials, the nativist-fueled prohibition movement easily overwhelmed wine's ethnic defenders. During the Progressive Era, wine-friendly legislation passed only in the state of California, where wine and grape groups were better organized.[15] Sbarboro's imprint on wine politics, however, persisted long after his death in 1923. Leon Adams, who would later direct the Wine Institute's publicity efforts, credited Sbarboro's *The Fight for True Temperance* for persuading him to make wine promotion his life's work. While reporting on the California grape industry in the 1920s, Adams interviewed Edmund and Robert Rossi about their extensive vineyard operations at the Italian Swiss Colony winery. During Prohibition, the second-generation Italian American winemakers set aside their winemaking operations and earned their living by shipping grapes and grape concentrate to eastern markets where home winemaking thrived.[16] The Rossis provided Adams with literature on the pre-Prohibition history of the winery, including Sbarboro's *The Fight for True Temperance*. After reading Sbarboro's defense of wine, Adams knew that he had found the "cause" he had been searching for since Edward Bernays' book *Propaganda* had inspired him to dedicate his career to shaping public opinion: he would educate Americans to drink light wine with meals and "civilize" American drinking.[17]

Adams's upbringing and progressive politics also sowed the seeds of his future career as a wine crusader. Adams spent part of his boyhood on his family's chicken and fruit ranch in Sonoma, picking the Zinfandel grapes from which his mother produced homemade wine. His father was a connoisseur of cognac and drinker of wine and beer, and as Adams recalled, he "indoctrinated us children on the subject of alcoholic misbehavior" by expressing disgust at "examples of alcoholic overindulgence."[18] A progressive at heart, Adams developed a strong impulse for reform when, as an undercover investigator for the San Francisco *Daily News*, he exposed brutalities at a reform school for juvenile delinquents. Adams advocated for penology reform for a short time before he began covering the San Francisco waterfront and Prohibition beats, first as a cub reporter for the *Daily News*, then as the *San Francisco Bulletin*'s young star reporter. Those experiences and a jaunt through the vineyards of Europe heightened his interest in wine. His reputation as a reporter well established, Adams started his own advertising and publicity firm with Robert Layton Smith, the waterfront beat reporter for the San Francisco *Call and Post*. Just as Adams and Smith began building their new business—the Pacific Advertising Staff—the campaign to repeal Prohibition delivered important new clients: California grape growers and winemakers seeking to secure the immediate relegalization of "Light Wines and Beer."

Many of the most spirited promoters of wine were public relations and advertising experts, who, like Adams, saw themselves as working to enhance people's daily lives by promoting better kinds of consumption and improving public tastes.[19] Wine also got a boost from etiquette counselors and cultural critics who, like earlier generations of wine promoters, championed the beverage as the nation's best hope of rescuing itself from drunken excess. These new exponents of the gospel of wine parted ways with Sbarboro in one crucial respect: they began to deemphasize wine's distinctive ethnic markers as the beverage of Frenchmen, Italians, Spaniards, and Germans and instead reclaimed a place for wine among the blessings of "ancient civilization"—a cultural category that embodied whiteness.[20] In *The Future of Drinking*, a book written in anticipation of Prohibition's repeal, the cultural critic Gilbert Seldes reminded readers that "ancient civilization" regarded wine as "an essential accompaniment to other pleasures: love, conversation, the appreciation of some of the arts." If Americans wanted to rescue the art of civilized drinking, Seldes argued, they would have to abandon their "supercharged cocktails" for a glass of wine, the "divine solvent" that loosed "tongues . . . but not Pentecostally."[21]

Other wine promoters believed that emphasizing the wine-appreciating customs of elites rather than the unceremonious wine-drinking habits of ordinary Europeans was bound to backfire. Contemptuous of the "vinous voodoo spilled . . . from the facile pens of household counselors, etiquette oracles, and journalistic hacks," wine and liquor importers Frank Schoonmaker and Tom Marvel complained that American wine writers had made wine seem like "an expensive and elegant something for special occasions, . . . ladies, and 'connoisseurs.'" In wine-drinking countries, they wrote, wine "ranks . . . with bread, cheese and the other simple staples of life. There is precious little talk of venerable vintages, of the proper glass, of musty bottles and the etiquette of drinking."[22]

Determined to seize control over wine's cultural representation and its regulation, California winemakers formed the Wine Institute in the fall of 1934, nearly a year after Prohibition's repeal.[23] Although membership in the trade association was in theory open to wineries across the nation, no wineries outside of California joined. Thirty-two vintners, representing about half of California's total wine production (but a miniscule number of the state's 654 bonded wineries), joined the Wine Institute and agreed to pay dues based on how many grapes they crushed (twenty cents per ton) and how much wine they sold (a fifth of a cent per gallon of table wine and a quarter cent per gallon of fortified wines with an alcohol content of 18 to 20 percent). The early joiners included veteran table wine producers with roots in the pre-Prohibition industry and several big Central Valley fortified wine producers who had entered the grape growing business during Prohibition. Fortified wine producers made their sweet wines (sold as port, sherry, tokay, muscat) by adding a small amount of grape brandy to arrest fermentation of the grapes' natural sugar and preserve the sweetness of their higher-alcohol wines. Bank of America president A.P. Giannini bolstered recruitment by encouraging the wineries he had financed to join and within a year 188 wineries counted themselves members. Although the Wine Institute represented nearly 80 percent of the state's wine production, large wineries far outnumbered small wineries, and fortified wine producers outnumbered table wine producers. These imbalances periodically hampered the Institute's efforts to craft an effective public relations strategy.[24]

The Wine Institute quickly moved to establish uniform state wine quality standards that exceeded those adopted by the federal government. The new rules banned the addition of sugar to the must (a common practice among winemakers in the eastern states), required that wines bearing the California label be made entirely from California-grown grapes, and compelled winemakers to submit samples for inspection. A month after the regulations took effect, the Department of Public Health confiscated forty thousand gallons of substandard wine.[25] The much tougher battle for consumers' pocketbooks lay ahead.

CREATING A MASS MARKET FOR WINE DURING THE GREAT DEPRESSION

During the Great Depression, the biggest wine producing countries turned wine promotion into an international project. Plagued by overproduction, shrinking export markets, and dwindling demand, France, Italy, the Soviet Union, and eventually the state of California all initiated state-backed campaigns to increase domestic wine consumption. In Italy and France—the two countries with the deepest wine-drinking traditions—new initiatives to eliminate wine fraud and protect wine quality, including France's creation of the wine appellation system, accompanied highly nationalistic wine marketing. French winemakers' troubles began in the 1920s, when US Prohibition, punitive European tariffs, and strained postwar finances dried up elite markets in the United States, the Soviet Union, Britain, and the Austro-Hungarian and German Empires. Overplanting in France and several other European countries and the development of viticulture in Chile, South Africa, and Australia added to the global wine glut. In response, the French government taxed high yields, prohibited new plantings for ten years, and aggressively promoted wine drinking as an essential component of what made France a great nation. Advertisements celebrated wine as a tonic for the body and soul that inspired France's great philosophers, poets, and artists. Radio broadcasts even cautioned that drinking too little wine could have dire consequences. According to one broadcast, the failed monarch Louis XVI suffered from poor thinking because "he added water to his wine" and his subjects rebelled because they "became too poor to drink wine every day." As part of the campaign, the *Médecins amis du vin*, an organization of physicians, championed the merits of moderate wine consumption over total abstinence and promoted wine as a healthy and hygienic beverage for all age groups.

Schoolteachers also joined the wine propaganda machine, making wine a part of children's geography lessons and math instruction, even as they rebuffed proposals to serve children wine with lunch.[26]

In the 1930s, French wine consumption was already the highest in the world, reaching an annual consumption of 206 liters per capita.[27] Although the French wine campaign failed to increase wine consumption, merely maintaining that level of consumption during the Depression was, from the vantage point of winemakers in other countries, an enviable achievement. A much different consumer landscape prevailed in Italy, the Soviet Union, and the United States, where bourgeois wine consumption was disappointingly low and popular tastes favored the "wrong" kinds of wine and spirits. Spurred by a desire to combat alcoholism, the new Soviet leadership maintained the tsar's wartime ban on 80-proof vodka in hopes of strengthening the thin market for dry table wines. Once officials lifted the vodka ban in 1925, however, consumer preferences for vodka and "falsified wines" adulterated with grain alcohol and sugar overwhelmed the state's fledgling efforts to bolster viniculture and a temperate wine drinking culture.[28] Fascist Italy's far more elaborate public relations and collective marketing campaign disavowed Italy's boisterous working-class wine taverns and reclaimed "wine's honor" as "Italy's wholesome, family-friendly 'national beverage.'" Like the French wine campaign, Italy enlisted "medical celebrities" to vouch for wine's "alimentary and hygienic virtues" and developed educational programs to disseminate knowledge of Italy's wine-growing regions and shared oenological heritage. Appealing to consumers' sense of patriotism, the Italian campaign exhorted middle-class women to buy reputable Italian wines instead of the inferior, unaged bulk wines. In an echo of wine discourse on the other side of the Atlantic, one leading Italian wine promoter assailed the increasingly popular American-style cocktails as a debasement of Italians' "physiological, artistic, and psychological tastes" and urged women to drink superior Italian wines as a matter of national duty.[29]

Like their French and Italian counterparts, American wine promoters also appealed to consumers' sense of economic patriotism, but the absence of a strong American wine-drinking tradition limited the emotional power of nationalistic appeals. American winemakers were also constrained by regulators who frowned upon the sort of health and medical arguments that French and Italian physicians had marshalled to great effect. In 1939, Leon Adams, now the Wine Institute's marketing director, established a Society of Medical Friends of Wine, but the group initially functioned as an elite social club for wine connoisseurs.[30] The invitation to the society's inaugural event at the St. Francis Yacht Club in San Francisco saluted the nine-course dinner, featuring lobster thermidor, filet mignon Bordelaise, and four premium California wines, as an occasion to practice "the more deliberate and relaxed way of living."[31]

American winemakers found their most formidable ally in newspaper magnate William Randolph Hearst. Few could have predicted at the start of Prohibition that Hearst, an early and enthusiastic supporter of the Eighteenth Amendment, would some dozen years later be heading the charge to slash wine taxes and persuade consumers to buy American wines. Hearst's disillusionment with Prohibition became apparent in the mid-1920s, when his newspapers devoted increasing coverage to Prohibition's violation of personal liberties and the spread of organized crime.[32] Hearst turned decidedly against Prohibition in 1929, when the Jones Act imposed prison sentences and hefty fines on citizens caught drinking. Calling the act "the most menacing piece of repressive legislation that has stained the statute books of this republic since the Alien and Sedition laws," Hearst concluded that Prohibition "had done nothing ... to advance the cause of temperance."[33]

When it came to temperate drinking, there was little daylight between the public Hearst and the private Hearst. Hearst permitted house guests no more than two cocktails before dinner, and he instructed his waiters to "watch carefully for signs of overindulgence" before pouring diners more wine. Weekend guests who could not control themselves often found their bags packed that evening or the next morning, with the "broad hint that they should leave."[34] Hearst's vision of temperance was decidedly wine friendly. In 1929, a New York City judge who supported the modification of the Volstead Act to permit state dispensaries for wine and beer claimed Hearst's $25,000 "Temperance Prize" for the best proposal to advance the cause of true temperance.[35]

The wine industry also benefitted from Hearst's staunch advocacy of economic nationalism during the Depression. Beginning in the fall of 1932, Hearst wrote daily editorials in support of the Buy American campaign and his twenty-seven newspapers prominently featured Buy American stories. Calls to "buy state" or "buy city" from women's clubs, manufacturers, and chambers of commerce quickly followed. Tainted by vicious anti-Mexican and anti-Asian immigrant bashing, the Buy American campaign drew strong support from American Federation of Labor unionists and others who wanted to save American jobs for "American-born" workers and keep foreign products out of the country.[36] As soon as repeal took effect, the California wine industry jumped on the protectionist bandwagon. In an hour-long radio talk, Judge Marion De Vries, an industry spokesman, called upon "every devoted Californian" to defend "American Markets for American Products" and support protective tariffs against "the menace" of foreign wine imports. De Vries linked the case for protection to the nation's unemployment problem, noting that coopers, printers, glass makers, farmers, agricultural laborers, railroad operators, merchants, distributors, grocers, restaurateurs, and even journalists gained employment from American wine.[37] Although New Dealers generally favored free trade, the federal government imposed a heavy tariff of $1.25 a gallon on imported wines—a hefty increase over the ten-cent federal tax on American table wines and twenty-cent federal tax on American fortified wines.[38]

With the threat of foreign wine imports at bay, California vintners invoked economic nationalism to target a menace closer to home: the persistence of home winemaking and the bootleg trade. How, they wondered, had sweet, fortified wines overtaken the table wine market in a dramatic reversal of pre-Prohibition patterns? After repeal, the higher alcohol dessert wines such as port, sherry, muscatel, white port, angelica, and tokay were outselling table wines by a ratio of three to one and by 1937 that ratio had increased to five to one—a sharp contrast to the pre-Prohibition pattern of selling six gallons of table wine to every four gallons of sweet.[39] A variety of factors explain this dramatic shift in consumer tastes. Not only had the popularity of sugary soft drinks and juice- or soda-spiked cocktails accustomed Americans to sweeter drinks, but the Prohibition-era practice of adding large quantities of sugar to grape concentrate had also made even homemade vintages sweeter than many commercial table wines. The sacramental wines that had circulated through bootleg channels were also significantly sweeter. Others gravitated to sweet dessert wines because they contained enough alcohol (18 to 20 percent) to still pack a punch but cost significantly less than heavily taxed spirits. Market analysts attributed the surge in dessert wine sales to "the poor man's whiskey trade."[40] Consumers also turned away from table wines because the vast majority produced in the mid-1930s had little to commend them. Sweet wines, even poorly made ones, were a more palatable and less risky purchase. A bottle of table wine, once opened, had a relatively short life span, but an opened bottle of fortified wine could last for weeks and months without spoiling.[41]

While vintners had entertained the possibility that consumers might initially favor sweet wine, the radical shift in consumer tastes caught them by surprise. The most logical conclusion, Robert Rossi charged in the trade press, was that "the real wine consumers of the nation are ignoring the repeal of prohibition . . . . They are continuing to make their own wine or to buy it from bootleggers."[42] California vintners based such charges on the assumption that about half of the fresh grapes shipped from California in 1934 went into homemade wine, in keeping with Prohibition-era patterns. That volume would have yielded 34 million gallons of homemade wine, about as much wine as the commercial wineries produced. Three years into repeal, much to the wine industry's dismay, home winemakers continued to make their own wine on a large scale—an entirely legal practice. In 1937, the Tariff Commission estimated that home winemakers produced some 29 million gallons of wine, about 30 percent of national consumption.[43]

Home winemaking remained popular not only in many urban immigrant districts but also in many Southern states and locales that still banned alcohol sales. Following a tradition begun by enslaved cooks, many African American women used the abundant local supply of scuppernong grapes to make their own wine. The classic recipe, calling for three pounds of white sugar for every gallon of juice, transformed the acidic and musky scuppernong grapes into a sweet, palatable wine similar to Manischewitz, the kosher wine that African American consumers helped to make a mass-market success in the 1950s.[44] Given the unreliable quality of California wines, most of which was sold in bulk to be blended and bottled by out-of-state distributors, many traditional wine drinkers likely found homemade wine a better and tastier bargain.[45]

When Robert Rossi, a second-generation Italian American, indicted the nation's "real wine consumers" for not patronizing the legitimate trade, he could barely disguise his frustration—perhaps even his sense of betrayal—that immigrant drinkers had forsaken their own ethnic community of wine entrepreneurs. Historically, the table wine market had traditionally consisted primarily of the immigrants and their descendants from Italy, France, Spain, Greece, and a few other European nations.[46] Rossi believed that traditional wine drinkers would abandon their bootlegger and basement wines if state and federal governments lowered excise taxes to make wine broadly affordable. Hearst papers amplified those calls. The *New York American* exhorted legislators to "put the country on a wine basis rather than on a whisky basis ... by slashing all taxes on mild alcoholic drinks."[47] Other hard-hitting Hearst editorials, conveniently ignoring the legality of home winemaking, characterized the widespread consumption of basement wines as a "startling abuse" akin to "BOOTLEGGING FOOD, for WINE IS A FOOD."[48] Positioning wine either as a food or as the benign alternative to hard spirits, Hearst papers sang the gospel of wine with enough force and conviction to move Congress to action. In August 1935, the House of Representatives cut federal wine taxes by half—the only taxes Congress reduced that session.[49] That same year fifteen states uncoupled wine from liquor regulations either by lowering state wine taxes or permitting table wines to be sold in retail food outlets instead of the state-run liquor stores.[50]

Building on the success of Hearst's appeals to economic nationalism, the Wine Institute styled its own buy California campaign. With help from the California State Chamber of Commerce, the Wine Institute encouraged railroads, civic groups, tourist offices, and allied industries to publicize California as the "Wine Land of America" and promote wine as the symbol of California's gracious hospitality. Railroads were a natural ally in this endeavor. In the late nineteenth century the Southern Pacific railroad had promoted California as a veritable Eden bursting forth with grapevine-lined hillsides and fruit-laden valleys.[51] The Wine Institute did not have to press too hard to get the Atchison Topeka & Santa Fe Railroad and the Great Western Railroad to include California wines on their dining car menus.[52] The trade association's ultimate goal was to make winemaking as distinctive a part of California as redwood trees, orange groves, and motion pictures.[53] Tapping regional pride, the Wine Institute urged loyal Californians to buy California wines for their state's benefit and to become ambassadors for California wine when traveling in other states.[54] Even Hollywood became a target of the Wine Institute's loyalty watch. At the institute's request, Universal Pictures agreed to eliminate a scene in *Sutter's Gold* (1936) depicting early California winemakers crushing grapes with bare feet, lest the public be reminded of the industry's inadequate attention to quality standards in the early days of repeal.[55]

American wine promoters shamelessly masked a genuine weakness—inconsistent and sometimes poor quality—by interweaving claims to superior wine quality with nationalistic appeals to Buy American. A cartoon distributed by Renault & Sons, the largest East Coast bottlers of California wines, boldly contrasted superior American wines, made with "modern production methods" and "American standards of

FIGURE 4. Cartoon distributed by Renault & Sons, East Coast bottlers of California wines, 1937.

quality," to imported wines, made with "obsolete production methods" and "cheap foreign labor" who crushed grapes with bare feet (see Figure 4). The cartoon depicted a consumer comfortably ensconced in the backseat of a car while an American wine wholesaler and retailer steered the automobile on the road to prosperity. Having chosen to buy American wines, the happy trio was guaranteed wines at the "right prices," made by "all American labor." Had the trio instead been lured by "ballyhoo!!" and veered off course to "buy foreign wines and promote the other fellow's prosperity," they would have encountered a higher-priced and unreliable product.[56]

Such boosterism, coupled with California's liberal wine policies, paid off handsomely in California, where residents drank on average three times more commercially produced wine than other Americans. Californians not only had easy access to wine—they could buy it in grocery stores or by the barrel directly from wineries—but they also paid considerably less for wine. California levied a modest two-cent per gallon tax on wine, a mere fraction of the taxes assessed by other states, peaking at $1.10 per gallon in Maryland.[57] Winemakers' success in California was not easily duplicated elsewhere owing to higher excise taxes, stricter trade barriers, and lack of consumer interest. The wine market was so limited, in fact, that three-fourths of the wine sold in 1934 was consumed in just five states—California, Louisiana, New Jersey, New York, and Michigan.[58] A massive investment in national advertising was the obvious next move.

THE BATTLE FOR COOPERATIVE WINE ADVERTISING

Throughout the 1930s, marketing authorities struggled to persuade vintners and grape growers to collectively advertise the pleasures and proper uses of wine. To achieve mass market success, they argued, the California wine industry needed to emulate the cooperative advertising campaigns of California's walnut, raisin, and orange growers. "Ten years ago there was no large natural demand for orange juice or mayonnaise," the *California Grape Grower* reported, "and it wasn't until the orange growers and the mayonnaise makers had used advertising space month in and month out . . . that sales began to grow and orange juice . . . became a national breakfast drink and [mayonnaise became a] salad dressing."[59] Cooperative advertising by the California Associated Raisin Company (reorganized as Sun-Maid Raisin Company in 1922) had similarly transformed raisins from a Thanksgiving and Christmas specialty item into a year-round staple.[60] Growers and winemakers who spent any time perusing advertising journals like *Printers' Ink* and *Printed Salesmanship* would have encountered numerous stories trumpeting the glories of cooperative advertising campaigns that enabled California walnut and citrus farmers to evade the depressed prices that afflicted other agricultural producers.[61] H. F. Stoll Jr., a merchandising authority and editor of *Wines and Vines*, advised vintners that it was a "fatal dream" to assume that dry wine consumption would increase once vintners had eliminated the problems of "high taxes, restrictions on bulk sales, home winemaking, [and] the bad quality of early shipments." Demand remained flat not just among the "well-to-do middle classes" and the younger generation, Stoll observed, but among second-generation Italian-Americans as well.[62] Noting the conspicuous absence of wine advertising in mass magazines, Stoll wondered "whether the consumer was conscious that Repeal also applied to the wine industry."[63]

The Wine Institute joined Stoll in underscoring the urgent need for collective action. Addressing vintners at the second annual wine conference in September 1935, Albert Paul, chairman of the Wine Institute's board of directors, asserted that wine would "take its rightful place on the dinner table of America" only when the industry "aggressively and dramatically [told] the people about the merits of wine." If "bread, butter, automobiles, furniture, neckties and even table salt have to advertise . . . wine is no exception."[64] Leon Adams, ghostwriting for Harry Caddow, the Wine Institute's secretary-manager, urged the trade to recognize advertising's essential role in courting skeptical women consumers who still doubted alcohol's respectability. If "the cigarette manufacturers (by stressing the smartness of cigarette smoking)" could weaken women's resistance to smoking, vintners could surely persuade women that "wine is essentially a food" and appeal to their interest in "serving smarter, more healthful foods."[65]

California grape growers and vintners strongly resisted such calls for cooperative advertising. Some recalcitrant producers calculated, as Ernest Gallo did, that they could more profitably spend money promoting their own brands than promoting wine collectively.[66] Others were advertising skeptics. Winemaker Louis M. Martini, who ultimately withheld his assessment for the collective advertising campaign launched in 1939, felt that "advertising is only good promoting something that is not up to the quality that people want. People buy what they want and make the market."[67] Trade associations in other industries encountered similar skepticism. Sunkist, the orange growers' association, constantly battled their members' wariness by heralding advertising "as the industry's white knight" that had enabled "exponential growth in production" to continue without disastrous price cutting.[68]

Disagreements over the merits of advertising obscured more fundamental internal industry divides among those who saw a future in the table wine market, those who catered primarily to the fortified wine market, and those who entered the winemaking business to provide an outlet for their surplus raisin and table grapes. These tensions arose because the wine industry's fortunes were bound to the vicissitudes of three separate commodity markets: table grapes, raisins, and wine. Dogged by chronic overproduction since the mid-1920s, when home winemakers' demand for juice grapes spurred overplanting, many San Joaquin Valley grape growers viewed wine in purely instrumental terms: as the most profitable outlet for their surplus grapes. If Thompson Seedless, a widely planted raisin variety, could not be sold at an attractive price in July as fresh table grapes, they could be laid out to dry in August as raisins. And if raisin prices proved unattractive, they could be left on the vines until October for delivery to wineries.[69]

Although this strategy enabled growers and wineries to adjust to market conditions, it had two major downsides: it lowered wine quality and it failed to discourage overplanting, thus perpetuating the chronic oversupply of grapes. Raisin grapes made especially poor table wines meant to accompany savory dishes, but they could be forged into a passable fortified wine (usually identified on the label as a port, sherry, tokay, or muscatel). Most fortified wine producers preferred the designation "sweet" or "dessert" wine to "fortified" wine, but all three descriptors aptly captured something of the essence of such wines. They were both sweeter and stronger than table wines because the winemaker added grape brandy to the wine sometime before the process of fermentation completed, yielding a wine with more residual sugar and more alcohol (18 to 21 percent). The habitual use of raisin grapes in fortified wines convinced Leon Adams that many Central Valley growers viewed wine merely as a "garbage pail" for their surplus grapes.[70] The fact that 80 percent of California wine in the 1930s was sold as bulk wine to out-of-state bottlers who sold them under their own labels, gives some credence to such views.[71]

Table wine producers often landed on the losing end of struggles to remedy the chronic surplus of table and raisin grapes. Since the surplus was mostly in raisin grapes, table wine producers and the coastal wine grape growers blamed the recurring crises of overproduction on Central Valley growers who overplanted Thompson Seedless and on Central Valley wineries who willingly salvaged their excess into mediocre fortified wines. Because consumer demand for fortified wines was three times greater than the demand for table wines, the big Central Valley wineries that made fortified wine had few incentives to uproot their existing grapes to make room for superior wine varietal grapes.[72]

As Leon Adams saw it, the biggest obstacle to spreading the gospel of wine boiled down to a "doctrinal" split between the table wine advocates and the large wineries who saw wine primarily as an outlet for surplus grapes.[73] Although many Central Valley growers and fortified wine producers opposed cooperative advertising, Adams oversimplified the array of calculations that fueled resistance to cooperative advertising. In the late 1930s, when constrained incomes, mediocre wines, and consumer preferences for liquor dampened enthusiasm for wine, it took a leap of faith to imagine that advertising could manufacture demand from such dim prospects. In the end, the California wine industry had to be dragged into the modern era of national advertising and mass merchandising by the key institutions that financed and regulated agriculture. The Bank of America and California's Department of Agriculture played pivotal, if belated, roles in compelling fractious growers and wine producers to support cooperative advertising. Since the 1920s, cooperation had been a "pillar of agricultural policy" at both the federal and state levels. Long experience taught policymakers that two crucial factors handicapped the success of cooperative marketing: cooperative associations had no effective mechanisms to deal with free riders or to control overproduction.[74] California walnut and citrus growers had succeeded where others failed because an overwhelming majority of producers had agreed to fund national advertising.[75] When participation fell below two-thirds of the total membership, resentment mounted against free riders—growers who enjoyed the benefits of cooperative advertising but did not share the costs—and participation faltered. In such circumstances, only the coercive power of additional "selective incentives" could mobilize support for collective action.[76]

California lawmakers provided just the incentives that cooperative marketing organizations needed to tackle the free rider problem. In 1937, they passed the California Marketing Order, which compelled all the growers in a particular industry to pay into an advertising fund once two-thirds of the industry, by number and volume, had consented.[77] To qualify for the program, the Wine Institute first had to convince a skeptical State Department of Agriculture, which administered the marketing orders, that wine was actually an agricultural commodity. Jefferson Peyser, counsel for the Wine Institute and a former San Francisco supervisor, was greeted with howls of laughter at an early Wine Institute meeting when he advised vintners to call themselves wine growers instead of wine manufacturers. The typical mocking response was, "I never saw any of this wine growing out of the ground."[78] Yet, Peyser's semantic innovation—an adaptation of the French term "vigneron" for a person who grows grapes or makes wine—proved crucial both to securing regulatory benefits from the state and to rehabilitating the industry's public image. As "wine growers," vintners could claim some of the virtue typically attributed to farmers while further distancing themselves from the maligned "liquor interests" targeted in local option elections. Such rhetorical positioning could also help vintners avoid the hostility so frequently directed in the 1930s against "big business." Thanks to Peyser's dogged persistence, Attorney General Earl Warren yielded to the Wine Institute's stance and the vintners won their marketing order.[79]

Sign-ups for the marketing order began gathering steam when Arpaxat Setrakian, the charismatic leader of Central Valley's raisin industry, endorsed wine advertising as the solution to the huge 1937 grape surplus.[80] The Bank of America, the industry's chief lending institution, also deployed its formidable leverage against holdouts. When the Bank of America, along with the Reconstruction Finance Corporation and several other California banks, agreed to finance a price stabilization program that allotted a portion of the crop to be distilled into brandy and set aside until more favorable markets emerged, the Bank of America did so on the condition that the national wine advertising program also get underway.[81] Having put up the lion's share of the $10 million dedicated to fund the set-aside program, the Bank of America signaled its willingness to enforce that stipulation if voluntary sign-ups lagged.[82] In some instances, bank managers threatened to retract the credit of holdouts.[83] Although such coercion was mild compared to the cloaked night-riders and fire bombings that had compelled Armenian raisin growers to join the raisin growers' cooperative in the mid-1920s, the bank's heavy-handed interventions undoubtedly helped the wine industry achieve nearly unanimous support for the wine marketing order.[84]

By the end of the 1930s, prospects for the American wine industry (and California vintners in particular) looked much brighter. Just as California vintners prepared to launch their $2 million "Wine for America Drive" in 1939, the Federal Alcohol Administration issued stronger wine quality standards, patterned after California's.[85] Wilford S. Alexander, head of the Federal Alcohol Administration, applauded the vintners' national campaign to educate Americans about the "tempera[te] ... use of [light] alcoholic beverages." In his address to Wine Institute members, Alexander admitted that he did not envision "making our America a nation of wine-bibbers"—a qualifier omitted from the institute's press release about Alexander's speech—but he did endorse the country's need for "a good, cheap table and culinary wine."[86] The vintners' wine promotion campaign, discussed in chapter 7, also garnered the ringing endorsement of John Boettiger, publisher of the *Seattle Post-Intelligencer* and Franklin Delano Roosevelt's son-in-law. "If you can teach Americans to linger longer at dinner," Boettinger said, and "[restore] the lost art . . . [of] drinking to each other's health . . . you will . . . be adding to . . . the neighborliness and brotherliness of our people."[87]

By the decade's end, the California wine industry had achieved something of its own new deal through its partnerships with banks, state legislators, and federal regulatory agencies. Although Leon Adams's republic of temperate wine drinkers was still a distant dream, Alexander and Boettiger both linked wine to a new cultural vision of the nation in which "good cheap table and culinary wine" fostered "neighborliness and brotherliness" and complemented the egalitarian sensibilities of the New Deal.

BEER AND THE GOSPEL OF MODERATION

Much as winemakers in France, Italy, Russian, and the United States had promoted the civilizing influence of wine, brewers in Europe and North America had long touted beer as a wholesome and healthful drink. The German immigrants who introduced lager to the United States in the mid-nineteenth century viewed beer as a food—or "liquid bread," as they called it—and they welcomed it into their homes and restaurants as a benign component of leisure and family life. When temperance reformers attacked beer, brewers in both Canada and the United States heralded beer as the temperate and healthful alternative to hard spirits.[88] "Whiskey makes a man ugly and corrupts his stomach," a US brewing journal asserted in 1880, while beer "mellows him . . . and makes him a friend to his kind."[89] Since its founding in 1862, the United States Brewers Association (USBA), one of the nation's oldest trade associations, had enlisted the gospel of moderation to defeat local option measures, fend off stricter regulations, and avert federal excise tax hikes.[90]

Brewing trade journals defended beer with the same reformist zeal that Nicholas Longworth, Andrea Sbarboro, and Leon Adams deployed to promote the "gospel of wine." The *Western Brewer* used its inaugural 1875 issue to announce its intention to "preach the gospel of BEER, against the Gospel of Puritanism, of Prohibition, of Personal Thralldom."[91] More than a decade later, the *Western Brewer* still hoped to persuade temperance activists that rising beer consumption was "doing more to drive out strong drink than all their preachments and ... agitation."[92] Although the *Western Brewer* correctly gauged consumption trends, it completely misjudged public opinion. By 1915 Americans consumed, on average, 20.2 gallons of beer each year (compared to 3.5 gallons in 1865)—and 1.2 gallons of whiskey each year (compared to 2.1 gallons in 1865).[93] Yet, voters continued to gravitate toward prohibitionism because they associated beer with the rapidly multiplying number of saloons.[94] When the brewers tried to blame public drunkenness on whiskey, the brewing industry's control of the saloons came back to bite them. "Who has encouraged the violation of law and the establishment of low drinking places?" the National Liquor Dealers' Association pointedly asked in 1906. "Certainly not the whisky ... trade," since the distillers controlled "very few saloons."[95]

Members of the USBA disagreed on how best to address the prohibitionist threat. While some members embraced saloon regulation and self-reform, others resisted aligning themselves with distillers, naively believing that beer would be spared from prohibition.[96] Many regional and local breweries "refus[ed] to believe" that prohibitionists "could possibly affect their operations in safe havens like New York City or Philadelphia." Pabst, Anheuser Busch, and other national shipping breweries feared prohibitionism more intensely because dry successes anywhere weakened the national market and threatened their "significant fixed investments in distant beer depots, saloons, and bottling facilities." Such fears proved warranted when the Webb-Kenyon Act in 1913 banned interstate transportation of alcoholic beverages to dry states, effectively cutting off national shippers from "existing markets and promising avenues of expansion."[97] Despite concerted efforts, the national shippers failed to convince their fellow brewers to fund a sustained campaign for saloon reform and, in a move that proved a fatal miscalculation, the USBA attempted instead to redirect prohibitionist ire against the distillers.[98]

After repeal brewers faced crucial questions about how to insulate themselves against future attacks and restore public confidence. In 1936, when the USBA hired Edward Bernays as their public relations counsel, the old intra-industry divides over whether the road to redemption lay in publicity, as Bernays believed, or in self-reform resurfaced. The obstacles to achieving unity in the brewing industry were more formidable than those that plagued the California wine industry. Because California produced 90 percent of the domestic wine, California's winemakers and grape growers did not have to reach agreement with producers in other states, with whom they competed for market share. By contrast, the structure of the brewing industry militated against cooperation. No single brewer sold "more than one-thirtieth of the nation's beer," and nearly two-thirds of the nation's seven hundred breweries served regional or local markets rather than national markets.[99] Plus, no external mechanisms comparable to the wine marketing order existed to compel cooperation.

Discord among the nation's brewers erupted into public view via press reports of personal rivalries and cutthroat competition for market share. The brewers began the post-repeal era with two national trade associations: the USBA, which had led the industry during the campaigns against the Eighteenth Amendment and for repeal, and the American Brewers' Association (ABA), which had formed during Prohibition to represent the producers of nonalcoholic "near beer." Although the USBA and ABA had both helped to write the new regulatory codes governing the legalized industry, the USBA antagonized newer industry members by limiting membership and leadership posts in the older trade association to breweries with pre-Prohibition-era roots. Headed by Colonel Jacob Ruppert, the owner of a large eastern regional brewery and the New York Yankees—a team then on the cusp of winning a long streak of World Series Championships—the USBA included among its members large national shippers like Anheuser-Busch, Schlitz, and Pabst, who had built beer fortunes before Prohibition. The alliance between the national shippers and regional breweries had long been fraught, and in 1936, with the ink barely dry on the USBA's contract with Edward Bernays, the large national shippers, led by August Busch of Anheuser-Busch, withdrew from the USBA to form a new trade association, Brewing Industry, Inc. (BII).[100]

The split between the BII and the USBA revived the factional divides that had impeded collective action to defeat the Eighteenth Amendment. Anheuser-Busch had withdrawn from the USBA in 1915, when the association refused to back saloon reform, and it led the revolt against the USBA again in 1936, when they learned that Bernays planned to promote beer as a "valuable food beverage" instead of as "whoo-pee fuel." Pabst and Anheuser-Busch took their dispute public, telling *Business Week* that such "ballyhoo" would "give the drys a large, clear target to shoot at." They believed that brewers should demonstrate social responsibility by "withdrawing their brands from outlets that besmirch the beer business."[101] BII's objections to the Bernays plan partly reflected the national shippers' understanding of history's bitter lessons: in the absence of measures to correct saloon abuses, selling beer's virtues stood little chance of changing hearts and minds. In an editorial announcing its opposition to the Bernays plan, the *Brewers Journal* insisted that bringing lawbreaking taverns in line had to come first.[102]

The national shippers' stand against lawbreaking taverns had as much to do with their interest in restricting competition and gaining market share as it did with their desire to score public relations points. The national shippers profited the most from the new post-repeal regulations that banned the tied house and limited the number of licensed drinking establishments. Before Prohibition, local and regional breweries had used the tied house to keep shipping beers out of their market. Because they supplied saloons with fresh draught beer that required minimal advertising and minimal transportation, local and regional breweries outcompeted shippers on both price and taste. Prohibitionists' attacks on the saloon persuaded the national shippers that beer's future lay in the home and in bottled beer, which in 1915 represented only 10 to 15 percent of all beer sales.[103] By 1933, the biggest breweries were well poised to exploit the home market for bottled beer. During Prohibition, Schlitz, Blatz, Pabst, and Anheuser-Busch expanded their bottling facilities and fleet of trucks and automobiles.[104]

Having bet their future on packaged beer, the national shippers used their influence on code-making bodies to dismantle the tied house and create new retail outlets that could compete with taverns. By requiring breweries to use wholesalers instead of supplying retailers directly, the new codes "eroded one of the cost advantages local breweries held over shippers." In another strike against the saloon, the new codes also enabled grocery stores to acquire a beer license for a fraction of the fee paid by taverns.[105] Some states prohibited sales of beer by the growler, further cutting into sales of draught beer.[106] All told, the new licensing arrangements promised to boost beer's respectability and the shipping breweries' bottom line. White middle-class women who would have scorned the notion of buying a growler of beer from the neighborhood tavern now had the more respectable option of placing beer bottles in a grocery cart loaded with other foods.

Although the national shippers preferred to see themselves as socially responsible firms who prioritized "corrective measures" over "ballyhoo," their own hands were not entirely clean. Even as the national shippers publicly denounced the tied house, they continued to give tavernkeepers trays, coasters, equipment, fixtures, and expensive electric signs to advertise their brands, often with the aim of obtaining exclusive selling contracts. Old habits died hard. Despite the risks to their public reputation, many breweries revived elements of the tied-house system because demand for packaged beer, though rising, was still untested and underdeveloped. By 1935, packaged beer represented less than a third of the market.[107] Taverns thus remained vital to the beer business and many breweries, including the national shippers, failed to maintain the mandated lines separating the retailing and manufacturing ends of the trade. In 1935, Schlitz and Anheuser-Busch both faced court orders to stop their giveaways. A year later federal officials threatened to appoint a brewery "czar" to help the industry enforce the regulatory codes it helped to write.[108]

The talk of brewery "czars" and the sharp uptick in dry local-option victories delivered brewers a clear message: clean house and make self-regulation work or face tighter state controls and possible federal oversight. Yet, for a host of reasons, members of the United Brewers Industrial Foundation (UBIF) and USBA hesitated to make tavern regulation the focal point of their public relations campaign.[109] More than half of the 112 breweries that formed the original nucleus of the UBIF, the organization that funded Bernays's work, came from the beer-producing states that transitioned most slowly to packaged beer: New York, Pennsylvania, New Jersey, Minnesota, and Wisconsin.[110] By 1940, nearly half of all beer sold in the United States was packaged beer. California, Michigan, and Missouri led the pack, with 79 percent, 60 percent, and 57 percent respectively of their production going into cans or bottles. New York breweries lagged well behind, as they still sold nearly three-quarters of their beer on tap in 1940. Likewise, breweries in New Jersey, Pennsylvania, Minnesota, and Wisconsin continued to sell approximately 60 percent of their beer in kegs.[111] The heads of New York's largest regional breweries—Jacob Ruppert, William Piel, and Rudolph Schaefer—used their leadership posts in the UBIF and the USBA to determine the focus and scope of the UBIF's public relations campaign. As long as draught beer was the mainstay of their business, brewers concluded that it made better sense to shift attention from the trouble with taverns to the delights of beer.

Brewers' cultural pride in the German-American tradition of enjoying beer in moderation with friends and family also explains their resistance to tackling the tavern problem. Many German-American brewers, especially those with roots in the pre-Prohibition-era industry, remembered well how wartime jingoism and xenophobia had stifled anti-prohibitionists and hastened their industry's demise. The UBIF campaign satisfied their yearnings to present the affirmative case for beer rather than battle their prohibitionist foes from a defensive crouch. At the USBA's annual convention, Sol Abrams, the general manager of Schlitz (one of the few national shippers to join the UBIF at its founding), lauded the foundation's plan to go on the offensive.[112] *American Brewer* similarly hailed the UBIF campaign as a welcome departure from the industry's previous pattern of "silently . . . suffer[ing] . . . slanderous attacks."[113] The UBIF campaign was thus in part a down payment on restoring brewers' wounded pride. As Colonel Ruppert explained, "To those self-respecting brewers who endured the distress of being outlawed during prohibition and who resented the injustice of being pilloried as a class apart, there is comfort and pride" in the foundation's plan "to depict the brewer for what he is, a manufacturer and a business man on a parity with other business men in our economic system."[114]

EDWARD BERNAYS AND THE REVAMPED GOSPEL OF MODERATION

When Bernays formally launched the UBIF campaign in April 1937, Bernays went heavy on offense, with nary a mea culpa in sight. He issued dozens of press releases that supplied material for stories about beer's contributions to government revenues and the economic recovery, its place in home cooking and gracious hospitality, its role in historic American events, and its value as "a bulwark of moderation and sobriety." Rural newspapers, metropolitan dailies, and the newswires picked up Bernays's beer-friendly story ideas. One such story, titled "Lack of Beer Caused the Pilgrims to Land at Plymouth Rock," put a new spin on one of the nation's origin myths. Women's page editors printed recipes for dishes that featured beer as both an ingredient and a complementary beverage. The UBIF hit pay dirt with a feature about the Arctic Expedition, led by meteorologist Clifford MacGregor in 1937–1938. Picked up by the Associated Press, the North American Newspaper Alliance, and 322 rural newspapers, the story informed readers that MacGregor and his crew drank beer instead of polar water to benefit from beer's superior mineral content.[115]

The UBIF campaign subtly retooled the gospel of moderation to appeal to housewives and rural voters—the two groups most likely to vote "dry" in local option elections. UBIF campaign materials presented beer as a food and a source of culinary adventure, partly with the goal of getting housewives to view beer as many brewers did: not as an intoxicating beverage but as a "liquid food" that belonged in the pantry "alongside the bread and other foodstuffs."[116] Anchoring beer more firmly to the food side of the food-drug divide also had distinct political upsides: it kept beer taxes low and allowed beer to be sold in delis and grocery stores.

The brewers' revival of the liquid food argument was both surprising and risky. Not only had the argument failed to gain traction during the crusade for national Prohibition, but it likely only further antagonized brewers' opponents. Consider the trade card advertisement that one Detroit brewer created in 1883 to advance the anti-prohibitionist cause. The color lithograph featured a cherubic toddler seated in a high chair, with a beer mug in hand, and the accompanying jingle left little doubt about the source of the babe's cheerful disposition: "the youngster ruddy with good cheer, serenely sips his Lager Beer" (see Figure 5).[117] The Detroit brewer clearly misjudged the audience he hoped to win over. Progressive Era reformers and public health authorities excoriated immigrant mothers who fed their babies beer and cabbage and created massive child welfare exhibits that promoted "clean and nutritious milk" as the appropriate beverage substitute.[118]

Despite obvious political risks, the UBIF campaign loudly trumpeted the liquid food metaphor. Advertisements that celebrated beer and ale as "Nature's Liquid Food" emblazoned the sides of fifteen thousand buses and trolleys in two hundred cities and small towns. Set against a pastoral backdrop of golden wheat fields dotted with grain stacks, the ad's imagery and headline—"America's Farmers supply both Wheat for your Bread, Barley for your Beer and Ale"—drew moral equivalencies between beer and bread and between brewing and farming. In the foreground of the ad, the enormous beer-filled pilsner glass with a voluminous foam head mirrored the fluffy-topped cinched grain stacks that filled the backdrop.[119]

The UBIF also developed a recipe booklet, *It's Smart to Serve Beer*, and hired Eloise Davison, a home economist, to write *Beer in the American Home*, a recipe-filled primer on beer's place in the modern American diet.[120] Davison's recipes for savory dishes like beer bread, ham cooked with beer, beer-based cheese sauces, and beer-braised beef kidneys were plausible (and possibly delicious) takes on standard beer-infused fare. More adventurous housewives might have tried their hand at Davison's chocolate beer cake or her sweet potatoes baked in beer or

FIGURE 5. Anti-prohibition trade card distributed by a Detroit brewer, 1883. Detroit Historical Society.

her potato salad with beer and milk dressing. Some of Davison's concoctions were hardly recipes at all. Mellon Balls in Beer Dressing consisted of a honeydew melon, doused with a cup of beer and left to soak in the refrigerator until serving time; Beer with Egg (a beaten egg stirred into a glass of cold beer) was billed simply as a "bland drink," with no hint of why homemakers might serve it.[121]

The twenty-one page history that preceded Davison's recipes endowed beer with a wholesome and patriotic past. Davison gave pride of place to the Pilgrims who brought beer to North America and the colonial ladies who put beer "on the table as regularly as bread" and used it to season foods.[122] She saluted the brews of William Penn, Samuel Adams, and Martha Washington—revolutionary era patriots all. Her omissions were telling. She bypassed the saloon era and failed to mention the German immigrants who developed Americans' favored style of lager beer. This, in essence, was beer's story in its most sanitized form: stripped of its ties to the saloon and immigrant drinking traditions and ennobled by its ties to America's revolutionary leaders and the lost art of colonial beer cookery.

The UBIF's courtship of housewives also fired the merchandising imaginations of allied trades. Department stores, makers of glassware and refrigerators, and producers of ham, mustard, and cheese all incorporated packaged beer in their print ads and displays. The tantalizing prospect of home refrigerators well-stocked with ice cold beer particularly excited the nation's electric utilities. More than 110 of them requested copies of Davison's book and planned to raise consumers' awareness of beer's uses in the home.[123] In all these ways, the UBIF and allied trades pointed toward a future in which the home—not the tavern—would become the dominant domain for beer consumption.

THE BREWERS' CRITICS AND A PUBLIC RELATIONS REBOOT

The UBIF's wave of beer publicity provoked a backlash from both expected and unexpected quarters. Several newspapers, even the wet-friendly papers, resented the UBIF's unwillingness to use paid advertising and refused to sacrifice newsworthy stories for free beer publicity.[124] *Christian Century*, a liberal Protestant magazine, decried the UBIF's campaign as a cynical move to stave off higher beer taxes, scapegoat hard liquor, and recast beer as "a home-and-family" food beverage.[125] One *Christian Century* editorialist particularly worried that the "beguiling prose" and menus in *Beer in the American Home* would convince housewives "that a home without beer is like a home without a mother"—an apt, if snide, summation of the brewers' goal.[126] As much a testament to the UBIF's success as its failure, the *Christian Science Monitor*, a national daily with high circulation, ran a scathing twelve-part series on the UBIF's "New Threat to Temperance."

Reviews of *It's Smart to Serve Beer* ridiculed the booklet's attempt to restore the lost art of beer cookery. Perhaps thinking of the recipes for such "tarty dishes" as Bohemian Lager Soup, beer-smothered celery, and beer pancakes for breakfast, the *Washington Post* observed that "some of Mrs. Schreiber's recipes call for question marks (until we have had time to try them)."[127] Other reviewers were not as polite. A Grand Rapids newspaper editorial feared that "the beer makers' press agents have been sampling something stronger than the mild amber fluid manufactured by their employers" and "hoped, for the sake of peace and quiet at dinnertime, that melon balls with beer, sweet potatoes in beer, beer cabbage slaw, and all the rest . . . will remain" uncooked and unsampled.[128] The advertising counsel for a Boston brewery urged the UBIF to abandon the "silly" beer cookery idea and promote beer as an accompaniment to "salads and steaks and chops."[129]

Bernays's decision to promote beer as a liquid food proved to be his biggest political miscalculation. Instead of solidifying beer's privileged position within federal regulatory frameworks, the beer-as-food argument provoked the head of the Federal Alcohol Administration (FAA), Wilford S. Alexander, to call for more stringent regulation of the brewing industry and beer advertising. Addressing the USBA at their "diamond jubilee" convention, Alexander criticized brewers for soft pedaling beer's intoxicating qualities. "Gentleman, beer is not Coca Cola. No campaign of education . . . will ever convince the American public that beer . . . should be regulated only to the same extent."[130] Alexander sought Congressional authority to ban alcohol ads from the airwaves and the Sunday papers and prohibit any references to alcoholic beverages as a medicine, tonic, or food. Although Alexander won the backing of the National PTA, the National Education Association, state alcohol administrators, and church-affiliated temperance organizations, he found little support within the Treasury Department, which oversaw the FAA, and he lost his post soon thereafter, when the Treasury's new Alcohol Tax Unit absorbed the FAA's functions. Stiff opposition from the National Association of Broadcasters, the advertising industry, the American Federation of Labor, and alcohol trade associations killed any chance of Congressional action.[131]

Although the brewers evaded tougher FAA sanctions, the pushback from friend and foe persuaded the UBIF to tackle the tavern problem more directly. The UBIF hired Newell-Emmett, an advertising firm with extensive experience promoting cigarettes, to publicize the new Brewers' Code of Practice. In a conference meeting with Bernays and UBIF members, William Reydel, Newell-Emmett's vice president, applauded cigarette advertising's unapologetic approach. "It has never been self-righteous, never talked back, and never crusaded. It has just gone on every day, everywhere getting more people to smoke cigarettes because they represent a thing to give pleasure, not a cause to be argued about."[132] The UBIF appeared to take that advice to heart. The UBIF's new code of practice, adopted in 1937, acknowledged the problem of disorderly taverns but declined to shoulder the entire blame. The eight-point code pledged to eliminate "anti-social conditions" in taverns and "prevent beer sales to minors" and intoxicated customers, but the brewers promised no concrete action beyond the vague pledge to "cooperate" with authorities.[133] Noting that brewers could not "effectively 'police' the quarter-million points where beer is sold (nor have we legal authority in many cases to do so)," the UBIF put the onus on the public to "restrict your own patronage to legal, respectable retail outlets."[134] In the short term, the UBIF's tavern work achieved at least one uncontested outcome: it managed to heal the fractious divides within the brewing industry. Satisfied that the UBIF had appropriately redirected its focus, the BII and ABA ended their boycotts of the UBIF and the three national brewing trade associations merged into one.[135] Shortly thereafter, the board unceremoniously fired Bernays.[136]

Despite the obvious upsides of promoting moderation, public relations experts, the editors of industry trade journals, and industry veterans struggled to rally key segments of the beer and wine industries to the cause. Some brewers and vintners resisted the gospel of moderation because, in their view, the drinking public wasn't buying it either. Americans preferred whiskey and cocktails to light wines and beer, they liked their wines sweet and fortified, and they easily passed up a 3.2 beer for a stronger brew. Some firms cashed in on the growing preferences for more potent forms of alcohol by hyping their brand's potency. One New York winery advertised its wine on subway cars with the simple slogan, "It's Fortified!"[137] Midwestern brewers touted the high alcohol content of "pepped up" or "winner" beer.[138] In the midst of the Great Depression, assessments of immediate economic self-interest often trumped concerns about long-term political survival, making the path to easy profits more alluring than the path to respectability.

Although economic crises often foster cutthroat competition and price-cutting spirals that doom efforts to find common ground, they can also spur industry-wide cooperation. Weak consumer demand and the cumulative impact of high excise taxes, restrictive retailing regulations, and dry activism pushed brewers and vintners to look beyond their competitive rivalries. Although some brewers and vintners questioned the moderation strategy, the industry's opponents feared that public relations experts had outmaneuvered "the temperance crowd" and "stolen [their] moral thunder." Charles Ferguson, writing for the *Christian Century*, denounced the industry's cynical "campaign" to "sanctify our impulses" and "make all of us feel upright, clean-living and manly about our indulgences."[139] Like Edward Bernays, Ferguson recognized that alcohol's moral rehabilitation hinged on broadening its social acceptance among middle-class elites unnerved by alcohol's associations with foreignness, criminality, and urban nightlife. To the dismay of many drys, not only did the modern tavern seem destined to remain, but alcohol's defenders had anointed new retail sites—the grocery store and the package store—as the guiding lights of the post-Prohibition regime. A packaged goods revolution that transported alcohol into the home—not via the growler or the drunken saloon-goer, but via the bottle, the can, and the housewife's hands—had smoothed the industry's path to moral rehabilitation.

4

Spiritous Beverages and the Muddled Meanings of Moderation

Reformers on both sides of the wet–dry divide have long imagined distilled spirits as the unruly alcoholic troublemakers that posed the greatest threat to public health and welfare. The eighteenth-century "gin craze" inspired William Hogarth, the English artist and pictorial satirist, to contrast the benign effects of beer with the destructive force of distilled spirits in his engraved and etched prints *Gin Lane* and *Beer Street* (1751). In *Gin Lane*, Hogarth portrays Englishmen engaged in street brawls, addicts reduced to skin and bone, and a drunken, negligent mother who has allowed her baby to fall off the railing, plunging to its death. The only thriving business is the pawnshop, where people trade essential possessions for money to buy more gin. In Hogarth's *Beer Street*, by contrast, order and industriousness prevail: the Englishmen and women are happy and well-nourished—some to the point of corpulence—and the only failed enterprise appears to be the empty, boarded up pawnshop.

On the other side of the Atlantic, the American Society for the Promotion of Temperance (ASPT), the first national temperance organization, drew similar contrasts between distilled spirits and fermented beverages. Founded in 1826, the ASPT sanctioned the measured use of wine and beer, but it urged citizens to abstain from ardent spirits and successfully campaigned to abolish soldiers' liquor rations in 1832. Many temperance advocates would come to believe that only total abstinence could guarantee personal salvation and ameliorate societal ills, but the ASPT refrained from endorsing total abstinence in the 1830s "for fear of outraging both the public" and their fellow reformers who still believed that wine and beer could be consumed in healthful moderation.[1] Over the next several decades, brewers and vintners worked hard to reinforce such convictions and defeat prohibitionists by casting wine and beer as the temperate alternatives to distilled spirits. In turn, dry propagandists invoked the specter of the slippery slope to combat the wets' gospel of moderation. Eventually, they argued, even drinkers of milder fermented beverages would join their whiskey-drinking peers on the path to misery, ruin, and death.[2]

Although whiskey's greater alcoholic potency made it a convenient target for both ardent drys and nervous wets, whiskey's defenders refused to surrender the moderation banner to their opponents. Instead they embarked on a campaign to retrain consumers' sensory expectations and teach them the etiquette (and imperative) of responsible drinking. Unlike the brewers and vintners, who relied heavily on trade association advertising to present their message of moderation, the distillers did not coalesce behind a collective public relations strategy until the end of the 1930s, when the Distilled Spirits Institute mounted an exhibition at the 1939 New York World's Fair. Seagram, the Canadian distiller, launched its own decades long moderation campaign in 1934 on behalf of the industry as a whole. Seagram's moderation campaign aimed first and foremost to build goodwill and rehabilitate the firm's reputation as a socially responsible company. Magazine ads bearing the company's moderation message exhorted alcohol consumers to avoid drinking while driving or hunting, to put the necessities of life ahead of the luxury of liquor, and to savor whiskey as a connoisseur rather than guzzling it. Seagram's reminders to drink responsibly also endeavored to jettison whiskey's much-maligned lower-class image and restore its dignity as the beverage of cultured gentlemen. Rather than rejecting old temperance discourses out of hand, Seagram heaped scorn on the male drunkard who squandered the family's income on liquor and lifted up the virtuous whiskey drinker—a financially secure, ambitious white male breadwinner in full command of his liquor—as a new exemplar of masculine respectability. In Seagram's vision, the possession of such masculine virtues better predicted a beverage's intoxicating effects than the potency of the beverage itself.

As historians of psychoactive commerce have demonstrated, the process of legitimizing and domesticating formerly controversial or illicit substances often proceeds on multiple political, social, and cultural fronts.³ In the case of whiskey, the intoxicant's chief redeemers sought to whitewash aspects of its past, reconstruct the image of its primary consumers, and reduce perceptions of whiskey's harm while amplifying perceptions of its public benefits. Such wide-ranging efforts to rehabilitate whiskey's reputation unfolded in newspaper and magazine advertisements, the potables columns of men's magazines, and the restaurants and exhibition spaces of the 1939 New York World's Fair. In these varied cultural realms, whiskey makers highlighted the industry's contributions to multiple sectors of the economy, elevated whiskey's status as a marker of class respectability and masculine virtue, and constructed more flattering narratives of whiskey's past. Seeking their own scapegoat for excessive drinking, whiskey makers sometimes blamed irresponsible breadwinners and sometimes warred with each other over which style of whiskey (blended vs. straight) best facilitated moderation.

All the while, whiskey makers did their best to muddle the meanings of moderation. Rather than attempting to quantify overindulgence, branded advertising and Seagram's moderation campaign promoted responsible drinking with a wink and a nod. They left the definition of moderation just vague enough to encompass drinking behaviors that could easily slide into excess. Despite such ambiguities, the distillers conveyed a clear political message through their muddled calls for moderation: the onus for managing the pleasures and perils of a potentially harmful commodity belonged not to the industry but to individual drinkers.

WHISKEY PURITY AND CIVILIZED DRINKING

Any advocate of moderation needs a good antagonist, one whose villainy exposes the sharp contrast between virtue and vice, purity and adulteration, and respectability and excess. For brewers and winemakers, whiskey was that antagonist. Whiskey distillers, on the other hand, searched for their antagonist within their own ranks. At the turn of the twentieth century, rivalries within the distilled spirits industry intensified when Congress and various federal agencies took up the question of food identity standards in response to growing public concerns about adulterated foods. The meat and milk supply got top billing at the Congressional hearings that eventually secured the passage of the Pure Food and Drug Act in 1906, but many of the subsequent debates on the act's interpretation and implementation turned on questions about what made whiskey whiskey. The key contenders in the debate—the manufacturers of straight whiskey and rectified whiskey—used different processing methods to achieve a well-balanced and flavorful whiskey. Straight whiskey makers distilled their whiskey to a proof of 100 to 110 and then aged it in new charred oak barrels for four to eight years to add flavor and convert the unpleasant-tasting and headache-producing higher alcohols (called "fusel oil") into less noxious compounds. Rectifiers, by contrast, produced unaged blended whiskey—a much less expensive beverage made from neutral grain spirits that were redistilled to 190-proof to eliminate the noxious fusel oil. The rectifiers then flavored and tinted their neutral grain spirits to resemble barrel-aged whiskey, sometimes by blending it with a small quantity of aged straight whiskey and sometimes by adding burnt sugar, prune juice, cherry juice, creosote (the oily substance that preserves wood utility poles) or cochineal (a red dye made from the crushed and dried bodies of the female cochineal insect).[4]

The rectifiers and straight whiskey producers each claimed that theirs was the purer whiskey. Pure whiskey, they argued, fostered civilized drinking while adulterated whiskey wreaked havoc on public health and social welfare. Whiskey makers became entangled in a three-year dispute, which began when rectifiers refused to label their bottles "imitation whiskey" in accordance with the 1906 Pure Food and Drug Act. President Howard Taft ended the dispute in 1909 when he ruled that both types of spirits could legally bear the name whiskey so long as the rectifiers' labels clarified that their whiskey was a *blended whiskey* made from redistilled neutral grain spirits. The Taft ruling entrenched public perceptions that straight whiskey was the superior product and the only whiskey suitable for consumption in respectable homes and private men's clubs.[5]

The debate over whiskey standards was as much about the politics of prohibition and the politics of class as it was about whiskey purity and whiskey quality. By the end of the nineteenth century, rectified whiskey, the whiskey favored by saloons and their largely working-class patrons, claimed 80 to 95 percent of the national market. Straight whiskey makers and their allies exploited the tight connection between rectified whiskey and saloon-going in hopes of shifting blame for public drunkenness from whiskey itself to a broader category of adulterated spirits that masqueraded as whiskey but were, in their eyes, "a scourge on society, answerable for violence and crime, murder, and the destruction of happy families." Straight whiskey deserved the public's trust, the

Kentucky Journal argued, because it had to "lie in the Government bonded warehouses season after season awaiting its maturity," but "unscrupulous" rectifiers deserved their scorn for doctoring "crude spirits of a week old ... with coloring matter" and other toxins to achieve some semblance of the real thing. Rectifiers rebutted such accusations with claims of their own superior purity. They noted that the process of redistilling whiskey at a higher proof removed the dangerous impurities and harsh flavors left behind in straight whiskey and that the subsequent addition of a few harmless coloring and flavoring agents produced a better-tasting and more wholesome beverage than barrel-aged whiskey.[6]

Dr. Harvey Wiley, the chemist who became known as the father of the Pure Food and Drug Act, gave straight whiskey advocates the moral upper hand in these disputes over whiskey purity. Referring to rectified whiskey blends as "rank poisons," Wiley claimed that "when a man gets drunk on spirits he is crazy drunk, and when he gets drunk on whisky [he] is a jolly good fellow."[7] Wiley's stance was not based on any opposition to the rectifiers' use of flavoring additives, which he judged harmless, but was instead a cynical ploy to keep prohibitionists aboard the political coalition that favored pure food legislation by casting the rectifiers as one of the bill's major foes.[8] Straight whiskey's Congressional allies did Wiley one better. They claimed the barrel-aged product could even promote temperance. Representative William Richardson, an Alabaman, testified before Congress that "it is the ... adulterated stuff ... that puts the very devil into men" and destroys families. Pure straight whiskey, on the other hand, promoted temperance.[9] Such rhetoric not only attempted "to redirect the odium of temperance reformers toward rectified spirits alone," but it also sought to normalize the expensive tastes of the upper- and middle-class men who consumed straight whiskey and marginalize the drinking practices of working-class and immigrant saloon-goers.[10]

Such arguments never made their way into the whiskey industry's formal organized campaign against the Eighteenth Amendment. Instead of attempting to sanctify whiskey as a beverage of moderation, as the brewers and vintners did, the distillers and liquor wholesalers formed "model license leagues" to push for stricter licensing requirements and stringent enforcement of saloon regulations.[11] After Prohibition, however, whiskey makers crafted a more elaborate gospel of moderation of their own—one that put a benign face on whiskey itself and called upon consumers to exercise greater self-restraint.

SEAGRAM'S MODERATION CAMPAIGN AND THE POLITICS OF THE GREAT DEPRESSION

In 1934, Seagram, the Canadian distilling giant headed by Samuel Bronfman, launched what would become a multi-decade advertising campaign to promote responsible drinking. Although Bronfman would later claim that he initially encountered skepticism when he pitched the idea to New York advertising agencies, the reasons for such skepticism remain a mystery.[12] Did advertising executives worry that such a campaign would irritate diehard drys who saw all alcohol consumption as irresponsible, or did they simply doubt that Seagram—or any other whiskey firm—was the right messenger? Seagram's moderation campaign aimed to address reputational problems that were both company specific and industry wide. Seagram and Schenley Distillers had both soiled their reputations by partnering with bootleggers during Prohibition. In addition, Seagram, Hiram Walker, and other Canadian distillers owed the United States government back taxes on the liquor their agents smuggled across the border during Prohibition—a claim that Seagram settled in 1936 for $1.5 million, about half of what Treasury Secretary Henry Morgenthau had hoped to recoup.[13]

The problem of poor whiskey quality also hindered the industry's efforts to build consumer demand and restore public goodwill. At the time of repeal, existing US stocks of aged whiskey "were critically low."[14] Whiskey makers flooded the market with cheap, poor quality whiskey. Throwing caution to the wind, some marketed unaged whiskeys as "pre-Prohibition blends."[15] Many drinkers, not well versed in the distinctions between a blended whiskey and a straight, assumed that blended whiskey was something akin to the adulterated or diluted bootleg whiskey they had imbibed during Prohibition.[16] Only Scotch whisky escaped Prohibition with its good reputation intact. Consumption of Cutty Sark and Ballantine's Scotch, both widely drunk in speakeasies, soared after repeal.[17]

The negative public perceptions of blended whiskeys were particularly devastating for Seagram, since it manufactured only blends, a type of whiskey made by mixing neutral grain spirits with 20 to 25 percent aged whiskey. Before Prohibition, about 70 percent of the whiskey Americans consumed was blended whiskey, but lingering memories of bootleggers' dubious mixtures badly damaged consumer demand for blends after repeal. Many of the "revived whisky companies fell in step with the prejudice," *Business Week* reported, producing straight whiskeys of a single age—that is, whiskeys made *without* the addition of neutral grain spirits—or what marketers confusingly called straight blends, mixes of straight whiskeys of different ages.[18] Lewis Rosenstiel, who headed the United States firm Schenley Distillers, gambled correctly that Americans, having suffered "an unrelieved diet of bootleggers' bastard blends," would gravitate toward "a blend of straight whiskeys, old and new." By blending differently aged straight whiskeys, Schenley stretched its small inventory of aged whiskey, and, as *Fortune* magazine put it, managed to "satisfy the drinker's taste for a potent brew without scorching his palate or griping his stomach."[19] Although consumer skepticism of whiskey blends added to Seagram's post-repeal marketing headaches, the Canadian firm, along with its Canadian and British rivals, retained one crucial advantage over US whiskey firms: Seagram's comparatively robust inventory of mellowed liquor enabled the company to deliver a quality product and strengthened its ability to shape consumer tastes.[20]

Seagram's moderation campaign gave many Americans their first introduction to the Canadian distiller and its brands. Seagram placed its first moderation ads in 165 leading newspapers and later purchased space in news magazines, business journals, and trade publications.[21] In taking up the task of courting public goodwill, Seagram joined "the public relations craze" alongside other large corporations. During the 1930s General Motors, Ford, Westinghouse, and AT&T launched major public relations campaigns to persuade a skeptical public that big business held the answers to the country's economic woes and could improve the standard of living for the common man. Eager to rescue the free enterprise system from government regulation and answer critics who blamed corporate greed for the economic collapse, such firms deployed populist imagery and rhetoric to befriend the masses and give the corporation a "soul."[22] Seagram similarly aimed to jettison its reputation as a soulless "merchant of booze."

For a variety of reasons, Seagram rejected the populist approach that dominated the public relations work of most major corporations. The whiskey industry's historical affiliation with working-class saloons, the association of problem drinking with financial insolvency, and the need to reassure status-conscious middle-class consumers all made populist appeals seem less apt. To transform whiskey drinking from a badge of dishonor into a badge of distinction, Seagram crafted its appeal not for the common man but for the well placed and the middlebrow. The model drinker in Seagram's moderation campaign was also deliberately gendered and implicitly racialized as an affluent white man. Like most liquor ads from the period, Seagram's moderation ads did not address or include women drinkers. Partly in deference to dry opinion, most distillers, in fact, observed the self-imposed industry ban on representing women in liquor ads until 1958. The decision to omit women—as well as Black and working-class men—from Seagram's ads also rested on the popular prejudice that none of these groups could responsibly manage their liquor. In *Fortune* magazine's 1966 retrospective on the Bronfman family dynasty, Samuel Bronfman told the reporter that the moderation campaign's inspiration came when he was lunching at the bar of the Commodore Hotel in Manhattan, where—to Bronfman's apparent horror and disgust—he witnessed tipsy women "bellying up to the bar." Aiming to associate whiskey with "respectability, responsibility and success," Bronfman, historian Michael Marrus explains, believed those "attributes ...were best protected within the sphere of male sociability." Where brewers and vintners staked their hopes for a new culture of moderation on the disciplining forces of domesticity, dining, and heterosocial leisure, Bronfman placed his trust in the capacity of affluent white men to discipline themselves.[23]

Seagram executives recognized that overplaying whiskey's respectability and the industry's dedication to the public good also carried risks. Some consumers would undoubtedly view the company's efforts to promote moderation with deep skepticism. How sincere could Seagram be, many might wonder, when the company also dedicated millions of merchandising and advertising dollars to boosting sales of whiskey? The moderation campaign would succeed as a PR venture, an in-house publication observed, only if it managed to "tread the line between sincerity and hypocrisy."[24] Seagram initially attempted to strike that delicate balance between "sincerity and hypocrisy" by aligning its interest in industry self-preservation with consumers' interest in preserving hard-won personal liberties. "There is a common problem which you as consumers and we as distillers share," a 1936 ad declared. "It is the *right use of liquor—drinking in moderation*. Your interest is in the continued enjoyment of your personal liberty. Our interest is the many millions of dollars we have invested in American plants, payrolls, grain and good-will."[25] Those words acknowledged that Seagram, like other members of the alcoholic beverage industry, had not fully earned the public's esteem, but the ad reminded drinkers that they, too, shared a responsibility for making repeal work. Seagram, in essence, defined the industry's social responsibility and the drinker's individual responsibility as flip sides of the same coin. The ad also suggested that promoting responsible drinking was just one dimension of corporate social responsibility. By reminding readers of the company's investments in plants and payrolls, Seagram also touted its contributions to economic recovery, undoubtedly hoping that this, too, would demonstrate its commitment to the public good.

Seagram's moderation campaign ultimately sought to reorient public debate from questions of corporate social responsibility to questions of individual responsibility. Instead of blaming the manufacturers and distributors of alcohol for problem drinking, as prohibitionists had done, Seagram placed the responsibility for managing the pleasures and perils of intoxicating beverages directly on the individual. The ethos of individual responsibility had deep historical roots in the Enlightenment and American traditions of individualism, but it acquired additional salience in the wake of repeal, as Americans confronted the challenge of reintegrating a previously illicit commodity into mainstream rituals of business, leisure time, and domesticity. Much as the alcoholism-as-disease paradigm shifted blame for problem drinking from alcoholic beverage producers to psychologically troubled individuals, the gospel of moderation performed similar cultural work by entrusting individuals with the responsibility for judging when one more drink was one too many.[26] The discourse of moderation naturalized the ethic of individual responsibility as the commonsense solution to problems of liquor control.

In Seagram's vision of moderation, responsible drinkers earned the privilege of enjoying whiskey only when they had achieved middle-class norms of breadwinning success and masculine virtue. A 1937 moderation ad titled "We Don't Want Bread Money" stressed that liquor was a luxury "to be bought and enjoyed only after the necessities are provided. . . . We don't want to sell whiskey to anyone who buys it at a sacrifice of the necessities or decencies." The advertisement's dramatic illustration, a black-and-white drawing of a woman's weathered hands cutting a slice of bread from a partially eaten loaf, consumed half of the full-page ad (see Figure 6). Showing only the hands and torso, the ad evoked the loneliness and despair of the woman who tightly grips an old loaf in order to slice it.[27] Particularly striking is the way Seagram's ad coopted the visual and verbal rhetoric of its prohibitionist opponents. The image of an impoverished woman struggling to feed her family on mere scraps played on old temperance imagery of the forlorn housewife, condemned to poverty by a husband who squandered his earnings at the saloon.[28] The reference to "bread money" in the ad's

WE DON'T WANT BREAD MONEY

Liquor is one of the luxuries of life, to be bought and enjoyed only after the necessities are provided. Whoever needs bread for himself or his family, should not buy whiskey.

The persons we want for our regular customers have definite incomes and definite obligations. They do not exceed the one nor neglect the other. We make sales to such persons with a clear conscience because Seagram whiskies are well worth all they cost to those who can afford the luxury of moderate use. We don't want to sell whiskey to anyone who buys it at a sacrifice of the necessities or decencies. We are not being idealistic. The House of Seagram counsels abstinence for some and moderation for all because such counsel is good business. Abiding prosperity for our business can be built only by the repeat orders of our wise friends. *We don't want bread money!*

THE HOUSE OF SEAGRAM

Seagram-Distillers Corporation, Executive Offices: N. Y.

FINE WHISKIES SINCE 1857

FIGURE 6. Advertisement from Seagram's moderation campaign, 1937. Courtesy of the Hagley Museum and Library.

title also evoked "blood money," suggesting that buying whiskey before necessities betrayed a man's honor as well as his breadwinning obligations. The man of little means who squandered family income on drink made for a particularly pathetic figure, one who, in the view of alcoholism experts, drank to "escape . . . the demands of true manhood and the husband/provider role it entailed."[29]

By stressing that Seagram sought only customers with "definite incomes and definite obligations," Seagram's "Bread Money" ad not only affirmed the distiller's own sense of social responsibility, but it also hinted at the type of men Seagram saw as its ideal customers and as consumers citizens worthy of emulation.[30] These were not wayward bachelors or lonely forgotten men, but affluent, responsible family men with a proven record of meeting financial obligations. The responsible, moderate whiskey drinker, in short, possessed the virtues of the iconic middle-class breadwinner: a man with a mortgage, a bank account, and a family to provide for. The emerging group of authorities on alcoholism made similar distinctions between moderate drinkers and problem drinkers. Unlike prohibitionists, who saw "drinking as an economic threat to all families or to society as a whole," historian Lori Rotskoff writes, the alcoholism movement based their assessment of problem drinking on "the degree to which a man's drinking interfered with his breadwinning obligations." Such assessments reflected experts' class bias against working-class drinking. According to one alcoholism expert, a normal drinker might even occasionally get drunk, but would still be regarded as a moderate drinker so long as his alcohol expenditures did not "jeopardize the economic welfare of his family or business." A man who spent money on alcohol "in disproportion to his budget," on the other hand, could not be considered a moderate drinker. Alcoholism experts, Rotskoff writes, "granted men the right to drink, but not at the expense of a family's right to consume desired goods."[31]

The text and illustration of "We Don't Want Bread Money" worked in conjunction to harmonize two dueling sensibilities in 1930s popular culture: sympathy for those who had fallen on hard times through no fault of their own and a yearning for the return of traditional values that valorized individualism and self-reliance.[32] Such contradictory impulses surfaced, for example, in *Gone with the Wind*, the 1939 movie blockbuster that gave us the iconic image of Scarlett O'Hara vowing with a clenched fist to never go hungry again after consuming the lone carrot buried in Tara's war-torn soils. Scarlett, at least in that scene, was at once an emblem of self-reliance and a sympathetic character with whom other Americans suffering through hard times could identify. Seagram's sympathy for the downtrodden, however, edged into contempt for the financially insolvent problem drinker. A rather scolding ad, titled "Pay Your Bills First," insisted that "No person should spend a cent for liquor until the necessities of living are provided—and paid for. Bills for groceries . . . clothes . . . shoes . . . rent . . . light . . . heat . . . doctors . . . have the first call on America's payroll." The ad reflected the whiskey industry's awareness that its legitimacy was probationary and subject to reversal: "The very existence of legalized liquor in this country depends upon the civilized manner in which it is consumed. In the long run . . . it is good business for us to say 'pay your bills first.'"[33] In Seagram's world of responsible drinking, the privilege of drinking whiskey was a privilege that only men of means should enjoy.

Seagram's moderation campaign also reminded drinkers of their responsibility to avoid harming others. One ad invited readers to join Seagram "in the crusade for safer, saner driving. . . . Think before you drink! *Don't drink before you drive.*"[34] Another warned against drinking while hunting, insisting that the "true sportsman . . . protects himself and his fellow sportsmen from tragic harm . . . *by obeying this personal code.*" Only after hunting was the time right "for the rich and honest pleasure of fine whiskey."[35] Avoiding harm to others also extended to the example fathers set for their sons. "Nothing is quite so disillusioning to the clear eyes of a youngster as the sight of a man—his own father—who has used liquor unwisely," one ad warned. Run on Father's Day in 1938, the ad portrayed a pipe-smoking, cane-bearing middle-aged father enjoying an afternoon walk with his preteen son. Much as fathers imparted wisdom to sons in such intimate moments, they also inducted sons into the realm of responsible manhood by way of example. "The coming generation will be less apt to use liquor intemperately," the ad continued, "if older people will regard it as a luxury and treat it as a contribution to gracious living."[36]

Many of the themes set forth in the moderation campaign ads deployed a tried and true tactic that many industries, from snack food makers to oil conglomerates, have used to deflect public criticism: they coopted the rhetoric of their opponents.[37] Like prohibitionists, Seagram associated problem drinking with poverty, unfulfilled breadwinning responsibilities, and deficient fatherly guidance. The essential difference, of course, was that Seagram enlisted these tropes in the service of promoting the pleasures and rewards of moderate drinking. It is striking nonetheless that during the 1930s Seagram did not wholly reject the temperance movement's paradigm of the problem drinker. Seagram executives reserved their harshest criticism not for the "unfortunate alcoholic" in need of medical attention but for unmanly drinkers who had not yet learned how much was too much. As Seagram president Frank Schwengel bluntly observed in a business talk, "In the vanguard of our enemies and contributing largely to the threat of prohibition is . . . the human pest 'who cannot handle liquor.'"[38] In the midst of the Depression, the habitual drinker who squandered family income mined especially deep reservoirs of anxiety about the demise of traditional male breadwinning and the loss of financial security.

By reviving temperance plots that cast women and children as the victims of self-indulgent men, Seagram aimed to beat prohibitionists at their own game. Fearful that such tactics were succeeding, *Christian Century* seethed that "a distillery, once conceived in the public fancy as a ravenous beast," could now be "cast in the conspicuous if somewhat ironic role of moral tutor."[39]

TO DRINK OR NOT TO DRINK: THE MUDDLED MEANINGS OF MODERATION

Promoting moderation was as much about teaching Americans *how* and *what* to drink as it was about teaching them when not to drink. Thanks to the limited availability of quality alcohol during Prohibition, many Americans came to value bathtub gins and basement wines more for their kick than their taste. If alcohol producers were to make repeal a success, they would also have to help consumers recalibrate their sensory perceptions and their drinking behaviors. To this end, Seagram's advertising frequently conflated drinking in good taste—that is, drinking in moderation—with drinking spirits that also pleased the palate. As a first step toward reeducating American palates and drinking behaviors, Seagram prodded Americans to own up to their bad drinking habits. Some of these bad habits were an inheritance from Prohibition-era excesses. Others, Seagram claimed, resulted from insufficient drinking experience and inadequate knowledge of quality brands. After Repeal, Seagram conceded in its first moderation ad, "Many bought unwisely. And drank unwisely." Instead of enjoying whiskey for its "mellow warmth and flavor," as good whiskey should be enjoyed, Americans guzzled the cheap stuff to get past "its rawness and harshness." Drinking in such a manner, the ad explained, was not "what any thoughtful person could desire."[40]

Seagram's brand advertising offered more specific pointers to retrain consumers' sensory expectations. Promising "a new deal for your throat," an ad for Calvert, a Seagram-owned distiller, encouraged consumers to

> Put your throat on a peace-time basis. Whisky is a pleasure, not a punishment now that CALVERT is here. Plenty of body to it, but doesn't get rough about it. CALVERT feels good going down—smooth and rich. Leaves no mean after taste.[41]

The accompanying illustration of a whiskey highball with a twist of barbed wire dramatized the contrast between Calvert and whiskey hot off the still. Calvert could boast of its whiskey's smoothness because it entered Repeal with a large inventory of aged whiskey, giving the firm a distinct advantage over its legal and illegal competitors. Brand advertising encouraged consumers reared on Prohibition-era hooch to adopt the habits of whiskey connoisseurs. Those who drank wisely, numerous ads instructed, sipped and lingered over their whiskey instead of bolting it down. One Calvert ad counseled moderation by instructing drinkers to "sup and sip" and "quench, don't drench, your thirst."[42] Another advised: "Don't hurry your first drink of CALVERT 'to get it over with.' . . . Most CALVERT converts never even think of a chaser."[43] The ad implicitly criticized Americans who drank solely with the intention of getting drunk—why else rush the first drink "to get it over with" and drink chasers to mask a nasty aftertaste? But it also implied, sympathetically, that consumers would inevitably adopt better drinking habits given the opportunity to purchase better whiskey.

Seagram's moderation campaign ads made the point more bluntly: "*Drink Moderately . . . Drink Better Whiskey.*" By consuming quality whiskey, Americans could drink less without sacrificing enjoyment. Moderate use of the finest, the ad insisted, was preferable to "the empty satisfaction that follows upon profusion of the second rate." Candidly admitting that quality-conscious consumers could expect to pay at least twice as much, Seagram assured consumers that the extra expense would be worth it. "A pint of good whiskey will bring you more enjoyment, more satisfaction, than a quart of whisky of dubious quality." Notably, the ad implied that consumers would be unable to drink themselves into oblivion if they mastered the "proper use of whiskey" and learned to take "pleasure in its aroma, its flavor, its mellowness."[44] A far cry from the vulgar saloon rituals of downing shots, moderate whiskey drinking, as Seagram envisioned it, was a leisurely genteel ritual—an essential facet of "gracious living."[45]

In both its moderation campaign and brand advertising, Seagram conspicuously avoided defining the line between moderate and excessive drinking in quantitative terms. Unlike later moderation ads that appeared during the 1980s, Seagram did not mention blood alcohol content or explain how much alcohol 86- or 90-proof whiskey actually contained. Nor did it suggest a number of drinks that exceeded the limits of sobriety, or draw equivalencies between a mug of beer, a glass of wine, and a jigger of whiskey, as Seagram's "A drink, is a drink, is a drink" campaign did in the mid-1980s. In fact, Seagram's definition of what it called "a sharp dividing line" between moderate and excessive drinking was exceedingly vague:

> *That dividing line is the extra drink that is 'one too many.'* . . . There comes a point when an extra drink brings no extra pleasure. For those who thoughtlessly or through good-natured response to a host's persuasion, drink more than they need for pleasure—there is this to remember: There can be no better judge of moderation than the individual himself.[46]

As the moderation campaign ad just quoted implies, Seagram's failure to quantify excessive drinking was not an unintentional evasion—it was largely the point. Such omissions enabled distillers to shift responsibility for drunkenness from the liquor makers, where prohibitionists thought it resided, to the individual. In the post-Repeal liquor regime, only the individual could monitor his own altered states.

If drinkers wanted to learn from liquor ads how much they could safely and responsibly consume, they would have to read between the lines. If so inclined, they could find permission to engage in drinking behaviors that routinely flirted with crossing the line between just enough and one too many. Consider, for example, Calvert's suggestion to "Linger over your first drink of CALVERT whiskey. Sip it, it's honey-smooth. That deep, rich flavor leaves pleasant memories of the good old days." The invitation to linger over the first drink, of course, implies at least a second and possibly a third and so on. Presumably the "pleasant memories of the good old days" referred to a time before bathtub gin and moonshine when quality liquor was not so hard to find, but the phrase could just as easily have referenced the nostalgic musings of the drinker who has cast all inhibitions aside.[47] Seagram achieved the epitome of ambiguity in a beautiful 1946 ad for Seagram's 7 Crown whiskey illustrated with a highball against a sunset backdrop. According to the text, the ad's title—"32,785 'Good Evenings'"—was "just another way of saying that for 89 years, the House of Seagram has been contributing to the good evenings of discriminating people . . . and that nothing less than 89 years of experience could have produced the smooth perfection of Seagram's 7 Crown." But the slogan "Designed for Your Pleasure Today, Tomorrow and Always" printed at the bottom suggested a less innocuous interpretation. True, the slogan touted the brand's consistent high quality, but it also intimated that whiskey drinking was a regular pastime—enjoyed "today, tomorrow and always" (perhaps not even just in the evening).[48]

Seagram's advertising also invited consumers to read between the lines by hinting at the altered states moderate whiskey drinking could induce. Euphemisms for a good buzz abounded in Seagram ads. A Calvert ad noted that its whiskey stimulated a pleasant but controlled altered state—"nothing but glowing comfort for the inner man."[49] Similarly, a moderation campaign ad spoke of the "friendly feeling" moderate drinking "engenders."[50] More indirectly still, another Calvert ad promised consumers they would find its "smooth, lower-proof blends not only most pleasing in their flavor and bouquet, but in *every* way most desirable," hinting at the pleasing altered states consumers might experience.

Seagram was perhaps most cynical in fudging the matter of whiskey proof. During the 1930s, Calvert heralded its 86- and 90-proof blends as lower-proof whiskeys. Drinkers might assume lower-proof provided some protection against excess. Never mind that, but for 100-proof bonded bourbons, Calvert's 86- and 90-proof blends were as potent as most whiskeys on the market.[51] What mattered, the ads implied, was that the genteel drinker knew to aim for the buzz without falling victim to the knockout punch.

Seagram's ads winked at the consumer so frequently that the ostensibly "sharp dividing line" between moderate and excessive drinking seemed to fade away before one could pin it down. If Seagram's concept of moderation evaded quantification, it did at least offer more clarity on questions of public appearance and social performance. In Seagram's vision, how much liquor individuals drank mattered less than how respectable and self-possessed they looked while drinking. A moderation ad, titled "We Who Make Whiskey Suggest: 'SAY "NO"' When It's One Drink Too Many," shamed men who could not handle their liquor. While most Americans had learned to exercise "discretion" and maintain "sobriety" in drink, the moderation ad asserted,

> here and there we still find the thoughtless individual whose excess discredits the moderate use of liquor by countless thousands. More often than not this thoughtless individual is not recognizably the 'enemy of society,' or the 'alcoholic.' He is just plain John Citizen, who takes just 'one drink too many.'[52]

Although Seagram's advertising liked to cast moderate drinking as a badge of affluence and gentility, it also retained some of the macho posturing of the saloon, in which drinking without losing self-control became a test of manhood.[53] As another moderation ad asserted, a real man "will not impair his mental and physical resources by excessive indulgence of his tastes. He will see to it that he becomes no burden to his associates. He bends the elbow, but not the knee."[54] Moderation became the measure of the man, but, as the next section will show, so too was his ability to camouflage excess.

BLENDS TO THE RESCUE

The whiskey industry never claimed, as the brewers and vintners did, that spirits were the "beverages of true temperance." But some whiskey makers like Seagram were brash enough to promote their blended whiskeys as the genteel alternative to "hard whiskey." In Seagram's version of the gospel of moderation, the key to moderation hinged less on *how much* whiskey one drank—that was left to the discretion of individual drinkers—but rather on the *type* of whiskey one drank. In both its brand advertising and the moderation campaign, Seagram touted the growing popularity of blended whiskeys as evidence that Americans were abandoning their Prohibition-era excesses and embracing moderation. In the late 1930s, a series of Calvert ads, titled "America is learning how to drink!," heralded "a great nation-wide trend ... toward the intelligent, moderate use of lighter, *blended* whiskies ... *better* whiskies." What made blended whiskeys better whiskeys was not just their smoothness and fine flavor, the ads claimed, but their lower proof. Such claims were highly deceptive: at 90-proof, the alcohol content reported in the ad's fine print, Calvert hardly qualified as a light alcoholic beverage.[55] Measured against the raw moonshine that Prohibition-era drinkers bolted down, however, a "lighter" blend signified a whiskey that smarter, better-mannered drinkers could leisurely enjoy.

By casting blends as the beverage of genteel sophistication, Seagram attempted to counter the popular perception of blends as imitation whiskey or an inferior alternative to straight whiskeys. To gain competitive advantage, Seagram's advertising boldly asserted that whiskey blends were superior to straights because they had fewer negative side effects. According to George Mosley, Seagram's marketing director, the strategy originated in a study by the Pease laboratory, which found that "blended whiskey was lower in congeners and better for you than straight whiskeys"—a claim rectifiers had made during the Progressive Era whiskey standards debates. Eager to capitalize on such findings, Seagram hired a psychologist to conduct experiments in the Adirondacks in upstate New York on 5,740 men after moderate drinking of Crown whiskeys the previous evening.[56] Conducted over forty-one days, the Adirondacks study measured restlessness during sleep and tested muscular control, mental accuracy, and appetite the next morning. It found that men were able to perform at 97.2 percent of normal and experienced no disruptions to their sleep or their appetite for a hearty breakfast. Notably, the study factored in a delay of several hours for sleep after imbibing the alcohol—a much looser standard of bodily competency than the wet-aligned scientists had adopted at the 1932–1933 Congressional hearings on proposals to modify the Volstead Act.

In a series of advertisements publicizing the Adirondacks study, Seagram insisted that the moderate pleasure-loving body could achieve the same vitality as the abstemious body provided that men drank the right kind of whiskey. Such claims echoed a pervasive theme in early twentieth-century corporate advertising: the assurance that consuming the right kinds of goods would enable the consumer's mind and body to function at peak efficiency. Unlike ads for antiseptics, toothpastes, laxatives, and foods that promised to eradicate the germs and "intestinal fatigue" that compromised peak performance, Seagram made no direct claims for whiskey's affirmative benefits.[57] Rather, Seagram informed middle-aged men that moderate drinking of blended whiskeys would not exact any next-day toll on personal efficiency: "Seagram's Crown Whiskies will be kind to *any* man who uses them moderately." Not unlike other Depression-era ads for cereal and packaged foods, the Crown whiskey ads read like a set of tips on the secrets to a happy and healthy middle-aged life.[58] "The Middle Years *will be kind to you*," one ad promised, if you "Sleep 8 hours. Eat less than you want. Take short rests throughout the day. Relax before meals." The point of the ads was not just to recommend drinking in moderation—it was to demonstrate that men could dodge the nasty side effects commonly associated with drinking whiskey by drinking *blended* whiskey. Whiskey could become a regular part of a healthy lifestyle, the ads asserted, so long as men "choose the form of whiskey that is best for you" and "use it moderately." Another ad, urging men to enjoy "moderate and sensible living," assured drinkers in their 30s, 40s, and 50s that they would "never feel your age" if they abstained from the extremes of overwork and hedonistic indulgence: "Avoid late hours, rich foods, overstrain, worry" and "be sure to choose the form of whisky that is *best* for you." Though described as "average men," the subjects featured in the ads all had degrees from prestigious universities and successful careers as engineers, businessmen, and professionals (see Figure 7).[59] They were, in other words, precisely the sort of men that Seagram's moderation ads upheld as the ideal whiskey consumers: affluent breadwinners who could appreciate fine whiskey without overdoing it or compromising their family obligations.

Seagram might have thought better of running the Adirondacks study ads had they genuinely feared stepping over the "line between sincerity and hypocrisy." Federal Alcohol Administration advertising regulations expressly prohibited misleading health claims and "statements relating to analyses, standards, or tests." In addition, the industry's own voluntary Code of Responsible Practices, adopted in 1934, barred any mention of liquor's physical effects "either directly or by implication."[60] These ads violated the spirit, if not the letter of the law. Seagram's competitors in the straight whiskey business cried foul, and the Treasury Department's Alcohol Tax Unit ruled against the campaign.[61] The makers of straight whiskeys, however, hardly shied away from making misleading advertising claims of their own. Schenley, for example, touted the superiority of straight blends by imprinting "It's ALL Whiskey ... No Alcohol or Spirits added" on its labels, clearly attempting to benefit from consumer's suspicions that blended whiskeys were adulterated with subpar alcohol. When the Distilled Spirits Institute, an industry trade association, protested that the slogan violated advertising regulations prohibiting the disparagement "of any brand, class or type of distilled spirits produced ... by another member of the industry," Schenley changed the label to "Whiskey—A Blend—All Straight Whiskeys."[62] Regulatory agencies and intra-industry pressure halted the most overtly misleading advertising claims, but as we shall see below, advertising agencies, well-versed in writing between the lines, found new, more covert ways to assure consumers that they could enjoy the pleasures of blended whiskey without the nasty side effects.

FIGURE 7. Seagram's Crown Blended Whiskies magazine advertisement, 1937. Courtesy of the Hagley Museum and Library. Image scanned from the author's collection.

The Adirondacks campaign presented consumers with the most seductive of enticements: a purchasable solution to the problem of consumer excess. What could be more convenient than consuming more of a good thing to counter the possibility of consuming too much of a bad thing? Might ad readers have assumed that since blends had fewer side effects they could drink more of them? If so, they would join the legions of American consumers who love to be told they can have their cake and eat it, too. They wouldn't be too different from dieters who convince themselves that just one more fat-free cookie or serving of low-sugar ice cream couldn't possibly do any harm—or from steak lovers who believe that chasing the steak with a broccoli "fat burner" will erase the meat's artery-clogging effects. In this respect Seagram's promise to deliver pleasure without repercussions was hardly unusual. Much like artificial sweetener makers, who promised consumers sweet indulgence without the caloric toll, American businesses have long worked marketing magic by telling consumers what they want to hear.[63] If blended whiskeys failed to deliver as promised, other consumer goods stood ready to erase their lingering effects. A 1938 ad for Bromo-Selzer, a stomach-calming antacid, assured *Esquire*'s male readers that one dose would "crack down on Morning Afters!"[64]

The emphasis in Seagram's advertising on avoiding negative side effects amplified well-established narratives about how drinking could both enhance and harm one's reputation. At stake were ideas about what constituted business success, personal honor, mental acuity, and physical vigor. If drinking threatened any of these masculine virtues, drinking would undermine the very essence of what constituted a successful middle-class man. This was not unlike the dilemma that confronted midwestern saloon-goers in the nineteenth century, who, as historian Elaine Frantz Parsons has shown, struggled to "reconcile saloon culture with their own standards of proper manhood." Although the ability to hold one's liquor affirmed a man's virility, drinking to excess threatened a man's ability to control his own body and preserve his standing as a provider, property owner, and autonomous decision maker.[65] Nor was "drunken comportment" permissible for middle-class men with "upwardly mobile class aspirations"—either before or after Prohibition. While socializing over drinks could yield valuable business contacts or cement relationships with clients, excessive drinking could ruin a man's prospects as a family provider and successful businessman.[66]

Because psychoactive substances have the potential to destabilize the male body (by dulling men's alertness and competitive drive), they often also raise concerns about their potential to destabilize masculine gender identities. Advertisers attempted to resolve this dilemma by presenting alcoholic beverages and prescription drugs as facilitators of masculine success. In the late 1950s, for example, drug marketers struggled to create a male market for tranquilizers because critics feared that anti-anxiety medications would further imperil the masculinity of white-collar men who had grown into soft and complacent conformists. In response to such criticisms, advertisers, historian David Herzberg has shown, presented tranquilizers as aids that would restore "masculine vigor, decisiveness, and achievement in office settings" by reducing excessive anxiety.[67] Seagram's advertisements addressed similar anxieties about alcohol's ability to imperil a man's ambition and business reputation. The taglines "Think of Tomorrow" and "Clear Heads Call for Calvert" succinctly summarized the main message: middle-class men who drank blended whiskeys could enjoy an evening of drinking and still be ready for work the next day. One such ad conveyed the point simply with a photograph of a squirrel, a visual metaphor for awaking bright-eyed and bushy-tailed after an evening of drinking.[68]

Even as Seagram's "Think of Tomorrow" ads encouraged moderation, a subtle undercurrent suggested that men who drank (but knew their limits) achieved more than those who abstained. "Lots of people who 'headline' at parties, get up the next day feeling like bad news," a Calvert ad observed. Not so the publisher who drank at the Press Club the previous evening, but "scooped every paper in town this morning." Ad readers could safely assume that the publisher got the scoop, thanks in part to his extensive and well-greased network of contacts maintained through social drinking (see Figure 8).[69] Successfully mixing business and pleasure required "gentlemanly restraint," of course, but it also required savvy about what kinds of drinks to order and how to drink them. Calvert ads advised men to drink "the Whiskey that *never wears out a Welcome*," implying that Calvert drinkers avoided whiskey's nasty side effects and the potential embarrassment of appearing drunk. The ad nodded approvingly of men who approached drinking with the same managerial discipline they displayed in business. Men who could pull off feats of late-night drinking yet still "drive a shrewd bargain" the next day had learned that drinking responsibly all came down to careful self-management and selecting the right whiskey: "Get a little system into your drinking, and a little less drinking into your system."

Another set of ads in the "Clear Heads Call for Calvert" series played on male anxieties about protecting their reputation in subtler yet even more subversive ways. At first glance, the ads read as a standard promotion of brand quality. Whiskey lovers seeking a "highly refined" whiskey will enjoy Calvert whiskey, the ads asserted, because "protective blending protects the flavor and good taste." This, no doubt, was the dominant intended interpretation. Why then did the ads compare

FIGURE 8. Calvert's "Special Reserve" Blended Whiskey advertisement, 1937. Courtesy of the Hagley Museum and Library.

Calvert blended whiskeys to the "protective blending" that camouflages animals from hunters and animal predators? Why attract the readers' attention with colorful drawings of mallard ducks blending into rushes and the Cinnamon Bear blending into foliage and fallen branches (see Figure 9)?[70] Unlike the banned Adirondacks study ads, which directly claimed that blended whiskeys protected drinkers against hangovers and next-day jitters, the "protective blending" ads alluded to similar effects metaphorically. Whiskey drinkers who read the ads against the grain might have assumed, more subversively, that Calvert would help them camouflage excessive drinking. They might have concluded that by helping to disguise a hangover—or at least minimize one—drinking a "protective blend" would also protect and safeguard their reputation.

Arriving at such conclusions did not require that much of an imaginative leap. During the interwar years, food advertisers had helped to popularize the idea that eating vitamin-rich "protective" foods could safeguard consumers against illness and disease. Perhaps consumers who had come to expect protective benefits from consuming Fleishmann's Yeast (touted as "richest known source of soluble vitamins") might be open to the possibility that a properly blended whiskey could deliver protective benefits as well.[71] More importantly, Prohibition had acculturated American consumers to veiled drug references in advertising for seemingly innocuous products. Like early twentieth-century advertisements for sex toys and contraceptives, advertisers for alcoholic beverages had perfected "socially camouflaged" advertising techniques that overtly promoted a product's socially accepted uses (say by recasting the vibrator as a health and beauty aid) while covertly providing subtle visual and verbal cues about the product's illicit or disreputable uses.[72] Sometimes the visual and verbal cues were not even all that subtle. Recall, for example, when California grape producers sold packages of pressed grapes called "wine bricks" with "a yeast pill to start fermentation and a printed warning not to use it 'because if you do, this will turn into wine, which would be illegal.'"[73] Although Anheuser Busch marketed Budweiser Yeast and Budweiser Malt Syrup separately for use in baked goods, consumers quickly figured out that the two in combination yielded a different sort of consumer delight.[74] Americans reared amid Prohibition-era hypocrisies had grown accustomed to reading between the lines.

Throughout the 1930s Seagram's preached the gospel of "all good things in moderation" without ever clarifying the boundaries between having a good time and having "one too many." In both its moderation

FIGURE 9. Calvert Blended Whiskey magazine advertisement, 1940. Courtesy of the Hagley Museum and Library.

campaign and brand advertising, Seagram left the definition of moderation vague enough to encompass drinking behaviors that could easily venture into excess. In a 1980 retrospective assessment of their nearly fifty-year-old moderation campaign, Seagram judged the campaign a success on at least one important count: the ads had managed to "tread the line between sincerity and hypocrisy."[75] Seagram's more notable achievement may have been persuading consumers to recognize that the tension between sincerity and hypocrisy was one they had to resolve within themselves. Consumers who read the moderation ads could acknowledge the industry's attempt to honor its social responsibility even as they winked back at the industry's invitation to enjoy the altered states that whiskey produced. Mac Shoub, who headed a Canadian market research firm that handled Seagram's moderation account, noted this precise psychological dynamic in 1980, when he assessed the moderation campaign's impact on Canadian drinking habits: "At the moment, most people seem perfectly able to applaud the virtues of moderation without undertaking to vigorously apply themselves towards changing their habits."[76] This, perhaps, was the moderation campaign's ultimate long-term victory: it shifted responsibility for treading the line between sincerity and hypocrisy from the industry to individual consumers. Consumers could appreciate the virtues of moderation but blame themselves when they failed to avoid one too many.

During the 1930s, the whiskey industry remained too divided internally over public relations strategies and legislative priorities to launch an industry-wide campaign promoting moderation. The bitter personal rivalry between Samuel Bronfman and Lewis Rosenstiel, which spilled over into Seagram's and Schenley's mutually disparaging advertising campaigns, spurred the formation of rival trade associations and impeded efforts to create a unified public relations campaign. For most of the 1930s, then, whiskey's gospel of moderation was carried forward under the aegis of Seagram's institutional and brand advertising.

Seagram's moderation campaign began the work of building goodwill and rehabilitating Seagram's reputation as a socially responsible company, but its own brand advertising and the brand advertising of numerous other distillers often muddled the message. While Seagram poured millions of advertising dollars into making whiskey the beverage of cultured gentlemen, others struck marketing gold by making a virtue of lower-priced whiskey for the masses. For most whiskey consumers during the Depression, the price of a bottle of whiskey mattered far more than its brand name or quality. In a study commissioned by

Schenley, the ad agency Lord & Thomas found that three-quarters of the whiskey purchased by consumers were young straights, priced at a dollar a pint and backed by no national advertising. These popularly priced whiskeys, the agency concluded, "appealed to a man with a dollar in his pocket and the certainty in his heart that the liquor wouldn't kill him." Schenley's Old Quaker brand, marketed with the populist slogans "You *don't* have to be *rich* to enjoy rich whiskey!" and "It doesn't take a barrel of money to buy it," "became the biggest seller in the U.S. whiskey market."[77] The white-haired Quaker in colonial garb on the label certainly looked the picture of virtue, but Schenley's assurance that "You *don't* have to be *rich* to enjoy rich whiskey!" almost seemed to snicker at the moralizing tone of Seagram's "We Don't Want Bread Money" and "Pay Your Bills First" ads.

WHISKEY AT THE WORLD OF TOMORROW

The distilled spirits industry's struggle to reconcile its marketing priorities with its public relations goals came to a head at the New York World's Fair in 1939. As planning commenced for the grand international exposition billed as the "World of Tomorrow" fair, North American distillers began to imagine how they could use the fair to their best advantage. In keeping with well-established tradition, some distillers envisioned the fair primarily as an enormous advertising venue that would bring their brands before a massive national and international audience. Since the mid-nineteenth century, international expositions had functioned in part as grand commercial trade fairs where corporate exhibitors introduced consumers to new products and promoted new ways of living. Over time, the influential businessmen and civic leaders who financed the fairs also came to appreciate their value as a public relations tool that could bolster public confidence in corporate and governing elites. According to historian Robert Rydell, the world's fairs of 1939 surpassed nearly all their predecessors as "revelries of corporate capitalism."[78] Arriving in the midst of an ongoing economic depression and intensifying global hostilities, the 1939 world's fairs in both New York and San Francisco enticed visitors with their optimistic vision of a better and more bountiful future—one centered not just on machine-age wonders but on a new American Way of living.

The presence of distilled spirits at the 1939 New York World's Fair was itself something of a novelty. Since the 1893 World's Columbian Exposition in Chicago, most world's fairs held on American soil had barred all intoxicants except beer from the fairgrounds. Thanks in part to New York State's more liberal liquor laws, some of the restaurants on the fairgrounds in Flushing Meadows, New York, sold whiskey alongside other alcoholic potables. North American distillers benefitted as well from their inside track with the fair president Grover Whalen, a public relations impresario who also served as Schenley Distillers' chairman of the board. Whalen's experience running large organizations made him a natural choice to take charge of planning the fair. He had served as the former general manager of Wanamaker's department store and as the former police commissioner of New York City. Whalen also knew how to put on a good spectacle. Known to many as New York City's "official greeter," Whalen had organized ticker-tape parades in the 1920s to honor Charles Lindbergh, Albert Einstein, Admiral Richard Byrd, and other dignitaries and celebrities. Wearing a top hat and dapper attire, Whalen invariably managed to capture some of the spotlight himself as New Yorkers feted these heroic figures. During Whalen's short stint as police commissioner (a post he held despite lacking any law enforcement experience), the police force went after communists so aggressively that the press dubbed them "Whalen's Cossacks." Despite his pledge to defeat organized crime, Whalen took a lighter hand with the city's speakeasies after concluding they were too numerous to police. He instead authorized raids on the small joints that sold "poison liquor"—a move that made him an appealing hire for Schenley when Prohibition ended.[79]

All of these experiences enabled Whalen to recognize the potential upsides and pitfalls of transforming the fair into a massive public relations spectacle for big business. "His job, as he perceived it," historian James Mauro writes, was to recruit companies to sponsor the fair "without actually permitting them to blatantly sell their product lines." If exhibitors made their interests too transparent, fairgoers might dismiss the fair as a naked advertising scheme for its corporate sponsors. But if corporate exhibitors focused more on building public goodwill than selling brands, the fair, Whalen thought, could help restore the public's diminished confidence in big business. Instead of vilifying big business for causing the Great Depression, the public might come to see corporations as public-spirited jobs creators and drivers of economic growth.[80]

The fair planners who worked under Whalen, however, did not always privilege public relations over advertising, especially during the planning stages when they were aggressively courting potential exhibitors. Laurence Herzog, the fair's director of exhibits, pitched an exhibit to the distiller Hiram Walker that promised to "explode" the whiskey "consciousness" of 50 million fairgoers and boost awareness of the Hiram Walker brand. Since most Americans lacked the "drinking vocabulary" to confidently answer the question, "What'll you have?," Herzog suggested that Hiram Walker create an exhibit that taught fairgoers how to order the "correct drink for the occasion." Properly edified visitors would leave the exhibit knowing the "right whiskey drink" to order when watching sports, conducting business, or relaxing at home.[81] Although the existing records do not reveal what Hiram Walker thought of the pitch, it is not hard to imagine why the proposed exhibit never materialized. An exhibit highlighting the wide array of occasions that demanded a whiskey cocktail or whiskey highball would have muddled the liquor industry's public relations messaging about the importance of moderation.

Selecting an appropriate site on the fairgrounds for the distillers' exhibit was also rife with potential public relations pitfalls. At one point, fair planners contemplated moving the Syria-Lebanon building next to the distillers' exhibition hall. On hearing that the building would include a replica of the Holy Sepulcher, Norman Baxter, the public relations director of the Distilled Spirits Institute trade association, voiced his concern that locating a religious exhibit in such close proximity to the distillers' building would offend devout fairgoers and intensify their opposition to the newly legalized liquor industry. Fair planners agreed to move the "Lebanon Building" a comfortable distance away in the International Zone.[82] Whiskey's dual status as a food and a drug also created conflicting opinions about whether the distillers' exhibit should be housed in the Hall of Pharmacy or in the Food Zone, one of the seven color-coded sectors that bundled exhibits into broad thematic categories. The well-established practices of selling whiskey through drug stores and prescribing whiskey as a medicinal aid made the Hall of Pharmacy a logical site, but the prospect of sharing space there with Tampax and Hollywood Bath-O-Bubbles—products distinctly at odds with whiskey's image as a masculine commodity—diminished the Hall of Pharmacy's appeal.[83] In the end, the distillers achieved something of a public relations coup when they secured a spot in the Food Zone alongside the nation's largest food manufacturers, including Wonder Bread, Kraft Foods, Heinz, Borden's, Swift, Fleishmann's Yeast, and Beech Nut. Three other producers of popular food-drugs joined the distillers in the Food Zone: Chase and Sanborn Coffee, General Cigars, and Lucky Strikes Cigarettes. Much as the brewers and the vintners had done in their own publicity, the distillers used their location in the Food Zone to amplify their product's association with the food side of the food-drug divide.[84]

In the initial planning stages, the distillers struggled to subordinate their strong instincts for marketing to their need for a unified public relations message. Several distillers, in fact, preferred to go it alone to better showcase their brands. Anticipating large throngs of "foreign visitors," Schenley's president Lewis Rosenstiel envisioned the fair as an opportunity to boost Schenley's sales at home and win new customers abroad.[85] Fair planners derailed all plans for independent, brand-centered exhibits, however, when they refused to license any other display or advertising of distilled spirits beyond the collective Distilled Spirits Institute exhibit.[86] By 1937, the Big Four (National, Hiram Walker, Seagram, and Schenley) and twenty-two more distillers, including Brown-Forman, Frankfort, and Glenmore, had signed on.[87]

The initial vision of the collective Distilled Spirits Institute exhibit attempted to merge the industry's marketing objectives with its public relations messaging. The exhibit planned to foreground both the distilling process and the retail spaces that distributed the finished product. Presented by Seagram's president Frank Schwengel, the plan would have allotted space for a giant model distillery, a temperature-controlled whiskey warehouse, and a chemistry lab. A collection of "primitive stills" would underscore the industry's technological advances and perhaps remind fairgoers of the raw moonshine they had only recently left behind. Should some visitors miss the point, a proposed exhibit on "The Price of Prohibition—The Reward of Repeal" would hammer the idea home. Once visitors grasped the social and economic costs of gangsterism, poisoned bootleg, "dry terrorism," and lost taxes, Schwengel argued, they would leave convinced of the industry's "moral right to live and prosper." Schwengel's plan set aside additional space for a model package store, a model bar, and displays of distiller's products. Unlike the other corporate exhibitors in the Food Zone, the distillers could not legally offer or sell their wares to fairgoers, but one can only imagine the business deals distillers might have hoped to seal in the proposed "club room" for the distillers' invited "guests."[88]

The finished Hall of Distillers that visitors toured diverged significantly from the original plan. Gone were the displays of branded spirits, the model package store, and the bar. Only the display cases of historic glassware remained to document how Americans had consumed whiskey in the nation's past. Bowing to federal and state regulations, the

Distilled Spirits Institute pledged that not a drop of liquor would be "advertised, sold, given away or promoted" in the distillers' building. Instead of highlighting whiskey's place in American leisure, the exhibit shined the spotlight on its place in the food system and the broader economy.[89] The most distinguishing feature of the building's exterior was a fifty-foot-high "structural banner" that depicted an ear of corn and blades of wheat and rye.[90] Representations of the finished spirit were conspicuously absent from both the building's exterior and interior.

The centerpiece of the exhibit was the spirascope—an immense revolving spiral stage forty feet tall and forty feet in diameter that occupied a fifty-foot vaulted chamber. The spirascope allowed visitors to stand along the perimeter and, without moving an inch, watch the industry's story unfold. According to the Distilled Spirits Institute's press release, the spirascope illustrated an important lesson: distilled spirits generated "employment and revenue—not only for those directly engaged in the production of whiskey, gin, and brandy, but for countless other[s] . . . in many lines of work."[91] Near the spirascope's base, mechanical animation depicted farmers harvesting the grain and lumbermen harvesting oak. As the spirascope turned, lumber mills cut the oak, cooperage plants forged the oak into barrels, and glass factories churned out bottles. Near the end of the full rotation, miniature railroads carried the goods to the distillery and the warehouses that sat atop the spirascope. Notably, the spirascope halted its narrative at the point of production, effectively sidestepping potential controversies as the post-production commodity chain moved spirits into the hands of wholesalers, retailers, and consumers.

The distillers attempted to cement their industry's centrality to the nation's economic development and political history through a selective retelling of the past. To reclaim control over their public representation in the present, the distillers reconstructed a more flattering narrative of alcohol's past. The exhibit highlighted distilling's origins in colonial America, its role in settling the "frontier" and promoting economic growth, and its storied connections to national figures. The Distilled Spirits Institute also heralded the scientific and technological advances that had improved whiskey quality. The history distillers erased was as crucial to their new public image as the history distillers privileged. Although the omissions were hardly surprising, the press release publicizing the exhibit (and the best surviving description of the exhibit's contents) did not mention the urban saloon or the Whiskey Trust (the large network of distillers that exerted monopoly control over prices in the 1890s while allegedly foisting an inferior product on the public). Nor did it mention the infamous Whiskey Ring, a Gilded Age scandal that exposed distillers' efforts to evade federal taxes via bribes to government officials.[92] Like all good whitewashes, the exhibit instead addressed the sullied moments in distilling's past by inference. If any fairgoer recalled that distillers had once exerted undue influence over government officials, the exhibit assured them that the government now had distilling under its watchful eye. From the setting of grain standards through the supervision of the warehouses where whiskey aged, the government now ensured that distillers preserved quality controls and made good on their taxes. Lest any visitors doubt the distilling industry's commitment to public welfare, the exhibit also enumerated the many social services that alcohol revenues helped to fund.[93]

The distillers' correspondence with fair planners underscored just how tall a sacrifice many whiskey firms thought they had made when they pledged to mount a "purely educational exhibit" that offered "no direct financial return" from brand advertising or sales. Dismayed by the marketing opportunities that Seagram had forfeited, Frank Schwengel telegrammed Grover Whalen to complain about the fair's disparate treatment of North American distillers and their foreign competitors. While Scotch whisky makers and other foreign exhibitors were permitted to advertise their alcoholic beverages and serve free samples, North American distillers had to content themselves with hawking their collective virtue in a "purely educational exhibit."[94] Even though fair planners had no standing to prevent foreign countries from advertising their wares, Seagram and other distillers still felt robbed.[95] When the fair's 1939 season concluded, the Distilled Spirits Institute chose to dismantle their exhibit instead of reviving it for the 1940 reopening.

Despite feeling shortchanged, the distillers gained far more than they acknowledged from their participation in the World's Fair. One might say they cried all the way to the bank. Although fairgoers could not purchase North American spirits directly from the distillers, they could easily buy a wide array of liquor in the largest restaurants on the fairgrounds. By itself, the inclusion of whiskey and cocktails on the beverage list counted as a big publicity win for distillers since most states in the union permitted restaurants to sell only wine and beer and some barred restaurant sales of any intoxicants. Fairgoers visiting from dry states or monopoly states glimpsed a more cosmopolitan consumer landscape in which alcohol flowed freely in all its various forms. The Ballantine Inn and the Schlitz Palm Garden—each run by a major national brewery—gave beer pride of place on the menu but by no means did their restaurants limit customers to the beer on tap. At the Ballantine Three Ring Inn restaurant, fairgoers found an impressive, even daunting, list of intoxicating potables. The beverage list included a selection of twenty cocktails made with 100-proof bonded whiskey; twenty-five mixed drinks made with other spirits; twenty-five different brands of North American ryes, bourbons, and blended whiskeys; nineteen brands of Scotch; seven brands of Cognac; fifteen imported cordials; and six Caribbean rums. A separate wine menu sold both "American" and "imported" wines by the bottle and half-bottle. To boost sales of American wines, Ballantine offered only the American wines in thirty-five-cent twelve-ounce splits (enough for two generous servings); a half bottle of imported French or Italian wine would have set diners back $1.50. At twenty cents a stein, Ballantine's popularly priced draught beer likely had more takers than the whiskeys or cocktails, which cost fifty cents on average (one quarter of the price for the sirloin steak). Customers who balked at the high price of Ballantine liquor could wander across the fairgrounds to the Schlitz Palm Garden, whose equally comprehensive beverage menu identified, in bright boldfaced red, five bourbons and cocktails that fairgoers could drink for thirty-five cents.[96] Wine and spirits also flowed at the international eateries. Fairgoers could sample several different vodkas in the Soviet Pavilion's "ritzy" dining room and enjoy regional Italian dishes paired with regional wines at the Italian Pavilion. The liquor menu at Heineken's on the Zuiderzee rivaled Ballantine's and the extensive wine list at the Romanian House surpassed them all.[97]

What should we make of the sheer variety and volume of spirits on the drink menus at the World of Tomorrow fair? To international and domestic fairgoers the drink menus signaled that the American alcoholic beverage industry, just half a decade after Prohibition's demise, was once again producing restaurant-worthy alcohol that merited a place alongside the esteemed wines and whiskeys crafted across the Atlantic. The diverse offerings also attested to alcohol's firmer place in modern leisure and its growing salience as an emblem of cosmopolitanism. Fairgoers who perused the drink menu and found their knowledge of intoxicants and global brands wanting may have realized that the standards for measuring culinary savvy had changed dramatically since the repeal of Prohibition.

The intermingling of wine, beer, and spirits on the same drink menu also exposed the challenge of attempting to forge distinctive cultures of drink for wine, beer, and spirits. Had the brewers gotten their way, beer, in keeping with previous tradition, would have continued to be the only alcoholic beverage sold at the New York World's Fair. Eager to control how visitors from the "Dry Belts" perceived the beer industry, the Brewers' Board of Trade had urged fair planners to ban concessions that sold spirits alongside beer. The trade group proposed instead to build "artistic pavilions" where fairgoers could drink beer with food while enjoying "restful music and constructive entertainment."[98] Although the brewers' vision of fairgrounds studded with beer gardens did not ultimately prevail, fair planners were not unsympathetic to the industry's desire to protect beer's wholesome image. Mindful of such desires, the director of concessions rejected several proposals to reproduce replicas of the old-fashioned saloon.[99]

The world of plentiful alcohol at the New York World's Fair did not long endure. By 1942, within months of the United States' entry into World War II, Americans found themselves navigating a consumer landscape rife with shortages of food and other goods, including shortages of alcoholic beverages. Shoppers found more U.S. table wine and Caribbean rum on the shelves but much less whiskey, if they could get it at all. The changing wartime political landscape also introduced new threats to alcohol's future as organized drys seized the moment to reinstitute and expand alcohol prohibitions. How brewers, winemakers, and distillers used the global conflagration to keep prohibitionists at bay and reimagine alcoholic beverages as an emblem of the good life is the story that unfolds in Part II.

PART TWO

The Politics of Pleasure

5

Beer Goes to War

Throughout World War II, American business saturated mass magazines with advertisements that joined calls for sacrifice to promises of a postwar future of consumer abundance. Ads for electric appliances, dream kitchens, and automobiles beckoned war-weary Americans to imagine a better tomorrow that would arrive when peacetime and production for civilian markets returned.[1] Industries that still served civilian markets had less incentive to stress the virtues and rewards of deferred gratification. While not completely abandoning appeals to sacrifice, these industries took a different approach. In their "Morale Is a lot of *little* things" collective advertising campaign, American beer producers tied the simple pleasures of drinking a "refreshing glass of beer" with "good friends" and a "home-cooked meal" to the broader war effort. In one such ad, a soldier, writing his sweetheart from the battlefront and dreaming of a better tomorrow, imagined himself lounging in his backyard hammock, enjoying a glass of beer, his wife's company, and "the kids playing in the orchard" (see Figure 10).[2] The soldier's longings represented beer drinking as a component of the idyllic domesticity that Americans were fighting to defend. It was a message that brewers hoped would advance their most urgent public relations goals. By reimagining beer drinking as a wholesome American domestic pastime, brewers aimed to distance beer from its earlier associations with the raucous working-class masculinity of the saloon and fend off renewed prohibitionist attacks.

FIGURE 10. Magazine advertisement from the Brewing Industry Foundation's "Morale Is a Lot of Little Things" campaign, 1944. Author's collection.

World War II gave new urgency to these types of appeals. As Americans mobilized for war in the winter of 1941–42, American brewers launched a massive public relations and advertising campaign to battle an old but newly energized foe. Prohibitionists were once again clamoring for wartime bans on alcohol production and distribution. Emboldened by memories of their previous victory in World War I, when the exigencies of war had swept national prohibition into law, drys saw the return of total war and food conservation as a tantalizing opportunity to revive Prohibition. Indeed, public opinion polls at the beginning of the war indicated that 40 percent of Americans favored some sort of emergency wartime prohibition.[3] Yet, despite drys' protestations that beer production wasted vital foodstuffs and diverted manpower from urgent wartime needs, government policies allowed beer production to continue largely unabated. Drys' efforts to ban beer from army training camps and create dry zones around them also failed in the face of strenuous opposition from military officials and the Secretary of War Henry Stimson. In fact, the government deemed beer sufficiently important to military morale that it required the industry to set aside 15 percent of its wartime production for the troops. Even more dismaying to drys, brewers' access to rationed goods such as rubber, gasoline, and tin cans gave brewing the stature of an "essential" wartime industry.[4]

How did brewing, an industry that barely escaped an outright ban during the previous world war, gain a privileged status in World War II? What explains such a dramatic reversal of fortunes? Historians have attributed brewers' securer position partly to the more hospitable political climate. For one, brewers no longer had to contend with the anti-German hysteria that had inflamed public opinion against them in World War I.[5] During World War II, official propaganda left room for the possibility of "good Germans" even as it demonized the Nazis and linked all Japanese to a broader "yellow peril."[6] Historians have also pointed to the federal government's reluctance to jeopardize a reliable source of tax revenues as it mobilized for total war.[7] Others have argued that brewers' more favorable treatment merely ratified a revolution in morals and manners that had been underway since the 1920s. World War II, in historian Jay Rubin's words, "only confirmed what repeal had already signaled—an end to decades of serious national conflict over the temperance issue."[8]

Such interpretations might lead one to conclude that brewers' wartime victories were a foregone conclusion—the predictable outcome of expedient regulatory policies and cultural shifts that rendered drys a nuisance but certainly not a serious threat. Brewers at the time did not see it that way. If they had learned anything from their failure to defeat national Prohibition it was to never underestimate the enemy. "The mental attitude that . . . pervaded the country concerning Prohibition was not stamped out with Repeal," *American Brewer* warned in 1942.

Now, "more than ever," the trade journal continued, "great effort is necessary to keep the Drys from dividing and confusing the public once again."[9] Dry victories in nine thousand of the fifteen thousand local option elections held between 1933 and 1945 attest to the legitimacy of brewers' concerns.[10]

Far from inevitable, the beer industry's enhanced wartime stature owed much to the intense marketing and public relations campaign that brewers undertook to *repoliticize* beer and link their fortunes to other wartime food crusades. Wars often create opportunities to reinvent and redefine the meanings of food precisely because they disrupt established social conventions surrounding eating patterns and access to food.[11] In some cases, previously suspect industries and consumer practices acquire new legitimacy, as happened during World War I, when the US military sanctioned cigarette smoking as the permissible "vice" that could reduce the allure of prostitution and excessive drinking.[12] The differing American approaches to food controls in the two world wars have special significance for how we understand changing conceptions of virtuous consumption and the shifting fortunes of beer. American food conservation programs in World War I, Helen Zoe Veit has argued, envisioned the true patriot as an ascetic, self-denying citizen and associated food conservation (and alcohol deprivation) with the moral purification of the individual and the nation.[13] Drys continued to embrace such notions in World War II, but brewers (along with many social scientists) stressed tolerance over moral purity and psychological well-being over self-denial as the keys to morale and victory. They envisioned the virtuous wartime consumer as a nutrition-conscious cultural pluralist, tolerant of diverse tastes.

Brewers also answered their dry critics by launching a food crusade of their own. Tapping the new science of nutrition, brewers convinced military and government officials that brewers' yeast, a byproduct of brewing, provided a rich source of vitamin B complex that could enrich soldiers' rations and boost the productivity of factory workers. Brewers' pledge to fortify the nation (mentally and physically) not only fortified the industry's links to government bureaucracies and disarmed drys of a key claim against beer—that it wasted vital foodstuffs—but it also helped to transform beer into an emblem of the American way of life. The brewers achieved such success not because repeal had already depoliticized beer but because the industry repoliticized beer in ways that exploited and sometimes harmonized key tensions in American national identity and American cultural values. Their campaign subtly distanced beer from its roots in ethnic, working-class drinking traditions, even while aligning beer with American virtues of tolerance and cultural pluralism. It embraced the softer appeals of masculine domesticity by shifting the class milieu of drinking from the saloon to the middle-class suburban home, yet it also preserved beer's associations with the virility of soldiers and industrial workers. Finally, it made the pursuit of private pleasures compatible with wartime sacrifice and victory over fascism and want. In all these ways, brewers positioned beer to survive the vicissitudes of war and flourish in the imagined postwar order of consumer plenty and suburban domesticity.

THE RESURGENCE OF PROHIBITIONISM

When the United States entered World War II, eight years had passed since the repeal of prohibition—a turn of events many drys treated more as a temporary setback than a permanent defeat. During these years, drys had won 7,700 out of 12,400 local option elections and the looming war encouraged them to step up the pressure.[14] In 1941, even before the United States declared war, the Woman's Christian Temperance Union, the Anti-Saloon League, Protestant ministers, and their congregations began flooding Congress with petitions supporting Senate Bill 860.[15] Introduced by Senator Morris Sheppard, chairman of the Military Affairs Committee and a major champion of the Eighteenth Amendment, S860 proposed to ban all alcohol from military training camps and create "moral zones" that would outlaw prostitution and alcohol from the vicinity of the camps. Though seeming to target only military personnel, the Sheppard bill was not a modest proposition: the wide, ten-mile dry zones could potentially encompass large chunks of San Francisco, New Orleans, Los Angeles, New York, and Chicago where the Army or Navy was stationed.

In urging passage of the bill, dry petitioners revived arguments they had successfully employed in the previous world war. Some petitions supporting the Sheppard bill issued broader calls for full wartime prohibition, arguing that the alcohol trade sabotaged the war effort by wasting manpower, grain, fuel, sugar, and shipping space.[16] Many other petitions invoked maternalist rhetoric to plea for the "Defense of our Defenders" against the twin evils of prostitution and intoxicating liquors, beer, and wine.[17] "Do not return [our boys] to us labeled CONTAMINATED, DAMAGED GOODS," one mother wrote to Congress. "A government that stops at martial training, and utterly ignores the moral and physical phase of the flower of our American manhoods placed in its care, is abetting the enemy."[18] The fall of the French Republic to Nazi control struck other petitioners as compelling evidence of alcohol's power to strip enlisted men—as well as nations—of their virtue, virility, and determination to resist fascism. One widely circulated petition, headlined "ALCOHOL—Hitler's Best Friend, America's Worst Enemy," blamed alcohol for the "downfall" of wine-loving France.[19] How could the United States in turn expect to defeat the Nazis if its own servicemen could not practice self-denial? "Germany bans beer from her army in order to win the war," one petition scolded, while "France admits she lost because her soldiers drank freely."[20] (Never mind that the Nazis requisitioned thousands of cases of French champagne to ship to the front.)[21]

Modern Brewery Age saw the Sheppard bill as an ominous sign that "the ghost of national prohibition has returned and will attempt to come to life under the guise of wartime need."[22] Opponents mounted a counter petition drive with the aid of beer wholesalers, the Liquor Dealers' Association, the International Brewery Workers' Union, and various hotel associations.[23] Petitioners cast the Sheppard bill as a conspiracy by professional drys to reinstate national prohibition and an unnecessary usurpation of military authority to regulate alcohol consumption in the armed forces. The National Council of State Liquor Dealers' Associations protested that the bill would furnish "a fertile field for bootleg operations" and "deprive those men who have made great sacrifice to protect us, of the personal liberties and privileges enjoyed by all Americans and which the Nation has vowed to defend."[24]

Although dry petitions to Congress outnumbered wet petitions, wets had one important advantage: most military officials—including several high-ranking officials—shared their views. The American Legion and the American Federation of Labor joined Secretary of the Navy Frank Knox and Secretary of War Henry Stimson in strenuously opposing the Sheppard bill and related amendments to the draft bill. Not only would such measures deliver a serious blow to morale, Stimson wrote in a letter to the Senate, but flat prohibition would likely also invite greater excesses as soldiers inevitably turned to speakeasies and bootleggers outside the camps. Temperance could be better attained, Stimson argued, through the current practice of selling light 3.2 percent beer on military premises, where beer consumption could be supervised and controlled.[25] Military officials believed that 3.2 beer, mild as it was, would compensate for the deprivations of military life and deter servicemen from pursuing less wholesome activities off the base.[26] The logic of providing access to 3.2 beer followed much the same logic the military used when they introduced cigarettes in World War I to divert servicemen from drink, prostitution, and gambling.[27] Unlike World War I, however, moral purification was not on their agenda. One of the military's strongest objections to the Sheppard bill was that it would compel the military to regulate the drinking habits of civilians who resided in the wide dry zones adjacent to military installations.[28]

Participants on both sides of the revived wet–dry war defined the stakes in highly gendered terms. While dry petitioners envisioned the military as a kind of surrogate parent, entrusted with guarding the morals of its charges, wet petitioners, who not coincidentally were predominantly male, chafed at the notion that army men needed such protection.[29] Anti-prohibitionists such as C. L. Chapin, secretary-treasurer of Repeal Associates, decried the Sheppard bill as an emasculating invasion of manly space and manly prerogatives: "A man is old enough to drive a tank, fly a bomber, but not manly enough to go and sit down in his barracks without someone saying: 'Now, Johnny, don't drink that stuff—it'll make you dizzy."[30] Echoing Chapin's sneering contempt for overbearing maternalism, an editorial in the *Chicago Daily News* surmised that "the roots of [dry] agitation probably lie in jealousy of the soldier by 'old women in pants'—and there is a word for it in the dictionary. We doubt if there ever was a time when the civilian average of sobriety was as good as the military and certainly there is nothing to justify branding our present Army as an infantile force needing a nursie."[31] Such sentiments resonated with the sentiments of Philip Wylie's best-selling 1942 screed *Generation of Vipers*, which decried the spread of overly protective mothering that made sons weak and passive. Wylie's quintessential mom closely paralleled Chapin's vision of the domineering, emasculating "old women in pants" who organized dry petition drives. "Mom," Wylie wrote, "builds clubhouses for the entertainment of soldiers where she succeeds in persuading thousands of them that they are momsick and would rather talk to her than take Betty into the shrubs. All this, of course, is considered social service, . . . patriotism, and self-sacrifice," providing "mom an infinite opportunity for nosing into other people's business."[32]

Despite the impressive showing of dry support, the Sheppard bill went down to stinging defeat, as did several similar measures that came before Congress in 1942, 1943, and 1944. Prohibitionists failed in part because they adhered too closely to their old political playbook. Their maternalist rhetoric had struck a powerful chord in World War I, but had grown stale by World War II, as the Progressive Era investment in moral purification gave way to a more pragmatic investment in controlling vice. The Progressive impulse to conflate public morale with private morality also diminished. As we shall see, new conceptions of morale—which elevated the importance of preserving ethnic traditions and maintaining at least some access to pleasure foods—conflicted with the previous emphasis on uniform standards of private morality.

Brewers still had their work cut out for them. Despite dry failures to enact prohibition measures at the national level, the drys continued to rack up local option victories.[33] Nor were brewers' fortunes entirely secure on the national front. Even if Congress rejected prohibitionist legislation, the government could still deny brewers access to railway lines and gasoline or reduce their supply of malt, which was also needed for livestock feed and industrial alcohol. Wartime concerns about food conservation and chronic shortages of tin, rubber, and gasoline limited the political mileage brewers could bank on from the tax revenues they generated. In fact, the real question was not *whether* brewers would face cutbacks in their rations but how severe they would be. Tin shortages required brewers to package domestic beer in glass bottles instead of cans and rely more on wooden kegs instead of steel or aluminum kegs.[34] Much to the irritation of drys, however, the government allotted brewers enough tin to make bottle crowns and to can beer for the troops overseas.[35] Conservation of gasoline and tires limited the number and scope of deliveries, prompting some brewers to put their Clydesdales and horse-drawn wagons back into operation.[36] Thanks to a modest 7 percent cut in brewers' allotment of malt and malt syrup, brewers had to mix in more corn and rice to stretch the supply.[37] The new blend produced a thinner and blander brew but still kept the breweries humming. The next sections analyze how and why brewers were able to maintain such advantages.

SOFTENING RURAL OPPOSITION TO BEER

The most important lesson brewers learned from their failure to defeat Prohibition was the fatal error of underestimating dry political power. In the lead up to national Prohibition, brewers had opted to douse prohibitionists fires as they erupted in states and municipalities instead of developing an aggressive national public relations campaign. Brewers did not let dry triumphs in rural local option contests overly concern them because the beer market was "almost entirely urban" and they believed the steady growth of urban populations was trending in their favor.[38] Brewers also gambled that tax revenues from beer sales, which had given brewers political leverage to fend off prohibitionist measures in previous wars, would do the same in World War I. Divisions within the United States Brewers Association further hindered the formulation of a consistent national strategy. While some embraced saloon regulation and self-reform, others persisted in believing that beer—the beverage of "true temperance"—would be spared from prohibition and resisted aligning themselves with distillers.[39]

World War II gave brewers the opportunity to revisit these failures and develop a coherent, multipronged national strategy. They endorsed self-policing and regulation of army canteens and taverns where beer was sold but also held fast to their conviction that promoting beer as a moderate beverage could enhance beer's respectability and blunt the effectiveness of drys. They also came to view local option contests in a more sinister light. Conceding any victory to drys in rural elections, they believed, would only abet prohibitionists in their quest to reenact prohibition piecemeal through a string of local option victories.[40]

The primary responsibility for creating a coherent national public relations campaign fell to J. Walter Thompson, a prominent advertising agency hired by the United States Brewers' Foundation (USBF) in 1942. J. Walter Thompson developed a multipronged media campaign aimed at distinct consumer and political constituencies. To reach a broad middle-class audience, the USBF ran full-page ads in mainstream mass magazines such as *Life, Liberty, Ladies' Home Journal, Woman's Home Companion, Colliers, Time, Newsweek,* and *U.S. News*. The beautifully illustrated ads, featuring paintings by American commercial artists, situated beer in wholesome Rockwellian scenes of domesticity and private life.[41] The USBF's campaign also targeted Americans who lived in small towns and rural areas where prohibitionist sentiments persisted and local option referendums frequently appeared on the ballot. To win over this more resistant rural audience, J. Walter Thompson created a recurring column entitled "From Where I Sit" that appeared in farm papers and small-town newspapers. Signed by the fictive Joe Marsh, an avuncular town leader, the column—an advertisement masquerading as an editorial—preached the virtues of tolerance through homey stories of small-town life.

Many of the Joe Marsh columns aggressively defended the beer industry against prohibitionist assaults. Throughout the war, drys maintained that drinking imperiled the war effort by wasting precious raw materials, encouraging "loose speech," and contributing to absenteeism and drunkenness in the army camps. Drys even blamed excessive alcohol consumption for the failure of American soldiers to defend Pearl Harbor against Japanese attack. To counter such arguments, brewers matched hyperbole for hyperbole. Turning the table on drys who decried loose-lipped drunks, one Joe Marsh column asserted that the "loose talk" of drys undermined morale "as much . . . as any rumor that the Axis could invent . . . You hear, for instance, talk about our soldiers drinking and carousing around Army Camps." Marsh debunked those claims by citing a 1941 Office of War Information report that characterized American soldiers as "the soberest, . . . best behaved in history"—a boast that would have strained credulity later in the war—and he urged patriotic readers to "spike that kind of sabotage before it spreads."[42] Other Marsh columns charged that rumors about excessive drinking in army camps were "lies planted by the Axis to destroy American morale."[43] "From where I sit . . . the Nazis would a heap rather face an army that already *lost* its rights than one that was fighting for freedom it could touch and taste and feel every day."[44] Here Marsh measured freedom not in terms of votes cast at the ballot box or in free speech but in the right to enjoy sensory pleasures that armies "could touch and taste and feel."

Generally, the brewers' campaign focused less on vilifying prohibitionists than on touting beer's positive contributions to the war effort. Marsh answered drys' claims that beer wasted precious resources by highlighting the government services and war materiel funded by beer tax revenues. "Right here in Iowa," Marsh wrote in 1942, "the taxes from beer last year alone were more than enough to pay for fourteen 4-engine bombers, seventy-four fighter airplanes, or one hundred and eleven medium tanks." J. Walter Thompson adapted the same column to reflect the buying power of beer revenues in the twenty different states in which the column appeared.[45] By forging such concrete connections between beer revenue and war production, the Marsh column might well have encouraged individuals to imagine their private beer consumption as a patriotic activity—perhaps not on par with purchasing war bonds, but nonetheless a guilt-free private pleasure with public benefits. Like much other wartime propaganda, the brewers' public relations campaign attempted to establish what historian Mark Weiner has called "the *moral equivalence* of consumer products." By connecting "the mundane objects of personal life with the matériel of national combat," Weiner has argued, wartime propaganda "symbolically transform[ed] what was private into what was public."⁴⁶

Central to the brewers' economic case for beer was their contention that the return of wartime prohibition would drain public coffers of beer tax revenues and place that money in unsavory hands. "It wasn't so long ago," Joe Marsh reminded readers, that "a lot of that money was going into pockets of bootleggers and gangsters."⁴⁷ In raising the specter of bootleggers and black markets, brewers not only aimed to remind readers of Prohibition's failures, but they also hoped to claim some of the same moral high ground as the government's wartime "Food Fights for Freedom" campaign, which called upon Americans to fight black markets for meat, sugar, and other rationed goods.⁴⁸ To reinforce the point, another Marsh column suggested that a "tangy ice-cold beer" could lessen the temptations of the black market by brightening the limited wartime menus of "unrationed foods and substitutes."⁴⁹

BOOSTING MORALE AND BEER'S PUBLIC IMAGE

Stressing beer's economic contributions was good PR, but it did little to promote the pleasures of beer drinking itself. That task fell to the "Morale Is a Lot of Little Things" campaign, a series of advertisements that appeared in mass magazines and nearly a dozen farm newspapers. The advertisements likened the pleasures of drinking beer to a host of other pastimes and consumer delights that "lift the spirits" and "keep up the courage" in trying times. For "millions of Americans," the copy noted, the "right to enjoy a refreshing glass of beer," though a "small thing," was nonetheless a cherished enjoyment akin to other morale boosting pleasures: "If you're a man, it's a shine on your shoes . . . the sweet feel of a fly rod in your hand. . . . If you're a woman, it's a tricky new hair-do maybe . . . or a change of lipstick. Morale Is a lot of little things like that. People can take the big bad things . . . the bitter news, the bombings even . . . if only a few of the little, familiar, comforting *good* things are left."⁵⁰ The accompanying illustrations rarely featured beer but instead painted Rockwellian scenes of wholesome domesticity and leisure: a man leaning back in a chair, casting his fishing line while enjoying a pipe; a husband carrying a tray of scrambled eggs, slightly burnt toast, and coffee for his wife to enjoy in bed; a "sweet old lady" placing a posy in a businessman's lapel to brighten his walk to work; a pretty woman admiring her new hairdo in the beauty salon (see Figure 11).⁵¹

FIGURE 11. Magazine advertisement from the Brewing Industry Foundation's "Morale Is a Lot of Little Things" campaign, 1943. Author's collection.

Brewers were not the only private industry to present consumer goods as aides to wartime morale. The makers of bridal apparel won an exemption from fabric restrictions after convincing the War Production Board that bridal gowns were essential to morale.[52] Other firms emphasized the critical role consumer goods played in shoring up both industriousness and good spirits. Simmons Mattress ads insisted that "Proper rest is not only a basic *right* . . . It is almost a duty."[53] Similarly, the United States Playing Card Company depicted card playing as an "inexpensive recreation" that provided a revitalizing respite from hard work.[54] Some of the brewers' ideas had the implicit backing of social scientists who helped to shape policies and ideas about morale management during the war. The National Research Council's Committee on Food Habits, a group of anthropologists, sociologists, and home economists charged with recommending ways to help Americans adjust to the rigors of food rationing, recognized that food and drink played a central role in "keeping up spirits."[55] The Committee on Food Habits cautioned policymakers that depriving adults of choice in matters of food could significantly lower morale by making adults feel like dependent children. "Wherever possible," the committee advised government agencies, "some choice, if only between type of bread or type of beverage, should be included."[56] In their *Report on the Morale Building Value of Specific Foods in the American Diet*, the committee specifically warned that the disappearance of pleasure foods—foods associated with relaxation, hospitality, and affection—"would impair morale." The committee even urged policymakers to ration ice cream, candy, soft drinks, and alcoholic beverages in the interest of quelling black markets and inflation.[57] Guided by pluralistic values, the committee advised against banning any foods (including beer and wine) that particular ethnic groups prized as "specially valued staples," noting that such prohibitions would undermine the sense of fair play essential to a democratic wartime food control system.[58]

Balancing the wartime demands for fair play with the wartime expectations of patriotic sacrifice, however, was no easy task. In fact, the brewers' invitations to relaxation and personal pleasure had the potential to backfire both with drys who saw beer drinking as an invitation to excess and with other civilians who believed that beer buying violated the government's requests to decrease luxury spending and buy more war bonds.[59] The brewers' call to relaxation might also have alienated the 70 percent of Americans who, according to an August 1942 poll, felt they "had not been asked to make enough sacrifices for the war."[60]

That brewers felt compelled to ease such guilt was most directly apparent in a Marsh column centered on the curmudgeonly Doc McGinnis, who complained at the church supper in Marsh's fictive town that "we oughtn't to be enjoyin' ourselves when American soldiers are over there fightin' a war."[61] Such sentiments echoed concerns raised by the Committee on Food Habits. In a memo to committee members, Margaret Mead observed that some groups in wartime—especially soldiers, but even defense workers—feel more entitled to pleasure foods because they bear heavier burdens and experience greater deprivations.[62] To be effective then, the brewers' advertising and public relations campaign could not simply affirm beer's value as a morale booster or stress beer's temperate qualities. It needed to give Americans permission to indulge while still preserving some notion of sacrifice. It needed, in short, to make beer consumption a patriotic activity.

Small variations in the "Morale Is a Lot of Little Things" campaign accomplished that goal by tying the morale of soldiers to the preservation of beer drinking traditions on the home front. For many GIs stationed overseas, ads observed, enjoying a glass of beer ranked among "the little things—the small familiar pleasures—that he thinks of when he dreams of home."[63] Small insets featuring a GI writing home about what he missed most shifted the advertising campaign's focus from the need for rest and recreation on the home front to the yearnings of soldiers on the battlefront. A thirst-quenching glass of beer appeared in the backdrop of some advertising images, but the primary illustration usually depicted the soldier's longing for the distant pleasures and comforts of civilian life: his "hammock . . . hanging in the orchard," his "spry old mare," or the family's pumpkin carving tradition on Halloween (see Figure 10).[64] Paradoxically, by making beer a secondary focus in the advertising images, brewers also elevated beer's cherished association with home. How better to Americanize beer than to associate it with images of American holiday rituals, lazy summer days, and a favorite animal on the farm? Even more strikingly, advertisements never depicted young men enjoying beer in uniform or in military settings, even though brewers dedicated 15 percent of their production to military needs. GIs consumed more Coca-Cola, Wrigley's gum, and Hershey's chocolate than beer, but the producers of all these goods, including brewers, won access to rationed goods because the military and government policymakers deemed their products good for morale.[65]

Brewers joined scores of other private advertisers who defined war aims in private, individualistic terms that associated citizenship and democratic freedoms with the enjoyment of home, family, and consumer abundance—the cornerstones of the American way of life. Although some copywriters worried that linking goods too directly to the war "would trivialize the sacrifices of servicemen and civilians alike," few resisted the impulse. As historian Charles McGovern writes, "advertisements inevitably connected the commodified fragments of daily life to the sacred mission at hand."[66] In one of the brewers' advertorials, Joe Marsh insisted that soldiers would want Americans to "keep up the little friendly customs they remember—like the evening get-togethers and a glass of beer with friends and all the little pleasures *they* look forward to enjoying."[67] "From where I sit," Marsh counseled, "one of our most sacred obligations here at home is to keep those little things exactly as they remember them—to keep intact the world they're fighting for."[68] Americans who felt guilty about enjoying beer while soldiers made bolder sacrifices on the battlefront could comfort themselves that their beer consumption was preserving a "right" cherished by GIs—the right to enjoy beer with friends and a good meal. Because the Marsh column targeted readers in areas where prohibitionist sentiments thrived, Marsh urged his readers to actively defend such rights against external threats. A vignette about Esther Curless, a soldier's mom who chased away a tramp sleeping in the hammock her son loved to lounge in with a cool glass of beer, made the point well. "It ain't only that I don't like laziness," says Esther, "'specially in wartime. It's that that particular hammock is Ned's hammock—and Ned's *fightin' for it* overseas!"[69] Just as the rolling pin wielding Esther Curless had chased away a freeloading intruder, brewers hoped that patriotic voters would deliver a knockout punch to prohibitionists in the next local option election.

Foregrounding the wants and needs of GIs also afforded brewers the opportunity to strengthen generational allegiances to beer. Brewers candidly acknowledged such ambitions—a little too candidly perhaps. Drys immediately pounced when a 1941 issue of *Brewers Digest* acknowledged that the establishment of army camps would enable brewers "to cultivate a taste for beer in millions of young men who will eventually constitute the largest beer-consuming section of our population."[70] For drys, the brewers' candid admission confirmed their cynical ambition to corrupt the nation's youth. The outcries of drys failed to dampen antiprohibition sentiment among GIs. Many GIs viewed prohibition, even as a temporary wartime measure, as an infringement on their rights and an affront to the principle of equality of sacrifice.[71] Much as the student sit-ins at Woolworth stores later in the 1960s "used the image of *denied* hamburgers and Cokes" to challenge the denial of Black civil rights, many GIs saw the denial of beer as a denial of personal liberty.[72]

The brewers linked support for beer to support for the troops with relative ease. Turning beer drinking on the home front into a patriotic act required a bit more imagination. The Marsh column frequently coupled beer drinking with notions of home front sacrifice by representing beer as deserved compensation for civilians' contributions to the war effort and compliance with rationing. In some columns, Marsh reported that the residents of his small town enjoyed beer after a "good day's work" collecting scrap metal or harvesting food.[73] Gasoline rationing and the use of trains by servicemen may have curtailed vacation travel, but Americans instead, Marsh testified, were learning to vacation at home and enjoy barbeques with family, friends, and a "glass of cold beer."[74] "We're all of us working hard at our jobs, doing our level best to pull our weight," Marsh wrote. "And we're learning the *little* rewards . . . are more welcome now than ever . . . because we've earned them!"[75]

Toward the end of the war, the USBF abandoned the defensive positioning of beer as a patriotic morale booster for a bolder assertion: "Beer belongs . . . enjoy it."[76] The "Home Life in America" advertising campaign, unveiled in *Time, U.S. News,* and the *American Legion,* targeted middle-class consumers, a market segment that brewers had struggled to capture since Repeal. The ads in this series forged new associations of beer drinking with Americanness by linking beer to time-honored American pastimes in various regions of the country: the community roof raising, the western barbecue, a Boston Pops concert (see Figure 12).[77] Beer also appeared in homier settings as the celebratory beverage that welcomed home an uncle from the West or toasted the arrival of Christmas when grandmother hung the mistletoe. Painted by leading American artists, the advertising illustrations evoked nostalgia for small-town life, where extended families, community involvement, and white picket fences symbolized the stability many Americans yearned for in the wake of wartime disruptions and separations. The popularity of Norman Rockwell and the small-town pastoral musical, a film genre that included *Meet Me in St. Louis* (1944) and *State Fair* (1945), attests to the powerful appeal of such nostalgic images in the final years of the war.[78]

Invoking the wholesomeness of small-town life to promote the wholesomeness of beer was not without its ironies. Brewers, after all, sought to reform small-town America—to inspire in its residents a more cosmopolitan tolerance for drinking. At the same time, brewers happily

FIGURE 12. Magazine advertisement from the Brewing Industry Foundation's "Beer belongs . . . Enjoy it" campaign, 1945. Author's collection.

appropriated nostalgia for small-town life to gain mainstream acceptance. The Home Life in America advertising campaign also traded on nostalgic images of family togetherness and material abundance that suffused wartime advertising and popular art, perhaps most famously in Norman Rockwell's painting of a joyful multigenerational Euro-American family gathered around the Thanksgiving table as a bespectacled grandmother places an enormous roasted turkey before the family patriarch. Produced at a time of rising global hunger, some viewers thought Rockwell's Thanksgiving scene better represented American extravagance than *Freedom from Want*, as Rockwell had titled the art, but the painting's immense popularity on the US home front attested to the allure of such visions of plenty and domesticity.[79] For many Americans in World War II, historian Amy Bentley has argued, observing familiar rituals, particularly those surrounding food, helped to ease feelings of uncertainty created by the social upheavals of war. Rockwell's depiction of a bountiful meat-centered meal, prepared and served by a woman and presided over by an "alpha male" seated at the head of the table, spoke to deeper yearnings for gender stability and the restoration of family mealtime.[80] Like Rockwell's *Freedom from Want*, the brewers' ads provided a reassuring vision of the private life and material plenty that Americans were fighting to preserve.

The USBF used nostalgic appeals to create new cultural expectations of the settings where beer belonged. Its ads muted beer's traditional masculine connotations by relocating beer consumption to the private sphere and public sites of heterosocial recreation, such as the Boston Pops concert. On the rare occasions when USBF ads showed beer in traditionally male settings, such as the iconic Western Barbeque, the USBF presented a domesticated vision of male sociability. How much tamer could beer drinking be with one ranch hand tending the grill (one of the few domestic duties assigned to men), two more absorbed in private reverie, and five others conversing with each other or with a cowgirl and the Native woman waiting their table (see Figure 12)?[81]

If the visual rhetoric of the brewers' campaign gestured toward Rockwell's Freedom from Want, its verbal rhetoric resonated more with the libertarian strains of the Four Freedoms. The Marsh column equated consumer freedom—be it the right to choose "beer or buttermilk," as Marsh frequently framed it—with the right to vote, freedom of speech, and freedom of contract. Even if Americans didn't agree with another's choices in matters of politics or personal consumption, Marsh counseled, the guiding American principles of "self respect and tolerance" entitled Americans to exercise those choices freely.[82] Brewers particularly emphasized the virtues of tolerance in ads that targeted women, who often decided how much—and what kind—of alcohol got purchased for the home. Countering older prohibitionist tropes, the USBF campaign encouraged women to view beer as an aid to marital harmony rather than a threat to it. The USBF's choice to use a gray-haired elderly woman to advocate for this view in a 1942 *Life* magazine ad was striking. The old-fashioned matron with her wire-rimmed glasses, pearls, and lace collar could have been drawn from central casting for the part of a temperance reformer, but she instead encouraged wives to indulge their husband's desire to relax "with a glass of mild and friendly beer." Modern wives could make the home a peaceful refuge from "the vexations and worries of the average man's daily work," she advised, if they made beer "an ally in keeping their men happy, fit, contented . . . and above all, men of moderation."[83] Similarly, the Marsh column counseled readers that tolerance for different tastes was the "recipe for happy marriage." Watching married friends toast their Golden Wedding Anniversary—"Dee with his glass of beer, Jane with her buttermilk"—convinced Marsh that "moderation, tolerance and understanding can build lasting happiness and solid homes."[84] Marsh's juxtaposition of beer and buttermilk—one the symbolic beverage of wets, the other a traditional temperance drink—underscored how tolerance could sustain marriages that united people with different tastes and political sensibilities. If the temperance agitators of an earlier era had envisioned the home as a refuge from vice and worldly corruption, the modern age now called for women to transform the home into a site of pleasure, emotional satisfaction, and mutual understanding.[85] Women could read similar advice from newspaper columnists. If a husband was spending too much time at the local tavern, the *Washington Post*'s Mary Haworth counseled, then his wife must have failed to make the home an inviting alternative. "Keeping beer in stock," historian Nathan Corzine astutely observes, was fast being reimagined as a wife's obligation to make "her home both private sanctuary and tavern."[86]

A wife's traditional duty to create a refuge from the outside world acquired additional importance in World War II. Advertisements and government bulletins entrusted homemakers with responsibility to provide the emotional and nutritional sustenance that could regenerate workers and boost their productivity on the home front.[87] The Marsh column echoed such mandates by valorizing acts of kindness to war-strained husbands as important war work on par with "work[ing] on salvage drives and lend[ing] a hand at the Red Cross."[88] Linking the morale boosting effects of beer to home front demands for boosting productivity not only provided a patriotic rationale for purchasing beer, but it also answered dry critics who complained that alcohol lowered productivity and raised absenteeism.[89]

The brewers' emphasis on tolerance resonated more broadly with other wartime rhetoric that stressed the United States' commitment to ideals of cultural pluralism. Newsreels, Hollywood movies, and government-sponsored war bond drives frequently contrasted American tolerance for diversity with Nazi totalitarianism and fascist theories of a master race.[90] Similarly, the Committee on Food Habits argued that respect for cultural differences and unfamiliar food practices separated Americans from the fascist enemy.[91] Although the United States failed to live up to these ideals—most dramatically in the incarceration of Japanese Americans and the racial segregation of the military—official propaganda, popular wartime films such as *Casablanca*, and the culture of swing music repeatedly represented cultural pluralism as an essential set of values and practices that Americans were fighting to protect.[92] Brewers amplified the patriotic appeal of beer in numerous Marsh columns that tied tolerance in the private sphere to the promise of peace in the postwar order. Intolerance in the home, Marsh asserted, "spreads to intolerance among neighbors, and intolerance among nations."[93] "Unless we make up our minds," Marsh counseled, "to respect the other fellow's rights and liberties—whether it's the right to enjoy a glass of beer occasionally or the right to vote according to our conscience—all our postwar planning won't be worth the paper that it's printed on."[94] More boldly still, Marsh claimed that beer itself fostered the tolerant mindsets that had contributed to recent military victories and that would eventually underwrite the postwar peace. "The success of our Invasion began months ago—when the English Tommies and the GI Joes got together over friendly beer, and games of darts—and learned to like each other in spite of differences in tastes and habits," Marsh wrote.[95]

Brewers' repeated appeals to honor American ideals of cultural pluralism highlight a significant tension within their broader advertising and public relations campaign. To win respectability and middle-class consumers, beer advertisements in mass magazines erased beer's roots in ethnic food traditions and relocated its consumption to homogenized white, middle-class settings. Such contradictions attest to the challenges brewers and advertising agencies faced as they negotiated the changing meanings of Americanness. Constructing imagined communities of beer drinkers required distinct appeals to rural and small-town Americans who continued to flirt with prohibition, and to middle-class women, some of whom still questioned beer's respectability for home consumption. It is not surprising then that the central tensions and strains in American national identity all surfaced in the brewers' wartime campaign: tensions between private pleasures and public obligations, tensions between visions of sacrifice and visions of consumer plenitude, and tensions between ideals of cultural pluralism and the continuing salience of whiteness as a marker of American identity. Brewers, like Americans themselves, straddled these competing visions of American national identity to define for themselves a more secure place in the economy and the postwar world.

BREWERS' YEAST FIGHTS FOR FREEDOM

The brewers' most innovative act of industry self-preservation was to position brewing as an essential *food* industry. Framing the debate over wartime prohibition as a contest over virtue and vice—the traditional battleground of the wet–dry wars—had lost much of its salience after repeal. Framing the debate as a fight over the nation's food supply, on the other hand, offered brewers and prohibitionists alike a better chance of gaining traction. In both world wars, American policymakers tied food conservation on the home front to victory on the battlefront. World War I posters assured Americans that "Food Will Win the War" if citizens planted war gardens and limited their consumption of scarce foods.[96] Unlike the mandatory rationing of coffee, butter, meat, and sugar instituted in World War II, however, compliance with the World War I food regime of "Meatless Mondays" and "Wheatless Wednesdays" was purely voluntary. World War II's more comprehensive "Food Fights for Freedom" campaign encouraged homemakers to avoid waste, starve black markets for scarce foods, and plan meals that skimped on rationed foods—all to guarantee a sufficient food supply for American troops overseas, the nation's allies, and peoples in countries newly liberated from Nazi control.[97]

Prohibitionists had good reason to believe that they could turn the "Food Fights for Freedom" campaign to their advantage. In World War I, drys scored a major victory when the government, citing concerns about the waste of vital foodstuffs, curtailed the production of whiskey and limited the production of beer, paving the way for wholesale Prohibition. Prohibitionist petitions to Congress in World War II hoped the same argument would accomplish similar results. In their view, equality of sacrifice demanded no less. "Since limitations are put upon automobiles, refrigerators, articles of clothing and even certain kinds of foods," the Prohibition Party of Lawrence Country, Pennsylvania, wrote Congress, "why should alcoholic beverages be permitted?"[98] In a contest between meat and sugar, on the one hand, and alcoholic beverages, on the other, the choice seemed clear. "Why is sugar rationed when it is used as a food," petitioners asked, "but is not rationed when it is distilled into liquor—a poison? Why are trucks which carry cattle and hogs to market to feed our nation and our allies restricted, while liquor trucks roll merrily along?"[99] Notions of food justice also galvanized prohibitionists across the Atlantic during World War II. Drys in Great Britain decried their government's hypocrisy in urging people to save food and grow their own while allowing "vast quantities of valuable food supplies . . . to be destroyed in brewing and distilling."[100]

This time around brewers had a ready—and inventive—answer for drys: brewers were not wasteful profiteers but ingenious recyclers who made every grain count (see Figure 13). The chief byproducts of brewing (spent grains, malt sprouts, and dried yeast), brewers argued, actually supplied beneficial nutrients, "superior in many ways" to those initially extracted from barley to produce beer. The trade journal *Modern Brewing Age* reported that the brewing industry's annual consumption of 50 million bushels of barley returned to farmers 720 million pounds of dry spent grains, 75 million pounds of malt sprouts, and 25 million pounds of dried yeast—close to one-third by weight of the original barley.[101] Brewers largely steered clear from the politically clumsy notion that beer itself was a "liquid food" and instead touted the nutritional benefits of brewers' yeast as a dietary supplement for humans and farm animals.[102] As a rich source of vitamin B complex, brewers' yeast could be added to a variety of foods to boost crucial nutrients often lacking in the American diet.[103] When added to commercial cattle feeds, irradiated brewers' yeast increased the milk production of cows as well as the fat content of their milk. Brewers' yeast also improved the nutritional value of pig and chicken feed.[104] British brewers also sought to fend off dry attacks by touting the nutritive value of brewing's byproducts for humans and animals, but unlike their American counterparts they did not shy away from extolling the food value of beer itself. A barrel of beer, a British trade journal hyperbolically claimed in 1939, was the nutritive equivalent to "10lbs of ribs of beef, 8lbs of shoulder of mutton, 4lbs of cheese, 20lbs of potatoes, 1lb of rump steak, 3lbs of

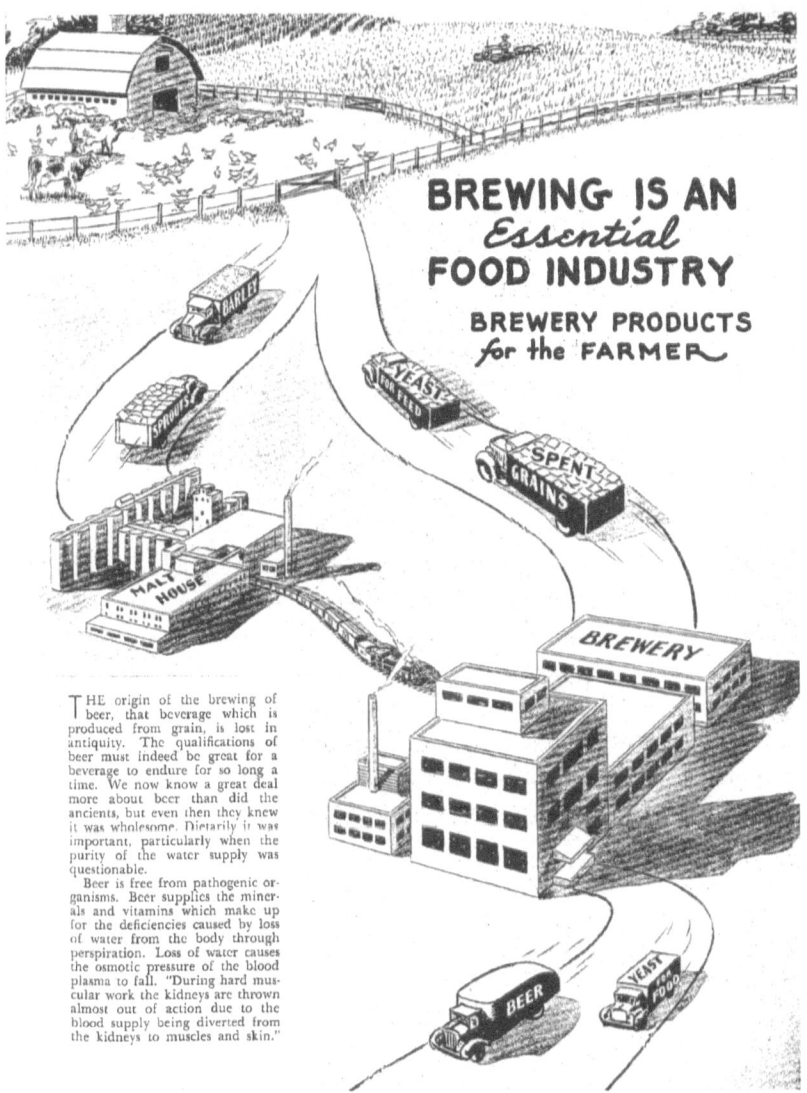

FIGURE 13. "Brewing Is an Essential Food Industry," illustration in *Modern Brewery Age*, April 1942.

rabbit, 3lbs of plaice, 8lbs of bread, 3lbs of butter, 6lbs of chicken and 19 eggs"—combined![105]

Brewers' yeast was much more than a convenient rhetorical weapon in the wet–dry wars. US brewers also hoped to persuade government and military officials that brewers' yeast could help win the war by boosting the productivity of defense workers and the nutritional value of soldiers' rations. Brewers had good reason to believe they would find a receptive audience for their bold claims. Maintaining a well-nourished work force and fighting force ranked high among the government's concerns, particularly in the wake of reports that 40 percent of the first million draftees had been rejected as physically unfit to serve.[106] Government officials worried, too, that a sluggish workforce, suffering the lingering effects of widespread malnutrition during the Great Depression, would impede production in key defense industries.[107] Policymakers recognized that victory in modern warfare hinged as much on industrial efficiency as it did on armies, navies, and air forces.[108]

Brewers' yeast was also not such a tough sale because cereal companies and vitamin manufacturers were already hyping vitamin B as a "pep" pill. In an address before a national conference on nutrition in 1941, Vice President Henry Wallace was even inspired to quote a radio announcer who described vitamin B as the "oomph vitamin" that "puts the sparkle in your eye, the spring in your step, the zip in your soul."[109] Dr. Russell M. Wilder, a physician at the Mayo Clinic, was an especially influential champion of vitamin B, as he also served on the National Research Council's Committee on Food and Nutrition, a group of physicians, home economists, nutritionists, and agricultural economists whose dietary recommendations helped to set government policies. Dr. Wilder had conducted a variety of vitamin B experiments at the Mayo Clinic in 1940 and 1941 that convinced him of vitamin B_1's importance to national defense. The studies found that thiamin deprivation caused a range of symptoms—many associated with neurasthenia—including depression, irritability, moodiness, sluggishness, indifference, fear, inattentiveness, and fatigue. Boosting thiamin in the diet, according to his studies, neutralized the negative effects of thiamin deprivation and increased productivity, mental alertness, and morale. Based on these findings, Wilder recommended supplementing the diets of defense workers by adding yeast, vitamin-rich oils, or rice polishings to juices and soups.[110] In 1942 the NRC's Food and Nutrition Board designated dried yeast as an "essential" wartime food and advocated the enrichment of white bread, corn grits, and flour with thiamin, niacin, and iron.[111]

The brewing trade press also trumpeted brewers' yeast as the miracle supplement that could "help win the war."[112] A feature article in *Modern Brewery Age* on "Brewers' Yeast in Industrial Nutrition" underscored the connection between industrial nutrition and military success

FIGURE 14. "Brewers' Yeast in Industrial Nutrition," illustration in *Modern Brewery Age*, September 1942.

with an illustration that recalled Soviet social realist poster art and the larger-than-life workers celebrated in WPA mural art (see Figure 14). Who could doubt that military victory was at hand after viewing the photograph of a heavily muscled, bare-shirted man swinging a sledgehammer? "Workers who don't eat the right food," the article argued, "slow up the production of the guns and tanks and ships needed to blast the Axis."[113] Thiamin deficiencies were even thought to reduce women's manual dexterity, an ability widely believed to make women industrial workers superior to men in performing precise and delicate work.[114] Fortified diets and supplemental feeding in industrial plants, on the other hand, guaranteed "greater working efficiency, fewer absences from work, and a decrease in the number accidents," according to Dr. Frank G. Boudreau, chairman of the Committee on Food and Nutrition and its sub-Committee on the Nutrition of Industrial Workers.[115] Dr. Wilder even went so far as to suggest that thiamin deficiencies in workers and employers could contribute to industrial unrest.[116] Although this controversial claim pushed the limits of credibility, the broader effort to promote B vitamins in industrial nutrition struck a positive chord. Coca Cola Company so feared that industry cafeterias might begin substituting more nutritious drinks for soda pop that they commissioned their own experts to dispute "unsubstantiated claims" about the morale value of vitamin B.[117]

While we cannot be sure how much direct influence trade journals such as *Modern Brewery Age* had on government policies, brewers would not have enjoyed as much credibility in asserting the national importance of brewers' yeast had policymakers not already given food such a prominent role in defeating the fascist enemy. *Modern Brewery Age* claimed the mantle of wartime patriot for the entire brewing industry when it hailed brewers' yeast as "an important weapon in the 'Food for Freedom' program." *Modern Brewery Age* even boasted that brewers' yeast would help the United States and other nations achieve Freedom from Want, one of the four freedoms that Americans were fighting to defend. "Not only will [brewers' yeast] help in the fight for the freedom of nations by taking its place in the food production line," *Modern Brewery Age* wrote, but it would also free nations from "the nutritional deficiency diseases which undermine the physical and mental health of millions everywhere."[118]

Public investment in vitamin education during the war facilitated the promotion of brewers' yeast as a food supplement. In the two decades before the war scientists on both sides of the Atlantic increasingly associated hunger not simply with the "hollow hunger" of caloric deprivation but also with the "hidden hunger" of nutritional deprivation.[119] Wartime pamphlets and posters issued by the US Department of Agriculture, the Bureau of Home Economics, and private industry promoted vitamins as the essential elements of a "Victory Diet." One company even created a "Vita-Min-Go" board game to help Americans of all ages learn which foods packed a nutritional punch.[120] The storm of vitamin publicity also aimed to help Americans cope psychologically with the dramatic wartime changes in the availability of valued foods. If Americans understood the nutritional equivalences of foods, the Committee on Food Habits surmised, then they would more likely accept unfamiliar—and sometimes odd—food substitutions.[121] Favorite dishes might not taste or look exactly the same—what counted now was the homemaker's ability to prepare nutritious, vitamin-packed meals, a task that many cookbooks touted as vital defense work.[122]

Home economists and nutritionists promised that brewers' yeast would transform ordinary foods into "Victory Foods." Some suggested that homemakers and defense plant cooks use brewers' yeast to fortify tomato juice, milk, and dehydrated vegetables, and to enhance the flavor of vegetable soups and purees.[123] Dr. Clive McCay of Columbia University's College of Home Economics recommended that industrial workers eat two mid-shift snacks that "provid[ed] protective foods rather than mere caloric pick-ups." Instead of the typical pastry cart fare, Dr. McCay advised, the plant snack cart might include milk and doughnuts fortified with brewers' yeast.[124] Others endorsed brewers' yeast as "health insurance" against bad cooks, time-challenged workingwomen, and constrained food budgets.[125] *Modern Brewery Age* imagined that brewers' yeast could provide compensatory nutrition for the families of women defense workers who cooked on the run and the casualties of inept homemakers who drained food of nutritive value by boiling it into a mushy pulp.[126]

The one downside of brewers' yeast—its bitter taste—tested the culinary imaginations of brewers' yeast advocates. Jane Holt, a *New York Times Magazine* food columnist, recommended adding brewers' yeast to gingerbread, baked beans, and meatloaf—foods with strong distinctive flavors that could mask its pungent taste. Some recipes, however, might have left readers wondering which was more disagreeable—the taste of brewers' yeast or the effort to disguise it. Consider "Miss Spinella's Sweetmeat," a mixture of sugar, vinegar, butter, cheddar cheese, dry skim milk, peanut butter, brandy, and brewers' yeast creamed and cooked into candy of fudge-like consistency and appearance. Developed in the medical nutrition laboratory of the Army Medical School, the candy, Holt noted, had a long shelf life, making it suitable for shipping overseas—perhaps to the horror of soldiers longing for a bit of mom's home cooking. Homemakers could purchase brewers' yeast in debittered form from health food stores, but culinary adventurers could also shop at Bloomingdales and other retail outlets for a new product called Bakon, a hickory smoke-flavored brewers' yeast that promised to spice up uninspired meatless meals and relieve the tedium of meat rationing.[127] Tired of porkless baked beans? Why not simulate the real thing, *Modern Brewery Age* suggested, by seasoning them with a bouillon of savory brewers' yeast—or jazz up kids' fare with a luncheon of deviled eggs, toasted muffins, and "zest[y]" cole slaw flavored with brewers' yeast?[128]

The brewers got favorable notices in the press for "supplying 'morale vitamins' to the armed forces, the war workers, and the people of nations liberated from Axis domination."[129] In early 1944 the Quartermaster Corps Subsistence Research and Development Labs began studying the use of brewers' yeast in military rations and foods to relieve starvation.[130] Brewers' yeast was an appealing prospect because it cost 40 percent less than primary-grown yeast, and the Quartermaster thought that it might provide a more appealing alternative to vitamin tablets, which only half the troops would eat.[131] Fortified food had downsides as well, however. Upon returning from a trip to the American fronts abroad in 1944, Margaret Mead informed the Food and Nutrition Board that the "sheer effort of eating" the notoriously tough fortified "biscuits wears them out."[132] At the end of 1944, after several months of testing and development, the Quartermaster Corps approved the use of debittered brewers' yeast in ration biscuits and crackers and within a few months combat troops in the Army and the Navy were consuming them. Soldiers still had to put up with tough biscuits, but the Quartermaster worked hard to assure that their taste, at least, was inoffensive. To win an Army contract, breweries had to persuade a taste panel of army officers and food technologists that soldiers would not detect any bitterness or off-flavors.[133]

Far from wasting vital foodstuffs, as drys contended, brewers had found a way to spin the byproducts of brewing into nutritional and political gold. Americans who had lived through Prohibition and were now being sold the virtues of brewers' yeast as a nutritional supplement likely greeted such claims with a mix of skepticism, amusement, and curiosity. After all, many Americans had first encountered brewers' yeast when they surreptitiously added it to malt syrup to make homebrew during Prohibition. Anheuser-Busch's Budweiser Yeast and Budweiser Barley Malt Syrup, ostensibly created in the 1920s for cookie makers and bread bakers, kept thousands of home brewers well supplied.[134] By the end of World War II, the once illicit connotations of brewers' yeast had begun to fade as brewers' yeast acquired entirely new patriotic associations with victory over fascism and the achievement of "freedom from want."

CONCLUSION

World War II may not have been the economic bonanza for beer that it was for food companies such as Coca-Cola, Hershey, and Wrigley, but "compared with many other industries," *Business Week* observed, "the brewers floated through the war tumults on a bed of hops and roses."[135] Beer consumption increased dramatically, with sales rising from 56,770,00 barrels in 1941 to 80 million barrels in 1945, well above the pre-Prohibition high of 66 million barrels.[136] Indeed, despite boosting its wartime production, brewers could not keep pace with demand. Rising disposable incomes, higher liquor prices, and the rationing of distilled liquor by state monopolies, *Business Week* reported in August 1943, had "transformed some whisky thirst into beer thirst."[137] Beer consumption by servicemen and women defense workers also fueled sales.[138] Brewers counted returning veterans among their staunchest supporters, both as beer consumers and readily mobilized opponents of postwar prohibitionism.

The brewing industry's changing fortunes cannot simply be explained by the government's need to protect tax revenues and minimize the social costs of black markets—although these were certainly major concerns. This explanation overlooks brewers' agency in protecting their access to rationed goods and their status as an essential wartime industry. While we cannot know for sure just how much the brewers' public relations campaign influenced federal policies, the brewers had clearly taken steps to remain in policymakers' good graces. They successfully aligned their interests with the military's needs to bolster the nutrition and morale of servicemen and they buttressed the recommendations of social scientists who argued for wartime food controls that preserved some measure of consumer choice. Brewers rendered the industry less vulnerable to shifting political winds not only by strengthening generational allegiances to beer, but also by forging new relationships with the military, social scientists, and other government bureaucracies.

Just as striking as the reinvigoration of brewers' ties to the state during World War II was the transformation of beer's cultural identity from a still morally suspect commodity to a symbol of the American way of life. World War II did much more than simply reaffirm the liberalization of attitudes toward drinking that had contributed to Prohibition's demise. The repoliticization of beer was part and parcel of the broader wartime politicization of food consumption and production. Brewers jettisoned the discourse of virtue and vice and created new associations of beer drinking with American liberty, the struggle for Freedom from Want, and the nation's pluralistic values. Perhaps the best testament to the brewers' success in reinventing the meanings of beer can be seen in the revised priorities of postwar prohibitionists, who now put a national ban on alcohol advertising—the brewers' most effective public relations tool—at the top of their agenda.[139] Even more than Repeal itself, World War II represented a transformative moment in which beer—and alcohol consumption more broadly—acquired new legitimacy as an emblem of American national identity.

6
Whiskey, Weapons, and the Wartime State

In 1942, *Time* hailed whiskey makers as "Patriotic Distillers" when they converted their entire production to industrial alcohol, a crucial ingredient for making smokeless gunpowder and synthetic rubber.[1] Unlike most industries commissioned for war work, whiskey distillers continued to serve civilian markets while producing around the clock to meet war needs. Consumers who wanted to buy a new car or replace a broken washing machine were usually plumb out of luck, but distillers still had plenty of liquor to deliver, thanks to their vast inventories of aging whiskey. Or so they thought. Robust consumer demand, fueled by fattened wartime paychecks, turned such enviable circumstances into an unanticipated liability for the whiskey industry. By the spring of 1943, whiskey shortages—and public complaints about them—had become pervasive. One *Newsweek* writer joked that Carry Nation, the legendary hatchet-wielding prohibitionist, "couldn't have been happier at the drought toward which the American drinker was drifting."[2] For whiskey makers and government officials, however, the liquor shortage was no laughing matter. Press reports of whiskey price control violations, revived bootlegging rings, and brazen liquor hijackings—conditions reminiscent of Prohibition-era chaos—damaged the whiskey industry's shaky reputation and created new headaches for the Treasury Department and other wartime agencies.[3]

The problem of whiskey black markets raised profound questions about how much consumer sacrifice wartime democracies could safely

FIGURE 15. Macy's Department Store, Manhattan, New York, c. 1942. The juxtaposition of the large billboard advertising Calvert Whiskey and the smaller billboard on top urging civilians to save scrap metals for the war effort encapsulates the tension between competing notions of consumer obligations and consumer entitlements on the home front. Historical via Getty Images.

demand without compromising morale and commitment to the war effort. If home front morale hinged partly on maintaining equitable access to scarce goods, how far, officials asked, should the state intervene to protect access not just to necessities but also to nonessential luxury goods like whiskey? Such questions cut to the heart of several concerns that shaped decision-making about wartime rationing and price controls. New Deal policymakers envisioned rationing and price controls as a form of shared consumer sacrifice that would safeguard economic fairness and preserve some measure of consumer choice consistent with the nation's pluralistic values.[4] Despite broad consumer support for price controls, Americans' commitment to shared sacrifice sometimes proved difficult to sustain as consumers chafed at buying restrictions and inferior substitutes for desired goods. Whiskey, perhaps more than any other scarce wartime commodity, highlighted the tensions between competing notions of consumer sacrifice and consumer entitlement on the American home front (see Figure 15).

Initially, public officials and policymakers treated the problem of whiskey black markets and liquor shortages as a distraction from more pressing concerns, but mounting public pressure and the growing scope of whiskey black markets compelled government officials to contemplate expanded federal regulation of the alcoholic beverage industry. Because the Twenty-First Amendment repealing Prohibition had given the states responsibility for alcoholic beverage control, historians have long assumed that the federal government steered clear of wet–dry controversies after Prohibition and limited its interest in alcohol questions to protecting liquor revenues.[5] When it came to whiskey, however, the federal government was hardly a neutral umpire. Although the federal government took punitive action against whiskey price control violators, its most consequential response to liquor black markets bestowed considerable favor on the whiskey industry. In the final year of the war, in recognition of the industry's importance for wartime morale and national stability, the federal government awarded distillers three separate month-long furloughs from war production to replenish dwindling whiskey stocks. That the government troubled itself over the whiskey question speaks volumes about the extent to which the US government, more than many other combatant nations, perceived civilian morale as vital to victory in a total war.[6]

Several important questions arise from this largely unexplored episode in World War II history. Why did wartime agencies abandon their initial reluctance to police liquor black markets? Why, despite the battered public image of distillers and liquor dealers, did the federal government authorize three "liquor holidays," allowing distillers to temporarily produce whiskey when other industries eager to return to civilian production received no such reprieve?

The answers to these questions complicate our narratives about the evolution of the New Deal state and the legacies of Prohibition.[7] First, the wartime battles over whiskey black markets reveal how the shadow of Prohibition continued to hang over federal policymaking long after Prohibition's repeal. Despite some policymakers' reservations about cutting breaks to an increasingly disreputable liquor trade, their even greater reluctance to adjudicate virtue and vice—rooted in liberal skepticism of Prohibition's attempt to legislate morality—tended to work in the whiskey industry's favor. Another powerful driver of policymaking was Treasury Secretary Henry Morgenthau's desire to preserve what he regarded as one of the New Deal's signature achievements: the repeal of Prohibition and the subsequent vanquishment of liquor black markets in the mid-1930s. In Morgenthau's view, failing to combat the resurgence of whiskey black markets not only undermined efforts to make Repeal work but it also risked eroding broader confidence in the efficacy of state action.

The wartime thirsts for whiskey's taste and psychoactive comforts generated consumer expectations that begged to be quenched and profoundly shifted the terrain of public debate over alcohol's place in the American good life. In the early 1930s, anti-prohibitionists had centered the case for repeal on pragmatic matters: the need to stimulate economic recovery and restore law and order. The World War II debates over whiskey shortages—and the whiskey lobby's well-articulated defense of the right to "decent" alcohol—brought the question of drinkers' freedoms and consumer liberties back to the forefront. The "right to drink," long submerged in public debates, now took center stage.

WHISKEY SHORTAGES AND BLACK MARKETS

Throughout the war Americans had to contend with shortages of food, gasoline, tires, shoes, and a host of other goods. Americans sometimes resented the inconveniences such shortages necessitated, but they understood the need to conserve scarce resources to win the war. Rationing essential fuels and foods (meat, sugar, butter, and coffee) helped to restrain home-front consumer demand, even if such policies failed to eliminate black markets in meat and gasoline altogether. Whiskey shortages, on the other hand, seemed to invite greater lapses in consumer discipline. Many Americans greeted the whiskey shortage not with sober acceptance but with all the irrationality of an inebriated binge drinker. Hoarding became widespread, two dollar bottles of whiskey traded for double and triple the price, and consumers continued to pay exorbitant prices even when they knew (or might have suspected) that bootleggers were selling cut whiskey. Black market dealers did especially big business near crowded defense plants, where a $1.75 pint could sell for $4 to $6.[8]

The shortages caught both the liquor trade and ordinary consumers by surprise. Early reporting had indicated that existing stocks of rye and bourbon would last another five years and that only gin would "feel the pinch sooner," since it was not typically set aside for aging.[9] Distillers underestimated the potential for shortages because they had expected demand to fall as young men departed for the battlefield.[10] Instead, bigger paychecks, full employment, and wartime shortages of other civilian goods, drove liquor consumption sky high. Having money to burn but fewer goods to spend it on, American consumers allocated a growing share of their disposable income to alcohol. In 1944, Americans spent $5.81 billion for beer, wine, and liquor, a 94 percent gain in real terms over 1939 levels of consumption and a sum that claimed nearly 9 percent of all spending on nondurable consumer goods (such as shoes, clothing, food, and entertainment).[11]

Whiskey shortages might not have been as dire if consumers had more enthusiastically accepted other alcoholic potables. Consumers could readily find gins from Cuba, Mexico, and other Latin American countries—or they might have turned to the more plentiful fortified American wines (port and sherry), a less alcoholic but still potent alternative. Soured by lingering memories of Prohibition-era bathtub gin, many American drinkers regarded any kind of gin—but especially Latin American and Caribbean gin—as a poor substitute for whiskey. California table wines, promoted more aggressively than ever by the Wine Institute and the Big Four distillers who acquired major wineries during the war, won new converts but also retained their image as the alcoholic beverage of last resort. When the media spoke of a "liquor drought," they were not describing the dearth of alcoholic beverages so much as they were bemoaning the shortage of good quality whiskey. As David Brinkley, the veteran Washington reporter, recalled, the drinks at a popular Washington, DC, nightclub were "something labeled 'Scotch type' whiskey, made in Chicago mostly of water and God knew what else, and tasting of brown grocery bags."[12]

The whiskey shortage did force some cultural adaptation. Drinkers sampled widely, egged on by advertisers, retailers, and potables columnists who promoted cocktails as liquor stretchers and touted Manhattans, Old-Fashioneds, and Sours made with rum or vodka instead of whiskey (see Figure 16).[13] Lawton Mackall, *Esquire* magazine's illustrious drink expert, advised men to stretch short whiskey supplies by doubling the ratio of vermouth to whiskey or gin in Martinis and Manhattans and drinking wine and beer with meals instead of cocktails.[14] Some seemingly unorthodox adaptations—like Mackall's recommendation to substitute California brandy for the bourbon in mint juleps—actually resurrected the early nineteenth-century formula for the beloved Southern cocktail.[15] The dramatic shifts in the wartime consumption of spirits attested to the adaptability of American drinkers. Many Americans sampled Mexican tequila for the first time and learned to substitute rum and brandy for their customary whiskey cocktail. Rum and Cokes, the

FIGURE 16. Old St. Croix Rum magazine advertisement, 1943. The whiskey shortage created new opportunities to promote rum as a satisfying substitute for whiskey in classic cocktails. Author's collection.

subject of the chart-topping calypso tune, became a popular wartime cocktail, helping to quadruple rum consumption between 1941 and 1944.[16] Drinkers who did not want to mix their own could buy ready-made bottled cocktails such as Cohasset Liquor 60 Proof, a blend of rum, red wine, fruit juice, and syrup.[17]

None of these alternatives dented American preferences for whiskey. Long the American favorite and an emblem of elite consumption in 1930s liquor advertising, whiskey acquired even more emotional resonance as an aspirational commodity during the war. Flush with cash from defense jobs, many drinkers used their windfall to trade up from beer to whiskey.[18] The liquor industry's promotion of gin, rum, brandy, and wine as whiskey substitutes tended to magnify whiskey's allure and stigmatize the proposed alternatives.

The whiskey shortages stimulated hoarding by consumers who intended to drink it themselves and those who intended to sell it for a higher black market price. Ironically, whiskey's disreputability aggravated both of those practices. Consumers who ordinarily hesitated to hoard scarce foods had fewer moral qualms about hoarding whiskey.[19] "The average citizen might turn in the guy who offers black-market sugar," *Collier's* reported, "but he takes an unholy joy in knowing the bootlegger . . . and . . . recommending him to others."[20] As happened in other countries, shortages of certain commodities forced consumers to discriminate between acceptable and dishonorable black market activities.[21] Some consumers may have considered hoarding whiskey and patronizing bootleggers less dishonorable because they saw the entire liquor trade as disreputable. Kenneth Baxter, executive director of the Conference of Alcoholic Beverage Industries (CABI), a trade association representing vintners, distillers, tavernkeepers, retailers, and hoteliers, believed the media criticized the liquor industry more harshly than any other industry afflicted with black markets. Newspapers never spoke of the "food traffic," Baxter complained, but they frequently assailed the "liquor traffic"—a term that linked alcohol to the drug underworld and the industry's sordid past.[22]

Defects in the federalist approach to liquor control also exacerbated black markets. The seventeen monopoly states with state-run liquor stores suffered the worst shortages because the state commissions, unlike independent dealers, did not accrue liquor backlogs. Distillers also tended to keep the licensed independent dealers in the twenty-eight open states better supplied because they could sell whiskey at higher prices.[23] During the war, most monopoly states limited customers to roughly one pint of whiskey each week, but the quantity ranged between a half pint and one quart of whiskey. Customers not sated by their weekly or bimonthly whiskey ration could typically also purchase limited quantities of wine and other spirits at state-run stores.[24]

The imbalanced supply of whiskey in the open and monopoly states created ideal conditions for liquor smuggling. Some private citizens who lived in monopoly states turned excursions to bordering open states into liquor buying sprees.[25] Operating on a much grander scale, organized bootlegging rings would purchase liquor in open states and then sell it at exorbitant prices in the surrounding monopoly states.[26] One such syndicate, supplied by retailers and wholesalers in Baltimore, extended its reach into New York, Pennsylvania, Maryland, Virginia, West Virginia, the Carolinas, and Texas. Two others, run by Prohibition-era bootleggers, monopolized black market whiskey sales in Washington, Oregon, Idaho, and Montana. Tempted by generous side payments of ten to thirty dollars a case, some retailers withheld whiskey from their customers to obtain the higher payments offered by bootlegging rings. A raid by local police and liquor board inspectors discovered that one Baltimore liquor retailer, likely acting as a front for a wholesaler, had 160 cases of whiskey in his warehouse awaiting delivery to bootleggers—despite the retailer's repeated protestations that he had none to sell.[27]

Squeezed by rising consumer demand and wholesalers' tightly rationed supplies, retailers in the open states struggled to prevent hoarders, black market buyers, and representatives from local bars from gobbling up the good whiskey before loyal, local customers had a chance to make a purchase.[28] Department stores, tavernkeepers, and other retailers sometimes allocated a limited volume for daily sales and shortened hours of operation to ration existing supplies. Others removed stock from shelves to save it for regular customers and men in uniform.[29] Whiskey firms came to despise under-the-counter sales because the hidden stock kept their brands out of the public eye and reinforced growing public suspicions that distillers were deliberately withholding whiskey. If you were not a regular, a Nashville liquor regulator reported, it was nearly impossible "buy a quart of Old Grandad or Johnny Walker" from a liquor store. For a small fee, however, unlucky customers could find someone to refer them to "a bellboy or somebody in the alley" who would charge "twice the regular price for a bottle of whiskey."[30] Though some liquor stores treated servicemen as privileged customers, servicemen frequently grumbled to commanding officers about the "chiselers" near army camps and nightclubs who gambled that soldiers would not "be stationed" in town "long enough to complain."[31]

The underground network of bootleggers and counterfeiters was only one dimension of the liquor black market. An even more pervasive form of black market activity was practiced by legitimate businessmen who devised various schemes to evade price ceilings. As whiskey became scarcer, retailers and tavernkeepers found themselves at the mercy of wholesalers who would supply them with popular brands of bourbon and scotch only if they also accepted deliveries of slower-selling brandies, wines, and Caribbean rums and gins. Retailers in turn pressured whiskey shoppers to buy less appealing wines and spirits.[32] The pressure to unload less desirable potables on consumers originated from the top of the distribution chain. During the war, the major distillers acquired California wineries and Caribbean distilleries, but they soon discovered they could not move wines, rums, and brandies unless they tied their purchase to whiskey allotments. According to the enforcement division of the Office of Price Administration (OPA), "purchasers all along the line, including ultimate consumers," could not obtain whiskey without also buying other alcoholic beverages from the distillers' product line.[33] The liquor trade was hardly unusual in using tie-in sales to evade price controls—such practices typified wartime food markets, especially for valued items like meat and poultry—but the practice incensed consumers and contributed immeasurably to the liquor trade's growing ill-repute.[34] Well into the postwar period, marketing research studies revealed that many New Yorkers and Californians continued to view liquor dealer recommendations as cynical ploys to move inventory or get the highest markup.[35]

Whiskey distillers evaded OPA price ceilings through two other tried and true techniques: "forced uptrading" and "the elimination of lower-priced lines of merchandise."[36] Under the General Maximum Price Regulation, the OPA froze prices for established brands at March 1942 levels but permitted companies to introduce new brands at prices compatible with the most comparable product. Distillers exploited such loopholes by withdrawing low-priced established brands and offering "new and unknown labels" at peak prices.[37] Some unscrupulous distillers bottled all their whiskey under high-priced labels so that even their lower-quality whiskeys could be sold under the OPA's highest price brackets.[38] Consumers soon had no choice but to buy high-end whiskey (whether or not the price accurately reflected quality), as the lower-priced options had all but disappeared. Although withdrawing lower-priced whiskeys disadvantaged consumers on tight budgets, Seagram encouraged retailers to view trading up as a pragmatic solution to the whiskey shortage and a long-range strategy for building postwar business. "Customers who trade themselves up today," a Seagram ad informed the trade, will *stay* traded up for good!"[39]

BLACK MARKETS AND STATE INTERVENTION

As the reality of widespread liquor shortages set in, the blame game began. "Until recently," *Business Week* reported, "Congress and the public have been disposed to accept . . . the semiofficial theory that whisky is a war casualty, and that complaining about it would do no good." The hefty profits reported by Seagram, Hiram Walker, National Distillers, and Schenley (known collectively as the Big Four) threw the industry under a cloud of suspicion.[40] Consumer complaints about price gouging and shortages of quality whiskey impelled the Senate Judiciary Committee to launch an investigation of the whiskey shortage and whiskey profits. According to *Business Week*, lawmakers had good reason to sympathize with consumers' pain. Thanks to the acute liquor shortage in Washington, DC, which claimed the highest per capita liquor consumption in the nation, politicians had grown "increasingly bitter about the scarcity of bourbon, rye, and Scotch, and the relative abundance of poor substitutes in unfamiliar labels at high prices."[41]

In the wake of intensified media and Congressional scrutiny, other government agencies also turned up the heat on distillers. John O'Connell, chair of the New York State Liquor Authority (NYSLA), accused distillers of hoarding whiskey stocks and creating an artificial shortage.[42] The Treasury Department began weighing punitive action to force the industry to release more whiskey. Adding to the distillers' troubles, the Department of Justice opened an antitrust probe against the Big Four following their moves to acquire smaller independents or purchase their whiskey inventories. By the end of 1943, the Big Four together owned 70 percent of the whiskey in storage, a 21 percent rise over their combined volume in 1939.[43] To round out their alcohol portfolios and relieve pressure on whiskey inventories, the big distillers also purchased one quarter of the California wine industry's productive capacity.[44] When their supplies of blending spirits ran low, Schenley purchased distilleries in Cuba and Puerto Rico, and Hiram Walker purchased Matfaldi-Simon, Argentina's largest grain liquor producer.[45] Some lawmakers viewed these diversification strategies as troubling evidence of the Big Four's monopolistic ambitions.

Whiskey firms, wholesalers, retailers, and consumers cast blame in all directions. Consumers had good reason to suspect that the liquor shortage originated at the top of the distribution chain, even if wholesalers, retailers, and hoarders helped to exacerbate it. In the fall of 1943 distillers sharply reduced deliveries to wholesalers by 50 to 60 percent of prewar volume.[46] They wanted to preserve enough aged whiskey, around 100 to 150 million gallons, to "avoid a repetition of using whiskey 'hot off the still,'" as happened immediately after Repeal.[47] Distillers also calculated that they could offset the lower sales with a corresponding reduction in the heavy wartime taxes on corporate income and excess profits.[48] Strict self-rationing at the top snowballed down the distribution chain. That did not stop distillers from blaming consumers for "refusing to switch from whisky to relatively plentiful drinks." A dismayed Hiram Walker executive complained, "When [consumers] go to a store and can't get butter they realize there's a war on. But when they can't get whisky, they raise hell."[49] And raise hell they did. According to an OPA report on the liquor situation, Americans expressed "more public interest and concern" about whiskey "than any other commodity, with the possible exception of gasoline."[50]

Despite the intense public complaints about whiskey shortages and liquor price control violations, the OPA and the Treasury Department were reluctant to divert limited enforcement resources from the food front to the liquor front.[51] Jurisdictional confusion and buck passing between agencies further delayed an effective, coordinated response. Treasury Secretary Morgenthau believed the OPA needed to step up its own enforcement since most black market activities violated price ceilings rather than internal revenue laws.[52] OPA officials and state liquor administrators concluded that black markets would continue to fester until the War Production Board (WPB) boosted supplies (by either granting distillers a furlough from war production or directing distillers to release more whiskey).[53] WPB officials for the most part agreed but could not release grain for whiskey production without the consent of the War Food Administration (WFA). State liquor administrators resisted getting involved with liquor price enforcement because their hands were already full monitoring alcohol sales to minors, eliminating bootlegging, and maintaining public order around drinking establishments in overcrowded defense centers.[54]

Bureaucratic inertia began to yield when politicians and policymakers discovered that ignoring the whiskey question imperiled other policy priorities. OPA officials worried that rising liquor prices would fuel inflation and undercut federal efforts to contain the cost of essential goods. Failing to police liquor black markets also threatened to undermine the agency's efforts to police food and clothing. As an OPA official explained, "Most decent people look down on the black marketer in meat, groceries and other necessities as a . . . chiseler, lacking in patriotism," but not so with liquor. If the Prohibition-era acceptance of the bootlegger "carries over to the new phase in liquor bootlegging," the official warned, "it may in time take the stigma off other black markets."[55] During his tenure at the OPA, Thomas Emerson, a Roosevelt Administration lawyer, feared that black markets of any kind would "discredit the whole war program" and "break down adherence to other wartime regulations." "As soon as any substantial number violated the laws," Emerson observed, others "simply took these unscrupulous violators as an excuse for violating themselves."[56]

The wartime resurgence of prohibitionism also prodded Morgenthau to act. As detailed in chapter 5, drys repeatedly petitioned Congress to ban alcohol from military training camps and drinking places located within a ten-mile radius of the camps. Although strong opposition from the Secretary of War, the Secretary of the Navy, and veterans' groups doomed such measures, prohibitionists outperformed in local option elections, especially in Georgia, Kentucky, and New York, where voters became fed up with shoppers from bordering monopoly states invading their states and depleting local whiskey stocks. By the fall of 1943, 83 percent of Georgia's previously wet counties and 72 percent of Kentucky's had voted to become dry. Exasperated citizens in Pike County, Kentucky—a wet county adjoining two monopoly states—privately admitted voting dry just to "spite the distillers."[57]

Morgenthau repeatedly raised the specter of Prohibition to underscore the urgency of combating black markets and the threat they posed to a signature accomplishment of the New Deal: Prohibition's repeal and the effort to drive bootleggers permanently out of business in the mid-1930s. The Treasury Department's aggressive moves to eradicate illicit distilling during Morgenthau's first two years at the helm marked him, in historian John Blum's estimation, as more "uncompromising toward bootleggers" than any federal official had been "during the entire history of prohibition." By 1936, Treasury agents had seized twenty-four thousand illicit stills and obtained as many convictions. Rigorous policing of the retail trade and international waters had dried up the illicit liquor traffic in most large cities and "reduced" liquor smuggling operations to "a mere trickle."[58] Morgenthau feared that public support for price controls would wane—and prohibitionists would gain more political leverage—if the wartime state failed to conquer liquor black markets.[59] Irked by the presumption that the Treasury Department had dallied on the liquor problem, Secretary Morgenthau urged Alcohol Tax Unit (ATU) agents to make sure that "every morning . . . an item [appeared] in every paper all over the country showing the results" of their crackdown on liquor black markets.[60]

In public pronouncements, Morgenthau cast the Treasury Department as a crime fighter rather than a moral crusader. His press releases stressed that the Treasury's efforts to defeat liquor black markets aimed not to settle "a question of morals, of drinking habits, of temperance" but to "preven[t] the old criminal gangs from taking advantage of the war situation to enrich and entrench themselves again."[61] Such statements give some credence to the argument that the federal government wanted to steer clear of wet–dry controversies, but this interpretation overlooks a more complex set of calculations. Battling greed and profiteering projected state competence; relitigating tired moral battles did not. Had Morgenthau characterized the spread of liquor black markets as "a question of morals, of drinking habits, of temperance," he might have also stirred broader debate about the state's failure to make repeal work and in turn tarnished an important legacy of the New Deal. Morgenthau's willingness to undertake dramatic state interventions against liquor black markets underscored his commitment to protecting this legacy.

The liquor trade's preferred solution was a temporary furlough from industrial alcohol production that would allow distillers to replenish whiskey inventories and release more whiskey for domestic consumption. The industry found support for the furlough from the Senate Judiciary Subcommittee to Investigate the Liquor Shortage, chaired by Nevada Senator Pat McCarran.[62] The McCarran Committee, as the subcommittee came to be known, was also willing to pursue tougher measures, however. It considered a draconian plan to push more whiskey onto the market by reducing the tax-free period for storing whiskey from eight years to four years. The idea for such punitive action arose from lawmakers' suspicion that whiskey distillers were creating artificial shortages by deliberately hoarding whiskey. Senator Walter George (D-GA), who proposed the four-year force out, believed distillers were hoarding whiskey to escape federal excise taxes (set to jump from six dollars to nine dollars per gallon in 1944). Supported by the McCarran Committee and the Treasury Department, the four-year force out would have immediately released 100 million gallons of whiskey for domestic consumption and raked in nearly $1 billion in taxes. Morgenthau relished the prospect that such a move "would just blow this whole black market up."⁶³

Despite Morgenthau's considerable enthusiasm, Treasury staffers doubted that the force-out would have its intended effect. Some predicted that whiskey supplies "would disappear as quickly as . . . the few people who have the limited ability to buy . . . [could] get hold of it."⁶⁴ Lawmakers pointed out the unfairness of forcing distillers to liquidate their business when their 90 percent tax bracket would eat up most of their profits. "In two or three years," the distillers would "be entirely out of business with millions invested in buildings and trade names and no whiskey with which to continue."⁶⁵ Distillers strongly opposed the force-out plan, believing it would jeopardize their postwar prospects and the quality of heavy-bodied bourbons and ryes, which required five-six years of aging.⁶⁶ Although the Senate Finance Committee ultimately rejected the four-year force-out, the mere threat of the proposed plan appeared to have prodded the industry to put more whiskey on the market in the closing months of 1943.⁶⁷

The McCarran Committee and the Treasury Department also contemplated a fairly radical demand-side solution to the problem of inequitably distributed liquor supplies: nationwide whiskey rationing. Although most monopoly states already limited customers to a quart of whiskey per month, Treasury officials proposed making the practice "uniform for the entire country," much like the OPA programs for rationed beef, sugar, and coffee. Morgenthau liked the plan because it addressed problems of equitability and excess: rationing would ensure fairer distribution while the limited liquor allowance would encourage people to drink "in moderation."⁶⁸ Strong opposition from top officials in the OPA and the WFA killed the rationing proposal. OPA head Chester Bowles informed the Treasury that he would "resist [rationing] to the very limits of his energy" since his agency was already shorthanded.⁶⁹ Alex Elson, director of OPA's Food Enforcement Division, opposed national liquor rationing because liquor was "a luxury" not "a necessity."⁷⁰ The WFA rejected the McCarran Committee's recommendation that the WFA oversee nationwide liquor rationing for fear of offending farmers who preferred an outright liquor ban.⁷¹

In weighing the best course of action against whiskey black markets, policymakers raised broader questions about the state's role in shaping mass consumption and protecting purchasing power. Should the federal government treat liquor as a luxury commodity and exempt it from price controls, as some policymakers argued, or should it take steps to keep whiskey prices within the reach of the ordinary consumer? Did full-fledged consumer citizenship entail access to intoxicating pleasures as well as the necessities of life? Although Morgenthau and Bowles vehemently opposed rescinding whiskey price ceilings, some OPA enforcement agents and Treasury Department staff strongly supported such measures. Proponents argued that allowing liquor prices to rise would absorb excess consumer spending power rather than unleash inflation.[72] Removing price ceilings would also free OPA enforcement staff to concentrate on essential "cost of living commodities" and "correct abuses . . . where the public really needs protection."[73] Newspapers and mass magazines were coming to similar conclusions. *Time* and *Life* called upon the OPA to stop wasting time enforcing "price ceilings on luxuries, such as fur coats, whiskey, jewelry," and instead focus on "the essential goods and necessities of life."[74] The seeming futility of policing whiskey black markets persuaded other OPA staffers that liquor price enforcement was not worth the effort. As one OPA enforcement agent concluded, "Nothing short of a large army of government agents" could battle the "well-organized, adequately financed, politically and legally fortified unscrupulous . . . underworld characters" who trafficked in black market whiskey.[75]

The proponents of rescinding whiskey price ceilings were hardly anti-statists—they fully supported food rationing and price controls on other essentials. State regulation of luxury markets was another matter. The case against price-controlled luxury goods candidly acknowledged the limited capacity of the wartime state and the advantages of allowing markets to find their own solution. If whiskey price ceilings were removed, proponents argued, distillers would stop withholding whiskey from the market, popular brand names would reappear, black market operators would disband, and the federal government would reap higher income taxes from law-abiding dealers who once again sold all their liquor through taxable channels.[76]

Other policymakers opposed rescinding price controls on both practical and moral grounds. Even if higher whiskey prices absorbed excess consumer spending, Chester Bowles argued, uncontrolled liquor pricing would still be inflationary because the distilled spirits industry, with annual sales exceeding $1 billion, represented a large part of the economy.[77] If whiskey makers were freed "to profiteer at will," some OPA officials worried that the entire edifice of price controls would crumble. Producers of other luxury goods would demand similar treatment and producers of essential commodities who continued to operate under price controls would grow more resentful.[78]

Policymakers also questioned the fairness of allowing whiskey prices to rise beyond the ordinary consumer's ability to pay. At Treasury Department staff meetings, staffers warned that without price controls only "the people with money" would be able to purchase liquor and the "ordinary fellow['s]" morale would suffer.[79] OPA officials took an even bolder stance. Some gauged the American standard of living by the affordability of decent liquor. As one OPA agent noted, in England, where liquor was not subjected to price controls, the lower classes could not "buy the same quality and high priced spirits which even the average American" could afford. Removing price controls, he implied, would lower ordinary Americans to the English standard.[80] For both the ordinary and the affluent, the enjoyment of good whiskey affirmed one's belonging in a consumer democracy and the superiority of the American way. Concerns about the equitable distribution of scarce whiskey supplies prompted John Galbraith to float the idea of requiring sellers to offer low-priced, medium-priced, and high-priced brands in the same proportions customers encountered before the war.[81] Although the OPA never enacted such a policy, Galbraith's proposal reveals how New Deal policymakers began to imagine equitable access to psychoactive pleasures as a dimension of consumer citizenship.

The proponents of maintaining whiskey price controls ultimately prevailed because this position best accomplished the wartime state's key economic priorities: containing inflationary pressures and preserving ordinary consumers' access to popular, but scarce, goods. Nevertheless, the politics of whiskey black markets continued to dog policymakers because whiskey occupied an ambiguous space in the American cultural imagination: it was at once a luxury for the upscale and a common pleasure for the masses. As we shall see, all sides of the whiskey question—wet, damp, and dry—exploited and muddied the distinctions between luxuries and everyday pleasures as the public campaign to grant distillers a "liquor holiday" from war production began in earnest in 1944.

LIQUOR ENFORCEMENT AND WHISKEY INDUSTRY PUBLIC RELATIONS

The wartime state enlisted the resources of multiple government agencies to execute its newly invigorated liquor enforcement campaign. Beginning in December 1943, the Treasury's Alcohol Tax Unit, along with the OPA, various state liquor administrations, the Anti-Trust Division of the Department of Justice, and even the US Army all cooperated to prosecute price control violators and tame whiskey black markets. To address the soaring cost of liquor, the OPA lowered fixed margins for wholesalers and retailers and took steps to close price ceiling loopholes that enabled distillers to introduce new brands at the highest price frozen under the General Maximum Price Regulation. The new price ceiling regulations established the same flat price on all new brands, blunting the incentive to concoct new (and often inferior) brands merely to gain a higher price.[82] At Secretary Morgenthau's behest, the ATU threw all "available forces" into the OPA's black market program.[83] To quell "vigorous complaints" about exorbitant liquor prices, the OPA's Cleveland Regional branch (which oversaw Kentucky, a significant center of liquor distribution) diverted staff from agricultural commodities to the liquor field.[84]

Recognizing the impossibility of policing the nation's 375,000 liquor dealers, the ATU and OPA focused much of their efforts on wholesalers, where most price control violations originated.[85] They hoped to achieve greater deterrence by prosecuting "a few well chosen" violators, freezing their assets, and demanding treble damages.[86] State liquor commissions in ten states suspended the licenses of liquor dealers who violated price ceilings.[87] None of this work was easy to carry out—or without risks. The presence of "criminal elements" among the black market operators, one enforcement agent cryptically observed, made it "difficult, if not impossible" to achieve compliance with liquor controls.[88] Nevertheless, by the fall of 1944, the OPA could boast that its Enforcement Department had broken large black market rings, jailed violators, and won several treble damage lawsuits.[89]

The US Army also conducted successful sting operations against black market operators and price-gouging taverns. Eager to exact retribution against liquor chiselers, soldiers in San Bernadino, California, and other army towns happily answered the Provost Marshall's call to help put away greedy profiteers. Not only did soldiers provide OPA investigators with leads on people and places that trafficked in black market alcohol, but they also entrapped taxicab drivers, shopkeepers, and bartenders known to sell servicemen bottled liquor above price ceilings.[90] The military's willingness to use soldiers in sting operations against black marketeers departed dramatically from the previous world war, when the military had declared alcohol off limits and barred sex workers and sales of alcohol within ten miles of a training camp.

Rather than banning certain kinds of pleasure-seeking, the World War II–era military doled out condoms and intervened (via liquor stings) to reduce commercial exploitation in the environs surrounding the camps.[91]

Whiskey firms and industry trade associations pressured retailers to end discriminatory practices and honor price controls. To counter widespread consumer complaints that liquor retailers favored certain customers, Seagram exhorted dealers to discourage quantity buying so that "no customer will go away empty handed because another man hoards."[92] Seagram's in-house magazine for salesmen underscored the urgency of monitoring retailers for price control violations. If Seagram salesmen failed to "smash" the retail "profiteer," the *Seagram Spotlight* warned, public demands for "government control of liquor rationing"—the "first step on the road back to Prohibition"—would only continue to grow.[93] Other distillers hired private shopping services to scope out the under-the-counter sales that kept nationally advertised brands out of view and made distillers "the 'goats' in the public mind."[94] Trade associations shamed retailers into compliance. Allied Liquor Industries placed ads in local newspapers that named retailers who pledged to observe ceiling prices, distribute merchandise fairly, and eschew tie-in sales in hopes of making the "derelicts . . . uncomfortably conspicuous by their absence."[95]

Whiskey distillers also attempted to repair damage to their reputation by publicizing their contributions to the war effort. Much of their messaging echoed the ongoing public relations campaign—initiated in 1940 by conservative business leaders, the National Association of Manufacturers, and other business groups—to convince Americans that free-market capitalism deserved credit for "the nation's massive military-industrial mobilization."[96] Whiskey makers heralded their "indispensable" contributions to the war production miracle in *Volunteer for Victory: The Story of How a Great Industry Enlisted for War*, a sixty-two-page booklet that explained how the distillers operated around the clock, seven days a week to produce explosive "cocktails for the Axis" and synthetic rubber for the military's tanks and fighter planes (see Figure 17). Had prohibition still been in place, the booklet stressed, the government would have wasted critical time and resources to build new industrial alcohol plants, resulting in "another case of 'too little, too late.'" *Volunteer for Victory* also heralded whiskey consumers' contributions to the war effort. In 1942 alone, the booklet boasted, alcohol excise taxes had yielded enough revenue ($1.4 billion) to build seventy aircraft carriers or two hundred destroyers or one hundred and forty thousand fighter planes.[97] Sympathetic magazine columnists ech-

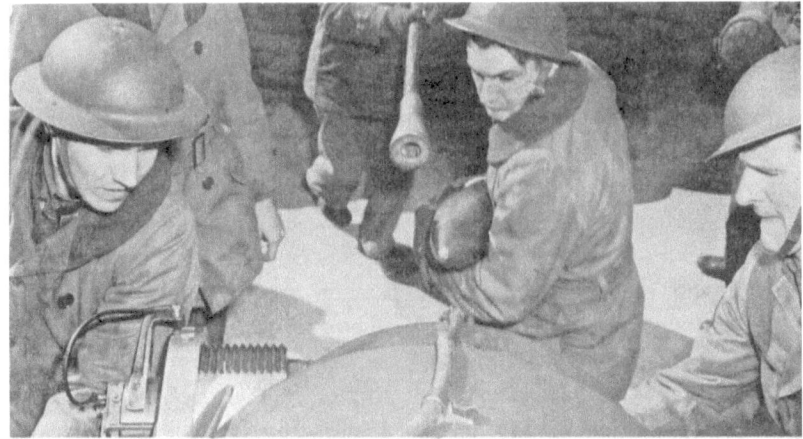

Loading large shore guns. The powder for these shells can be traced to many former whiskey distillers

A COCKTAIL for the AXIS
War Alcohol for the Smokeless Powder That Keeps Big U. S. Guns in Action

FIGURE 17. Illustration from *Volunteer for Victory: The Story of How a Great Industry Enlisted for War*, an industry-sponsored booklet, published in 1943, that aimed to defuse public anger over whiskey shortages and publicize the distillers' contributions to the war effort.

oed the distillers' talking points. *Esquire*'s Lawton Mackall suggested that distillers had earned the deserved "satisfaction of being a national lifesaver in the scrimmage we're going through." *Life* counseled patience with liquor shortages, explaining that after holding some 100 million gallons for postwar reserve, "the remaining 203,000,000 ... would vanish ... in less than a year" unless distillers rationed their supply.[98]

Tougher liquor enforcement produced results, but, as many policymakers had predicted, the scale of consumer demand and the scope of the liquor trade outmatched the limited capacity of the state to police the market. In the face of such challenges, the demands for a liquor holiday that would temporarily release distillers to produce whiskey instead of industrial alcohol continued to grow.

THE POLITICS OF LIQUOR FURLOUGHS

Whiskey firms recognized that campaigning for a liquor furlough was fraught with moral peril. Doing so would rile prohibitionists and invite accusations that whiskey distillers (and allied industries) were putting profits ahead of the war effort. It also risked industrial and civilian discord. If the government granted the whiskey industry a reprieve from war production, what would stop other industries from making similar demands? How could the government effectively demand shared sacrifice in conserving essential commodities if it granted special privileges for a commodity that many regarded as a luxury—and a morally debasing one at that? These questions required business, consumers, and the state to address a central dilemma in the politics of wartime consumption: how to reconcile consumers' yearnings to purchase freely with the state's mission to encourage restrained and responsible consumption.[99]

Putting such concerns to rest required deft manipulation of what historian Mark Leff has called the "politics of sacrifice"—a "political process" by which various interest groups invoked the rhetoric and imagery of sacrifice to "gain political advantage or ... shift war burdens to others." At various points during the war, consumers, labor, business, farmers, and high-income earners all seized the politics of sacrifice to correct inequities and demand greater equality of sacrifice.[100] Morgenthau's mere mention of a possible liquor holiday in March 1944 prompted prohibitionists to condemn the government's misplaced priorities. "A rationed people and a starving world," the Reverend Edwin Field wrote, "need food and clothing—not liquor as a substitute."[101] If distillers championed the liquor holiday, the ensuing political storm might well bury the idea. It thus fell to allied groups, those better able to risk playing with "political 'dynamite,'" to take up the cause.[102]

Most of the pressure for a liquor furlough came from Tavern Leagues, Liquor Dealer Associations, the Society of Restaurateurs, and state liquor administrators.[103] At its emotional core, the case for a liquor holiday boiled down to an argument about consumer rights and freedoms—not just the right to drink alcohol, but "the right to decent whiskies," as Paul Henkel, president of the Society of Restaurateurs, put it.[104] A *Tavern News* editorial likened the quest for a liquor holiday to a "crusade" to "[protect] the American public" and satisfy "public demand for properly manufactured liquor potables" and "good grain-made whiskey." Instead of drinking quality aged American whiskeys, the editorial lamented, Americans had to find satisfaction in "a flood of Cuban rum, Spanish and Portuguese brandy, gin from South America and Australia and certain mysterious-tasting liquor from Mexico"—much of it tasting something akin to the "bathtub nectar" of Prohibition days.[105] *Tavern News* leaned heavily on nationalistic tropes to justify a liquor holiday, but it did not exaggerate about the deteriorating quality of wartime whiskey. Schenley Distillers Company and other whiskey producers stretched their dwindling supply by blending the aged whiskey on hand with inferior spirits made using potatoes, cane sugar, or redistilled brandy rather than grain. The resulting blended whiskey was, by many accounts, odd tasting, unpleasant, and physically punishing.[106] Schenley Reserve's "Black Label" blended whiskey gave wartime consumers such "terrible hangovers" that some dubbed the brand the "Black Death" and "sw[ore] they wouldn't drink the stuff" after the war.[107]

By invoking the language of consumer rights, the advocates of a liquor furlough transformed whiskey from a luxury good for the upscale to a common pleasure for the masses. John O'Connell, chair of the NYSLA, defended access to decent alcohol as a right that the federal government should protect—even in wartime.[108] The fact that high demand for whiskey had pressured "five governmental bureaus and the U.S. Senate" to investigate the whiskey shortage persuaded *Tavern Weekly News* that whiskey should be treated as "a necessity . . . to maintain morale."[109] The danger of such arguments was that they divorced the notion of consumer rights from any conception of wartime sacrifice. To avoid seeming whiny and selfish, the *Tavern News* insisted that "loyal, patriotic citizens wouldn't want that [quality] drink if it detracted from the war program in the slightest degree."[110] Proponents of a liquor holiday attempted to shield themselves from accusations of selfishness by demanding greater sacrifice from liquor drinkers in allied countries. Clark Gavin, the editor of a leading liquor trade journal, extended the principle of equal sacrifice to the timing of beverage "respites" in Canada and the UK, where liquor black markets also raged out of control. Canadian distillers had already received a three-week holiday in early 1944, but fairness and Allied unity, Gavin argued, demanded that future holidays be "undertaken in concert."[111] If Americans weren't getting good whiskey, Gavin might well have said, why should the Brits and Canadians?[112]

The liquor trade also justified a liquor holiday on the grounds that American whiskey was no less essential or worthy than other civilian commodities that used war alcohol. If the government had enough industrial alcohol to allocate a share to makers of toiletries and other consumer products, why should the government not allot whiskey makers their fair share? "The average citizen," Henkel said, "cannot understand . . . why [the government allotted] millions of gallons of so-called war grain alcohol [for] anti-freeze, hair tonics, rubbing alcohol, [and] shoe polish . . ., while he must content himself with . . . inferior gins and rums from Cuba and other Caribbean ports."[113] Simply put, Americans who wanted quality whiskey were no more extravagant than those who wished to polish their shoes or tame their hair. Seagram President Frank Schwengel made a similar point at a March 1944 Liquor Control Conference organized by Treasury Secretary Morgenthau. Noting that the government gave cosmetics makers about half of their prewar alcohol requirements in the interest of protecting women's morale, Schwengel argued that the government should grant whiskey makers the same consideration in the interest of bolstering public morale.[114]

Whiskey makers and the broader liquor trade returned to the cosmetics analogy time and again to legitimize their demands for a liquor holiday. In seeking special wartime dispensations, cosmetic firms and whiskey makers both championed the socially redeeming and morale boosting dimensions of their products. Although genteel norms had previously associated women's use of cosmetics with prostitution and lower-class promiscuity, aggressive mass marketing and the widespread use of close-up shots in Hollywood films had largely normalized cosmetics use by the 1920s and 1930s. Wartime advertisements accelerated the mass acceptance of cosmetics by making their use seem downright conventional. Magazine ads assured women who worked in defense factories and the military that wearing lipstick and rouge would preserve their femininity.[115] From the distillers' perspective, the morale-boosting, gender-affirming effects of whiskey—the drink of respectable, manly men—easily rivaled those of cosmetics. Whiskey's defenders amplified the injustice of denying whiskey makers a liquor holiday by highlighting how the current allocation of industrial alcohol for civilian markets privileged women's consumer preferences. The *Tavern News* complained that the government had put women's desires ahead of men's by allotting a portion of the nation's war alcohol for "making milady's rouge" while allowing "NONE of it" for "my-man's highball."[116] Some whiskey makers, perhaps sensing this was an unwise tack, instead urged men to adjust to life with fewer bottles of whiskey, just as women had learned to do with fewer shoes. "Only through the united efforts and unstinted sacrifices of all of us," a liquor ad counseled, "will the day of abundant shoes ... and G & W Five Star [Whiskey] ... dawn again" (see Figure 18).[117]

The liquor trade found a sympathetic audience among key government officials who similarly preferred not to judge certain consumer preferences as more worthy or more moral than others. At the Congressional hearings on the liquor shortage, WPB chief Donald Nelson, a

FIGURE 18. G & W Five Star Whiskey magazine advertisement, *Wine and Liquor Retailer*, 1943. Courtesy General Research Division, New York Public Library.

former Sears executive, testified that the WPB "tried . . . religiously to avoid calling anything in this economy non-essential" but instead assessed "relative essentiality."[118] In Nelson's view, cosmetics and whiskey both met "essential civilian requirements."[119] The refusal to define one civilian commodity as any more essential than another also informed the government's response to prohibitionist demands that whiskey production be halted for the duration. At the beginning of the war, prohibitionists had urged the government to spare the housewife's sugar bowl by seizing existing whiskey stocks for redistillation into war alcohol. (Doing so would presumably relieve industrial alcohol plants from needing to distill molasses into war alcohol and would thus expand sugar supplies.) *Christian Century*, a liberal Protestant magazine with strong dry sympathies, warned that "a good many American housewives . . . will start asking why they should be called on to deprive themselves of a food necessity while the distillers hold their stocks of booze inviolate."[120] The OPA threw cold water on the plan.[121] Addressing the General Federation of Women's Clubs, Leon Henderson, the OPA's first chief administrator, bluntly refused to sacrifice men's consumer pleasures to feminine moralizing. "Some Americans," Henderson said, "would rather have liquor than sugar and this is still a democracy."[122]

The liquor holiday idea received strong support from the Treasury Department, the WPB, and the McCarran Committee. The latter in particular shared the liquor trade's frustration with the dearth of decent whiskey.[123] In its first report on the liquor shortage the committee insisted that the "tremendous public demand for quality spirits" should not "be ignored or 'prohibited'" or frustrated by exploitative "foreign and domestic promoters" of overpriced "inferior products."[124] The McCarran Committee's support for the liquor holiday by no means represented an endorsement of the whiskey industry itself. The committee's public report on the whiskey shortage concluded that distillers had deliberately hoarded better-known brands, with the intention of selling them at higher prices after the government had lifted price controls and relaxed excess profits taxes. The McCarran Committee's most serious charge accused the Big Four of "monopolistic tendencies," citing their ownership of 70 percent of the whiskey supply; their absorption of smaller distilleries, breweries, and California wineries; and their purchase of distilleries in Cuba and Puerto Rico.[125] Nevertheless, even the McCarran Committee supported a liquor holiday for the sake of satisfying public demand.

The biggest obstacles to a liquor holiday came from the WFA and military planners. Even with the backing of the WPB and the McCarran

Committee, the fate of the liquor holiday ultimately rested with the WFA, the lone agency with the authority to allocate grain for military and civilian use. Distillers, in short, could not be liberated from war production until the WFA liberated grain for beverage production. For this very reason, some industry personnel preferred the term "grain holiday" to "liquor holiday." Orville Schupp, who headed distillery operations at Schenley, recalled that distillers "pressured" employees to send telegrams to Washington, DC, "imploring" their representatives to support a "grain holiday."[126] Despite such lobbying, for most of 1943 and 1944 the WFA refused to sanction the use of grain for whiskey, preferring to hold it in reserve for the war alcohol program, livestock feed, and underfed peoples in war-torn countries.[127]

WPB chief Donald Nelson, while generally sympathetic to the liquor furlough, bowed to military planners who feared that any early reconversion to civilian production would breed complacency and make Americans less receptive to demands for further sacrifices. The clash between the military and civilian heads of war agencies "over resuming civilian production ... was so intense and dragged on for so long—from mid-1943 to 1945—that it came to be known as 'the war within a war.'"[128] The industry's hopes for a liquor holiday were repeatedly raised and then dashed in the midst of this "war within a war." In January 1944, Nelson, previously a furlough supporter, warned that the industrial alcohol stockpile had become dangerously thin, and announced his opposition to the liquor furlough. The synthetic rubber program remained fully dependent on industrial alcohol, as the petroleum-based butadiene plants—the only viable alternative for making industrial alcohol—were operating far below expected capacity.[129]

Relief, as it happened, was just months away. On June 20, 1944, Donald Nelson, acting on Rubber Director Bradley Dewey's assurances of adequate war alcohol supplies, announced that distillers would get their long-awaited furlough in August.[130] In the absence of adequate corn supplies, distillers were not able to produce bourbon, but they nonetheless hailed the liquor holiday as a nationalistic victory for American consumers who would gladly accept "any grain liquor" over "the cane and fruit spirits they've been forced to take."[131] The timing of the announcement, coming on the heels of the successful Normandy invasion on June 6, was not coincidental. More than any other factor, planning for D-Day explained why the government had postponed the liquor furloughs. In the seven or eight months before D-Day, synthetic rubber production had kicked into overdrive to supply, among other things, rubber tires for the six hundred thousand wheeled vehicles that would land on the Normandy beaches. Marvin Jones, the head of the WFA, recalled being "called over to the White House [in December 1943] and told, 'We've got to have two hundred million bushels of wheat, and a hundred and sixty thousand tons of sugar to make synthetic rubber.'" Commanded to complete secrecy, Jones could not reveal to housewives or whiskey distillers why allocations of sugar and grain would remain tight.[132] In the absence of such information, the liquor trade hatched their own conspiratorial theories, speculating (perhaps correctly) that Jones, a devout Methodist, was "a dry at heart and will[ing] to do his best to cross up any resumption of liquor manufacture."[133] Jones remained a staunch opponent of liquor furloughs until the end of the war. Donald Nelson suspected that Jones would have denied whiskey makers a holiday in December 1943, regardless of the rubber situation.[134]

Although military planning dictated the timing of the furloughs, the electoral calculations of the Roosevelt Administration determined their scope and generosity. The distillers, as it turned out, owed their furlough to friends in the highest places. Franklin Delano Roosevelt, who had won the presidency in 1932 partly on the promise to repeal prohibition, wanted the liquor situation under control before his fourth reelection campaign got underway.[135] The generous terms of the August furlough suggest that the Roosevelt Administration aimed to give the distillers and whiskey-deprived consumers as big a boost as possible. Distillers initially feared that they would not be able to reach their optimal goal of producing 50 million gallons of spirits because existing laws prohibited whiskey making on Sunday and between sundown and sunup. The WPB lifted all of those restrictions and sweetened the deal by allowing the molasses-based industrial alcohol producers to sell distillers and rectifiers 50 percent of their August production for use in blended whiskeys.[136] Distillers received a second furlough in January 1945 even though military setbacks in late 1944 had abruptly halted reconversion to civilian production in other industries.[137]

Although the McCarran Committee blamed whiskey firms for the whiskey shortage, the culpability of consumers, retailers, and hoteliers who had hoarded whiskey by the caseload also became apparent. Shortly after officials announced the furlough in late June, "well-known brands of whiskies and gins almost miraculously reappeared in many liquor stores, not only in single bottle displays but in case lots." The big hotels began "drink[ing] down their inventories" and retailers slashed prices on California wines and low-grade whiskeys, gins, and rums as they struggled to unload goods acquired through forced tie-ins. Exuberant citizens deluged the McCarran Committee with letters of gratitude.[138]

In October 1944, OPA chief Chester Bowles announced that the liquor black market had been broken. The combined effects of the liquor holiday, higher excise taxes, tighter OPA ceiling prices, tougher liquor enforcement, and widespread expectations of additional furloughs drained whiskey of its speculative allure and discouraged further hoarding. Lawton Mackall, editor of *Esquire*'s potables column, summed up the results of the liquor holiday in a burst of staccato exclamations: "Black market boffed. Favorite brands available again—and visible. Cats and dogs being cut-rated to little more than their true worth. Bootleggers brokenhearted. Dry Martinis that taste like Dry Martinis."[139] The biggest losers—aside from the drys and bootleggers—were the retailers who now struggled to unload California wines and low-grade rums and gins acquired through forced tie-ins. As John Crimmins, an Alcoholic Beverage Control Administrator in Jefferson County, Kentucky, recalled, some retailers ultimately decided that the best way to get rid of their rum surplus was to set it on fire.[140]

CONCLUSION

Distillers emerged from the war richer in finances but poorer in reputation. In many respects World War II completed the economic reconstruction of the industry that had begun after Prohibition. The major distillers had paid off their bank loans, expanded their plant capacity, eliminated destructive price wars, and diversified their domestic and international holdings in alcoholic beverage companies. Yet, even as the major distillers consolidated their economic power, they remained vulnerable to charges of corruption and predatory practices. Despite the demise of liquor black markets toward the war's end, lingering resentment over tie-in sales and the "terrible concoctions" that commanded high prices during the war continued to fuel suspicion of the industry long after.[141] That lingering resentment partially explains why crowds greeted the war's end on V-J Day by shattering liquor store windows and ransacking their shelves. All across the country, liquor retailers "boarded up windows and doors ... to protect their supplies."[142] The crowds who pillaged liquor store shelves may have simply wanted an intoxicating beverage to toast victory, but they may have also used the occasion, as often happens in food riots, to deliberately attack retailers who had treated customers unfairly while profiting from the shortage of a prized symbolic food.[143]

During World War II the federal government involved itself in alcohol questions to a greater extent than at any other time since repeal. Conventional wisdom holds that the federal government steered clear of wet–dry controversies and limited its interest in alcohol questions to protecting vital tax revenues. The conventional wisdom is partly correct. Excess profits taxes and excise taxes more than doubled over the course of the war, making the whiskey industry a dependable cash cow for the government. The government was not about to forfeit that revenue to appease drys. A "wet" war was a better financed war.[144]

The state's vested interest in protecting a valuable cash cow from dry attacks did not invariably guarantee the industry favorable treatment. At times, the state showed a remarkable willingness to muscle the whiskey industry into submission. The Treasury Department's four-year force out plan, though ultimately rejected, attempted to tame black markets by taxing valued industry assets on terms that would have damaged whiskey makers' long-term prospects. The WPB was willing to make even bolder interventions if changing circumstances threatened military victory. In his testimony at the Senate hearings on the liquor shortage, Nelson affirmed that the WPB "would not hesitate" to reconvert "every bit" of whiskey in storage into war alcohol if the United States were ever unable to meet military requirements.[145]

Even if the federal government had wanted to divorce itself from wet–dry controversies—and the evidence on that score is decidedly mixed—market conditions made it impossible to do so. Initially, the OPA did not involve itself in policing liquor black markets or subjecting liquor to federally mandated rationing because whiskey's status as a dispensable luxury—and a morally suspect one at that—made it difficult to regulate whiskey as an everyday commodity. Ironically, the federal government's attempt to steer clear of wet–dry controversies created new, equally thorny problems to contend with. The more that citizens hoarded liquor and paid above price ceilings, the more the OPA worried that such economic behavior would spill over onto the food and clothing fronts. In other ways, however, the federal government profited from moral qualms about whiskey. Such qualms, after all, partly justified the huge gap between the relatively low federal excise taxes for wine and beer (60 cents a gallon on 14 to 21 percent wine, and 25.8 cents a gallon on beer in 1944) and the dramatically higher excise taxes for whiskey ($9 a gallon in 1944).[146]

As much as organized drys, state liquor administrators, and the liquor trade liked to frame the alcohol question as either a struggle to protect drinking freedoms or a struggle restore moral standards, many government policies boiled down to questions of military planning and material resources. Prohibitionists and the whiskey industry could put a conspiratorial spin on nearly every government decision, but practical considerations often proved more consequential. Was there enough rubber for the Normandy invasion? Did it make sense to build new grain distilling plants (to ease the burden on whiskey distillers) when metals and time were in short supply and when whiskey makers could achieve the necessary productive capacity for manufacturing industrial alcohol with a few simple changes to plant equipment?

Nevertheless, prohibitionists did correctly discern a favorable federal government bias toward the whiskey industry. The decision to grant distillers not just one but three liquor holidays offered compelling evidence that the federal government did not act as a neutral umpire on the liquor question. The Roosevelt Administration was sufficiently invested in getting liquor flowing freely again that it even encouraged another industry—the molasses-based industrial alcohol industry—to sell half of its production of neutral spirits during the liquor holidays back to distillers. The liquor holidays, timed to provide relief to whiskey drinkers before the 1944 elections, affirmed the modern Democratic Party's embrace of cosmopolitan values and its cultural heritage as the multiracial and multiethnic coalition that defeated Prohibition.

Those cosmopolitan values now included not just a right to drink but the right to "decent whiskey." Repeal had implicitly conceded that the right to drink alcohol ranked among the personal liberties protected by the constitution, but in the midst of the Great Depression other arguments—that Repeal would create jobs and end lawlessness—had carried more weight. In their quest for a liquor holiday, state liquor administrators, distillers, and the hospitality trades defended the right to drink more forcefully and forthrightly. By framing such rights in highly nationalistic terms—the industry and its allies invariably cast the right to "decent" whiskey as the right to enjoy "American" whiskey over inferior Caribbean substitutes—they also made alcohol consumption an emblem of the American standard of living. Such rights-oriented rhetoric easily harmonized with other wartime propaganda that equated the defense of American freedoms with the defense of the consumer-oriented "American way of life."[147] More than a few wartime consumers who waited out whiskey shortages or downed mysterious wartime concoctions likely imagined that a highball filled with "decent" whiskey would become a staple of their postwar future of consumer abundance.

Yet considerable ambivalence toward the whiskey industry remained. John O'Connell's call to regulate the industry as a "public utility" in the interest of protecting the consumer's right to decent whiskey perfectly captured that ambivalence. In the NYSLA chief's view, the distillers had an "obligation" to put more whiskey on the market much as other utilities, like the electric company or the water company, had an obligation to serve the public interest. O'Connell's intent to regulate the industry as a public utility expressed the widely shared distrust of distillers' commitment to good corporate citizenship. But it also acknowledged the centrality of alcohol in American life: alcohol was now as much a part of the country's basic cultural infrastructure as water and electricity were the backbones of its hard infrastructure.[148]

In a much broader sense, the liquor holidays were emblematic of the reorientation of American liberalism, in Alan Brinkley's formulation, "from a preoccupation with . . . confronting the problem of monopoly and economic disorder . . . toward a preoccupation with 'rights' (a commitment to the liberties and entitlements of individuals)."[149] Even if the New Deal's reform impulse had kicked into high gear with the formation of the OPA, by the war's end a different tenor was readily apparent.[150] Instead of asserting greater government control over whiskey supplies (as WFA-administered national rationing or the four-year force out would have done), the liquor holidays sought to maximize consumer choice by giving private enterprise the means to expand supplies. The McCarran Committee huffed and puffed about the distillers' monopolistic practices, but the major policy outcome that emerged from their recommendations was a liquor holiday to assure the consumer's right to decent whiskey. The liquor holidays delivered on the promise of a "Consumers' Republic" that increasingly prioritized freedom of consumer choice over government investments in protecting purchasing power and consumer welfare.[151] What the liquor holidays couldn't do—and what the distillers had not yet done for themselves—was to redeem the whiskey industry in public opinion.

7

Wine and Culinary Innovation on the Kitchen Front

Shortly after the United States entered World War II, Marjorie Mills, a popular radio broadcaster and food columnist, began receiving letters from women eager for advice on how to cope with wartime shortages of meats, fats, and sugar. As the women's page editor of the *Boston Herald Traveler*, Mills was soon inundated with queries from "stumped" women seeking a cookbook with "good meatless main dishes, recipes low in fat and sugar, hearty soups and chowders, and above all meals that won't take too much time to prepare." Like many other civilians, the women who wrote Mills quickly realized that the massive mobilization of food resources needed to wage total war would require wholesale changes in daily living. Urged to follow rationing guidelines, observe price ceilings, and eschew the black market, Americans changed how they thought about food and even how they fantasized about food. City dwellers, long accustomed to procuring their produce from the local grocer or supermarket, planted fruits and vegetables in their backyard, tended community gardens, and learned to can their own. Many mastered the new guidelines that taught shoppers and cooks to substitute nutritionally equivalent foods for prized rationed foods such as meat, sugar, and butter. In her new cookbook, *Cooking on a Ration: Food is Still Fun*, Mills delivered her answer to home cooks who found themselves pressed for time but still yearning for gastronomic pleasure. Promising readers that wartime food could still satisfy families even without "whipping cream, pounds of butter, sirloin steaks and rib roasts," Mills encouraged home cooks to use savory seasonings, herbs and "good domestic wines" to achieve "brilliant camouflage and enticement."[1]

American vintners were surely pleased that Mills elevated wine—and good American wines at that—as the "brilliant camouflage" or secret sauce that would make less desirable meats and meatless dishes taste delectable. It amplified the message that wine promoters were sending through recipe booklets, in-store display cards, and magazine advertisements. Winemakers hoped that the changing wartime food landscape would inspire wartime eaters to cook with wine and drink it with meals. In some cases, food shortages and food controls did inspire culinary innovation. Egged on by cookbook authors, food trade associations, and government bulletins, many household cooks and eaters experimented with unfamiliar foods and invented new recipes to enliven leftovers and use foods in plentiful supply. Wine promoters, however, repeatedly butted up against a competing consumer impulse: the desire to cling to familiar foods that provided comfort and reassurance in turbulent times. Just as tea deepened its hold on drinkers throughout the British empire, Coca-Cola expanded its market reach and allure by appealing directly to wartime yearnings for the familiar.[2]

Of all the alcoholic beverages sold domestically, wine made in the United States faced the most daunting marketing challenge and the greatest potential for cultural reinvention. Backed by their new collectively funded advertising campaign and the deep pockets of the distillers who had recently acquired California's largest wineries, California vintners now had the means to bring their message to a national audience. Consumers encountered wine advertising on outdoor billboards, in glossy magazines, and on radio variety programs.[3] Restaurateurs, home economists, food writers, and novelists—many of them echoing the wine industry's own promotional materials—rounded out the wine propaganda machine. By 1942, US vintners also faced a less crowded field of competitors. The war had halted whiskey production and dramatically slowed the importation of European wines. Even the supply of homemade wine—long a source of frustration for the wine industry—began to dry up thanks to the military's requisitioning of raisin grapes for soldiers' K rations and government restrictions on the transportation of California grapes to East Coast home winemakers.[4]

Despite these considerable advantages, wine promoters struggled to get American consumers to buy US wines. Instead of greeting wine as an enticing novelty, many white Americans continued to view wine as a stigmatized foreign beverage. As *Wines and Vines* explained in 1941,

Americans typically associated wine with "luxurious living—or something that people from the old country mistakenly believed 'good for the blood and good for the appetite.' . . . One was beyond the purse . . . of the Smith and Jones families, the other disdained with slight contempt."[5] World War II created new opportunities for wine marketers to deepen wine's roots in American culture and demonstrate wine's value to the war effort. Championing wine as the secret ingredient that could tenderize cheap cuts of meat and redeem low-ration point dishes, wine advertising and recipe booklets promised to help homemakers fulfill their duties on the Kitchen Front.

Patriotic appeals, however, were only part of the cultural work wine promoters undertook to divest wine of its associations with foreignness and earn wine a welcome place in American restaurants and homes. As detailed in chapter 3, wine promoters had initially attempted to enhance wine's respectability by instructing readers about proper serving glasses and serving temperatures and proper food and wine pairings. When these highbrow approaches backfired in the mid-to-late 1930s, trade associations, cookbook authors, and restaurateurs approached wine promotion as a kind of Americanization campaign. Seeking to divest wine of both its highbrow and lowbrow associations, wine promoters found new ways to align wine with symbolically American foods and the more dominant American culture of enjoying cocktails before dinner. They set their sights, as one hotel manager put it, not on the upper crust who ordered Chateaubriand, but on the average customers who ordered "Shrimp Cocktail or Tomato Juice, . . . Steak and French Fried Potatoes—Chicken or Turkey—a piece of pie and a cup of coffee."[6]

These more populist approaches grasped what anthropologists have long known: that acquiring a taste for unfamiliar foods—especially foods with foreign origins—often involves a process of refashioning their uses, forms, and meanings in ways that echo and subtly modify preexisting food and dining practices. As recent scholarship attests, acquiring a taste for foreign foods may not even require the experience of sensual pleasure if the *social* pleasures associated with certain foods and beverages override their perceived sensual deficits.[7]

As much as this chapter is a story about the cultural reinvention and "Americanization" of wine, it also contributes to a larger story about how wars compel societies and entire industries to adapt to widescale disruptions in the global food supply. We know much about how governments, nutrition scientists, and home economists encouraged civilians to view food as a tool for maximizing nutrition, fitness, and stamina, but much less about how wartime food controls transformed the ways states and civilians thought about pleasure.[8] As this chapter demonstrates, a network of wine publicists that included American winemakers, trade associations, food and drink columnists, cookbook authors, and home economists worked in concert to promote gastronomic pleasure and conviviality as the defining features of a good meal. Their varied approaches to selling wine reflected the contradictory impulses that shaped wartime visions of the good life. Consumers desired familiar comforts but also yearned for novel tastes; they valued the affordability of mass-produced foods but also prized the romance of the artisanal; and they sought convenient remedies to monotonous wartime diets while sometimes grasping for a taste of the gourmet. Wine promoters navigated all of these competing consumer desires while working to convince women that wine could both ease and enliven their wartime duties on the Kitchen Front.

LAUNCHING THE "WINE DRIVE FOR AMERICA"

In the summer and fall of 1939, as the storm clouds of war gathered over Europe, California vintners unveiled their collectively funded wine marketing campaign. Since California vintners produced 90 percent of the nation's wine, it made sense that the Golden State's winegrowers (rather than those in Ohio and New York) would use their funds to focus a national spotlight on wines. The Wine Advisory Board (WAB), a fifteen-member panel appointed by California's director of agriculture and chaired by winemaker Herman Wente, oversaw the vintners' "Wine Drive for America." They enlisted Wine Institute staff and the J. Walter Thompson advertising agency to develop the campaign. Although the initial outlay of $2 million was quite modest next to the $7.5 million brewers spent on advertising in 1939 and the $16.5 million spent by distillers, the campaign's scope and ambition was impressive. Advertisements for California wine appeared on billboards and in monthly mass magazines such as *Life, Collier's, Red Book*, and *Cosmopolitan*. A wide array of supplementary promotional materials—educational pamphlets, menu stickers, restaurant table cards, and recipe booklets—maximized wine's visibility in restaurants, grocery stores, and liquor shops.[9] In 1941 alone, wine retailers distributed 6 million wine recipe booklets and the WAB received requests from some 26,770 women for copies of its *Wine Cook Book*.[10]

The WAB's efforts to elevate wine's public image went hand in hand with a parallel campaign to elevate the public image of vintners themselves. As the campaign's launch date approached, leaders in the Wine Institute and the WAB goaded winegrowers to become more effective public ambassadors for wine. Aware that some industry members preferred whiskey to wine, Wente exhorted wine men to "Drink wine with your meals at home. Order it at restaurants," and "Entertain with wine in your homes." If restaurants didn't carry wine, Wente continued, "insist that they put it in" and "see that your friends entertain with wine."[11] Aiming to mold Central Valley's growers into country gentlemen, Leon Adams, the Wine Institute's chief publicity director, staged a black-tie champagne ball in Fresno for the growers and their wives and ghostwrote wine-friendly speeches for them to deliver at Kiwanis Club and Rotary Club luncheons.[12] If one of the campaign's aims was to glamorize wine, it made sense, in Adams's view, to glamorize the winegrowers themselves—enough that they might net an invitation to speak at white, male service clubs.

The "Wine Drive for America" sought to elevate wine's respectability while normalizing its place in the American consumer landscape. Wine menu stickers and table cards suggesting wine with dinner greeted restaurant diners. WAB broadsides and window streamers lured shoppers into liquor stores, where shoppers found WAB recipe leaflets for hot spiced wine and summer wine coolers made with seltzer water, fruit, sugar, and ice. Display cards pitched wine as the beverage of hospitality: "Guests Tonight? Let us help you select from our assortment of fine Wines of California." Outdoor billboards called out to summer travelers enjoying road trips to the New York World's Fair and the Golden Gate International Exposition in San Francisco.[13] Picturing scenic California vineyards with thirst-quenching wine coolers in the foreground, the billboards urged travelers to "Beat the Heat with California Coolers."[14]

California's vintners attracted big crowds at the San Francisco world's fair when hundreds of curious fairgoers ventured to the Wine Temple to watch the wine industry's weekly cooking demonstrations. Lured by the promise of a free wine cooler, many visitors learned new tricks of the culinary trade from famed chefs and home economists. Fairgoers learned how to make the classic Italian dessert, Zabaione (a sweet-wine based custard), and the French dessert Pruneaux au Vin (red-wine spiced prunes). Chef George Mardikian, the owner of three Omar Khayyam's Armenian-American restaurants in California, taught an overflowing crowd how to prepare Haigagan Kebab (lamb cooked in sherry). Some of the recipes demonstrated in the Wine Temple emerged from partnerships between the wine industry and other food manufacturers. Home economist Ann Welcome, working on behalf of the Golden State's vintners and prune growers, demonstrated recipes for prune wine cake and prune pie with Sherried whipped cream. Martha Lee, a home economist on the payroll of Standard Brands (the makers of Royal Gelatin), showcased recipes for wine gelatin, wine jelly, and baked ham with wine sauce. The cooking demonstrations in the Wine Temple asked fairgoers to take a leap of faith that wine could transform ordinary mass-produced industrial foods into dishes with all the "subtle flavorings" Americans had come to expect from restaurant meals. Rather than presenting wine cookery as a gourmet alternative to industrial foods, the demonstrations found a culinary middle ground that embraced both the familiarity of American convenience foods and the cosmopolitan allure of the gourmet.[15]

The title of the vintner's "Wine Drive for America" campaign announced their intention to raise the nation's wine consciousness while stripping wine of its perceived foreignness. From a pure marketing standpoint, however, American winemakers concluded that some aspects of wine's foreignness were worth preserving. Instead of giving their wines American place names and varietal designations, they stubbornly clung to the practice of borrowing European appellations (Burgundy, Rhine, Chablis, Port, Sherry). Much to the dismay of European winemakers, who resented Americans' usurpations of their prized appellations, winemakers in California and New York long resisted adopting American regional and varietal designations because they regarded the European names as "generic" and were reluctant to sacrifice the Old World cachet that such names commanded.[16] Rather than attributing wine's foreignness to its Europeanness, the Wine Institute and the WAB sought to reclaim wine's Americanness by identifying connoisseurship as an elitist affectation foreign not just to most Americans but also to most European wine drinkers. To demystify wine and broaden its appeal, the Wine Institute embraced a populist culinary discourse that encouraged American consumers to follow the dictates of their own tastes. A short quiz that appeared in display cards created by the WAB encouraged American consumers to "make your own rules":

> Q—What is the best wine? A—The wine *you* like best.
> Q—What wines with what foods? A—Any wine *you* like best.
> Q—What glasses for wine? A—Any kind of glass *you* happen to have.
> Q—Serve at what temperatures? A—Serve any wine the way *you* like it—that's the *right* temperature for *you*.[17]

Assuring consumers that "the best wine drinkers of Europe" eschewed fancy wine rules, the quiz promised that nobody would "slap you on the wrist" for enjoying "red wine with fish or white wine with red meat."[18] Such rhetoric cast the wine populists as the true inheritors of the European tradition—one centered not on the stuffy rituals of Continental etiquette but on the simple pleasures of drinking wine with meals.

The Wine Institute also struck a populist note in the press releases and publicity materials it distributed to journalists and magazine writers. *Nation's Business* reported that "American vintners don't care whether the stuff they sell is sipped from thin stemmed goblets . . . or quaffed from paper cups at high noon."[19] If Americans preferred to drink red and white wine at the ice-cold temperature they liked to have their sodas and cocktails served, so be it.[20] Home economist Mary Frost Mabon and the author of *ABC of American Wines* issued much the same advice to the women readers of *Harper's Bazaar:* "Your own palate is the final infallible criterion."[21] Making wine less complicated also allowed California vintners to present their wines as equal to, or even superior to European wines. The WAB's *Wine Cook Book* suggested that consumers need not trouble themselves with knowledge of "vintage years" because every year in sunny California was a vintage year. While European winemakers needed to "mark the every-so-often good vintages . . . when the grapes thrive," California's "uniform climate" produced "luscious [grapes] *every* year" and good wine "year in and year out."[22]

Even *Esquire* magazine's witty potables columnist, Lawton Mackall— a restaurant critic, gastronomy expert, and unofficial ally of the California wine industry—affirmed that individual taste preferences trumped the standard wine conventions. He informed his predominantly white, upper-middle-class male readers that drinkers "throughout our thirsty land" were "ousting oppression and setting up gullet government by consent of the taste buds." Men could indulge their fondness for sweet wines, Mackall assured, without jeopardizing their masculinity or white racial respectability. Mackall's proposed "Covenant of the Better World League for Flavor Freedom and Felicity of Refreshment" promised to administer a "swift kick . . . to any blahster feigning superiority by belittling sweetness in beverages where it belongs . . . If you are a sweet-toother wine lover, go ahead and have your fun, even with rare roast beef, Burgundy's playmate." The aspiring sophisticates who read Mackall's column would still know that Burgundy was the conventional choice, but if sherry, port, or something sweeter pleased their senses, Mackall would not shame them.²³ For men who knew the rules, flouting the rules was merely an assertion of masculine culinary independence.

Pushing wine populism too far, however, risked alienating potential wine drinkers. Most housewives, home economist Dorothy Rankin argued, needed basic guideposts to make them comfortable trying something new. "Rules, recipes, directions, are part and parcel of a woman's life. Set her adrift without them and she will pass the whole thing up rather than take a chance on making a mistake."²⁴ Rankin's skepticism of the industry's populist appeals underscores the difficult task that vintners faced in appealing to varied taste communities. Vintners sought to broaden wine's appeal by drawing upon a democratic culinary discourse that rejected "arbitrary standards of distinction based on a single, elite French notion of culture."²⁵ Rankin, however, believed that the consumers most inclined to break elite wine drinking rules were those already in the know. For the aspiring middlebrow consumer who lacked such cultural capital, mastering a few simple rules may have made wine both more alluring and more accessible.

As Rankin's concerns revealed, wine promoters often struggled to find the right balance between appealing to consumers' distaste for fussy rituals and their yearnings for respectability. Food writer Jeanne Owen, who authored *A Wine Lover's Cook Book* in 1940, assured the upper-middle-class readers of *House Beautiful* that the "chi chi" wine rituals of the past "[had] all gone by the board," even as she recommended serving plain jug wine in fashionable decanters that had returned to "the best dining rooms."²⁶ In Owen's view, even ordinary jug wine merited the ceremonial niceties of an elegant glass decanter. Nowhere was the effort to merge populist rhetoric with appeals to genteel respectability more clumsily executed than in magazine ads the WAB placed in *Life, Colliers, Liberty, American, Red Book*, and *Cosmopolitan* between 1939 and 1941. J. Walter Thompson, the ad agency handling the WAB account, recruited famed athletes, Hollywood celebrities, and luminaries in arts and letters to endorse wine as the beverage for "busy, active people" who like to enjoy "genial, leisurely evenings" without overindulging.²⁷ Following the longstanding practice of using society women and celebrity endorsers to sell products that had not yet come into wide acceptance, J. Walter Thompson assembled an impressive roster: golfer Lawson Little, baseball hall of famer Ty Cobb, author John Steinbeck, painter Norman Rockwell, actress Lynn Fontaine, radio host Gabriel Heatter, photographer Margaret Bourke-White, and sportswriter Grantland Rice. In some cases, the fashionable wives of renowned actors (Mrs. Basil Rathbone), poets (Mrs. Ogden Nash) and writers (Mrs. Edgar Rice Burroughs) stood in for their more famous spouses.[28]

By using prominent Americans to vouch for wine—as Mrs. Edgar Rice Burroughs did when she claimed that "so many of my guests now choose wine" because they prefer "not to overdo when they relax"— J. Walter Thompson imagined that the ad campaign would "appeal to families of every income group."[29] But in a country slowly emerging from the Depression, the image of Mrs. Basil Rathbone entertaining elegantly dressed guests seated at a lavishly appointed table in her Bel Air, California, home—to say nothing of the uniformed white maid pouring their wine—did little to divest wine of its associations with luxurious living (see Figure 19).[30] J. Walter Thompson likely calculated that it was more important to first disentangle wine from its lowbrow associations with southern and eastern European immigrants and indigent "winos." Situating wine in refined domestic interiors—the settings that etiquette books had long viewed as emblems of whiteness and middle-class respectability—was one way to do that.[31]

Not all of the WAB's celebrity endorsers reinforced wine's highbrow image. One in particular—the baseball great Ty Cobb—fulfilled the symbolic function of both elevating and democratizing wine. Though better known for his hot temper, aggressive playing style, and penchant for profanity, Ty Cobb exuded cosmopolitan sophistication in his role as a wine pitchman (see Figure 20). Photographed wearing a three-piece suit and serving Sherry to male guests in his tastefully decorated living room, the wine-loving Cobb may have struck some ad readers as a genteel pretender. Others might have concluded that wine could confer genteel respectability on the unlikeliest suspects. Noting that Cobb enjoyed hunting and fishing as well as good food, the ad may have helped others see wine drinking as more manly and more American. In his guise as a wine endorser Cobb exemplified the new ideals of middle-class masculinity, championed by *Esquire Magazine*, that valorized male connoisseurship in food and drink and the hedonistic pursuit of these and other bodily pleasures.[32] The choice of such a masculine spokesman to sell California sherry, a drink more commonly associated with female tastes, was likely no accident. The Ty Cobb ad inspired Lansing McCurley, a sportswriter for the Philadelphia *Daily News*, to devote a third of his column to other star athletes like race car driver Ralph De Palma and world featherweight boxing champion Benny Bass who also regularly drank wine with meals. Federal regulations barred

FIGURE 19. Magazine advertisement from the Wine Advisory Board's campaign to promote California wines, 1939. Author's collection.

FIGURE 20. Magazine advertisement from the Wine Advisory Board's campaign to promote California wines, 1940. Author's collection.

winemakers from touting wine's potential health benefits in their ads, but they were surely pleased to have sports columnists do that work for them.³³

AMERICANIZING WINING AND DINING

The Wine Institute and WAB recognized the crucial role that American restaurateurs could play in developing the market for American wines, but many restaurateurs had to be convinced that American wines merited a place on their menus. Although wine could have harmonized well with typical American restaurant dishes—broiled steak and lamb chops, roast chicken, fries and mashed potatoes, canned peas or frozen vegetables—many Americans contentedly paired the "tasteless, colorless" fare, as novelist John Steinbeck (a WAB wine endorser) described it, with coffee and soda.³⁴ Apart from restaurant goers in San Francisco, New York, New Orleans and other great food cities that boasted Wine and Food Societies, "interest in fine dining" faded after repeal, even among the upper class.³⁵ Americans' strong preference for whiskey and spirits-based cocktails also dampened restaurant wine sales. Even among groups who wine promoters imagined as promising prospects, the preference for liquor was overwhelming. The Hotel Carlyle in New York City recommended fine sherries to women guests, but most stuck by their preferred cocktails: dry Martinis, Scotch highballs, and Old Fashioneds.³⁶ Many restaurateurs preferred the higher immediate profits on liquor sales to the less certain long-term gains from teaching diners to enjoy wine with meals.³⁷ Some even credited pre-dinner cocktails for stimulating a taste for luxury and greater spending in the dining room. According to D. T. Touhig, who headed the liquor department at Child's restaurant, "a beef stew might satisfy a customer who hadn't ordered a cocktail," but "only a charcoal-broiled steak on a dinner complete from soup to demitasse will satisfy a customer who has whetted his appetite with a Manhattan or a Martini."³⁸

In the 1930s and 1940s, American restaurateurs pursued a variety of strategies to boost sales of American wine. Some picked up the populist baton and turned the Depression-era backlash against pretentious wine rituals to their advantage by casting connoisseurs as "un-American" snobs who favored expensive European wines over their humbler American counterparts. Although imported wines never constituted more than 5 percent of the US wine market in the 1930s, thanks to a hefty protective tariff of $1.25 on each gallon, imported wines, especially those from France and Italy, enjoyed far greater prominence on upscale restaurant menus than American wines.[39] In a column for *Restaurant Management*, Mrs. J. Molera, the wine manager for the Edgewater Beach Hotel in Chicago, called upon waitstaff to proudly recommend American wines. Though admittedly not "GREAT wines," American wines, Molera insisted, were better suited to the simple American restaurant fare of chicken or "Steak and French Fried Potatoes." Molera applauded the patriotic loyalty and populist virtue of diners who opted to "DRINK AMERICAN" and "BUY AMERICAN." To insist on drinking only imported wines, Molera contended, "would be like telling people that they . . . should hear only the works of great composers."[40] Molera's efforts to Americanize winning and dining shared the same democratizing impulses that enabled middle-class consumers in the late nineteenth and early twentieth centuries to transform dining out from the exclusive privilege of the wealthy into a common middle-class pastime. As historian Andrew Haley has shown, middle-class diners "challenged nineteenth-century elite ideas that French cuisine was the only cuisine of merit" and pressured restaurateurs to abandon ostentatious multicourse dinners, simplify menus, and lower prices.[41]

Other restaurateurs discovered that they could sell more wine (regardless of its national origin) by allowing wine to ride the cocktail's coattails into the dining room. Some even designed menus and wine tips specifically with the cocktail-drinking set in mind. Frederick Anderson's "Wining and Dining" column in *Restaurant Management* recommended that menus offer wine recommendations based on the types of cocktails patrons ordered before dinner. Diners who had already consumed "several cocktails," Anderson noted, would greatly appreciate a note on the menu suggesting, "If you have had an Old-Fashioned you'll enjoy a bottle of Moselle with dinner . . . This could be carried further with suggestions for wines that are friendly to Martinis and Manhattans." Although Anderson conceived such menu notes as "merely another way of bringing wine to people's attention," they also underscored wine's subordinate status within the hierarchy of alcoholic beverages. In Anderson's view, wine best served restaurants' bottom line as an adjunct to cocktails. Rather than bother patrons with tips on wine and food pairings, Anderson offered tips on which wines paired best with which liquors.[42]

In the short run, the most important contest for American wine's supremacy on the restaurant dining table was not the battle between wine and cocktails or even the battle between American wines and European imports. Wine's real enemies, *American Restaurant Management* proclaimed, were "the coffee pot and the water tap." To combat coffee's dominance as a mealtime beverage, some restaurateurs endeavored to make wine and coffee culturally and economically equivalent. "The 400" on Fifth Avenue in New York City priced wine by the glass because that "unit of sale ... match[ed] coffee by the cup."[43] Ted's Grill in Santa Monica sold wine and coffee for the same price.[44] Similarly, some restaurateurs added wine to the standard list of options (alongside coffee, tea and milk) on the table d'hôte menu.[45] Restaurants also elevated wine's mealtime presence by restaging the dining table. The Wine Advisory Board encouraged restaurateurs to set their tables with wine glasses (in addition to the customary water glasses or coffee cups) and place an "unopened half bottle of wine on each table," with a bottle topper saying, "Ask your waiter to serve this bottle."[46] By claiming a place on the table, where customers ordinarily encountered condiments and seasonings, the wine glasses and the unopened wine bottle symbolically affirmed wine's mealtime role as a complement to the food on the plate.

For some wine promoters, the goal was not just to situate wine next to the condiments but to get consumers to think of wine itself as a condiment or sauce that improved their entire sensory experience of the meal. As Harry Caddow, the Wine Institute's secretary-manager, explained in *Wines and Vines*, wine added flavor to the meal much as "ketchup and other bottled sauces" did, but instead of pouring bottled condiments on the food, diners consumed wine as "a delicious sauce ... taken by the glass." For wine to serve its "sauce-function" and its lightly intoxicating one, too, Caddow concluded that restaurants had to offer enough wine to satisfy customers' sense of gustatory taste as well as their yearnings for "laughter and relaxation." Caddow determined that a six-ounce split bottle was the ideal size for a neophyte wine drinker—small enough to invite sampling but big enough to deliver bodily pleasure and allow wine's "sauce-function" to last through the entire meal. Anything smaller would fail to deliver the multilayered sensory experience that might convert wine neophytes into regular wine drinkers.[47]

All of these pricing, bottle sizing, and table setting strategies aimed to entice consumers with the promise of a novelty while also easing their apprehensions about wine's foreignness. As historians and anthropologists have demonstrated, most peoples around the globe rarely adopt new food tastes wholesale. In the United States, native-born Americans embraced Americanized versions of foreign foods that toned down the spicing, added the new flavors "as 'sauces' for their still-familiar 'core' foods," and "domesticated [the new foods] with familiar markers such as ketchup or mustard."[48] Similarly, Britons transformed Indian curry into British food by reimagining it as a "gravy" for high-status metropolitan foods like beef, shrimp, and lobster.[49] Wine merchandising in the United States attempted to erase wine's foreignness by hyping wine as a base for cocktails, setting the wine bottle alongside the bottled condiments, and offering customers a choice of wine, coffee, tea, or milk on the fixed-price menus. These varied ways of modifying and recontextualizing foreign foods reflected the competing impulses that often guide food choices: the desire for variety and the exotic, on the one hand, and the desire "for the reassuringly familiar" on the other.[50] What native-born American restaurant goers wanted, historian Audrey Russek has written, was "a kind of packaged authenticity, a cultural reproduction that was different enough to feel foreign, but familiar enough to be non-threatening."[51] Wine merchandising attempted to do just that.

These merchandising innovations ultimately succeeded more in getting wine a place at the table than in promoting the temperate wine-centered drinking culture championed by drinking reformers. Increasingly, the American tradition of wining and dining came to mean cocktails before wines with dinner. Although several gourmet dining societies prohibited cocktails before dinner in deference to their ideal of temperate civilized dining, by the early 1940s even *Gourmet* magazine, which relied heavily on whiskey advertising revenues, had "reshaped gourmet dining to accommodate Americans' liking for the cocktail" and "publish[ed] equal numbers of articles on wine and cocktails."[52] Tourist guidebooks also affirmed the marriage of wine and cocktails in fine dining establishments. In her 1939 guide to New York, written for the "woman vacationist," Marjorie Hillis mentioned wine only once in the chapter on "Cocktails, Dinner, and No Escort" when describing a lavish "gourmet" meal enjoyed by two female diners at the French restaurant Lafayette. Starting with dry Martinis, "unsurpassed for stimulating the appetite," the diners next ate clear consommé with a dry sherry, then for the main course enjoyed grilled pompano, new potatoes, and peas with a Pouilly Fuisse 1929, followed by salad and cheese, and Pot au Crème for dessert, with coffee.[53] Stretched over a leisurely meal, the Dry Martini, glass of sherry, and bottle of wine for two may not have left the diners three sheets to the wind, but it certainly put the culture of moderation to the test.

WINE COOKERY ON THE KITCHEN FRONT

The wartime disruptions to established food traditions and popular recreations created new opportunities for vintners to make wine drinking both more respectable and more accessible. Wine promoters hoped the war would advance the industry's long-term objective of persuading Americans to view wine as many Europeans did: as a daily part of "eating," rather than "an occasional part of dining."[54] Such hopes rested in part on the expectation that home cooks would seek new foods and beverages to fill the cultural and gastronomical voids created by the rationing of meat, sugar, butter, and coffee and shortages of other prized foods. Some California vintners even fantasized that the wine glass would displace the coffee cup at the dinner table as coffee rationing compelled Americans to seek an alternative to a favored dinnertime beverage.[55] American vintners also anticipated that disruptions in the global supply of alcoholic beverages would redound to their advantage. Thanks to the wartime shortages of whiskey and dramatically reduced shipments of European wine, California vintners had fewer competitors in the alcoholic beverages market. As early as 1940, when the number of European wine imports precipitously dropped, Napa Valley's quality winemakers began to see increased purchases of their wines in Boston, New York, and Chicago.[56]

Though not by deliberate design, the government's newly instituted food and price controls particularly advantaged California's table wine producers. The perpetual surplus of raisin grapes that had plagued the California wine industry since the 1930s ended when the federal government requisitioned the entire crop for the Allied military forces. Instead of landing in the same crushers as the higher quality wine grapes, the nutrient-dense raisin crop landed in soldiers' K rations. Table wines benefitted the most from the market fallout of the government's raisin grape restrictions. Not only did the absence of raisin grapes improve their quality, but it also cut the supply of dessert wine nearly in half, prompting consumers who had long favored dessert wines to give table wines a try.[57] The tighter wartime grape market also shrank the semi-licit market for wine.[58] By 1943 the production of so-called "basement" wines from California grapes had declined from an estimated 20 to 30 million gallons per year in the 1930s to 9.5 million gallons. Although home production rose to 19.5 million gallons in 1944 when the government relaxed "wartime restrictions on refrigerator cars, shipping containers, and price ceilings," even the 1944 high was substantially lower than the prewar peak.⁵⁹ Finally, government price controls provided yet another inducement to improve wine quality, as vintners could reap the maximum set price only by aging their wines longer.⁶⁰

Not all was clear sailing for California vintners. Vintners also had to contend with the wartime resurgence of prohibitionism. In keeping with the public relations strategy of the brewers and distillers, American vintners seized the mantle of patriotism and touted the industry's contributions to the war effort. They stressed wine's value as a revenue generator and morale booster, hailing wine in one ad as "one of the better ways" to "ease up and . . . to keep up good morale and good cheer."⁶¹ Vintners also publicized the industry's production of crucial matériel for the military's ground and airborne operations. Tartrates, a byproduct of winemaking, facilitated the production of rayon, a synthetic fiber used to make parachutes and tents. California's brandy makers reconfigured their distilling equipment to make industrial alcohol for the synthetic rubber program and they supplied the military with enough real brandy to outfit the emergency kits of pilots, navigators, and bombardiers.⁶² Whether officers used the brandy to steel nerves, relieve boredom, alleviate pain, or treat wounds in a pinch, the fighters in the sky had brandy on hand to meet the war's daily demands.

In their marketing and promotional materials, vintners found additional ways to burnish their patriotism while simultaneously selling more wine. Much as the brewers had linked brewers' yeast to wartime food crusades, California vintners aligned wine with the government's Food Fights for Freedom campaign. While the brewers promised to fortify the nation nutritionally (with vitamin B-boosting brewers' yeast), vintners promised to fortify consumers' compliance with food rationing and food conservation by teaching home cooks how cooking with wine could enliven drab wartime dishes. Strengthening the link between wine and food was also good wartime politics. Early in the war, uncertainty about how the government would define and regulate luxury goods prompted vintners to reinvigorate their efforts to establish wine as a "grocery item." They did so partly out of fear that government regulation of luxury goods might eventually "force out the liquor stores" and partly because women were more likely to buy wine from a grocery store than a liquor store.⁶³ Vintners were especially keen to curry favor with women since they comprised the majority of the wartime electorate, giving them more sway in local option elections.⁶⁴

For most women on the home front, more help in the kitchen was precisely what they needed. A constant drumbeat of government propaganda on the radio and in film and print media encouraged women to do their bit for the war effort by assuming a host of new responsibilities. The government encouraged women to help the men at the front by taking their place in defense factories and conserving meat, sugar, and butter—foods essential to protecting servicemen's morale and stamina. To guard against inflation and guarantee fair shares for all (including United States allies abroad), the government asked Americans to avoid food waste, adhere to rationing guidelines, pay no more than price ceilings, and starve the black market. Eating the right foods with the right nutrients also became an obligation of wartime citizenship. The government's new Basic 7 dietary guidelines urged all Americans to consume vitamin-packed "protective" foods from each of the seven categories to preserve the health and good spirits of civilians and defense workers. In the eyes of nutritionists and cookbook authors, achieving these goals made the job of preparing attractive, nutritionally balanced meals women's most important wartime defense work.[65]

Many wartime recipe writers were less interested in introducing home cooks to novel taste sensations than in teaching them how to stretch their sugar and meat rations while making sure meals met the recommended daily allowances of vitamins, minerals, and macronutrients. The mostly Anglo-American-inspired recipes collected in the *Ladies' Home Journal's Wartime Homemaking Manual* flavored savory dishes with bacon fat, meat drippings, onions, and modest sprinklings of salt, but said nary a word about the flavor-enhancing potential of wine (to say nothing of garlic and herbs).[66] Nor did wine appear in the *Victory Meat Extenders* recipe pamphlet produced by the National Live Stock and Meat Board. Perhaps fearing that recipes for wine-infused meats might offend teetotalers, the meat trade association stuck to politically and gastronomically neutral territory, recommending that cooks use water to braise, stew, and pot roast meats. Some recipes added tomatoes or vinegar to the cooking liquid, but wine was conspicuously absent.[67]

Although far from a ubiquitous presence in wartime food culture, wine cookery danced its way into the imaginations of cookbook authors, food writers, and the newly founded *Gourmet* magazine, whose first issue in 1941 urged readers to treat "the expected wartime shortage of European wines" as an opportunity "to experiment with American wines."[68] Most of the new wartime cookbooks were not nearly as wine-centered as the recipes found in *Gourmet* magazine and the wartime reissue of *The Original Picayune Creole Cook Book*, which restored all the recipes using wines and liquors from the pre-Prohibition editions of the popular cookbook. A compendium of New Orleans cuisine that blended the culinary traditions of France, Spain, Africa, and the New World, the *Picayune Creole Cook Book* featured recipes created and adapted by enslaved and free Black women. Unlike other wartime cookbooks, the *Picayune Creole Cook Book* made no apologies for dishes that incorporated animal organs and unusual proteins.[69] The revised 1941 issue of Cora, Rose, and Bob Brown's *The Wine Cook Book* (originally published after repeal) similarly emphasized wine cookery's exotic racial and geographic origins, touting recipes for "almost every conceivable" wine-infused dish "from the village kitchens of France, from the archives of famous inns, from Dinahs and Sams in our own epicurean South, from the Far East and the Near."[70]

While the Louisianan authors of the *Picayune Cook Book* and *The Wine Cook Book* presumed an audience largely presold on the benefits of cooking with wine, Ted Hatch's *The American Wine Cookbook*, published in 1941, set out to convince the uninitiated that wine cookery was neither "too difficult for the ordinary homemaker" nor "too expensive." In fact, Hatch claimed, readers would discover that it was "*easier to cook with wine than without it.*" Yet, even as Hatch rejected the American tendency to associate wine with luxury—insisting that "the humblest European peasant . . . uses wine as matter-of-factly as we use sugar or butter"—he also created a new kind of wine connoisseurship: one centered not on mastery of vintages and "Chateau" bottlings but on knowledge of wine's multiple uses in flavoring food. Noting that wine's "*natural* flavor" varied from both its "*cooked* flavor" and its "*simmered* flavor," Hatch invited his readers to develop their palates and raise their "favorite recipes . . . to new heights with . . . just a touch of wine."[71] Hatch treated his readers to plenty of French- and Creole-inspired dishes, but the four separate recipes for barbecue sauce (quadruple the number in the other wine cookbooks) underscored the Americanness of his *American Wine Cook Book*.

While *Gourmet* and the other wine-centric cookbooks set their sights on upper-middle-class readers with time and money to spare, the Wine Advisory Board and other cookbook authors and food writers aimed for a more popular audience. Offering a distinct alternative to the nutrition-centric (and often bland) Anglo-American diet, this more populist set of wine promoters promised gastronomic pleasure without the fuss or the expense. Mary Taylor's *Economy for Epicures: A Practical Menu and Recipe Book* sang wine's praises as a "subtle and potent" flavoring agent. Acknowledging that Americans were not "a wine-drinking people,"

Taylor assured her readers that American wines would add distinction to their dishes at a more affordable price than the bottled sauces Americans "habitually" used to season food.[72] Taylor's pitch echoed the California wine industry's: American wine was good, inexpensive, and as trustworthy a flavor booster as the customary condiments Americans set on the table. As Marjorie Mills, the author of *Cooking on a Ration*, had discovered from the hundreds of "stumped" women who wrote her seeking cooking advice, the wartime appetite for advice on how to prepare pleasurable meals without scarce meats, fats, and creams was real.[73]

Like *Economy for Epicures* and *Cooking on a Ration*, the Wine Advisory Board and other wartime food writers stressed that glamorizing dishes with wine did not require a huge investment of time, a big budget, or mastery of the art of French cooking.[74] The WAB's *Hostess Book of Favorite Wine Recipes* made a direct play for busy wage-earning women and "kitchenette cooks" who needed to pull a meal together at a moment's notice using the ingredients at hand.[75] Promising extraordinary results for ordinary cooks, the WAB also presented wine as an ally in the government's mission to discourage food waste and recycle leftovers.[76] According to the WAB's *Hostess Book of Favorite Wine Recipes*, "a few spoonfuls of California Wine" could invigorate "thrift dishes" and a Burgundy marinade could transform cheaper, tough cuts of meat into tender delights.[77] The WAB's full-color advertisements in middle-class magazines similarly pledged that wine would "[do] wonders for wartime foods." Brief recipes appeared alongside mouth-watering photographs of such dishes as Spaghetti Baked with Burgundy, Macaroni Stuffed Peppers with White Wine, and Meatloaf flavored with red wine. While most ads featured dishes that centered on pasta, fish, and other unrationed proteins, the WAB also suggested that wine marinades could amplify the pleasure of special occasions, when consumers had "saved up the 'points' to set out a tempting" roasted leg of lamb.[78] Invariably, the ads also reminded cooks and diners to enjoy a glass of wine with their wine-infused stews and casseroles.

The Wine Advisory Board leaned heavily on the wine cookery angle because it addressed a central marketing challenge—women's reluctance to purchase a bottle that might not be finished the same evening—while simultaneously positioning wine as a valiant ally in the nation's Food Fights for Freedom campaign. Writing for *Wines and Vines*, home economist Mary Frost Mabon informed vintners that women could be persuaded to buy more wine if they understood that unused wine (even wine that had already soured) could tenderize cheaper cuts of meat and transform leftovers into inspired new creations.[79] Vintners also touted wine cookery as the solution to one of the government's most challenging food problems: getting Americans to purchase and consume less desirable meats and protein substitutes. Americans had long associated organ meats and other animal parts—pigs' feet, oxtails, ham hocks—with the food of the poor and the cuisine that African Americans had created during slavery and later embraced as "soul food."[80] During World War II, foods that many Americans had previously viewed as inedible discards filled part of the protein gap created by the military's hefty consumption of red meat. Sixty percent of the choice cuts of beef went to the military. Government bulletins reminded civilians that reducing their red meat consumption was an essential sacrifice to ensure that servicemen had "the energy to outfight the enemy." Despite the weekly allotment of two and a half pounds of meat per person—an amount that exceeded what most Americans ate during the 1930s—and despite sharp condemnation of those who purchased more than their share, the strong desire for meat often thwarted government efforts to control the meat supply. Consumers smuggled meat across the Canadian border, grocers sold meat above ceiling prices, and butchers and "meat-leggers" kept the black market well supplied.[81] Government campaigns to promote nutritious protein substitutes, including soybeans and "variety meats"—an umbrella term that covered an array of animal organs and body parts—fared little better. Even though consumers could obtain variety meats without sacrificing ration points, social scientists who studied wartime food habits found that many Americans avoided unfamiliar meat proteins, especially when nutritionists touted them as "healthy."[82]

The Wine Advisory Board gambled that wine cookery's emphasis on pleasure stood a better chance of enhancing the appeal of organ meats than nutritionists' emphasis on good health. Advertisements in mainstream magazine prominently displayed images of "Stuffed Heart Burgundy" and "Oxtail Stew" above the caption "Wine changes war dishes into 'food for kings'" (see Figure 21). Cooks who added wine to their culinary arsenal, the WAB assured, could transform oxtails and organ meats into regal food that even manly beef eaters would enjoy. Owing to their lower expense, such delectable low-ration-point dishes would also enable cooks to entertain at home more often and without embarrassment.[83] Although government publications depicted variety meats as a temporary solution to wartime meat shortages, the WAB implied that these unfamiliar, wine-flavored proteins were tasty enough to warrant a permanent place in the home cook's repertoire. The WAB also

FIGURE 21. Magazine advertisement from the Wine Advisory Board's campaign to promote California wines, 1943. Author's collection.

supplied wine merchants with display posters and "take-one" recipe pads that featured both traditional and unconventional American fare. For the average Anglo-American cook, the recipes for one-pot vegetarian meals (bean casserole with sherry) and organ meat dishes (kidney sauté with wine) likely seemed a bigger gamble than the recipe for fish with white wine sauce.[84]

The WAB's advertising and merchandising strategy was both savvy and risky. On the one hand, the strategy offered home cooks an inventive, relatively inexpensive solution to a common dilemma: how to make low-status proteins more appetizing. In sidling wine up to beans and kidneys, the WAB diminished some of wine's older associations with luxurious living, but it also amplified wine's foreignness by associating it with vegetable and meat proteins that disrupted mainstream ideas of what a meal was supposed to be. Neither one-pot casseroles nor organ meat sautés conformed to the traditional iconography of a good meal centered on a higher-status protein plus two separate but complementary sides.[85]

The WAB was hardly a lone culinary voice calling upon home cooks to experiment with novel foods and novel tastes. Mary Taylor and Majorie Mills included wine-infused recipes in the meat and desserts sections of their cookbooks, precisely the sections where red meat and sugar—the rationed foods Americans struggled the most to do without—had starring roles.[86] Mills called for generous portions of wine in her recipes for Braised Beef, Braised Ox Joints, Baked Liver with Apples, and Gourmet Kidneys, and she incorporated sherry or muscatel in her recipes for Zabaglione with Baked Peaches, Banquet Pudding, Muscatel Jelly, Wine Sauce, Grilled Grapefruit, and Strawberries Flamingo. Taylor added sherry by the spoonfuls to her soups and wine by the cupfuls to her organ meat stews and fruit desserts.

Wine cookery introduced Americans to culinary traditions and ideologies of pleasure that the dominant Anglo-American food culture eschewed. None of the wine-oriented cookbooks produced during the war did this better than M. F. K. Fisher's *How to Cook a Wolf*. Published in 1942, the book critiqued conventional dietary advice and passionately defended the necessity of gastronomic pleasure even (and perhaps especially) in hard times. Like Mills and Taylor, Fisher aimed to inspire home cooks befuddled by food shortages and the wartime demands for thrifty living. Her ideas also put her at odds with many wartime food authorities. As a leading exponent of the new gourmet movement, Fisher argued that the contemporary dietary obsession with vitamins and "the bugbear of meal-balancing" strained the home cook's pocketbook and patience and failed to satisfy the human hunger for sensual pleasure. Inviting home cooks to awaken "their palate ... to new pleasures," Fisher encouraged home cooks to experiment with wine, cast aside the monotony of meal-balancing three times a day, and enjoy better health in the process. She criticized white American food culture as unadventurous, disdainful of pleasure, and overly wedded to food rules. Acknowledging that the thought of "eating anything but the actual red fibrous meat of a beast" horrified "at least eight out of ten Anglo-Saxons," Fisher assured readers that "a stuffed bull's heart, or a grilled lamb's brain" could "become gastronomic pleasures" with the simple addition of wine or sherry along with herbs and vegetables. If extreme economizing were required, a pigeon roasted with red wine and bacon and served with bread and a glass of the humble wine used to cook the bird would keep hunger at bay. Such advice severed the connection between wine and luxurious living, even as it suggested that thrifty consumers could—and should—luxuriate in the pleasures of eating inexpensive wine-flavored meals and drinking inexpensive wine. Fisher particularly disdained the "American Anglo-Saxon" tradition of frowning upon children and others who displayed pleasure in eating and drinking. Such scorn encouraged Americans to eat "without thought, without comment, and, worst of all, without interest" in the sensual and spiritual value of food.[87] While other wine promoters sought to divest wine of its ethnic associations by integrating it more firmly within white, middle-class culture, Fisher suggested that a genuine pleasure revolution could not take hold without also attempting to transform "American Anglo-Saxon" culture. Eager to sign onto Fisher's brand of gourmet populism, the WAB featured Fisher's recipe for short ribs and fixings and a small drawing of the renowned food writer in one of its wartime ads.[88]

Since the 1930s gourmet writers had viewed nutritionists' obsessive focus on vitamins, calories, and well-balanced meals as the "enemy of pleasure."[89] A similar critique of the sensually impoverished American diet of processed industrial foods emerged in the Federal Writers' Project's *America Eats* series, which nostalgically celebrated the persistence of tasty homemade regional and ethnic dishes that Americans enjoyed in the communal settings of church dinners, family reunions, political barbecues, and clambakes.[90] The critique of contemporary cooking took on a distinctly masculinist bent in *Esquire* and *Gourmet* magazines, which habitually denigrated women as recipe-bound, nutrition-obsessed cooks who lacked the good taste and improvisational spirit of the male cook.[91] Although a majority of *Gourmet*'s readers were likely women, its editors publicized their new venture as a magazine for men that emphasized the pleasures of food and alcohol, including cooking with wine.[92] A 1941 ad for *Gourmet* promoted the new periodical as a "man's magazine on food that men enjoy. No vitamins, no calories. Just good food—yes, and good drinks."[93] *Esquire* similarly envisioned its upper-middle-class male contributors and male readers as the vanguard of the pleasure revolution. Isles Brody, the author of Esquire magazine's recurring "Man in the Kitchenette" column, touted wine cookery as the "acme of culinary refinement" and the key to unlocking female sexual desire. Dishes prepared with wine, Brody assured, "make strong women weak, and weak women willing."[94] Reimagining wine cookery as a tool of sexual conquest that "bachelors with just a single burner in a small-one-room apartment" could pull off, Brody suggested that wine connoisseurship and sexual connoisseurship went hand in hand.

While *Esquire*'s predominantly male readership surely included many homosexual men, the magazine's primary mode of address imagined the reader as a heterosexual bachelor whose cosmopolitan tastes in fashion and good living were as keen as his attraction to the long-legged, buxom pinup girl that Albert Vargas painted for each new issue.[95] The magazine's practice of denigrating women's taste while objectifying women's bodies may have made it easier for Brody to call men to action on the Kitchen Front without impugning their masculinity. In one column, Brody envisioned thrifty cooking (with the aid of wine) as a test of masculine "ingenuity" that just might put women's waste of vital foodstuffs to shame. Observing that "an American housewife's garbage would feed a whole European family," Brody urged his male readers to follow instead the lead of New York's "finest" chefs who daily "rack their famous culinary brains" to make tasty dishes from kitchen discards. One chef-inspired dish—a stew served over rice dubbed the "Axis Downfall"—involved little more than simmering leftover cooked meats and browned onions for a half hour in "a glass of white wine" and "a tablespoon of tomato sauce."[96] Having mastered such culinary tricks of the trade, the thrifty bachelor could revel in his superiority to the wasteful, recipe-bound housewife.[97]

Hollywood films of the era also valorized the wine-savvy male chef. In *Christmas in Connecticut* (1945), viewers learn that Elizabeth Lane, a celebrated food writer who barely knows how to flip a pancake, has, unbeknownst to her readers and publisher, been getting all of her recipes from her friend, the Hungarian restaurateur Felix Bassenak. Lane's charade is revealed early in the film when Elizabeth asks Felix, "Oh, did you write up those recipes for next month's article?" Felix replies that he has, prompting Elizabeth to inquire, "What am I cooking?" His reply would have delighted budget gourmets and meat rationing boards: "Breasts of grey dove sautéed with peaches Grenadine, no points, chicken soup with Moselle wine, no points."[98] Though less biting than Brody's snide attacks on the wasteful American housewife, the lighthearted *Christmas in Connecticut* shared *Esquire*'s masculinist sensibilities. As a counterpoint to masculine culinary ingenuity, Lane, the inept but lovable woman cook, helped viewers to imagine thrifty wine cookery as a suitably masculine domain.

The Wine Institute seemed to have cultivated a relationship with Brody, as many of the recipes that he featured in his column—Pruneaux au Vin, Oxtail Stew with American Burgundy, Baked Beans with Wine, fruit salad with Port, and Sabayon sauce over sponge cake—also circulated in the Wine Advisory Board's ads and cookbooks. Surely the Wine Institute would have beamed when Brody confessed his preference for American wines and judged French wines "over-rated."[99] Given how extensively the Wine Institute courted restaurateurs, novelists, and home economists, the trade association likely had male potables columnists on board. However tightly or loosely coordinated, the wine publicity machine struck a remarkably harmonious chord.

The war gave food writers and trade associations new opportunities to recast the enjoyment of intoxicating pleasures as a civic virtue. Although California vintners had long argued that dining with wine promoted "good fellowship" and "moderate, heart-warming cheer," the wartime ads characterized wine's contributions to "good cheer" as a patriotic contribution to the war effort. "When you sit around your table and share a wartime meal with friends," one ad proclaimed, "you ... find you can work harder next day. So can the folks who've been to your house for dinner."[100] As industry insiders saw it, wine's great virtue—in wartime or not—was its capacity to "releas[e] tense nerves" without compromising efficiency.[101] Like the cookbook authors who conflated good cooking with vital defense work, WAB ads invoked military imagery to suggest that mildly intoxicating pleasures also advanced the war effort.[102] Far from undercutting the war effort, good cheer, one ad insisted, "is a weapon, too! ... for building morale."[103]

Almost by necessity, the war turned liquor store proprietors into the wine industry's most enthusiastic and inventive promoters of cooking with wine. Forever short on whiskey and long on wine (thanks to distributors' insistence that retailers accept cases of wine in exchange for a few bottles of whiskey), some liquor dealers urged disgruntled male whiskey seekers to give wine a try while they waited for whiskey to come back in stock. Other retailers set their sights on an entirely new base of "culinary customers": women who were "timid" about stepping foot in a liquor store but eager to try their hand at wine cookery.[104] Columnists in the trade press encouraged retailers to make their stores a welcoming place by hiring women salesclerks, advertising in the cooking pages (rather than the sports pages), and handing out simple wine recipes.[105] To ease the angst of women customers who feared the scorn of nosy neighbors and judgmental clubwomen, columnists also encouraged retailers to master the art of concealment and wrap their packages "to look like Grandma's old yo-yos, or a recapped bath brush, or anything with an alcoholic content under 3.2."[106]

Liquor store proprietors made good use of the WAB's recipe booklets and talking points—assuring women shoppers that wine sauces would relieve the monotony of wartime fare and improve the flavor and texture of cheap meats—but they also innovated new merchandising techniques that aimed to soften the liquor store's rough, masculine edges.[107] Otis & Lee, a "swanky Michigan Avenue" liquor store in Chicago, created a luxurious Women's Department outfitted with padded aqua-green leather walls, a cookbook library, and a lengthy wall seat flanked by a coffee table and upholstered chairs. Customers could peruse the cookbooks and wine bottles before meeting with Mary Jane Keiss, a culinary advisor who chatted with women about "their wine-cooking problems" and helped them select the right wines and recipes for the occasion.[108] Retailers also expanded their female customer base by embedding wine in the everyday consumer spaces where women regularly congregated. Art Morris, a liquor store proprietor in Syracuse, New York, dropped off literature at local beauty shops so that women could pick up tips on wine and food pairings and wine's use in cooking while they waited under the dryer.[109] Other retailers circumvented women's timidity about entering a liquor store by bringing the wine storeroom straight to their front doorstep. Enchanted by the idea of a "wine cellar on wheels," Max Miller hired a saleswoman to make home deliveries in Ogdensburg, New York, from a station wagon packed with wines. The saleswoman delivered bottles to customers who had placed phone orders in advance, and she cultivated new business via door-to-door sales made between 4:00 and 5:30pm, the dinner prep hours when many home cooks welcomed suggestions on an appropriate wine to accompany the meal.[110]

Retailers took note of women's increasing wartime presence in liquor stores and began to imagine a postwar future in which women customers and wine sales were both more abundant.[111] Yet, even as the wartime fortunes of wine and liquor became more tightly intertwined (through forced tie-in sales, winery ownership, and the courtship of women liquor store shoppers), wine's leading promoters remained determined to distance wine and winemaking from the "merchants of booze."

A MAKEOVER FOR THE WINE INDUSTRY

Key industry leaders believed that wine's cultural reinvention could not be fully accomplished without also highlighting the wine industry's cultural distinctiveness from the distilled spirits industry. Even though most wines were mass produced (as liquor was) and even though the Big Four distillers had by 1943 acquired nearly one-quarter of California's wine production, the Wine Institute remained determined to cast the wine industry in an agrarian glow. If the American public could be made to see vintners as fashionable farmers rather than as industrial manufacturers, then perhaps Americans might imbue vintners with some of the virtue Americans had long associated with small independent farmers.[112] Throughout the war varied contributors to the industry's publicity machine—novelists, journalists, and the Wine Institute itself—deployed agrarian metaphors to associate wine with the romance of artisanal farming and distance wine producers from their less savory reputation as merchants of booze.

The effort to reimagine vintners as artisanal farmers reflected the Wine Institute's dream of what the wine industry could be more than the reality of how the industry was organized. Only twenty or so vintners produced wine from vineyards they owned and cultivated. The largest producers purchased grapes cultivated by others and turned out such huge quantities of wine that credible observers often saw them as wine plants or wine factories. Roma Winery flaunted its bigness as a badge of pride, billing itself as the "world's largest winery" on the Fresno winery's gargantuan welcome sign. Roma even hired Jack Earle, the world's tallest man, to be their salesman. Towering at eight-and-a-half-feet, Jack Earle carried a six-by-ten-inch calling card and never failed to place an order for Roma wines.[113] Such publicity stunts were good for Roma's bottom line, but they hampered the Wine Institute's efforts to alter the industry's public image. In 1941 *Fortune* magazine likened the largest wine producers—Roma, Fruit Industries, Italian Swiss Colony, Central Winery, Earl Fruit Co., and Petri Wine Co.—to a "$2.98 dress factory. . . . A certain amount of [their production] is good, sound highly palatable wine. A very little of it" (the 2 percent set aside for long aging) "even approaches the exceptional . . . For the present," *Fortune* concluded, "most of it is neither good nor bad, but just plain ordinary."[114]

Changes in winery ownership during World War II reinforced these trends toward bigness. The Big Four distillers moved to acquire California wineries when the war halted domestic whiskey production and reduced the importation of European wines, eliminating a portion of their distribution portfolio.[115] By 1943, Seagram, Schenley, National Distillers, and Hiram Walker "owned or leased eighteen, mostly big, California wineries, with a total storage capacity of almost 50 million gallons"—nearly one quarter of California's wine production.[116] Many wine producers and wine merchants welcomed the distillers' investment in the industry, believing they would use their well-oiled distribution machine and deeper pockets to cut distribution costs, buy new equipment, and pour huge sums into national advertising.[117] Others worried that the distillers' mass production sensibilities and unfamiliarity with winemaking would set back the industry's quest for quality. Still others did not trust the distillers to safeguard wine's emerging image as the beverage of moderation.[118]

These perceived threats to wine's cultural distinctiveness reinvigorated the Wine Institute's efforts to amplify wine's agrarian mystique. Aware that the absence of well-trained wine dealers and restaurant wait staff deprived the industry of crucial public ambassadors, Leon Adams, the Wine Institute's publicity chief, developed a wine study correspondence course in 1943 to educate waiters, retailers, restaurateurs, and wine-curious consumers about the fundamentals of wine. As Adams recalled, during the 1930s many retailers hid "wine under the counter" because "they only wanted to sell liquor" and "were ashamed to sell wine. Only the cheaper stores had wine on display. Wine moved so slowly that labels became flyspecked."[119] The wine study course aimed to teach waiters and retailers a new vocabulary that "digni[fied] the honored occupations of wine grower, vintner and dealer."[120] Students who correctly answered the accompanying test questions about wine types and wine terms—including terms like "domestic," "fortified," and "manufactured" that "should never be used when talking about U.S. wines"—received a diploma certifying them as a wine expert.[121] The course instructed industry personnel to call wine producers "wine growers" rather than "wine manufacturers," because saying "wine is 'manufactured' . . . deprive[s] wine of its true character as a pure agricultural product."[122] It urged course takers to use the term "winery" instead of "plant" or "wine factory"—terms that diminished wine's agrarian allure and implied that the wine was "shipped without aging."[123] By 1945 the wine study course had enrolled twenty-six thousand students and graduated fifty-five hundred—about four times higher than the average completion rate for correspondence courses. Half of those who enrolled were salesclerks, including many women who boosted in-store sales by promoting wine's use in cooking. Winery personnel, wholesalers, writers, and admen also signed up.[124]

Trade associations hoped that purging negative wine terminology from consumers' and retailers' vocabulary would also retrain consumers' sensory perceptions of wine. *House Beautiful*'s "Wine Dictionary for Brides," created with WAB materials, taught women conventional wine appreciation terms ("aroma," "body," and "bouquet") as well as words and phrases to avoid. Even if consumers' preferences for sweet beverages conditioned them to perceive dry table wines as "sour," the dictionary advised them to never use the term, since sour wine was a "disagreeable acid, spoiled wine." In a similar vein, the dictionary urged brides to substitute "American wine" for "domestic wine" since the latter implied "cheapness and inferior quality."[125] Just as important, in the eyes of the Pennsylvania Liquor Board, was stripping "imported" wines of their presumed cachet—a view that prompted the board to reclassify wines as "United States" and "Foreign" rather than "Domestic" and "Imported."[126]

Promoters of American wine especially despised the term "fortified" wine, as it led some consumers to assume that winemakers "deliberately 'spiked' [sweet wine] to give it an alcoholic 'kick.'" Noting that prohibitionists had weaponized the word to portray winemaking as a predatory industry that profited from alcoholism, an editorial in *Wines and Vines* urged industry personnel to banish "fortified" from their vocabulary. Instead, the editorial suggested, they should explain that winemakers added only "a little *pure* grape brandy" to arrest fermentation of the grape's *natural* sugar and preserve the sweetness of port, sherry, and other higher-alcohol wines [emphasis added].[127] As producers of "fortified" wines, vintners (in some consumers' minds) occupied the same moral plane as merchants of booze. The purity of vintners' motives was harder to doubt when they were imagined instead as producers of "pure" and "natural" sweet wines meant to be consumed with appetizers and desserts. For Leon Adams, wine nomenclature mattered because language influenced sensory perceptions of quality. Acquiring a taste for wine was easier when consumers learned to call wines "dry" instead of "sour." Language could also influence how consumers perceived wine's intoxicating effects. Even if the alcohol content of "sweet wines" and "fortified wines" was exactly the same, the consumer's mindset and the settings in which consumers drank "sweet wines" (presumably with appetizers or dessert) might produce a different psychoactive experience than a "fortified wine" drunk primarily for its intoxicating effects.[128]

Two best-selling wine novels published in 1942—Alice Tisdale Hobart's *The Cup and the Sword*, set in Napa Valley during and after Prohibition, and Idwal Jones's *The Vineyard*, set in pre-Prohibition-era Napa Valley—furthered the Wine Institute's efforts to promote wine growing as a virtuous agrarian enterprise. Although unscrupulous winemakers entered the storylines of both novels, Jones and Hobart both upheld artisanal wine growers as heroic figures who placed their devotion to the soil, the vines, and making good wine above pecuniary interests. The Wine Institute supplied both authors with research materials and lent a hand with publicity. In private correspondence with Jones, Harry Caddow, the Wine Institute's secretary-manager, applauded the novelist for depicting "the small wine grower just as he is"—not as "a manufacturer" concerned with "short cuts and money-making methods" but as "a man dependent on the soil and the vagaries of climate for his existence, and ... a producer with a strong and traditional pride in his product."[129] A *New York Times* book reviewer expressed similar sentiments about *The Cup and the Sword*, noting that while Hobart "is perfectly aware that many inferior wines have been foolishly foisted on the public, ... she conveys superbly the sense of dedication, the craftsmanship and the tradition that can be found in the wine industry, too." Swayed by Hobart's portrait, the reviewer commended readers to "buy as many bottles of California wine as your purse can afford."[130]

The politics of agrarian virtue ultimately provided too thin a veil to mask the realities of large-scale wine production. Despite positive portrayals of California's producers of quality, estate-bottled wines in *Fortune* magazine and in best-sellers like *The Vineyard* and *The Cup and Sword*, postwar market research studies found that most American consumers still thought of California wine as cheap, "synthetic," and "mass produced."[131] As late as 1955, even in the context of a relatively flattering article touting the "heady" sales of California wine, *Newsweek* referred to California's vin ordinaire as "conveyor-belt wine."[132] During World War II, American consumers may not yet have been sold on wine's agrarian mystique—that triumph awaited the postwar era of wine country tourism—but the politics of agrarian virtue helped to determine whether, how often (and at what price) their wine glass got filled. In states where the Wine Institute and other wine promoters persuaded lawmakers of wine's value to the agricultural economy and its merits as a moderate mealtime beverage, lawmakers usually lowered wine taxes and made wine easier to purchase. Californians consumed three times more wine than consumers in other states thanks to lower wine taxes, wine's availability in grocery stores, and consumers' ability to purchase wine from roadside wineries.

WINE PROMOTION AND CULTURAL CHANGE

By 1945, the Wine Advisory Board could boast measurable success in broadening wine's mass market appeal. Rising incomes, liquor rationing, steady advertising, and improved wine quality all increased table wine sales, which grew by roughly 20 percent in 1944. Compelled by gasoline rationing to restrict their travels, some Americans discovered that wine added the "festive touch" that made entertaining guests at home a satisfactory substitute for a night on the town.[133] The most sanguine assessments of the US wine market came from importers of European wines. Wine importer Peter Greig applauded California wine producers for breaking down "the absurd mystery" and "snobbery" that "clouded the simple matter of wine drinking." Thanks to those efforts, "people who like wine (and a great many people who a few years ago didn't know they would like wine)" now drank "various kinds fairly regularly."[134] Importer Frank Schoonmaker saw a particularly bright future for the dozen or so California fine wine producers: "Even the so-called 'sophisticates,'" Schoonmaker observed, "no longer serve American wine (as they certainly did four years ago) with an apologetic smile, or a shrug."[135]

Others were dismayed that wine consumption had not risen more dramatically. If ever there was a moment when wine consumption should have taken off, the war should have provided it. Curtailed liquor production, reduced imports, vigorous wine advertising, and rising disposable incomes had given vintners an enviable competitive advantage.

Wine consumption initially saw sharp gains, rising from 0.753 gallons per capita in 1941 to 0.84 gallons per capita in 1942, but consumption quickly leveled off and eventually fell to 0.73 gallons per capita in 1943 and 0.68 gallons per capita in 1944. The shortage of dessert wines in 1943 and 1944 explains some of the overall drop-off, but this provided little comfort to the vintners who saw table wine consumption as key to the industry's long-term fortunes. Even with the decline in dessert wine consumption, Americans preferred sweet dessert or appetizer wines to table wines by a 1.4 to 1 ratio in 1944—a sharp decline from the 2.5 to 1 ratio in 1942 but an indication that the table wine market was still underdeveloped.[136]

Several factors explain why, despite the increasing wartime demand, wine consumption did not rise more dramatically in World War II. Government mandates that grapes be turned into raisins sharply curtailed the production of California wines in 1942 and 1943, creating a scarcity of dessert wines and white table wines.[137] The complex regulations governing wine distribution also thwarted the development of a national wine market. Regulations for wine shipping, taxing, labeling, advertising, selling, and serving varied so widely from state to state, *Wines and Vines* reported, that "a California winery with nation-wide distribution of its brand" operated more like "an exporter shipping to forty-six different foreign countries."[138] Such widely divergent regulatory practices produced highly misleading national aggregate figures of per capita wine consumption. The aggregated statistics, in fact, obscured both the bright spots and the dark spots in the national wine market. Wine sales were anemic in the South, sluggish in the Midwest, and vulnerable to sharp downturns in both regions during the "liquor holidays" in 1944 and 1945, when the government temporarily released distillers to produce whiskey instead of industrial alcohol.[139] Wine sales fared much better in the twenty-seven states that permitted sales of wine in food or drug stores—a shift encouraged by persistent Wine Institute lobbying; such outlets accounted for 15 percent of all wine sales. In Ohio and California—two of the largest wine-producing and highest wine-consuming states—consumers purchased more than one-third of all the wine sold from food stores.[140] Validating the WAB's strategy to link wine and food, wine sales increased by 75 to 100 percent in Cincinnati and Chicago grocery stores that displayed wine in the produce section.[141]

The drop in aggregate national wine consumption after the wartime peak in 1942 raised another troubling possibility: advertising had succeeded in getting Americans to try wine, but consumers had little desire to keep coming back for more. For wine proprietor Horace Lanza, the solution was clear. Having failed to convince consumers that table wine was "dry" when their "taste buds" told them it was "sour," vintners needed to gear production to the "national sweet tooth." Lanza urged vintners to produce more "light sweet wines"—wines with the potency of traditional table wines (12 to 14 percent alcohol) but a higher sugar content that could please palates acclimated to sweetened beverages. Once consumers developed the habit of taking light sweet wines with meals, vintners could then introduce them to the drier reds and whites.[142]

In some parts of the country, substandard wine quality also hindered vintners' efforts to build a mass market for table wine. Admittedly, California wine quality improved when the military's requisitioning of raisin grapes forced some winemakers to stop adding raisin grapes to the crushers. Even so, quality problems occurred along various points of distribution, far removed from the winemaker's oversight. Wine sold to consumers directly from barrels was especially at risk, as some "unscrupulous dealers diluted, or cut, the wine to meet the unprecedented demand" in some regions and locales.[143] Bottled wine was less vulnerable to tampering, but even if bottles left California as palatable wine, vintners could not guarantee the wine's continued palatability when retailers exposed the bottles to excessive heat or excessive cold.[144] Bootlegged wines also undermined the reputation of California wines. In Eastern cities, where bootleggers still commanded a portion of the wine market, some bartenders would refill empty California wine bottles with cheap homemade wine and postpone reordering commercial wines until the original label had worn off from repeated handling.[145]

The industry's most sanguine wine promoters overestimated the war's potential to deliver dramatic cultural change in drinking habits and preferences. Commodity shortages, rationing, and full-scale economic mobilization compelled cultural adaptation in so many areas—food choices, gender roles, and uses of leisure—that Americans sometimes clung more fervently to tradition when the choice was purely voluntary. Whether overly optimistic or needlessly dispirited, none of the wartime winemakers and wine promoters who sized up the industry's future fully grasped the enduring impact of the vintners' wartime campaign on postwar food fashions. The popular postwar practice of using wine to glamorize casseroles or doctor dishes concocted from canned goods and frozen foods extended the wartime practice of using wine to flavor sauces and add pizzazz to fruit desserts.[146] Likewise, the postwar resurgence of home-centered entertaining, fueled by a baby boom that kept young parents homeward bound, reinforced wartime trends toward domesticating both the pleasures and the perils of alcohol consumption. Although the war did not produce the wine boom some had anticipated, it laid the cultural groundwork upon which future postwar growth, nurtured by improved wine quality, could build.

8

Rank Privilege

The Politics of Intoxicating Pleasures in the US Military

By the time most US servicemen had completed basic training in World War II, they had been pushed past the limits of their physical endurance and subjected to humiliating tests of their obedience to top command. They capped off the grueling weeks of training with one final initiation rite: drinking beer with their unit.[1] For the US army's youngest recruits—and those who had not yet sampled alcohol—this particular initiation rite promised the softest of landings. The 3.2 percent beer that the army permitted was so weak that seasoned servicemen would stock up for the "occasional three-cans-per-man beer parties" on the off-chance they might get lightly buzzed.[2] The US military's decision to provision enlisted men with 3.2 beer represented a sharp departure from the outright ban on alcohol that the military introduced in 1900. Even so, the military's alcohol policy was still relatively restrictive. While other imperial powers doled out daily rations of rum, wine, or whiskey, the US military made 3.2 beer available as an optional treat. For a mere eight cents a can, soldiers could buy the beer at an Army Post Exchange—so long as they purchased no more than three twelve-ounce beers within a three-day period.[3]

The long shadow of Prohibition hung over these policymaking choices. Fearing that an official (and more potent) alcohol ration would arouse the ire of organized "drys" at home, the US military instead met the infantryman's daily needs for pleasure and release through its generous rations of cigarettes and chocolate. If World War II was a "wet

FIGURE 22. US Navy Seabees drink 3.2 percent beer at a rest camp in the South Pacific. National Archives and Record Administration.

war," as one historian has dubbed the war, it was most meaningfully so for the officers.[4] Those with stars and bars on their uniform could enjoy cocktails, wine, and beer in the officers' mess, plus a monthly ration of whiskey, scotch, gin, and brandy. Ordinary GIs, lacking consistent access to an Army Post Exchange, were left to fend for themselves. Whether serving behind the lines or protecting US positions in countries liberated and occupied by the US military, infantryman faced long bouts of alcohol scarcity followed by unexpected windfalls—circumstances that often invited excess and dangerous experimentation.

When it came to intoxicating pleasures, the principle of "fair shares for all" that governed food rationing on the home front had little purchase in the racially segregated and hierarchically structured US military. Instead, race and rank determined the types of intoxicating beverages that military personnel could enjoy as well as when, where, and how often they could indulge such pleasures. The unequal distribution of pleasure had far-reaching social and political consequences. It intensified racial discord between Black and white soldiers and reinforced divisions between enlisted men and their officers; it prompted some white servicemen and Black personnel of all ranks to question the United States' commitment to upholding democratic values at home and abroad; and it stoked their desires for more equitable treatment within the military and beyond.

The story of alcohol's cultural reinvention unfolded not just in the civilian marketplaces over which American advertisers and merchandisers exerted some control but also in the distinctive consumer marketplaces that servicemen encountered in US training camps and in the European and Pacific theaters of operation. The industry's fantasy that GIs would return from war with more worldly and abundant appetites for wine and beer did not entirely pan out as anticipated. For most of the war, the world of alcohol plenty that some imagined would lay within the average enlisted man's grasp never materialized. In both the Pacific and European theaters, military personnel encountered consumer marketplaces for alcohol limited by the unpredictable availability of 3.2 beer, the constrained scope of indigenous production, the extensive requisitioning of local supplies by the Nazi regime, and looting by the German army. In the face of such scarcity, the quality and quantity of the alcoholic potables that soldiers imbibed often hinged on the vibrancy of the local black market and the creativity of GIs who distilled and mixed their own concoctions.

The consumer marketplaces for alcohol in war-torn countries were also shaped by something more intangible: servicemen's yearnings for the brands and types of alcoholic potables, especially whiskey, that were now the hardest to procure. Emotionally bound to the consumer world they left behind, GIs followed news about whiskey shortages in the United States and peppered war correspondents with questions about the pleasures civilians still enjoyed on the home front.[5] Remarking on American GIs' unceasing talk of food and alcohol while covering the Italian front, Margaret Bourke-White, the pioneering photojournalist, concluded that "Four-inch steaks and eggs with shells on them had become symbols of home."[6] She might have said the same of good quality American beer and whiskey.

Historians have frequently commented on the ways militaries transform diets and cultivate new tastes across the globe for both foreign cuisines and processed industrial foods.⁷ Equally compelling are the ways that military policies and wartime food scarcities politicize access to beloved foods and drinks and often unwittingly amplify their prestige. The various obstacles that servicemen encountered in their quests for recreation, intoxicating pleasures, and some semblance of dignity indelibly shaped how they fought in the war and remembered the war; how they perceived racial and class inequalities; and how they battled for a better postwar order. In all these ways, conflicts over military provisioning and access to alcohol expanded and redefined the politics of pleasure.

ERNIE PYLE'S VIRTUOUS BEER-LOVING GIS AND THE MYTH OF THE GOOD WAR

In wartime popular culture, representations of the wholesome American GI often bore only passing resemblance to the real flesh-and-blood GIs who fought on the front lines. The reassuring image of the homesick, beer-loving GI—an image that wartime beer advertising and war correspondents helped to popularize—stood starkly at odds with the aggrieved, alcohol-seeking GI who surfaces in memoirs, oral histories, and the gripe letters of army newspapers. American civilians glimpsed the virtuous, beer-loving GI in the brewing industry's collective wartime advertising campaign, which touted beer as one of "the small familiar pleasures" that GIs thought of when they "dream of home" (see Figure 23 and earlier Figure 10).⁸ They also encountered the beer-loving GI in the hugely popular syndicated columns of Ernie Pyle, a war correspondent who reported from various posts in the North African and European theaters. Appearing six days a week in nearly seven hundred US newspapers, Pyle's columns gave readers a front seat to daily life on the battlefront, indelibly shaping their perceptions of the ordinary soldier's experience of war. Pyle's column was also a beloved staple of *Stars and Stripes*, the army's main news source for GIs stationed abroad. By 1943, Pyle's dispatches from North Africa and Italy had made him a household name, and before Pyle was killed by enemy fire while covering the war in the Pacific, two books of Pyle's collected columns—*Here Is Your War* (1943) and *Brave Men* (1944)—had become best sellers.⁹

Apart from a few effusive profiles of General Omar Bradley, Pyle rarely wrote about servicemen above the rank of captain.¹⁰ Instead he focused on the infantrymen—"the mud-rain-frost-and-wind boys," as he called them. Fighting without comforts and sometimes "without the

FIGURE 23. Magazine advertisement from the Brewing Industry Foundation's "Morale Is a Lot of Little Things" campaign, 1944. Author's collection.

necessities," the infantry, Pyle wrote, were "the guys that wars cannot be won without." In a departure from the anonymity of most war reporting, Pyle's columns also included the names and addresses of the soldiers he interviewed. His vivid depictions of soldiers' daily lives gave readers thousands of miles from the front lines a glimpse of how GIs weathered the monotony and dreariness of war and why they longed for the simple pleasures of "ice cream, beer [and] clean clothes."[11]

Many of Pyle's stories helped to create the wartime image of the GI as "stoically heroic under trying circumstances."[12] The deprivation of alcohol was a recurring feature of such trying circumstances. In one column Pyle sympathized with the American soldiers aboard a British ship who found plenty of soft drinks at the bar but no liquor to slake their thirst for the entire voyage to North Africa. The stash of whiskey officers brought aboard, Pyle reported, was "all gone after a day or two and from then on it was probably the driest ocean voyage ever made." An American soldier added his own folksy take on the lamentable situation: "We can't smoke in the dining room because it's a British ship, and we can't buy liquor because it's an American trooper."[13] Instead of presenting gripping stories of battlefield heroism, Pyle portrayed modern warfare as hard, unrelenting toil. In a column from the Tunisian front, Pyle concurred with journalist Hal Boyle's observation that in wartime the experience of perpetual physical discomfort dominated men's existence more than the experience of endangerment. "You're always cold and almost always dirty," Pyle wrote. "Outside of food and cigarets you have absolutely none of the little things that made life normal back home. You don't have chairs, lights, floors, or tables . . . There are no newspapers, milk, beds, sheets, radiators, beer, ice cream or hot water. You just sort of exist . . . The velvet is all gone from living."[14]

Pyle's focus on the sensory experiences and yearnings of ordinary GIs was partly a product of the material and political conditions under which he and other wartime journalists operated. Many reporters wrote human interest stories rather than battlefield accounts because military censors barred reporters from including details about troop numbers, troop movements, and the location of combat in the interest of withholding information from the enemy. Delays in transmitting stories gave reporters an additional incentive to produce "stories with a longer shelf life, ones that could be sent by mail rather than by cable or wireless."[15] Pyle's human interest stories highlighted both the pleasures soldiers could indulge and the ones they had to forgo. Although the GIs Pyle profiled were not as a rule a teetotaling bunch, alcohol was, for the most part, an infrequently indulged pleasure. Instead, soldiers incorporated more innocent (or officially approved) psychoactive pleasures into their daily routines. Pyle's readers learned, for example, that the men dug in on the Anzio beachhead regularly brewed "coffee or hot chocolate just before bedtime."[16] They also learned that many GIs who had never touched cigarettes before the war now "smoked one after another," prompting Pyle, himself an avid smoker, to concede that "a guy in war has to have some outlet for his nerves."[17]

As members of a liberating and occupying army, GIs encountered supplies of alcohol considerably more diverse and potent than the 3.2 beer on offer at the Army PX. There was the occasional windfall when troops dug out piles of exotic liquors from the rubble—enough to fill "a dozen company and battalion command posts" in Italy with "a shelf full of the finest stuff imaginable." But "a windfall like that [did not] come often," Pyle recalled.[18] In Pyle's accounts of the North African and European theaters, most of the alcohol supplies had already been ransacked or requisitioned by the German army or failed to satisfy the tastes of the troops. When the US military arrived in Oran, a major port city in Algeria, GIs found poorly stocked stores and locals on the verge of starvation. Inexpensive wine "was about the only thing left to buy," but "most Americans," Pyle observed, had not yet "learned to drink wine with relish."[19] In other locales, the remaining liquor supplies were either too dangerous or too punishing to consume. The first American troops in Naples found stores well stocked with several coveted items—fine watches, sweaters, and real silk stockings—but an "almost exhausted" supply of "good liquor" and "considerable bootlegging of . . . dangerous booze."[20] The *eau de vie* that Pyle and some troops sampled at the invitation of a French café owner in the small Normandian town was so harsh that Pyle likened it to boiled "barbed wire" with "a touch of nitroglycerine for flavor." Although Pyle appreciated the Frenchman's generosity—the Germans had depleted his other alcohol stocks—the sensory shock that he and the GIs experienced prompted Pyle to proclaim that "every American who connects with a glass of *eau de vie* should get a Purple Heart."[21]

In recounting how GIs coped with alcohol scarcity and chronic deprivation, Pyle helped to normalize drinking as a justified reprieve from an otherwise dreary existence. From his post aboard a Naval vessel in March 1945, Pyle reported that the sailors had spent weeks sailing the "vast Pacific" with little to occupy them but "their work, and their movies, and their mail." Their only respite from "the isolation and monotony" were three brief trips to "remote, lifeless sandbars," where they would "sit under palm trees and drink three cans of beer."[22] Reports of sailors consuming government-sanctioned 3.2 beer were unlikely to raise eyebrows, but even when the enlisted men Pyle profiled drank more potent alcoholic beverages, the men still seemed relatable, if not virtuous. In Pyle's telling, fighter pilots rarely drank because they flew "so frequently," but when a popular fighter pilot "was killed right on the home field, in an accident, some of them assuaged their grief with gin."[23]

The US military's own efforts to downplay the extent of GI's drinking may have influenced Pyle's tendency to do the same. Military officials publicly touted the salutary effects of selling 3.2 beer in the army post exchanges, noting that the availability of light beer had prevented soldiers from drinking hard liquor in nearby towns and engaging in destructive behavior.[24] Such claims, however, did little to quell the persistent complaints from drys. The Army repeatedly had to quash rumors that the military was issuing rations of beer and whiskey to servicemen and clarify that it merely permitted the PXs to sell "nonintoxicating" 3.2 beer to off-duty servicemen.[25] Fearful of further antagonizing drys, Army public relations had a vested interest in concealing certain "facts about military drinking from the public," including the military's practice of issuing officers two bottles of hard liquor a month.[26]

Even as Pyle downplayed drinking among the troops, he also represented the drinking GI as an entirely sympathetic and even fun-loving figure. In one column, Pyle joked that the American soldiers in Sicily were known to fill some of their water canteens with "a strange red fluid known colloquially as 'vino,' to be used, no doubt, for rubbing fleabites."[27] Rather than representing drinking as an encumbrance to military discipline, Pyle represented drinking as an infrequent but restorative indulgence. Drinking "some vino" was just one of the small pleasures "the boys" could enjoy on their five-day junket in Naples, where they could also "get a bath and a good bed, go sightseeing, ... and maybe even have a date."[28] Much as brewers depicted beer drinking as one of the "little things" that boosted morale on the home front, Pyle depicted drinking as one of the small comforts that sustained GIs on the battlefront.

In Pyle's telling, the GI's experience of war was typified by alcohol scarcity—whether measured in absolute terms or by the absence of preferred potables. The officer class had a much different sensory experience of the war. Not limited to 3.2 beer or the alcoholic remnants discovered amid the rubble, officers enjoyed access to a well-diversified, though not always plentifully stocked, bar. Writing two months before the Normandy invasion, Pyle described a liquor rationing system at the thousand-seat Army officers' mess in London. Owing to widespread liquor shortages in London, the bar at the mess "would sell whisky and gin for about fifteen minutes and then hang up the 'all out' sign, leaving only beer and wine." Once the thick crowd at the bar dissipated, the mess would start "selling whisky and gin again for about fifteen minutes." Although Pyle wanted his readers to know that the liquor ration "wasn't much"—a maximum of two drinks enforced by the honor code—it is not hard to imagine why Pyle reported that the system "seemed to work out to everybody's satisfaction." For one, the two-drink maximum appeared not to include the unrationed wine and beer. Pyle's column failed to mention that the enlisted men's mess had no bar or that many of the officers' messes (especially the small exclusive ones) were racially segregated. If the system really did "work out to *everybody's* satisfaction," it may have done so because American servicemen regularly frequented London's pubs and had little trouble finding alcohol in the UK.[29]

Despite such conditions of relative alcohol abundance for higher-ranking personnel, Pyle endeavored to present officers' drinking as restrained by both circumstance and officers' sensitivity to unit morale. Pyle shared with readers that General Omar Bradley "drank and swore in great moderation" and that "he and Mrs. Bradley probably took one drink a month before supper" back home. An exemplar of moderation and generosity, the general even gave away his cigarette rations. In England, where liquor supplies were low, "he drank hardly ever, but he did pour a dust-cutting libation for visitors who showed up at suppertime."[30] Another Pyle column profiled a captain who refused a lieutenant's offer of gin because the lieutenant did not have enough gin to share with the enlisted men under the captain's command. Readily conceding that not all officers demonstrated such gallantry, Pyle viewed the incident as evidence that "the battlefield does produce a brotherhood. The common bond of death draws human beings toward each other over the artificial barrier of rank."[31]

No matter how vividly Pyle or any other war reporter reconstructed the loneliness, monotony, and misery of daily life on the battlefront, there remained a vast gap between civilians' sensory perception of the war and soldiers' sensory perceptions.[32] Many of the false impressions that Pyle and other war reporters created—that men of all ranks fought together as a band of brothers, that the GI's drinking was relatively restrained, that the enlisted men yearned for nothing more than to simply return home—helped to burnish World War II's image as the "good war." As historian Richard Fine has written, Pyle's "long-suffering and non-ideological 'citizen-soldier' rests at the very heart of this collective view of the American soldier."[33]

Wartime reporters' portrait of the virtuous, heroic GI performed critical political and cultural work. War reporting gave civilians "a sense of vicarious participation in battle, a sense of identification that would harden" their commitment to the war effort and "ease their irritations over war-born regulations."[34] Surely some civilians experienced a twinge of guilt for complaining too much about whiskey shortages when they read about the simple pleasures that GIs pined for on the battlefront or learned that GIs routinely peppered Pyle with questions wondering whether it was still possible to "get a glass of milk" or "buy a drink" at the bar, or "have any fun" on the home front.[35] By casting GIs as men who more than anything yearned for "chocolate milk shakes, cokes, iced beer, and girls," historian John Blum writes, war reporters suggested that it was home, not "freeing the oppressed" and "making the world safe for peace or democracy," that "spurred the G.I. to fight."[36]

Pyle's image of the "stoic, naturally pacific and duty-bound" soldier who fought alongside his comrades and superiors as a "band of brothers" distorts as much as it illuminates.[37] As the next sections reveal, the pursuit of alcohol and the military's unequitable provisioning of alcohol exposed the darker sides of the war. Although alcohol provided a much-needed release and respite from the traumas of war, the quest for alcohol and the denial of alcohol could also incite and intensify class and racial conflict within the segregated US military. While some GIs undoubtedly fit Pyle's image of the "long-suffering and non-ideological 'citizen-soldier,'" conflict over the inequities of alcohol provisioning also had deeply politicizing effects.

ALCOHOL AND THE ENLISTED MAN'S WORLD OF WAR

If the Army intended to minimize excessive drinking by allowing off-duty troops to purchase 3.2 beer wherever enlisted men trained and fought, the Army failed on multiple counts. Even under optimal circumstances, the monthly allocation for each man—one case of 3.2 beer or twenty-four bottles—was too slim to meet the average soldier's need for release and relief from the stresses of war.[38] Further, Army beer was not always available when soldiers wanted it, thanks to delays in establishing post exchanges near new fronts and the logistical challenges of securing sources of supply.[39] To save shipping space for vital equipment and food, the Army requisitioned breweries overseas to produce 3.2 beer and hired civilians in occupied countries to operate the breweries.[40] Although this arrangement guaranteed a consistent supply, GIs sometimes struggled to develop a taste for local brews. Some complained that the Egyptian "Stella" beer tasted vaguely of onions; many condemned the beer produced by the field brewery in India "as undrinkable."[41] Officers and enlisted men stationed at Port Moresby in Papua New Guinea could not enjoy even the meager 3.2 beer allotment because the "New Guinea Force, the highest allied command in Papua and New Guinea, prohibited alcohol." The allied command eventually relaxed its dry regulations to permit beer in the Australian canteens and American PXs, but only after liquor smuggling and drunken escapades fueled by hazardous moonshine had gotten out of hand.[42]

The troops' response to alcohol scarcity in Papua was replicated throughout the European and Pacific theaters. In the absence of adequate alcohol provisions, enlisted men found ways to provision themselves. They distilled and fermented their own home-brewed concoctions. They sampled the local production, some of it gifted by the recently liberated, some purchased, and some obtained via looting. Left to fend for themselves, servicemen also created and sustained a lively barter trade in war souvenirs and branded whiskey. Although the war correspondent Ernie Pyle painted a picture of alcohol scarcity broken only by the occasional windfall, soldier's own memoirs and postwar accounts suggest that alcohol indelibly shaped and even helped to structure soldiers' experience of the war. In hindsight, the military's policy of supplying the troops with 3.2 beer, though despised by prohibitionists, bent too far to accommodate "dry" opinion—sometimes with disastrous results. As historian Michael Adams writes, "it must be the ultimate act of willful naïveté to pretend that a man engaged in killing other men will be morally corrupted by a bottle of liquor. Only the American army tried to keep its ranks dry . . . The result was an army obsessed with obtaining booze."[43]

The average soldier rarely experienced Europe as the land of alcohol plenty that some historians have imagined. Stephen Ambrose surely exaggerated when he wrote that "every liberated village in France, and later in Belgium, Holland, Germany, and Austria was full of wine, cognac, brandy, and other fine liquor, of a quality and in a quantity quite unknown to the average enlisted man."[44] Nor was "the profusion of names, brands, labels, and appellations" so vast, as another historian has suggested, that it "made the GIs' heads spin."[45] Closer to the mark was historian Lee Kennett's observation that the GI was "doomed to see Europe at her worst": buildings and infrastructure neglected or destroyed, food and alcohol in short supply, and shops closed or emptied of merchandise.[46]

Instead of finding a veritable Land of Cockaigne, soldiers in the European theater found an erratically supplied consumer marketplace for alcohol offering unfamiliar and not entirely trustworthy potables, often at prices beyond the average GI's pay. As Edward Toles, reporting for the *Chicago Defender*, observed, the known brands of liquor were "so expensive that one had to pay through the nose for even a moderate drink or it was absolutely unobtainable or it was 'bootleg' stuff drunk only at the drinker's risk of death or blindness!" In England, black marketeers and loose-spending GIs drove the price for a quart of Scotch to twenty-five dollars, five times its set price.[47] The premium for British whiskey was considerably less in North Africa, but the bottle usually contained something else altogether. Bill Mauldin, an enlisted man whose wildly popular cartoons in *Stars and Stripes* satirized army life, discovered that Arab merchants would "gather discarded British whisky bottles, fill them with unmentionable substances," and sell them to unsuspecting Americans for ten dollars. In Italy, where repairs to a big brewery in Naples had delayed the promised allotments of 3.2 beer, GIs developed a taste for the local wine—or guzzled it to avoid the "questionable" water. Others jury-rigged distilleries from "barrels of dug-up vino, gasoline cans, and copper tubing from wrecked airplanes." Despite their "crude apparatus," the "unauthorized gin mills," Mauldin recalled, produced a fiery grappa "much less corrosive than the bootleg stuff the Italian civilians offered."[48]

Weak military oversight of white GIs' drinking enabled GIs to broaden the consumer marketplace for alcohol beyond 3.2 beer. The commanders at Anzio, Mauldin recalled, "usually looked the other way when they spotted" an unauthorized distillery; some became regular patrons.[49] Nor did soldiers have to work too hard to maneuver around the Military Police who guarded access to underground wine dens. On the Anzio beachhead, black marketeers had turned the underground caves into "speak-easy dens." Although the MPs marked the caves off limits, soldiers managed to evade the guards, amble down the steep steps, and purchase *vino bianco* drawn straight from the cask. GIs returned to camp with big wicker-wrapped flasks of wine to share with their comrades. "A 'slug of the old *vino*' before going to sleep," one GI recalled, "gave a good many people on the Beachhead enough 'catacomb courage' to face the anguish awaiting them next morning."[50] Apparently drinking hot chocolate before bedtime—the homey ritual that Pyle documented on the Anzio beachhead—was not the only nightly drinking ritual that infantrymen observed.

The soldier's sensory experience of war was shaped by the exotic and unfamiliar foods and beverages they discovered as they liberated and occupied distant lands (see Figure 24). Some learned to adapt their own drinking practices to the customs of the country. After attending several

FIGURE 24. A Sicilian policeman offers a jug of wine to an infantryman with the first US Army patrol to enter the town of Troina, 1943. Bettman via Getty Images.

drinking and dancing parties hosted by Italians, Sergeant Eugene Lester, a Black medic with the 365th Infantry Regiment, was eventually able "to drink their wine all night without getting drunk. The secret was to sip it because the minute your glass was empty they refilled it."[51] Other enlisted men learned about the perils of imbibing unfamiliar intoxicants the hard way. After training all day in the hot North African desert, Alex Carrillo, a soldier with the Mexican-American Company E, purchased a bottle of wine from a local grocer. When he fell ill after drinking nearly half the bottle, his fellow GI Nacho Rosemond offered to taste the wine, quickly spat it out, and informed Carrillo he had been drinking vinegar.[52] Soldiers' encounters with the calvados produced by Normandian peasants also produced disastrous results. The homedistilled apple brandy was potent enough (140 proof and higher) to fuel soldiers' lanterns and cigarette lighters.[53] As Major Dick Winters recalled, French peasants drank calvados "between courses to clear the palate and then as a finale to a good meal. If not aged ten to fifteen years, calvados will take the skin off your throat, as many Allied soldiers discovered within days of the invasion."[54] Unaware of its customary uses, many soldiers drank too much and turned into belligerent drunks.[55]

In the Pacific theater, the limited availability of imported alcohol, including 3.2 beer, and the more limited indigenous production created even more opportunities for dangerous encounters with home-made spirits.[56] Faced with scanty options, enlisted men did their best to provision themselves using the ingredients at hand. James Jones recounted how the men in his outfit "got blind asshole drunk every chance we got" on "raisin jack" or "swipe," a "Hawaiian word for bootleg liquor." Using "a fivegallon tin of canned peaches or plums or pineapple [stolen] from the nearest ration dump," the men would add "a double handful of sugar ... to help it ferment," cover it with cheesecloth or mosquito netting, and "then leav[e] it in the sun" to work its magic. Describing swipe as "godawful stuff to drink, sickly sweet and smelling very raunchy," Jones recalled getting the "most terribly awful bar-none hangover" from a late-night "'swipe' party."[57] GIs also exhibited their panache as creative mixologists. They concocted a citrusy cocktail by blending the Aqua Velva aftershave lotion from their toiletry kit with canned grapefruit juice. Tasting something like a Tom Collins, Jones claimed that "everyone loved it."[58]

GIs' inventiveness did not stop there. "One of the handiest things in a K-ration," GI moonshiners discovered, was the fruit bar, which, according to *Yank* magazine, yielded "a very tasty ... bottled product." Other GI distillers made "a drink called Cherry Squeezins" from the Army's supply of canned cherries and juice. That *Yank*, the weekly magazine written by and for GIs, reported on such creative uses of fruit bars and canned cherries, signaled to readers that even if the Army did not "condone this kind of sport" it was willing to look the other way so long as the yields remained small.[59]

Alcohol scarcity in the Pacific gave rise to a robust semi-licit barter trade that transformed alcohol and other foods into a form of "community currency." Soldiers used this form of community currency to achieve the sorts of masculine prestige and sensory satisfactions that the military's rigidly hierarchical structure denied them.[60] Much of the barter trade centered on the exchange of war souvenirs for high-quality liquor. In both the Pacific and European theaters, soldiers collected a variety of battlefield keepsakes to provide tangible proof of their victorious military service. Some prized gas masks, Luger pistols, helmets, and Samurai sabers as battlefield keepsakes. Others delivered one last humiliation to their defeated foe by robbing the war dead of body parts, as US marines did when they took skulls as war trophies or made necklaces from Japanese gold teeth and pickled Japanese ears.[61] The souvenirs-for-alcohol trade in the Pacific satisfied the disparate emotional needs of its participants. Those fighting behind the lines could acquire a keepsake to memorialize their military service and affirm their martial valor, while those at the front could acquire psychic relief and masculine prestige by drinking hard whiskey instead of weak 3.2 beer. By transforming whiskey into a form of community currency, ordinary GIs removed whiskey from the exclusive preserve of the officer class and dealt a small, symbolic blow to the military's rigid hierarchies.

Demand on both sides of the whiskey–souvenir trade was sufficiently high that bartering took place every afternoon when the supply plane from Australia landed with milk, meat, and cheese. The flight crews, Jones recalled, "stuffed every available bit of space with bottles or cases of Scotch" to keep the souvenir trade going. A bloodstained silk battle flag fetched three Imperial quarts; a rifle merited only a pint. "A typical, *normal* 'Samurai saber' was always worth five Imperial quarts at least, and the ... ones with gold and ivory chasing could bring ... nine Imperial quarts." Men who had no souvenirs to trade paid as much as fifty dollars for a quart of Scotch.[62] The sheer volume of whiskey that enlisted men consumed fueled the vigorous barter trade. According to Jones, "almost everyone put away at least an Imperial quart a day, many quite a bit more."[63]

The existence of a shadow liquor economy indelibly shaped the enlisted men's sensory experience of the war. Some enlisted men established new drinking rituals to mark the passage of time and the beginning and end of combat. As some historians have noted, modern warfare often obliterates "the fighting man's sense of time," erasing the meal hours, bedtimes, and other recurring events that structure daily life.[64] Drinking alcohol created new structures in the absence of familiar ones. Some soldiers relied on alcohol for liquid courage when combat began.[65] Others "looked forward to jungle juice ... after harrowing combat patrols" in the Pacific, finding it "a stupendous reviver."[66] In France and Germany, soldiers "frequently sought out a cache of cognac or schnapps to finish the day's fighting with celebrating, relaxing, or just putting the war out of their minds."[67] James Jones described a platoon in the Pacific that used alcohol to both mark and blur the passage of time. The platoon would begin the day, Jones recalled, with "a good stiff jolt of Australian Scotch, wash up at the trough, have another jolt, then report with mess gear to the kitchen tent.... Breakfast was the only rollcall of the day..., and after that ... most preferred to sit in the tents or in the sun with their shirts off drinking from their Imperial quarts and refighting the great battle."[68]

Looting was another important feature of the enlisted man's shadow liquor economy. Although the locals of many liberated towns and villages in Europe often greeted US troops with gifts of alcohol and other sweets, GIs also took it upon themselves to liberate the wine and liquor cellars of the countries they occupied.[69] When the troops reached Germany, the scale of looting increased substantially, and many participants defended their actions as just retribution for Nazi atrocities and Germany's massive looting of other countries.[70] Some GIs were particularly incensed by the German army's sabotage of wineries. "What they couldn't eat or drink or carry away," Mauldin recalled, "they messed up so nobody else could use it."[71] David Webster, a private in an airborne unit, recalled that "GIs searched tirelessly for hidden bottles of cognac, schnapps, champagne, and wine" as they made their way across Germany. When they arrived in a new town, infantrymen often first searched the local brewery or distillery for stashes of alcohol. Although "civilians went to great pains to conceal their valuables, alcohol included, in hidden niches," this only added to the sport of hunting for alcohol.[72]

The best looting opportunities came when the Allied forces reached the mountain town of Berchtesgaden, home to the highest-ranking Nazi leadership and Alderhorst (Eagle's Nest), Hitler's retreat atop the eight-thousand-feet tall mountain. There Major Dick Winters discovered Hermann Goering's Officer's Club and its massive wine and liquor cellar, which held an estimated ten thousand bottles from around the world, stacked from floor to ceiling. Major Winter's discovery of the cellar on May 6, one day before the Germans surrendered to General Dwight D. Eisenhower, made the Allied victory even sweeter as men celebrated with the cellar's stock of champagne and other potables.[73] Although the Supreme Headquarters Allied Expeditionary Force issued edicts against looting, "subordinate commands rarely enforced" them.[74]

The sheer variety of methods enlisted men used to obtain alcohol attests to their determination to provision themselves. Whether by looting, trading war souvenirs for whiskey, distilling their own, or engaging in off-label uses of aftershave lotion and buzz-bomb fluid, enlisted men evaded the military's efforts to bar their access to liquor and confine drinking to off-duty times and spaces. The army's generous allotment of cigarettes and chocolate may have provided some relief, but not the kind that would enable soldiers to calm their anxieties and blot out the horrors of war. As historian Gerald Linderman has observed, many soldiers came to understand "that any chance of survival lay in totally inuring himself to the world within war. Thoughts of that other, fading world would only resuscitate hope of returning to it" and "revive . . . the aching futility of wishing that [they] could."[75] This was one element of the soldier's mindset that the popular wartime image of the homesick GI failed to grasp: sometimes soldiers coped with the stresses and strains of war not by thinking about the comforts of home but by putting home out of mind.

Even as alcohol helped to meet the psychic needs of GIs, excessive drinking by GIs endangered their health, fueled sexual assaults and other violent crime, and created ill will among civilians in both the United States and occupied countries.[76] Some servicemen experienced agonizing deaths after unwittingly consuming wood alcohol or knowingly drinking buzz-bomb fluid from a captured German cruise missile.[77] Between October 1944 and June 1945 more combat troops died from alcohol poisoning than communicable disease.[78] It is not clear what set of carrots and sticks would have tempered the excessive drinking of soldiers who sought to blot out the horrors of war, but by trying to control too much (permitting only off-duty consumption of 3.2 beer), the military brass also compromised their ability to guide drinking behaviors.

CLASS AND BRASS

Military officials, white enlisted men, and Black servicemen of all ranks saw the military's alcohol problem through entirely different lenses. Eager to quell dry outrage at home and shore up the US army's reputation as a benign occupying force abroad, military officials addressed negative publicity about intoxicated GIs and rising crime by instituting curfews in occupied countries, curbing sales of calvados, fining intoxicated GIs, and limiting off-duty GIs to 3.2 beer.[79] White enlisted men and Black servicemen of all ranks, on the other hand, defined the military's alcohol problem primarily as a problem of inequitable access to the pleasures that made military service bearable. In the gripe sections of army newspapers, white enlisted men voiced their dissatisfactions with the widely maligned army "caste system" and called for corrective legislation. The satirical cartoons and comic strips that enlisted men created for *Stars and Stripes* and *Yank* lampooned the officer class while empathizing with enlisted men's dreary, pleasure-deprived existence. Yet, even as white enlisted men invoked democratic values to condemn officers' undue privilege, they rarely indicted the military's pervasive racism and racial discrimination. As the next section reveals, it fell to Black enlisted men and Black officers to connect the politics of pleasure to broader struggles for racial equality and democracy both at home and abroad.

Resentment of officers' access to liquor of enviable quality and quantity was hardly the only objectionable inequity that stoked enlisted men's ire and frustration. Officers got better food, better accommodations, better entertainment, and even bested enlisted men in competition for women.[80] Fully conscious of the myriad ways rank had privilege, GIs were outraged that they put their bodies in the line of fire while officers secured faster releases from service, excluded soldiers from high-end brothels and strip clubs, and forced them to run errands and polish their shoes. All too often, the GI "felt more like a tool, cog, or disposable object than a soldier."[81]

Many GIs condemned the disparities between the quality and quantity of liquor that officers and soldiers enjoyed as an affront to democratic values. "Last night," one soldier fumed, "the soldiers were given about one swallow schnapps apiece. I know for a fact that the officers had two bottles apiece. Is this democracy?"[82] These inequities grated because soldiers could measure their disparate treatment in bottles, swallows, and dollars and cents. Myles Babcock, who served in the Pacific, recalled that soldiers paid forty-five dollars for a quart of brandy that cost officers a dollar and a half.[83] Whiskey's associations with masculinity, white privilege, and higher-ranking military officials made it a particularly powerful symbol of servicemen's frustrations with class and racial inequalities in the military. The exorbitant price soldiers paid for whiskey underscored what the enlisted men lacked: the social currency of rank. Echoing the US hospitality trade associations that championed a "liquor holiday" to preserve the "right to decent whiskey," some GIs viewed the occasional drink of American-made whiskey as just compensation for their arduous battlefront duties. Insisting that "A guy's entitled to a drink once a month in the jungle," Corporal Robert E. Wilson proposed that the military find a way to dehydrate whiskey so that it could be shipped in larger quantities. "They dehydrate everything else," Wilson said. "If they put up cans of whiskey powder, it wouldn't take up much space in the ships and all we'd have to do is add water and get drunk."[84]

The gripe sections of *Yank* and *Stars and Stripes* gave enlisted men space to vent their frustrations without fear of reprisal. Although criticisms of the brass and the military's undemocratic practices sometimes sparked controversy, the gripe sections ranked among the most popular features of the soldier newspapers. General George C. Marshall's endorsement of *Stars and Stripes* as a "symbol of . . . the free thoughts and free expression" the military was "fighting to preserve" likely helped to preserve the popular "Mail Call," Mail Bag," and "B-Bag" columns as venues for airing grievances.[85] Some gripe letters seethed with resentment. "Many officers can't figure out why the EM [enlisted men] are so prejudiced against them. What we EM can't figure out," one corporal complained, "is what God given reason or military order says officers shall eat steak and drink whisky while their subordinates eat hash."[86] Other letter writers called upon the military to eliminate the liquor ban in the interest of protecting enlisted men's health. "If whisky were rationed to EM," Sergeant E.J. Damico (and six other signers) argued, soldiers in the Pacific would jettison their unhealthy illicit habit of drinking substandard and dangerous replacements for "good liquor." Damico plainly explained why the officers' "whisky ration" made the enlisted man's "small beer ration" even more intolerable: "Who in the hell wants to sit and drink warm beer when someone else is enjoying good mainland whisky?"[87]

While some enlisted men demanded greater access to decent whiskey, others aimed to bring officers down to their level. The "number one gripe" of enlisted men stationed in China was not the food, slow mail, or bare PX shelves but the officer's monthly "jungle ration" of North American-made booze. The GIs complained so vociferously that the military eliminated the officers' ration of leading whiskey brands such as VO, Old Grand Dad, and Black & White, forcing everyone to make do with what *Yank* implied were inferior local alternatives: "Chinese whiskeys, rum, and wines . . . dreamed up by the wildest imaginations of Cathay distillers."[88] Another GI, fantasizing about payback, urged enlisted men to use their "numerical strength" and lobbying power to secure veteran's benefits for themselves while denying them to officers, who had already been amply compensated with better liquor, better pay, and better food.[89] Some officers who regularly shared their monthly liquor ration with enlisted men (and assumed other officers did, too) were taken aback by the depth of GIs' resentment.[90]

Aggrieved soldiers found solace and vindication in the editorial cartoons and satirical comic strips that appeared in *Yank* and *Stars and Stripes*. Sergeant George Baker's "Sad Sack" comic strip, a recurring featuring in *Yank*, followed the travails of a bumbling and perpetually pleasure-deprived infantryman whose desires for liquor and women were invariably thwarted by bad luck or malicious officers. In one strip, Sad Sack (military slang for "sad sack of shit") secures a coveted pass into town and giddily contemplates the women and alcohol that await him only to find the town in ruins when he arrives.[91] Just as often sadistic, pleasure-hoarding officers foiled Sad Sack's pursuit of pleasure. In one strip, an officer rummages through Sad Sack's possessions and seizes his lone bottle of liquor. In the next still we see Sad Sack scrubbing the floors of the officer's club while the officers drink the confiscated liquor in his presence.[92]

Bill Mauldin's editorial cartoons in *Stars and Stripes* voiced similar complaints about officers' undue privileges and the infantryman's difficulty accessing good liquor. Combat infantrymen loved the cartoons because Mauldin, a sergeant in the 45th Infantry Division's press corps, shared the same gripes about the dreary monotony and restrictiveness of Army life.[93] Mauldin centered his cartoons on Willie and Joe, two dirty, unshaven, coarse-speaking infantrymen who, as Mauldin wrote, lived "a life stripped of conventions and niceties."[94] His cartoons about the infantryman's persistently disappointed hunt for booze ranked among his most popular. At a 1999 Medal of Honor Society Convention a recipient recalled his favorite Mauldin cartoon: the one in which Joe and Willie happen on a liquor cellar only to discover that the Germans had already plundered all the booze. The caption captured their outrage and disappointment: "Them rats! Them dirty, cold-blooded, sore-headed, stinkin' Huns! Them atrocity-committin' skunks" (see Figure 25). The other veterans in attendance roared with laughter.[95]

Willie and Joe occasionally secured alcohol for themselves and their compatriots, but they also encountered cities and towns that the MPs had "plastered with 'prohibited' and 'off limits' signs." As was often the case, once US troops occupied a city, the MPs would restrict the best hotels and restaurants for the officers' exclusive use, leaving infantrymen with few places to enjoy their leave from combat duties.[96] In one cartoon, Willie and Joe arrive in town for rest and recreation but find an officers' bar for "A.M.G. [American Military Government] and base staff officers only" and a "Soldiers Club" guarded by an MP who admits only soldiers wearing ties (see Figure 26). The caption sums up their

"*Them rats! Them dirty, cold-blooded, soreheaded, stinkin' Huns. Them atrocity commitin' skunks . . .*"

FIGURE 25. Bill Mauldin cartoon in *Stars and Stripes* (Mediterranean edition), February 22, 1944. Copyright by Bill Mauldin (1944). Courtesy of Bill Mauldin Estate LLD. Image Courtesy of Fantagraphics.

"The hell with it, sir—let's get back to the front!"

FIGURE 26. Bill Mauldin cartoon in *Stars and Stripes* (Mediterranean edition), January 11, 1944. Copyright by Bill Mauldin (1944). Courtesy of Bill Mauldin Estate LLD. Image Courtesy of Fantagraphics.

dismay: "The hell with it, sir—Let's go back to the front."[97] In another cartoon, Willie and Joe mock an observer who completely misjudged the infantryman's condition: "Them wuz his exack words—'I envy th' way you dogfaces git first pick o' wimmen an' likker in towns.'"[98]

Even as Mauldin's cartoons condemned officers for keeping the best liquor for themselves, Mauldin also mocked the infantryman's appetite for alcoholic beverages of suspect origin. When soldiers purchased Cognac or drank an unclaimed bottle of the spirit, they could never entirely be sure that the label accurately reflected the Cognac bottle's contents. Cognac, as a result, acquired a reputation as a harsh and punishing spirit, sufficiently potent to fuel hangovers and possibly motor vehicles. One cartoon, captioned "We should have drank the cognac and walked to get gas," showed Willie and Joe stranded with their jeep, two empty bottles of cognac on the ground and the engine on fire, their attempt to refuel the jeep with cognac having backfired.[99] Jokes about cognac and calvados circulated widely in soldier humor. Mauldin recounted in *Up Front*, "The dogfaces love to tell the story of the curious soldier who sent a bottle of Cognac to a chemist friend for an analysis. In due time the report came back. It informed the soldier that his horse had kidney trouble."[100] In a *Yank* story written by an army private, a soldier's dry wit consoles his platoon mates who pined for the congratulatory bottle of whiskey given to their captain: "Aw, you prob'ly wouldn't like the stuff anymore. You got a calvados throat by now."[101]

Mauldin's own experience in the infantry made him deeply skeptical of the military's decision to ban liquor for enlisted men. Viewing the policy as misguided and counterproductive, Mauldin surmised that the only plausible reason for the ban was the military's fear of inciting a prohibitionist backlash "at any hint of the clean-cut lads overseas besotting themselves."[102] American civilians did not understand that most soldiers drank to "dull the sharp memories of war," Mauldin explained. By contrast, European armies, cognizant that soldiers will drink, "get good hooch" to wet "their soldiers' whistles . . . just enough to satisfy the boys, but not enough to souse them."[103] Mauldin welcomed the idea of a liquor ration for the enlisted men, noting that the British and French sated their soldiers' appetites for more dangerous intoxicants by regularly giving the French soldier wine and the British soldier "a spot of whisky" and beer. By soothing the French and British soldier's "palate . . . with honest liquor," the modest ration "makes him unable to bear the smell, let alone the taste, of the home-distilled stuff the Americans are forced to drink because they can get nothing else."[104]

TESTING THE COLOR LINE AT HOME

When white enlisted men complained about the military caste system, they typically understood the concept of caste in terms of class rather race. They attributed their inequitable treatment to undemocratic policies that favored the pleasures and needs of higher-ranking white officers over those of lowly white enlisted men. Most white servicemen perceived the military as a system built on the privileges of rank rather than race, even though the privileges of whiteness guaranteed them better lodging and amenities than Black soldiers and more opportunities for advancement. In the integrated training camps, Black troops lived in inferior quarters, ate in separate mess halls, and watched movies from the segregated section of the movie theater. Barred from the main post exchange, Black servicemen shopped at smaller PXs that carried limited supplies of beer and other desired goods.[105] The white (and often Southern) officers who commanded Black troops addressed them as "boy" or "[n____r]" and consigned them to menial jobs. Although some seven thousand Black servicemen earned promotions to the officer class, the military routinely passed over Black officers "for promotions that would rank them above white officers."[106]

When Black troops ventured off base for rest and recreation, the humiliations of serving in a segregated military followed them. In the towns surrounding US military bases, Black soldiers had to contend with capricious, racist, and often brutal local law enforcement. Adding insult to injury, the military reserved the better bars, restaurants, and liquor stores for white officers and enlisted men and permitted Black soldiers to patronize the small number of establishments located in the Black quarters or on the outskirts of town. Black officers and troops who hoped to see a Double Victory against fascism abroad and racism at home instead witnessed efforts by white servicemen and military officials to reconstitute the rules and racial logic of Jim Crow in the European and Pacific theaters of operation.

Official propaganda heightened Black Americans' expectations that the wartime state would protect their consumer rights and civil rights. Not only did official propaganda cast the war as a battle to defend freedom and democracy, but it also criticized fascist theories of the master race as antithetical to American ideals of cultural pluralism. In addition, rationing and price controls aimed to democratize the wartime political economy with the express purpose of ensuring equal access to basic goods.[107] Time and again, however, Black Americans' heightened "expectation of fair treatment within the consumer marketplace" went unfulfilled.[108] The military's efforts to restrict their access to alcohol and leisure became a particularly potent symbol of the wartime state's failure to fulfill such expectations. Each time a Black soldier or officer was banned from obtaining beer in an army canteen or was excluded from the more desirable bars near the base or in an occupied town, the military undermined the democratic principles its troops were ostensibly fighting to protect. The resentment and bitterness that such racial disparities aroused intensified Black Americans' determination to expand equality and democratic freedoms. Both at home and abroad, Black servicemen and officers resisted efforts to deny their access to intoxicating pleasures via peaceful protests and nonviolent acts of military and civil disobedience. They also answered acts of white violence and intimidation with their own acts of violence and intimidation.

The pervasive racial discrimination that Black officers and enlisted men encountered in military training camps and the towns surrounding US military bases was both profoundly demoralizing and deeply politicizing.[109] More than 80 percent of Black soldiers trained in military camps located in the South, but wherever they trained—whether in California, Arizona, Michigan, or Texas—discriminatory policies limited their mobility and access to local recreation, including bars, restaurants, and liquor stores. As the US military established bases in new locales across the country, it carried the racial logic of Jim Crow with it. The military did not merely accommodate or acquiesce to local prejudices; it actively spread Jim Crow to places where segregationism was not as deeply rooted. "Since the War Department could issue only one rule," General Frederick H. Osborn explained, it applied the "'Jim Crow' rule ... to the South and North alike."[110] Southern racial mores, in essence, established the default for the entire Army in the early years of the war.

White civilians residing in the towns surrounding military bases also played their part in making racial discrimination national policy. When white civilians complained that too many Black soldiers from nearby bases were entering their town, the military responded by declaring those areas off limits to Black soldiers.[111] Black soldiers who chose to ignore the "off limits" signs posted in the small Mohave Desert towns near Camp Clifford knew they were taking a big risk. As Second Lieutenant Walter Green recalled, "Some [restaurants] would serve you, and others would not; but they had the upper hand."[112] Military policies also conspired to keep Black servicemen on base and limit their time in town. At Camp Barkeley in Texas, the buses for white soldiers made nightly passes into town, but the two buses allotted for Black military personnel ran only on Saturdays and Sundays. Without a pass into town, Black servicemen had to make do with the paltry recreational options on base: unplayable basketball courts; a service club reserved for white patrons; and a small PX that might stock enough goodies for a Black soldier to enjoy a single bottle of 3.2 beer and a box of ice cream.[113] In the few cases where Black and white soldiers shared a PX, the Black soldiers had to take their drinks outside since they were not permitted to share the counter inside. Master Sergeant Warren Bryant, stationed at McDill Field in Florida, "bitterly resented" the myriad ways that military segregation interfered with the pleasure seeking of Black servicemen. If Black soldiers wanted to go into town, Bryant recalled, they "had to wait until all of the white soldiers who wished to go had been taken to their destinations; then we were crowded like sardines into a couple of buses and driven directly to the colored section of the nearby town."[114]

Black officers quickly learned that rank had few privileges when the body in a decorated uniform was Black. At the base in Midland, Texas, army officials essentially demoted Black officers to enlisted men's status by excluding them from the officers' club and requiring them to eat at the cadets' mess. The separate Black officers' club at Selfridge Field in Michigan, First Lieutenant Alexander Jefferson recalled, was "a small wooden building with a bar that literally shouted, 'Okay "[n____r]" this is good enough for you.'" The two-star general in charge of Selfridge Field quashed any hope for a better officers' club, insisting on "no socializing between white and colored officers" under his command.[115] Tellingly, the general also refused to allow the segregated Black officers' club to have its own fully stocked bar—a privilege to be bestowed only on high-ranking white men.

White officers were particularly invested in preserving whiskey drinking and liquor connoisseurship as an exclusively white, male domain. They aggressively patrolled Black soldiers' access to whiskey, a beverage that many white servicemen (especially Southern white troops) viewed as either too prestigious or too potent for Black consumers. As one white captain told the Black soldiers under his command, "Whiskey is a white man's drink, so you colored boys let it alone."[116] In another instance, a white officer from Georgia refused to obtain ration books for Black soldiers, thus denying them the means to purchase liquor from state stores in North Carolina.[117] Such attitudes recalled the white "drinking prohibitionists" of the South who ratified national

Prohibition to block Black Americans' access to intoxicating beverages but never intended to abandon drinking themselves.[118]

The long tradition of state-sanctioned violence in the American South gave police greater license to respond aggressively and without provocation to Black servicemen who ventured into town to enjoy the local theaters, bars, and cafés. Richard Jennings, who eventually became a major in the Air Force, recalled venturing into the Black quarters of Biloxi, Mississippi, "one night on pass" and almost being run over by a police car. After that near miss, Jennings decided "to stay on the base" and abandon his pursuit of urban nightlife—precisely the intended effect of police intimidation. The mere presence of armed, uniformed Black troops in towns surrounding Southern army bases—to say nothing of their desire to eat in the same restaurants and enjoy the same alcoholic beverages as white soldiers—prompted white servicemen to accuse Black troops of "abusing their military privileges."[119] The most shocking indignity for many Black military men stationed in the South was witnessing German POWs enjoy better living quarters, obtain town passes more frequently, and use restaurants and facilities that barred Black servicemen.[120] Both Black and white troops would have been dismayed to learn that the 173,000 German POWs interned at Fort McClellan in Alabama could also drink a quart of 3.2 beer each day (about three times the amount allotted to US servicemen).[121]

When Black officers and enlisted men protested these wide-ranging inequities, many drew inspiration from a decades old tradition of protesting Black citizens' exclusion from amusement parks, skating rinks, and public swimming pools. As the color line in recreation solidified across the nation, the NAACP and ordinary Black civilians made equal access to urban leisure a central demand of the civil rights movement. In the 1920s and 1930s, Black Americans filed petitions and lawsuits, entered swimming pools and beaches designated white only, clashed with private police, and threw punches when simmering conflicts erupted into violence. They risked white violence because they deeply resented the myriad ways that segregated leisure "circumscribed their citizenship and consumer rights."[122] During World War II conflict over access to intoxicating beverages and urban recreations intensified, sometimes provoking racial violence against Black and Mexican Americans, as happened in the June 1943 Los Angeles Zoot Suit Riots.[123]

Black civilians and Black servicemen instigated lawsuits against tavern owners who refused to serve them beer and they enlisted the aid of leading Black activists and the Black press to publicize the persistent discrimination that Black servicemen faced.[124] A letter signed by "A Group of Soldiers" hoped the *Pittsburgh Courier* would "start the ball rolling" by printing their short missive describing the limited recreational opportunities and poorly stocked PXs reserved for Black soldiers at Camp Barkeley in Texas.[125] Black servicemen also used the Black press to applaud communities that bucked the color line. Several Black soldiers reported to the *Chicago Defender* about a small Western Oregon town that opened their churches, theaters, beer taverns, and soda fountains to them. Perhaps hoping that the exception to the rule could also be politically instructive, the *Chicago Defender* noted that the warm reception made Black soldiers "feel as though they have something to fight for."[126] On other occasions, Black servicemen forged effective alliances with clergy to demand integrated public accommodations. When beer taverns and other businesses in San Bernadino, California, plastered their entrances with "We Cater to White Trade Only" signs—sometimes at the army's behest—Black soldiers pressured the army to change course. The army held firm, but the collective efforts of a priest, a rabbi, and a Black clergyman convinced many businesses to remove the signs.[127]

Black servicemen who engaged in nonviolent direct action risked white backlash and disproportionate punishment. At Freeman Field in Seymour, Indiana, sixty-one Black officers staged a sit-in to desegregate the white-only officers' club. Operating in small groups, the officers walked into the club and politely requested service only to be denied service and arrested. For this act of disobedience, the Army court-martialed and convicted one officer and officially reprimanded the others.[128] The Army sentenced Private Alton Levy to hard labor, ostensibly for circulating a rumor that the base commander's wife controlled base policy, but his real offense was agitating for more equitable recreational facilities at Lincoln Air Base in Nebraska. The Black soldiers stationed there were barred from entering the main USO canteen and buying beer from the main rec center. But for "a hole in the wall on Ninth Street," all other bars in town were closed to them.[129]

Agitation and nonviolent direct action sometimes gave way to violence, especially when conflict centered on highly symbolic masculine drinks such as whiskey.[130] In Arizona and California the persistent refusal of white merchants to sell Black servicemen liquor provoked Black soldiers to "wreak havoc" on white businesses, causing thousands of dollars in damages.[131] In San Luis Obispo, an infuriated Black soldier began "hurling bottles and glasses" when a white liquor retailer denied him service. Other Black soldiers joined in, and a "battle raged" for two hours, ending only after firemen tear gassed the building.[132] Black Americans' determination to claim equal treatment often put them directly in harm's way. In Walterboro, South Carolina, the specter of lynching hung over a group of Black Air Force pilots when their ranking officer, Lieutenant Colonel Henry Peoples, persisted in requesting beer from a white waitress. Two white sailors and a marine at the counter urged the men to heed the waitress's refusal, prompting one of the pilots to hit the sailor and the shaken waitress to give the pilots beer so long as they consumed it off premises. Within minutes of leaving the shop, thirty cars with white men carrying pitchforks, blunderbusses, and high-powered rifles encircled the Black Air Force pilots. Fortunately, an associate of Lieutenant Colonel Peoples had also called in reinforcements and the white lynch mob disbanded. Although the Black pilots escaped physical harm, the FBI created a file for Lieutenant Colonel Peoples noting that he had started a "race riot."[133]

TESTING THE COLOR LINE ABROAD

When Black troops shipped overseas, many Europeans greeted Black troops as liberators and acknowledged them as American citizens, giving Black Americans a taste of the dignity and respect that a postwar order based on racial equality might bring. Ivan Houston, a member of the Army's 92nd Division, recalled being showered with "hugs, kisses, and wine" in Italy. "Our color was no issue at all. . . . To the Italians we were first class."[134] The British also warmly welcomed Black troops. Affectionately calling Black troops the "Black Yanks," the British invited Black Americans to their "homes, churches, and trade union meetings" and included them in their leisure activities, sometimes with the hope and expectation that Black servicemen would teach them the lindy hop. According to the Black journalist Roi Ottley, who covered the war in Europe for *Liberty Magazine*, *PM*, and the *Pittsburgh Courier*, the British preferred the company of Black troops to white servicemen because they displayed good manners, adopted the local customs, and did "not come here to 'take over.'"[135] Some pub owners, Ottley wrote, would even "save whiskey for Negro troops and refuse it to white soldiers."[136]

Not all Britons and Europeans were so welcoming, however. The official British policy toward Black American troops tried to carve out a middle ground that accommodated Jim Crow in the US military without explicitly condoning it. Following extensive Cabinet discussions, the British government settled on an ambiguous message, advising British troops and citizens to treat Black Americans politely and as equals but avoid becoming too friendly and offering Black troops drinks.[137] A local newspaper in Cherbourg similarly advised French citizens against socializing with Black troops or selling them wine and liquor.[138] The US military's censorship of Black reporters reflected its own dueling sensibilities on race questions. Fearful of engendering negative publicity and eager to calm racial animosities on base, the military censored stories about violent clashes between Black and white soldiers both at home and abroad; some commanders even confiscated Black newspapers that found their way to army bases.[139] At the same time, the military also censored Ottley's reporting on the warm reception Black troops received from the British, perhaps attempting to avoid inflaming white Americans who disapproved of interracial social intimacy or perhaps attempting to suppress evidence that other western democracies were more liberal and tolerant than the United States.[140] Although Britons were hardly free of race prejudice, stories about their kindness toward Black troops heightened the "mystique of British anti-racism"—myths that "silenced a broader imperial history of anti-Black violence" while allowing Britain to "claim the moral high ground associated with being regarded as a tolerant nation."[141]

The most vicious and insidious attacks on Black troops abroad came not from locals but from US servicemen and the military brass. White servicemen became enraged when Black troops enjoyed the pleasures of drinking and socializing with white women—activities that in white soldiers' eyes enabled Black men to claim social equality with white men. US Army officers threatened to lynch Black troops who met up in pubs, and fights between Black and white troops, Roi Ottley observed, frequently broke out "when whiskey and white women [were] about."[142] In Bremen, Germany, white servicemen from the 29th Division, a notoriously racist division, violently obstructed Black mobility and pleasure seeking. Black "soldiers did not go out on the streets alone at night," Staff Sergeant Chester Jones recalled, because "members of the 29th had been known to beat and kill Blacks."[143] The intensity of the white backlash against the Black troops serving abroad stemmed from white anxieties that the sexual color line would lose its moral force and that more equitable treatment would, as Ottley put it, make Black soldiers "mighty difficult to remold into the Jim Crow pattern" when they returned home.[144]

Army leaders at the highest command, seeking to quell racial violence and calm the white racial anxieties that fueled it, sanctioned policies that strictly segregated Black and white troops in public sites of leisure. General Dwight D. Eisenhower directed local commanding officers in Great Britain to avoid racial discrimination but "use their own best judgement" to "minimiz[e] causes of friction between White and Colored Troops." General John Clifford Hodges Lee, a deputy theatre commander whose grandfather had been a captain in the Confederate Army, believed such directives gave him license to discriminate against Black troops "when it concerned women and liquor."[145] Like other white Southern Army officials, Lee feared that the absence of Jim Crow abroad would agitate white Southern troops.[146] Their determination to replicate Jim Crow in Great Britain reproduced the violence and intimidation that sustained segregation in the American South. Some white Army officials and servicemen threatened boycotts and deployed other ugly forms of coercion to stop Black patronage of British pubs and restaurants. White commanders informed the proprietors of the best cafes, restaurants, theaters, and hotels that the Army would declare their premises "Out of Bounds" for both white and Black soldiers if they failed to bar Black soldiers. Such strong-armed tactics, Ottley reported, effectively relegated Black troops "to the worst sections on the outskirts of town or along the waterfront."[147] White American soldiers also became enforcers of the color line. They harassed, bullied, and bruised a white British woman who worked in a Red Cross club for Black soldiers and urged her to stop working there, warning, "We string up women like you in Georgia!"[148] One clearly intimidated pub owner pleaded with a longtime Black customer to stop visiting the pub, noting that white Americans had threatened to "break up his place" if he served Black patrons.[149]

Although such racial discrimination was intended to humiliate and demoralize Black soldiers, it also strengthened their resolve to make a stand for racial equality and align reality with the war's stated democratic aims. When Army officials set up two bars for American troops in Cherbourg—one for white soldiers in the center of town and another for Black servicemen on the outskirts of town—Black soldiers launched a consumer boycott in protest. Not one of the ten thousand Black troops in Cherbourg entered the Jim Crow bar, and their sustained boycott forced the army to open the bar at the center of town to them.[150] Black troops also took up arms to defend themselves against violence from white servicemen. Staff Sergeant Jones recalled an incident in Bremen, where white servicemen in the 29th Division used guns and ritual humiliation to reclaim a bar as a white-only space. The white soldiers forced two Black soldiers "to do a jig while these crackers shot at their feet, the ceiling, everywhere." When word of the event spread, twenty-five Black soldiers returned to the bar and "shot it up," leaving five or six dead or seriously injured. MPs arrested all the Black soldiers they saw within blocks of the café, but none of the white soldiers could identify their assailants. Making Black soldiers "do the jig," Jones surmised, "did not long remain a favorite form of entertainment among the men of the 29th."[151]

Not all white soldiers were avowed segregationists. In some instances they joined Black soldiers to protest segregated recreation. When a Filipino bar owner posted a Whites Only sign at the behest of one white soldier, some white troops objected, saying 'We're fighting the same war, ain't we?'" Although local residents, the Filipino bartender, the Chinese cook, and Black war reporters pressured the bar owner to remove the sign, he refused to comply, perhaps betting that segregationist opinion was strong enough to keep the bar in business.[152]

The determined efforts of white military personnel to preserve white privilege and the determined efforts of Black officers and servicemen to resist it created perpetual conflict over Black troops' access to recreation and intoxicating pleasures. For many Black soldiers, the experience of racial discrimination in sites of leisure and consumption fortified their resolve to continue the battle for racial equality and civil rights after the war. The last straw for Lieutenant Christopher Sturkey came when he returned to the United States and was still denied service at a restaurant, despite appearing in full dress uniform decorated with "his battle stars, campaign ribbons, the works." For Sturkey the incident highlighted that the battle for civil rights needed to begin in retail sites "where little people . . . [tell] us we are not good enough to eat in, drink in, shop in . . . their little places of business."[153] It was no accident that the "repeated indignities over eating and drinking" experienced by Black civilians and servicemen "made access to dining establishments one of the earliest front lines in the civil rights movement of the 1960s."[154] It was also no accident that Black veterans became key players in the NAACP, CORE, and other civil rights organizations after the war.[155]

The war itself delivered only modest and weakly enforced changes for Black men serving in the military. The government's response came relatively late, following the rash of racial violence in 1943 on military bases and in Detroit and Los Angeles. That same year, the adjutant general of the army ordered the military to open recreational facilities to all races. The following year, army bus services between military camps and nearby towns took passengers on a first-come, first-serve basis regardless of race. None of these responses significantly disrupted segregation, as base commanders could still assign facilities by unit. The new policy did, however, give Black soldiers more leverage in pressing for greater access to recreation.[156] Racial conflict spurred by blatant discrimination against Black GIs who tried to patronize bars in Germany, South Korea, and Vietnam would continue to plague the army well into 1960s and 1970s.[157] Although the wartime state failed to protect Black consumer rights and civil rights, World War II did lay the groundwork for future activists and Black GIs "to demand new rights from the federal government," seeding the field for the "rights revolutions" of the 1960s.[158] Those rights revolutions were also intimately tied to expectations fueled by the pleasure revolution: the idea that access to recreation and psychoactive pleasures were also meaningful ways of measuring citizenship and belonging.

CONCLUSION

World War II transformed what military personnel drank and how they imagined alcohol's place in both army and civilian life. While stationed overseas, servicemen sampled an array of exotic new beverages—from the rice wines of China and Japan to the cognac, wine, calvados, and schnapps of Europe. Although the US military minimally and inconsistently provisioned GIs with 3.2 beer, the Army's pocket guides to the cities of Southern France and Italy, published in 1944, encouraged GI travelers to sample the local wines and offered tips on the best Bordeaux wines. The pocket guide to Italy, however, assured GIs that they needn't venture far beyond their sensory comfort zone. "If you like to drink a sweet wine with meat," the pocket guide advised, "don't let it bother you."[159] The pocket guide's advice to "suit your own taste" echoed the populist sensibilities of the California wine industry's wartime advertising campaign with its injunction to "make your own rules" and drink "the wine *you* like best."[160] Some American troops undoubtedly did come home, as Wayne Curtis has argued, with "a new taste for French brandy and wine, as well as for German schnapps" and rum and cokes.[161] Many also returned with "a strong penchant for heavy drinking" and helped to swell the postwar membership of Alcoholics Anonymous.[162]

Many white GIs, however, did not return with more cosmopolitan tastes and outlooks. Instead, as Lee Kennett's study of GI letters found, they "compared what they saw [abroad] with what they already knew, and ... confirmed ... that the American way of doing things was the right and the normal way." The authors of *The American Soldier*, a comprehensive study of GI attitudes conducted after the war, echoed that conclusion, noting that returning veterans "came home as they went out, indubitably American."[163] A cartoon in *Collier's* magazine similarly implied that the spirit of culinary adventurism had not yet taken hold of the average GI (see Figure 27). Simultaneously satirizing soldiers' desires for all things American and the California wine industry's relentless campaign to elevate the status of American wines, the cartoon joked that soldiers stationed in Paris now preferred American wines. Rejecting their waiter's offer of French wine, two servicemen seated in a Parisian café informed the gracious garçon, "We don't want that domestic stuff. Haven't you got some New York or California wines?"[164]

Once back on home soil, many white GIs reclaimed the trusted and the familiar in gender relations, race relations, and alcoholic beverage preferences. Beer remained the go-to for a night on the town, and whiskey, by virtue of its wartime scarcity and masculine cachet, acquired even greater prestige. Although many Southern white officers and enlisted men continued to view whiskey as the white man's beverage, many Black servicemen also longed to reexperience the pleasures of decent whiskey upon their return. Fondly recalling his enjoyment of Four Roses Bourbon, one Black GI facetiously asked Santa Claus (via the *Pittsburgh Courier*) to bring him a "sweet young ... Lena Horne type" and "one large-sized quart of mild whiskey with four roses tied around it."[165]

The conventional view of Europe as a land of alcohol plenty did not square with the average GI's experience abroad.[166] In Britain and on the continent, black markets priced decent spirits beyond the average soldier's pay. Much of the good quality wine and liquor had been seized and consumed, deliberately adulterated with toxins, or stretched and redistilled into a wretched spirit. By the time GIs arrived in occupied Berlin, the high-priced cocktails served in nightclubs were, according to one *Yank* reporter, "nothing more than water faintly colored with wine and tea."[167] When the army's stingy provisions of warm 3.2 beer could not suffice, GIs found new ways to provision themselves. Some participated in the robust barter trade in alcohol and war

FIGURE 27. A liquor trade publication reprinted this cartoon by Michael Berry, which originally appeared in *Collier's* magazine, 1944. General Research Division, New York Public Library.

souvenirs; others learned to convert K-ration fruit bars, Aqua Velva aftershave, and jumbo-sized cans of army peaches into potent intoxicants. Yes, GIs enjoyed a few glorious windfalls along the way, but the experience of alcohol plenty represented only a temporary reprieve from the far more politicizing experience of deprivation and inequity (see Figure 28).

Many servicemen from the generation that came of age after Prohibition's demise came to view alcohol consumption as a right of citizenship

FIGURE 28. These men at a US naval base in Manila, the capital of the Philippines, received four beer cans each (quadruple the usual allotment) to celebrate the war's end, August 15, 1945. James Benton via Getty Images.

and a pleasure to which they were entitled. They regarded the repeal of Prohibition as a defining generational event—one that had spared them from bootleg liquor, speakeasies, and the injustice of selective prohibition enforcement. One notable expression of such sentiments appeared in a tribute to President Franklin Delano Roosevelt published in *Yank* a month after his death. Saluting the president as "the Commander in Chief, not only of the armed forces, but of our generation," the memoriam praised various aspects of the president's leadership, including the jobs programs that had given many servicemen the first paychecks of their youth. Most significantly, the second line of the obituary highlighted the repeal of Prohibition as the deed that sealed young servicemen's bond to Roosevelt. "We never saw the inside of a speakeasy," *Yank* observed, "because he had prohibition repealed before we were old enough to drink."[168] The great irony of that statement was that World War II embedded servicemen in a consumer marketplace abroad that exhibited many features of the Prohibition economy: exorbitant black market prices for high quality liquor, the illicit production of potent spirits, deaths from poisonous booze, and the growing acceptance of wine and brandy as substitutes for more highly desired spirits.

On the home front, organized drys had hoped to seize the wartime emergency to reimpose prohibition on large swaths of the country, but servicemen's own sense of justice and entitlement shifted the political center of gravity on alcohol matters in an entirely different direction. Increasingly they imagined equal access to intoxicating pleasures as a right to defend. Consider the returning airman who proposed that the government purchase existing liquor stocks and sell them to returning veterans at a fair price. Although many home front Americans, in his view, earned enough to pay "exorbitant" black market liquor prices, he thought veterans "deserve[d] special consideration," as they had been deprived of liquor abroad and had "earn[ed] only soldier's pay."[169] For many white GIs and Black military personnel of all ranks, the absence and denial of intoxicating pleasures ranked high among the daily injustices that made the military a fundamentally undemocratic institution. White GIs voiced their resentment of the gap between the officers' club's well-stocked liquor cabinet and their own meager supply of warm 3.2 beer in gripe letters to army newspapers. Soldier humor, especially the satirical cartoons of Bill Mauldin and George Baker, pilloried such inequities. Black servicemen used the media as well to shame military officials into changing course by alerting Black journalists to their unequal treatment.

More remarkably, Black military personnel channeled their resentments into direct political action, using boycotts, sit-ins, and violence to protest discriminatory practices at home and abroad. Although Black military personnel scored a few modest wartime victories, the forces of white supremacy proved stubbornly resilient. Nevertheless, the military policies that assured inadequate and inequitable access to pleasure had enduring politicizing effects. The experience of unequal pleasures helped to nurture a rights consciousness that energized the postwar civil rights movement, especially the struggles of Black citizens to integrate public sites of recreation. Alcoholic beverages could be politicized in all these ways because they so profoundly shaped the ways Americans experienced pleasure and leisure in the world of war and beyond.

Epilogue

The Power and Limits of Reinvention

In 1984, some fifty years after launching its advertising series extolling moderation as the hallmark of the modern whisky drinker, Seagram debuted another campaign that aimed to reverse Americans' growing preference for beer and wine over spirits. Faulting "years" of misleading publicity, Seagram set out to correct the widespread "impression that liquor is, in itself, strong drink, whereas beer and wine are drinks of moderation."[1] The company's new campaign claimed that spirits were equivalent to wine and beer because an average serving of each contained the same amount of alcohol. The print and billboard ads dramatized the point with elegant simplicity, showing a twelve-ounce can of beer, a five-ounce glass of wine, and a one-and-a-quarter ounce shot of liquor—each joined to the other by an equal sign. Although many who viewed the ads mistook them for a disinterested public service announcement, the Wine Institute and the Beer Institute howled in protest.[2] Having spent decades and millions of dollars fashioning distinctive cultural identities for wine and beer, their dismay was understandable. The equivalency campaign's slogan—"A drink, is a drink, is a drink"—attempted to erase all such moral and cultural distinctions. Although the irony was surely lost on the company's executives, Seagram's new slogan revived a central assumption of the prohibitionists, who also believed "A drink, is a drink, is a drink," irrespective of usage.

The controversy sparked by Seagram's equivalency campaign reveals much about the power and limits of reinvention. As the alcoholic beverage industry continually relearned, reinvention was—and is—an ongoing process. In different times and places, changes in consumer tastes, social norms, addiction paradigms, and regulatory regimes have all unsettled the ground on which tastemakers and trade associations had forged previous cultures of drink. Seagram's alcohol equivalency message was conceived in just such a moment of flux. During the 1980s, consumption of distilled spirits—already diminished by countercultural rebellions that identified highballs and martinis with white-collar conformity—declined further as new generations of consumers discovered the pleasures of craft beers and varietal wines. Improved quality continued to lift wine's popularity in the years following California's surprise victory over French wines in the Paris Wine Tasting of 1976. The market outlook was not all rosy, however. Some industry members railed against the rising threat of "neoprohibitionism" as state and federal legislation raised the drinking age, stiffened penalties against drunk driving, and mandated new warning labels on alcohol containers. The real brilliance of Seagram's alcohol equivalence message was its ability to hide a marketing ploy within a public relations appeal. The message was pliable enough to earn the approval of anti-drunk driving crusaders and also reassure liquor fanciers that cocktails were no less virtuous than wine or beer.[3]

Seagram's equivalency campaign diminished, but hardly erased, wine and beer's reputation for moderation. After two years of steady print and cable TV advertising, the percentage of adults who believed in alcohol equivalence rose from 12 percent in 1982 to 38 percent in 1985. More striking, however, was the Gallup Organization's conclusion that most consumers, with the exception of college graduates, continued to believe that standard servings of spirits contained more alcohol than standard servings of beer and wine.[4] Perhaps consumers recognized that Seagram's idea of a standard pour wasn't all that standard. Or perhaps they recognized, as brewers and vintners had attested at the congressional hearings to modify the Volstead Act, that the social and temporal contexts in which drinking occurred also influenced a drink's intoxicating effects. Whatever the source of their skepticism, consumers did not easily relinquish beliefs honed by personal experience, shared communities of taste, and decades of industry propaganda.

The marketing and public relations challenges that Seagram confronted in the 1980s paled in comparison to the challenges that alcoholic beverage producers faced during the Great Depression and World War II. Although the repeal of Prohibition ended the debate over the efficacy of broad alcohol bans, it raised new, thorny questions about how states should best regulate the sale of intoxicating pleasures and accommodate their growing popularity. Popular culture and history textbooks have so frequently portrayed the repeal of Prohibition as the triumph of cultural liberalism over puritanical Victorianism that we often fail to grasp just how modest and constrained repeal actually was. Repeal did not end the deep and lingering suspicion that alcohol producers and sellers put profits ahead of the public interest. It did not override the new tastes for soft drinks, sweet cocktails, and potent spirits that consumers had acquired during Prohibition. Nor did it end the continuing allure of homemade wine in a depressed economy or remove the class and ethnic stigmas that made wine a tough sale. Perhaps most significantly, repeal did not eliminate the lingering influence of prohibitionists on the new regulatory regimes that governed when and where alcohol could be sold and who could access it. In the early years of repeal, many localities simply returned to the status quo ante of the 1910s, when local option elections had already turned large swaths of the country dry. Even in states where prohibitionists had less clout, repeal suppressed segments of urban nightlife that had flourished in the 1920s. Instead of making selective enforcement a relic of the Prohibition era, state liquor authorities heightened their surveillance of bars that catered to gays and lesbians.

It took a world war and a battalion of mass marketers, public relations experts, and tastemakers to uproot prohibitionist mythologies and fully launch alcohol's journey to mainstream acceptance. Alcohol's contributions to wartime food crusades, civilian morale, and the production of essential war matériel stoked fantasies of market expansion and reputational redemption that partly came to fruition. Wine enjoyed a sales boomlet in 1942, and, for a brief time, sales of table wines overtook dessert wines as gourmets and ordinary home cooks discovered the pleasures of drinking wine with meals and the flavor-enhancing benefits of adding wine to their soups, stews, and spaghetti sauce—a practice that grew in popularity after the war. Beer acquired more American hues as trade association advertisements embedded beer in the nostalgic settings of the small town homecoming, the western barbecue, and the community roof raising. The military's provisioning of 3.2 percent beer strengthened generational allegiances to beer, fulfilling *Brewers Digest*'s prediction in 1941 that military service would "cultivate a taste for beer in millions of young men who will eventually constitute the largest beer-consuming section of our population."[5] Few returning veterans likely longed for the warm, sensorially muted, and erratically supplied 3.2 beer on offer in the training camps and far-flung theaters of operation, but male consumers kept lager sales humming throughout the postwar years. On the home front, civilians awash in cash from good-paying defense jobs traded up to better brands of whiskey (when they could find them) and learned to order by brand name.

The war, however, also revealed the limits of reinvention. Despite their heavy investments in advertising and public relations, circumstances that the industry thought would redound to their benefit did not invariably play out to their advantage. At the beginning of the war, Lewis Rosenstiel, who headed Schenley Distillers, was certain that turning their facilities over to the production of industrial alcohol would burnish distillers' reputation as patriotic corporate citizens. As it happened, however, whiskey shortages and forced tie-in sales only deepened public suspicions that profiteering distillers were deliberately withholding whiskey to gin up prices. The *American Wine Merchant* anticipated that the "continental" practice of drinking wine with meals would eventually rub off on "the average G.I.," but a Europe awash in decent wine was not the land GIs encountered and the veteran-induced wine boom failed to materialize.[6] As soon as North American whiskey distillers resumed whiskey production in late 1944 and 1945, aggregate national sales of table wine flattened.

Sales statistics provide only one measure of alcohol's reinvention. We can also assess alcohol's representation in popular postwar films to gauge how deeply the work of tastemakers and trade associations had penetrated the popular imagination. Few might guess that whiskey executives would actively promote *The Lost Weekend* (1945), a critically acclaimed film about an alcoholic writer's nightmarish five-day drinking binge. Yet that is precisely what Seagram did, despite the staunch objections of other whiskey makers who feared the box-office sensation would unleash a wave of attacks.[7] In every large city where the film was released, Seagram placed large newspaper ads urging moviegoers to see Ray Milland's "magnificent performance" as the alcoholic Don Birnam, a role that earned the actor an Academy Award. Seagram was certain the story of a failed writer who depends on his brother's financial support and loves the bottle more than his devoted girlfriend would convince moviegoers that "*some men should not drink!*"—a sentiment that Seagram's moderation ads endorsed in the 1930s.[8] Don, as played by Milland, elicited both empathy and disgust. Desperate for alcohol after his brother Wick confiscated his hidden stash, Don steals the ten dollar bill Wick had left for the cleaning lady and heads out for Nick's bar. On his way, he drops by the liquor store, where the clerk apologetically declines Don's request for two bottles of rye, explaining that Wick would no longer pay Don's tab. When Don flashes the ten dollar bill, the clerk asks, "What brand?" Don's short-tempered reply played right into whiskey makers' hands: "You know what brand, Mr. Brophy. The cheapest. None of that twelve-year-old, aged in the wood chi-chi. Not for me." By Seagram's lights, Don lacked all the virtues that idealized whiskey drinkers possessed in abundance. A failed, financially insolvent writer who guzzled liquor for the effect, Don the drunk was the perfect foil for the ambitious, gregarious bread-winner who, in keeping with Seagram's moderation message, savored his liquor but "paid [his] bills first."⁹ Even the film's camera work affixed blame where whiskey executives thought it belonged: not on the liquor store's whiskey bottles that blurred into the background, but on Don's brightly lit face in the center of the screen. Don's faults, the scene emphasized, were his own.

Wine frequently appeared in wartime films as an accoutrement of urban nightlife and heterosexual romance, but on rare occasions, wine also acquired deeper political meanings. In the Christmas classic *It's a Wonderful Life* (1946), directed by Frank Capra, wine comes to symbolize the virtues of pluralism, neighborliness, and broadly shared prosperity. Wine makes its first appearance when the Martinis, a large Italian American family, move from the Potter's Field slums to a new single-family home in Bailey Park, a burgeoning suburban development in the small town of Bedford Falls. Thanks to generous loans from the Building and Loan run by the golden-hearted George Bailey, townsfolk who aspired to home ownership no longer had to "live like pigs" in shacks rented from Henry Potter, the town's greedy real estate mogul. When the Martinis arrive in Bailey Park, George Bailey and his wife Mary warmly greet them with gifts of bread, salt, and wine and a blessing for their home: "Bread, that this house may never know hunger. Salt, that life may always have flavor. And wine, that joy and prosperity may reign forever." Moviegoers might not have known the blessing's origins in Jewish and Slavic culture, but they likely would have recognized the gift of wine as a meaningful acknowledgment of the Martini's Italian heritage. Much as official wartime rhetoric celebrated cultural pluralism as a distinguishing feature of American national identity, George and Mary Bailey welcomed the Martinis—and their wine-drinking traditions—into the mainstream of white, middle-class American life.

The film's depictions of alcohol were not uniformly flattering. George's bumbling, forgetful Uncle Billy drinks too much and misplaces an eight-thousand-dollar bank deposit, precipitating a crisis that threatens to bankrupt the Building and Loan and land George in jail. Now suicidal, George comes to believe that he is worth more dead than alive. To show George what the world would look like had he never been born, George's guardian angel conjures Pottersville, a dystopic inversion of Bedford Falls. Bailey's Building and Loan no longer exists, and the land where Bailey Park homes once stood has become a cemetery, a figurative graveyard for the townsfolks' middle-class aspirations. Mr. Potter's unrestrained capitalist greed has turned Pottersville into a garish, vice-ridden town awash in cheap liquor. Jazz blares from sleazy bars and nightclubs. Flashing neon lights advertise fight clubs, pool halls, pawnshops, and burlesque joints. The building that used to house Martini's, the wholesome Italian restaurant that served wine, beer, and spaghetti dinners, is now home to Nick's, a seedy saloon where unescorted (presumably disreputable) women sit at the bar, cigarette girls sell smokes, and couples dance to boogie-woogie performed by a Black pianist (a cameo by the famous Meade "Lux" Lewis). The stage directions in the final script make the intended contrast between Martini's "warm, welcoming spirit" and Nick's "hard-drinking . . . honky-tonk" clear. In Nick's bar, the script notes, the checkered tablecloths and "the cheerful Italian feeling [are] gone" and the clientele are "lower down and tougher."[10]

Like many of his fellow Italian Americans, Capra represented wine as liquor's virtuous antithesis. The full depravity of Nick's bar is revealed when Clarence, George's 293-year-old guardian angel, enrages the bartender by requesting "mulled wine, heavy on the cinnamon and light on the cloves." Nick blusters, "We serve hard drinks in here for men who want to get drunk fast." Mulled wine hardly fit the bill. Wine reenters the story in the film's concluding scene, when the townspeople rally to George's side and donate their savings to spare the Building and Loan from bankruptcy. Moved by the festive mood, Mary calls out to Mr. Martini, "how about some wine?" and the crowd gathered by the Christmas tree bursts into song. In marking the celebratory occasion, wine symbolically affirmed the redemptive power of neighbors coming together for the common good.

It's a Wonderful Life oozed with so much nostalgia and sentimentality that neither its idealization of small-town life nor its portrait of a morally bankrupt Pottersville rang entirely true. Capra's decision to associate Pottersville with swing and boogie-woogie—music that had entertained the armed forces and boosted civilian morale throughout the war—was particularly puzzling. James Agee, *The Nation*'s film critic, remarked that Capra's vision of "a twentieth-century American town . . . uses so little of the twentieth and idealizes so much that seems essentially nineteenth-century."[11] Another critic, finding *It's a Wonderful Life* "the latest example of Capracorn," similarly lamented that the director's portrait of small-town "American life" mirrored "the *Saturday Evening Post* covers of Norman Rockwell."[12] Perhaps Capra was inviting viewers to associate the blackness of jazz with Pottersville's moral decay, but for some viewers the joyful sounds emanating from Nick's Place and the downtown nightclubs likely made the ostensibly nightmarish Pottersville seem more alluring than Bedford Falls with its lone movie house and quaint Italian restaurant. Nevertheless, Capra's nostalgia was a powerful strand in wartime popular culture, evidenced by the popularity of Rockwell's art and the commercial success of the small-town pastoral musical, a film genre that included *Meet Me in St. Louis* (1944) and *State Fair* (1945). Capra's racial politics and his take on alcohol's proper place in modern American life largely echoed the carefully crafted image that brewers and vintners had cultivated for wine and beer. When the USBF ads asserted that "Beer Belongs!," beer drinkers appeared not in public crowds that might evoke memories of the saloon but in homier settings where extended families, community involvement, and white picket fences symbolized the stability many wartime civilians yearned for. Wine's connections to ethnic food cultures sometimes augmented its allure, but the Wine Advisory Board also situated wine in distinctly white, middle-class settings to cultivate wine's respectability and broaden its mass market appeal. Brewers and winemakers were all too happy to hitch their wagons to the redemptive power of whiteness and small-town nostalgia.

The Best Years of Our Lives (1946) offers yet another gauge of the power and limits of alcohol's cultural reinvention. Praised for its realistic and humanizing treatment of veterans' postwar readjustment, the film won seven Academy Awards and became the highest-grossing film of the 1940s. *Best Years* resonated deeply because it forthrightly acknowledged—and eased—widespread anxieties about how discharged veterans would cope with the challenges of readapting to civilian life. Particularly alarming were the predictions of medical authorities and other experts that the postwar dislocations and traumas of war would unleash a wave of alcoholism.[13] *Best Years* tracks the intertwined stories of three veterans—US Navy petty officer Home Parrish, Army sergeant Al Stephenson, and Air Force bombardier captain Fred Derry—who meet for the first time awaiting a flight to their hometown. From the opening scenes, references to alcohol and depictions of excessive drinking allow audiences to glimpse how the war has changed both the discharged veterans and the small midwestern city they have returned to. On the taxi ride home, Homer marvels that his uncle's tavern now bears a neon sign—an indication of his hometown's modernity—and he informs Al and Fred that Uncle Butch is a "swell guy—only the family don't think he's respectable because he sells liquor." Hailing Butch's Place as "the best joint in town," Homer clearly does not share his family's assessment. That short bit of dialogue acknowledged alcohol's contested respectability, yet the film's many moments of comic relief also affirmed alcohol's broad social acceptance. When the taxi drops Al off at his posh apartment building, Fred jokes, "Some barracks you got. What are you? A retired bootlegger?" Al responds, "Nothing as dignified as that. I'm a banker."

In later scenes, *Best Years* invites viewers to contemplate the line that separates normal alcohol consumption from problem drinking. On their first evening home, the three veterans meet at Butch's Place by happenstance after each has experienced an awkward family reunion. Delighted to find Fred at the bar, Homer orders a whiskey, a drink he thinks befits his veteran status. "Before I went to the service," Homer tells Fred, "Butch wouldn't let me have any liquor. He used to read me lectures on the curse of drink. But it's different now. I am a veteran." Butch, still playing the protective uncle, orders the bartender to "draw a beer," and Homer jokingly threatens to "take my trade to another joint where I don't have relatives." Al arrives last at Butch's Place, the final stop of his night on the town touring swing nightclubs and drinking with his wife Milly and adult daughter Peggy. Although already tipsy from drinks at four nightclubs, Al is still raring to go. Butch instructs the bartender to give Fred and Al "anything they want" and Homer "any kind of beer." Hilarity ensues when Milly—and then a male waiter—gamely dance with Al and Al switches out his nearly empty highball for Milly's cocktail when she looks the other way. While Homer leaves the tavern in full command of his senses (and with a ride home from Butch), Fred and Al continue drinking until closing, leaving the good-humored team of Milly and Peggy to get the sloshed veterans safely home. When Fred and Al pass out in the backseat of the car, Milly jests, "They make a lovely couple, don't they?" Peggy retorts, "I think they'll be very happy together."

The humorous antics and dialogue do a lot of cultural work in these scenes. Brewers would certainly have been gratified that Uncle Butch endorsed beer as the beverage of moderation. The fact that Homer could enjoy a few glasses without losing his moral and physical bearings seemed to confirm that oft-stated claim. At the same time, the tavern scene suggested that beer, in some veterans' eyes, did not share whiskey's masculine prestige. Indeed, returning enlisted men might have laughed or groaned at the familiar scenario of the lowly petty officer getting stuck with beer while Fred, the higher-ranking officer, enjoyed whiskey. The frank depictions of excessive drinking made the film's broad acceptance of alcohol all the more significant. While *It's a Wonderful Life* cast Pottersville's neon lights and jazzy nightclubs as symptoms of moral decay, the neon lights and swing nightclubs in *Best Years* confirmed that Al was, as he put it, "back in civilization." *Best Years* also painted the liquor business in a more benign light than Capra did. Unlike Nick, the bar owner in Pottersville who served "hard drinks . . . for men who want to get drunk fast," Butch understood the "curse of drink" and made sure his customers did not drink and drive. *Best Years* did not whitewash the problem of alcohol abuse. In later scenes, Milly gently chides Al for drinking too much, a habit fueled by Al's dissatisfaction with his soulless banking career. But *Best Years* also suggested that women, at least initially, ought to take veterans' excessive drinking in stride. Instead of scolding Al for his homecoming drinking spree, Milly and Peggy modeled the feminine patience and understanding that experts believed would help veterans reacclimate to civilian life and domestic routines.[14]

Despite their depictions of excessive drinking and alcohol abuse, these three postwar films attest to the efficacy of the alcoholic beverage industry's public relations and advertising strategies. The cinematic format made Hollywood's portrait of alcohol vulnerable to contestation and misinterpretation, but it also dramatized industry messages more powerfully and memorably than a trade association advertisement or publication. Amid its horrifying depictions of alcoholism, *The Lost Weekend* also took time to remind moviegoers that responsible men who savored their whiskey and embraced their breadwinning obligations could avoid Don Birnam's plight. *Best Years* and *It's a Wonderful Life* reassured moviegoers that wine and beer—and even liquor with women's careful stewardship—could be safely reintegrated into the rituals of domesticity and heterosocial public leisure. Collectively, the films affirmed what wets, drys, and damps well understood: that the enjoyment of intoxicating pleasures had become a meaningful measure of white, middle-class respectability and cultural belonging.

Yet, the work of cultural reinvention remained incomplete. The falloff in wine sales when whiskey became available again suggested that wine had made more cultural headway as a cooking aid than as a mealtime beverage. Nevertheless, in significant pockets of the country wine promoters had laid a durable foundation for expanding the table wine market. After the war, the Wine Advisory Board continued its campaign to downplay connoisseurship and strip wine of its foreignness by marketing wine as a base for cocktails, a flavorful addition to classic American dishes, and the thrifty housewife's secret to fuss-free hospitality. This approach, in conjunction with improved wine quality, yielded substantial gains in table wine sales during the 1950s and 1960s.[15] Beer's reinvention, though more dramatic than wine's, was also unfinished. Although the war had strengthened beer's connections to national identity and servicemen's allegiances to beer, brewers continued to struggle after the war to broaden beer's middle-class appeal, especially to women drinkers. Eventually, marketing experts recognized the diminishing returns of hyping beer's genteel respectability and lost interest in women as a primary market.[16] In the early 1960s, when memories of rowdy saloons had long since faded and brewers no longer needed to nudge homemakers to add a six-pack to their shopping cart, the United States Brewers' Foundation discontinued its collective advertising campaign and beer marketers reembraced beer's masculine image and working-class appeal. Beer belonged in the home, for sure, but the domestic housewife and suburban husband, who had dominated beer ads in the 1940s and 1950s, faded from view in later decades as the sports enthusiast, the convivial male bargoer, and the sexy female bar companion took their place.

Whiskey exited the war with the biggest reputational gains and losses. Whiskey shortages on the home front and the battlefront had amplified whiskey's prestige and masculine cachet, but lingering memories of forced tie-in sales and degraded whiskey quality had damaged public goodwill and the reputation of some brands. Even so, the reigning consumer preferences for cocktails and highballs assured whiskey's place atop the hierarchy of alcoholic beverages in the postwar period. By 1958, whiskey makers had become so confident in whiskey's broad respectability that the Distilled Spirits Institute officially abandoned the industry's self-imposed ban on representing women in liquor ads.[17]

If World War II was not the final stage in alcohol's cultural reinvention, it was the most significant moment in that process. The war demonstrated the alcoholic beverage industry's pivotal role in boosting civilian and military morale, supplying the raw materials to wage total war, and furthering the aims of wartime food crusades. Trade associations mobilized a vast alcohol publicity machine to create a new politics of pleasure. They jettisoned the older rhetoric of virtue and vice on which the previous century's war on alcohol had been waged and embedded alcohol in new national mythologies about the US's commitment to cultural pluralism, tolerance, and personal liberty—the very characteristics that set the United States apart from its fascist and totalitarian enemies. Buoyed by the yearnings of ordinary consumers and military personnel who demanded a more equitable distribution of intoxicating pleasures, the industry more forthrightly articulated a right to decent alcohol than they had at any point during their crusade for repeal.

More than that, the industry and allied trades convinced the federal government to treat alcohol as an essential wartime industry that merited furloughs from war production and access to rationed goods. Decades later, when lockdowns shuttered schools and nonessential businesses during the global COVID-19 pandemic, every state but Pennsylvania protected access to intoxicating pleasures and kept liquor stores open—a display of government priorities that would have antagonized drys during World War II but that elicited relatively little public commentary in 2020. Although some officials cited public health rationales for keeping liquor stores open, the decision to designate liquor stores "essential businesses" during the COVID lockdowns was also a direct legacy of the industry's decades-long effort to unshackle intoxicating beverages from their older stigmas and transform them into emblems of the American good life.[18] By the end of World War II, alcohol had become deeply insinuated into the fabric of everyday life, the corridors of power, and the agendas of government agencies. Freed from previous associations with vice and corruption, alcohol would continue to take on new and varied cultural meanings in subsequent generations.

Abbreviations

ACC   *American Consumer Culture: Market Research and American Business, 1935–1965*, Adam Matthew Digital, online

BP   Bernays Papers, Manuscripts Collection, Library of Congress, Washington, DC

CFH   Committee on Food Habits Papers, National Research Council, Washington, DC

DAC   Domestic Advertising Collection, J. Walter Thompson Company Archives, Duke University, Durham, North Carolina

FDRPP   Franklin D. Roosevelt Papers as President, Official File, Franklin D. Roosevelt Presidential Library, Hyde Park, New York

FNB   Food and Nutrition Board Papers, National Research Council, Washington, DC

HMD   Henry Morgenthau Diaries, World War II Era, Franklin D. Roosevelt Presidential Library, Hyde Park, New York

HR   Records of the US House of Representatives, 77th Congress, House Committee on Military Affairs, Petitions and Memorials, HR77A-H12.1, Various Subjects, Center for Legislative Archives, Washington, DC

NYWF   New York World's Fair, 1939–1940 Collection, New York Public Library Manuscripts and Archives Division, New York City

OPAPB   Office of Price Administration, Office of the Administrator, Administrative Subject Files of Prentiss Brown, Entry UD-3, Record Group 188, National Archives, College Park, Maryland

OPAPD	Office of Price Administration, Price Department, Food Price Division, Grocery Products Branch, Beverage Section, General Correspondence Files, 1942–1946, Entry PI-95 386, Record Group 188, National Archives, College Park, Maryland
OPAED	Office of Price Administration, Enforcement Department, Food Enforcement Division, Agricultural Commodities Enforcement Branch, Records Relating to Commodity Programs, 1943–1946, Entry A1 E150; Monthly Reports by Field Offices, 1944–1945, Entry A1 E151, Record Group 188, National Archives, College Park, Maryland
RTC	Rexford F. Tugwell Collection, Franklin D. Roosevelt Presidential Library, Hyde Park, New York
SEN	Records of the US Senate, 78th Congress, Committee on Military Affairs, SEN78A-J14, Center for Legislative Archives, Washington, DC
SFEC	San Francisco Ephemera Collection, San Francisco Public Library, California
SMC	Seagram Museum Collection, Hagley Museum and Library, Wilmington, Delaware
SCP	Seagram Company Papers, Hagley Museum and Library, Wilmington, Delaware
UL	Archives and Special Collections, University of Louisville, Kentucky
USBF	United States Brewers' Foundation
WPB	War Production Board, Policy Documentation Files, 1939–1947, Entry PI-15 1, Record Group 179, National Archives, College Park, Maryland
WAB	Wine Advisory Board

Notes

INTRODUCTION

1. Cohen, "Jim Crow's Drug War," 55–79; Spillane, *Cocaine*.
2. For sweeping global and comparative accounts of anti-alcohol and anti-drug crusades, see Tyrrell, *Woman's World/Woman's Empire*; Courtwright, *Forces of Habit*; Chrzan, *Alcohol*; Phillips, *Alcohol*; Schrad, *Smashing the Liquor Machine*. For studies of the prohibition crusade and anti-alcohol propaganda in the United States, see Kerr, *Organized for Prohibition*; Lender and Martin, *Drinking in America*; Pegram, *Battling Demon Rum*; Parsons, *Manhood Lost*; Martin, *Devil of the Domestic Sphere*; McGirr, *The War on Alcohol*; Lerner, *Dry Manhattan*; and Okrent, *Last Call*. On cocaine, cannabis, and opium, see Spillane, *Cocaine*; Himmelstein, *The Strange Career of Marihuana*; Bonnie and Whitebread II, *The Marijuana Conviction*; Campos, *Home Grown*; Campos, "Mexicans and the Origins of Marijuana Prohibition in the United States," 6–37; Courtwright, *Dark Paradise*.
3. Many excellent studies have examined how previously illicit psychoactive substances acquired mainstream respectability, but they tend to focus on the factors that paved the way for their legalization or decriminalization more than the process of cultural reinvention that continued after legalization. Excellent studies of the mainstreaming of previously illicit substances include Courtwright, *Forces of Habit*; Mendelson, *From Demon to Darling*; Richert, *Strange Trips*; Ferraiolo, "From Killer Weed to Popular Medicine," 147–179. Other scholars have examined how once disreputable or controversial licit psychoactive substances achieved mainstream acceptance (even as they continued to court controversy): Schivelbusch, *Tastes of Paradise*; Tate, *Cigarette Wars*; Herzberg, *Happy Pills in America*; Brandt, *The Cigarette Century*; Milov, *The Cigarette*; Herzberg, *White Market Drugs*.

4. Sinclair, *Prohibition*; Asbury, *The Great Illusion*; Kobler, *Ardent Spirits*. For a useful summary of the historiography, see Mark Edward Lender, "The Historian and Repeal," 177–205.

5. Allen, *Only Yesterday*; Clark, *Deliver Us from Evil*, 168–180; Burnham, *Bad Habits*, 35–49; Leuchtenberg, *The Perils of Prosperity*, chap. 9; Murphy, "Bootlegging Mothers and Drinking Daughters," 174–194.

6. Mumford, *Interzones*, 133–135, 150–158; Heap, *Slumming*, 189–191, 194–204.

7. Allen, *Only Yesterday*, 204.

8. Burnham, *Bad Habits*, 67–69, 82.

9. Phillips, *Alcohol*, 281–282.

10. Films such as *The Public Enemy* (1931), *The Great Gatsby* (1974, 2013), *The Cotton Club* (1984), and HBO's television series *Boardwalk Empire* (2010–2014) are but a few examples of such representations.

11. Roizen, "How Does the Nation's 'Alcohol Problem' Change from Era to Era?," 61–87.

12. Lender, "The Historian and Repeal," 187; Lender and Martin, *Drinking in America*, 170–171.

13. Pegram, *Battling Demon Rum*, 187; Roizen, "How Does the Nation's 'Alcohol Problem' Change from Era to Era?," 61–87.

14. McGirr, *The War on Alcohol*, xxii, 249–252.

15. Appadurai, ed., *The Social Life of Things*; McCracken, *Culture and Consumption*; Enstad, *Ladies of Labor, Girls of Adventure*; Belasco and Scranton, eds., *Food Nations*; Guy, *When Champagne Became French*; Watson and Caldwell, eds., *The Cultural Politics of Food and Eating*; Rappaport, *A Thirst for Empire*; Enstad, *Cigarettes, Inc.*; Burke, *Lifebuoy Men, Lux Women*.

16. Burnham, *Bad Habits*, 67.

17. Pegram, *Battling Demon Rum*, 186.

18. Historians of gender, sexuality, and the family have long been attuned to the ways that new restrictions often accompany new liberations of social and sexual behaviors. See, for example, Chauncey, *Gay New York*; Jacobson, *Raising Consumers*, chaps. 2, 5; Mumford, *Interzones*; Calder, *Financing the American Dream*.

19. Chauncey, *Gay New York*, 334.

20. Burnham, *Bad Habits*, 258. Burnham contends that repealers and other "merchants of the minor vices" successfully deployed ridicule to drown out and coopt the sincere voices of reform.

21. The leading women's repeal organization offered few specific prescriptions for drinking reform, but it repeatedly stated that Prohibition had set back the cause of "true temperance." Rose, *American Women and the Repeal of Prohibition*, 2, 4, 85–86, 89; Neumann, "The End of Gender Solidarity," 42.

22. Historians who study the alcoholic beverage industry as a business have been more attuned to the industry's cautiousness after repeal and the continuing influence of prohibitionists on post-repeal regulatory regimes. See, for example, Pennock and Kerr, "In the Shadow of Prohibition: Domestic American Alcohol Policy Since 1933," 390; Dighe, "A Taste for Temperance," 4, 19; Corzine, "Right at Home," 843–866; Pinney, *A History of Wine in America*, 49–52. By

contrast, historians who focus more on the politics of Prohibition and the social history of alcohol consumption have tended to view alcohol as a largely settled question after repeal.

23. Pennock, *Advertising Sin and Sickness*, 43–47.

24. "The Gentle Revolution in America's Package Stores," *Package Store Management* 27 (August 1960), 19; "Milt Cohen: Master of the Gentle Sell," *Package Store Management* 27 (October 1960), 26.

25. Dighe, "A Taste for Temperance," 1–32.

26. Edensor, "The Social Life of the Senses," 32–33.

27. Wilson, *Destructive Creation*, chap. 3; Henthorn, *From Submarines to Suburbs*.

28. Sparrow, *Warfare State*, chap. 2; Westbrook, *Why We Fought;* Duis, "No Time for Privacy," 17–45; McGovern, *Sold America*, 327–353, 363; Fox, *Madison Avenue Goes to War*.

29. Reinarman, "Policing Pleasure," 54–57; Schivelbusch, *Tastes of Paradise*, 148, 153, 156; Chrzan, *Alcohol;* Rappaport, *A Thirst for Empire*, chap. 2.

30. In the French language, the word "alcohol" (*alcool*) applied only to distilled spirits but not to fermented beverages such as beer, wine, and hard cider; even temperance reformers referred to wine as "a *boisson hygiénique*, a healthy drink." Guy, *When Champagne Became French*, 32–33.

31. For more on cooperative advertising campaigns by California fruit growers, see Woeste, *The Farmer's Benevolent Trust;* Sackman, *Orange Empire*.

32. For more on food rationing and wartime propaganda to promote compliance with food controls, see Bentley, *Eating for Victory;* Biltekoff, *Eating Right in America;* Collingham, *Taste of War;* Rappaport, *A Thirst for Empire*, chap. 9; Veit, *Modern Food, Moral Food*. For more on war and food deprivation, see Goldman and Filtzer, eds., *Hunger and War;* Collingham, *Taste of War;* Cwiertka, *Cuisine, Colonialism and Cold War;* Davis, *Home Fires Burning;* Helstosky, *Garlic and Oil;* Trentmann and Just, eds., *Food and Conflict in Europe in the Age of the Two World Wars;* Seikaly, "A Nutritional Economy," 37–58; Nordstrom, ed. *The Provisions of War*.

33. For more on wartime black markets and compliance with price controls in the United States, United Kingdom, and France, see Mouré, *Marché Noir;* Rockoff, *Drastic Measures;* Mills and Rockoff, "Compliance with Price Controls in the United States and the United Kingdom," 197–213; Jacobs, " 'How About Some Meat?' " 910–941; Cohen, *A Consumers' Republic*, chap. 2; Jacobs, *Pocketbook Politics*, chap. 5; Mouré and Paula Schwartz, "On Vit Mal," 261–295; Rockoff, *America's Economic Way of War;* Mouré, "Capitalism's Black Heart in Wartime France," 139–156.

34. Cross, *An All-Consuming Century;* Cohen, *A Consumers' Republic;* McGovern, *Sold American;* Jacobs, *Pocketbook Politics;* Sparrow, *Wartime State*.

1. THE POTENT POLITICS OF WEAK BREWS

1. "Ask 'Tax for Prosperity': Bands Play Drinking Songs as Pretzels Are Strewn in Marchers' Path," *New York Times*, May 15, 1932, 1, 3; "Mayor James J. Walker leads the great Beer Parade in New York City," HD Stock

Footage, CriticalPast Archive. www.youtube.com/watch?v=rXyldRD9WcU. For more on how opposition to Prohibition produced a new multiracial and multiethnic working-class coalition that gave rise to the modern Democratic Party, see McGirr, *War on Alcohol*, chap. 6, 240–246; Materson, "African American Women," 63–86. For more on Walker, see Mitgang, *Once Upon a Time in New York*; Peretti, *Nightclub City*.

2. "Ask 'Tax for Prosperity'," 1, 3.

3. US Congress, House, Committee, *Modification of the Volstead Act*, December 10, 1932, testimony of Rep. Clarence F. Lea, 278.

4. Quoted in Okrent, *Last Call*, 330.

5. Phillips, *Alcohol*, 271–277.

6. US Congress, Senate, Committee, *Amendment of the Prohibition Act*, January 8, 1932, testimony of Sen. Hiram Bingham, 4.

7. Pauly, "Is Liquor Intoxicating?," 305–313.

8. McGirr, *War on Alcohol*, chap. 3, 164–187.

9. Kyvig, *Repealing National Prohibition*, 59, 68–69.

10. Kyvig, *Repealing National Prohibition*, 54.

11. Barr, *Drink*, 183; Kyvig, *Repealing National Prohibition*, 68. For more on working-class resentment of Prohibition see McGirr, *The War on Alcohol*, chaps. 3, 6; Levine and Reinarman, "From Prohibition to Regulation," 465–466.

12. The federal government deliberately added poison to industrial alcohol to prevent it from entering bootleg channels as beverage alcohol; bootleg liquor contained antifreeze, Sterno, and other toxins that produced long-term medical damage. Lerner, *Dry Manhattan*, 259–260; McGirr, *The War on Alcohol*, 60–61, 101–102.

13. Constantine Panunzio, "The Foreign Born and Prohibition," *Annals of the American Academy of Political and Social Science* 163 (September 1932), 149.

14. Rose, *American Women and the Repeal of Prohibition*, 57–59.

15. Kyvig, *Repealing National Prohibition*, 49; Lerner, *Dry Manhattan*, 231.

16. Dighe, "Pierre S. Du Pont and the Making of an Anti-Prohibition Activist," 97–118 (quoted at 108).

17. For a more extended analysis of the AAPA, see Kyvig, *Repealing National Prohibition*; Dighe, "Pierre S. Du Pont and the Making of an Anti-Prohibition Activist"; Burk, *The Corporate State and the Broker State*.

18. Rose, *American Women and the Repeal of Prohibition*, 67–68.

19. Rose, *American Women and the Repeal of Prohibition*, 2–4, 81–89, 142–143 (quoted at 85). For more on the WONPR, see also Murdock, *Domesticating Drink*, 137–158; Neumann, "The End of Gender Solidarity," 31–51; Kyvig, "Women Against Prohibition," 465–482; Kyvig, *Repealing National Prohibition*, 118–127, 160–161, 169–170.

20. Davis, *Jews and Booze*, 191.

21. Kyvig, *Repealing National Prohibition*, 59, 68–69.

22. John B. Kennedy, "Loaded for Beer," *Collier's* 90 (July 16, 1932), 16, 43; Louis Hacker, an economic historian and professor of economics at Columbia University, disputed many of these optimistic claims. See Hacker, "If Beer Returns," 385–392.

23. Lerner, *Dry Manhattan*, 291–292.

24. US Congress, Senate, Committee, *Amendment of the Prohibition Act*, January 20, 1932, testimony of Matthew Woll, 277.
25. US Congress, Senate, Committee, *Amendment of the Prohibition Act*, January 20, 1932, testimony of Matthew Woll, 261.
26. US Congress, House, Committee, *Modification of the Volstead Act*, December 7, 1932, letter from August A. Busch, 34–35.
27. Wilbur White, a US representative from Ohio, testified that homebrews contained as much as 11% alcohol: US Congress, House, Committee, *Modification of the Volstead Act*, December 10, 1932, 292.
28. US Congress, House, Committee, *Modification of the Volstead Act*, December 7, 1932, letter from August A. Busch, 34–35.
29. US Congress, House, Committee, *Modification of the Volstead Act*, December 7, 1932, article by A. B. MacDonald in *St. Louis Star*, 57.
30. Larson, "The Drinkers Dictionary," 87–92; Douglas, *Terrible Honesty*, 101; Levine, "Vocabulary of Drunkenness," 1038–1051.
31. US Congress, House, Committee, *Modification of the Volstead Act*, December 10, 1932, testimony of Rep. Wilbur White, 292.
32. "Nation Prepares for Return of Beer," *Newsweek* 1 (March 25, 1933), 4.
33. "Nation Prepares for Return of Beer," 4.
34. The final bill included lager but not the more alcoholic porters, stouts, and ales; see US Congress, House, Committee, *Modification of the Volstead Act*, December 8, 1932, testimony of Rep. William H. Stafford, 88. On the intoxicating effects of 6 to 8% percent beer, see US Congress, House, Committee, *Modification of the Volstead Act*, December 10, 1932, testimony of Prof. Yandell Henderson, 98.
35. US Congress, House, Committee, *Modification of the Volstead Act*, December 10, 1932, testimony of Judge Marion De Vries, 264.
36. US Congress, House, Committee, *Modification of the Volstead Act*, December 8, 1932, testimony of Prof. Yandell Henderson, 101.
37. US Congress, House, Committee, *Modification of the Volstead Act*, December 10, 1932, testimony of Judge Marion De Vries, 264.
38. US Congress, House, Committee, *Modification of the Volstead Act*, December 8, 1932, testimony of Prof. Yandell Henderson, 105.
39. US Congress, House, Committee, *Modification of the Volstead Act*, December 10, 1932, testimony of Edmund A. Rossi, 309–310.
40. US Congress, House, Committee, *Modification of the Volstead Act*, December 10, 1932, testimony of Judge Marion De Vries, 265–266.
41. Pinney, *A History of Wine in America*, 21–23; Teiser and Harroun, "The Volstead Act, Rebirth, and Boom," 50–51; Barr, *Drink*, 170–171; Okrent, *Last Call*, 112; Mendelson, *From Demon to Darling*, 72.
42. US Congress, Senate, Committee, *Amendment of the Prohibition Act*, February 2, 1932, testimony of Amos W. W. Woodcock, 351; Pinney, *A History of Wine in America*, 23.
43. Barr, *Drink*, 171.
44. US Congress, House, Committee, *Modification of the Volstead Act*, December 10, 1932, testimony of Rep. Clarence F. Lea, 282.
45. Pauly, "Is Liquor Intoxicating?," 306.

46. Pauly, "Is Liquor Intoxicating?," 307–308.
47. Pauly, "Is Liquor Intoxicating?," 311.
48. Pauly, "Is Liquor Intoxicating?," 308.
49. US Congress, Senate, Committee, *Amendment of the Prohibition Act*, January 8, 1932, testimony of Prof. Yandell Henderson, 29.
50. US Congress, House, Committee, *Modification of the Volstead Act*, December 10, 1932, testimony of Prof. Yandell Henderson, 98, 102.
51. US Congress, Senate, Committee, *Amendment of the Prohibition Act*, January 8, 1932, testimony of Prof. Yandell Henderson, 29.
52. US Congress, Senate, Committee, *Amendment of the Prohibition Act*, January 8, 1932, testimony of Prof. Yandell Henderson, 26–27.
53. US Congress, Senate, Committee, *Amendment of the Prohibition Act*, February 12, 1932, statement of Dr. Oliver T. Osborne, 509.
54. US Congress, Senate, Committee, *Amendment of the Prohibition Act*, January 20, 1932, testimony of Matthew Woll, 282. Consumption of Coca-Cola tripled between 1920 and 1933; Lender and Martin, *Drinking in America*, 147.
55. US Congress, House, Committee, *Modification of the Volstead Act*, December 8, 1932, testimony of Prof. Yandell Henderson, 98.
56. US Congress, House, Committee, *Modification of the Volstead Act*, December 12, 1932, testimony of Mrs. Harvey Wiley, quoting Dr. Richard Cabot, 377–378. Anna Kelton Wiley, a suffragist who picketed the White House in 1917 and chaired the National Woman's Party, was married to Harvey Wiley, the chemist who championed the Pure Food and Drugs Act (1906) and became the first Commissioner of Food and Drugs; Roxie Olmstead, "Anna Kelton Wiley, Suffragist," *Turning Point Suffrage Memorial*, https://suffragistmemorial.org/anna-kelton-wiley-suffragist/.
57. Veit, *Modern Food, Moral Food*, 30–31.
58. Biltekoff, *Eating Right in America*, 22, 30, 32.
59. US Congress, Senate, Committee, *Modification of the Volstead Act*, January 7, 1933, Edward B. Dunford, brief in opposition to H.R. 13742, 27–28.
60. US Congress, Senate, Committee, *Amendment of the Prohibition Act*, January 20, 1932, testimony of Matthew Woll, 257.
61. US Congress, Senate, Committee, *Amendment of the Prohibition Act*, January 19, 1932, testimony of Mary T. Norton, 246. Sociological studies of immigrants in the United States echoed Norton's claims. See Panunzio, "The Foreign Born and Prohibition," 147–154.
62. US Congress, Senate, Committee, *Amendment of the Prohibition Act*, January 8, 1932, testimony of Prof. Yandell Henderson, 34–35.
63. See, for example, US Congress, Senate, Committee, *Amendment of the Prohibition Act*, January 8, 1932, testimony of Dr. Charles Norris, 47; US Congress, Senate, Committee, *Amendment of the Prohibition Act*, January 20, 1932, testimony of Dr. Alfred Stengel, 292–293.
64. US Congress, House, Committee, *Modification of the Volstead Act*, December 10, 1932, testimony of Prof. Yandell Henderson, 103.
65. US Congress, Senate, Committee, *Amendment of the Prohibition Act*, January 8, 1932, testimony of Prof. Yandell Henderson, 30.

66. Gusfield, "Passage to Play: Rituals of Drinking Time in American Society," 73–90 (quoted at 78, 86); Janet Chrzan, *Alcohol*, chap. 5.

67. US Congress, House, Committee, *Modification of the Volstead Act*, December 8, 1932, testimony of Yandell Henderson, 110–111.

68. US Congress, House, Committee, *Modification of the Volstead Act*, December 8, 1932, testimony of Prof. Yandell Henderson, 100; see also US Congress, Senate, Committee, *Amendment of the Prohibition Act*, January 20, 1932, testimony of Dr. Alfred Stengel, 292.

69. US Congress, Senate, Committee, *Amendment of the Prohibition Act*, January 8, 1932, testimony of Sen. Hiram Bingham, 24.

70. Gabaccia, *We Are What We Eat*, 79.

71. US Congress, House, Committee, *Modification of the Volstead Act*, December 10, 1932, testimony of Yandell Henderson, 100; "worst feature . . ." quoted in testimony of Yandell Henderson, December 8, 1932, 110–111.

72. US Congress, Senate, Committee, *Amendment of the Prohibition Act*, January 8, 1932, testimony of Prof. Yandell Henderson, 31; US Congress, House, Committee, *Modification of the Volstead Act*, December 10, 1932, testimony of Yandell Henderson, 100. Ironically, winemakers in Fascist Italy, taken aback by the growing popularity of American-style cocktails among bourgeois Italian consumers, also campaigned against the "cocktail craze" by urging Italians to forsake "foreign" concoctions and reembrace the family-oriented Italian custom of drinking wine; see Griffith, "(Inter)National Spirits: On the Cultural Politics of the 'Cocktail Craze' in Fascist Italy."

73. US Congress, House, Committee, *Modification of the Volstead Act*, December 10, 1932, testimony of Yandell Henderson, 100; US Congress, Senate, Committee, *Amendment of the Prohibition Act*, January 8, 1932, testimony of Prof. Yandell Henderson, 34–35.

74. US Congress, House, Committee, *Modification of the Volstead Act*, December 8, 1932, testimony of Rep. William H. Stafford, 87.

75. US Congress, House, Committee, *Modification of the Volstead Act*, December 10, 1932, testimony of Edmund A. Rossi, 310.

76. The criminal syndicates trafficked mostly in spirits since they delivered the highest profits and were easier to smuggle and hide. Mendelson, *From Demon to Darling*, 50–51.

77. Kerr, *Organized for Prohibition*, 28–29, 161–163, 165.

78. US Congress, House, Committee, *Modification of the Volstead Act*, December 7, 1932, article by A. B. MacDonald in *St. Louis Star*, 59–60.

79. US Congress, Senate, Committee, *Amendment of the Prohibition Act*, January 9, 1932, testimony of Rep. William H. Hull, 52.

80. Edward B. Dunford, an attorney for the Anti-Saloon League, cynically observed that although proponents argued that "beer should be legalized as the 'poor man's beverage,'" the bill "discriminates against the poor man" by allowing consumers to buy beer only by the case and not by the drink. He believed the bill "would not satisfy either wets or drys." US Congress, Senate, Committee, *Amendment of the Prohibition Act*, February 9, 1932, statement of Edward B. Dunford, 460.

81. Stack, "Liquid Bread," 194–197.

82. US Congress, Senate, Committee, *Amendment of the Prohibition Act*, January 9, 1932, testimony of Rep. William H. Hull, 58.

83. Bushman, *Refinement of America*; Grier, *Culture and Comfort*.

84. Quoted in Davis, *Jews and Booze*, 58–59.

85. US Congress, Senate, Committee, *Amendment of the Prohibition Act*, February 2, 1932, testimony of Amos W. W. Woodcock, 345–346; US Congress, House, Committee, *Modification of the Volstead Act*, December 12, 1932, testimony of Ida B. Wise Smith, 416; US Congress, Senate, Committee, *Amendment of the Prohibition Act*, January 28, 1932, testimony of Louis J. Taber, 316.

86. US Congress, Senate, Committee, *Amendment of the Prohibition Act*, February 9, 1932, statement of Edward B. Dunford, 459–460. For more on how the discourse of family destruction reverberated in the temperance movement, see Martin, *Devil of the Domestic Sphere*; Parsons, *Manhood Lost*.

87. US Congress, Senate, Committee, *Amendment of the Prohibition Act*, January 28, 1932, testimony of Mrs. Arthur C. Watkins, 335–336.

88. US Congress, Senate, Committee, *Amendment of the Prohibition Act*, February 19, 1932, testimony of Rev. William Sheafe Chase, 536.

89. "Nation Prepares for Return of Beer," 3–4.

90. Kyvig, *Repealing National Prohibition*, 167–168.

91. "Wets and Drys Line Up for the Beer Battle," *Literary Digest* 114 (November 19, 1932), 8–9.

92. "Beer as a Budget Balancer," *Literary Digest* 115 (March 25, 1933), 7.

93. "Beer Nearer," *Business Week*, November 30, 1932, 3–4.

94. Lerner, *Dry Manhattan*, 303–304.

95. McGirr, *The War on Alcohol*, 246–247.

96. "How Beer Returned to the Nation," *Christian Century* 50 (April 19, 1933), 538.

97. "Nation Prepares for Return of Beer," 3–4.

98. Levine, "Birth of American Alcohol Control," 30.

99. U.S. Representatives Hawley, Timberlake and Crowther, "Should the Sale of Beer Be Legalized?: Minority Report I" *Congressional Digest* 12 (January 1933), 11.

100. "Drys Face Dilemma, Accuse Brewers of Plotting," *Newsweek* 1 (April 22, 1933), 7; testing conducted by the Anti-Saloon League revealed that most beer in New York contained only 2.2 percent alcohol by weight. Six New York beers tested by the *American Journal of Public Health* had an alcohol by weight content of 2.48, 2.67, 2.28, 2.67, 2.22, 3.05; the author converted the journal's alcohol by volume statistics into alcohol by weight using this formula: ABV × 0.8 = ABW. "Analysis of Six New York Beers," *American Journal of Public Health* 23 (July 1933), 704.

101. "Beer: Preparation for Early Sales Made in Many States," *Newsweek* 1 (April 1, 1933), 8.

102. "Nation Prepares for Return of Beer," 3–4.

103. McGirr, *War on Alcohol*, chap. 5, quote at 136.

104. Lender and Martin, *Drinking in America*, 88–92; Pegram, *Battling Demon Rum*, 58–64; Parsons, *Manhood Lost*, 55–57, 165–169. Parsons notes

that the line between moral suasion and coercion was not always clear-cut in the nineteenth-century temperance movement.

105. "How Beer Returned to the Nation," 536–537.

106. The Rockefeller Report also echoed many of the central recommendations made thirty years earlier by the Committee of Fifty to Investigate the Liquor Problem, an upper-class policy organization; Levine, "The Birth of American Alcohol Control," 2, 17.

107. Pauly, "Is Liquor Intoxicating?," 311.

108. DeGrandpre, *The Cult of Pharmacology*, 27.

109. Lerner, *Dry Manhattan*, 29–34.

110. Davis, *Jews and Booze*, 190–191.

111. Gabaccia, *We Are What We Eat*, 136.

2. A NEW DEAL FOR ALCOHOL?

1. Ray Tucker, "Goin' Through the Rye," *Collier's* 90 (October 7, 1932), 57.

2. Eleanor Kinsella McDonnell, "Wine, Washington, and War Debts," *Saturday Evening Post* 206 (December 23, 1933), 29, 50, 51. For more on the falling European demand for French wines, see Phillips, *Alcohol*, 286.

3. Elliott, *Quiet Drinking*; Whitaker, *Bacchus Behave!*. Other titles from 1933 included Carlisle and Dunn, *Wining and Dining with Rhyme and Reason*; Drex, *ABC of Wines, Cocktails, and Liqueurs*; Drinkwater, *How to Serve Wine and Beer*; Gray, *After Repeal: What a Host Should Know*; Stoll, *Wine-wise*; Street, *Wines: Their Selection, Care, and Service*; Stringer, *Wines: What to Serve, When to Serve*. Even the government published a book on the subject: Hartman, *Wine and Liquor*.

4. Rexford G. Tugwell, "Wine, Women, and the New Deal," address to the Women's National Democratic Club, February 5, 1934, pp. 1–5, Box 56, Rexford F. Tugwell Collection (RTC).

5. National Institute on Alcohol Abuse and Alcoholism, "Table 1: Apparent Per Capita Ethanol Consumption, United States, 1850–2018"; Kay, "Balance-Sheet of Repeal," 20–24.

6. Speech by Edward L. Bernays to meeting of brewers, October 1937, UBIF file Jan–Feb 1937, 6–8, Box 352, Bernays Papers (BP).

7. Teiser and Harroun, *Winemaking in California*, 182, 189.

8. Ernest Wente noted that most of California's cooperage after repeal was full of tourne, a type of bacteria, and had not been properly sanitized. Wente, *Wine Making in the Livermore Valley*, 56.

9. Amerine, *The University of California and the State's Wine Industry*, 15.

10. Adams, *Wines of America*, 27.

11. "The Wines of the U.S.," *Fortune* 9 (February 1934), 118.

12. Edward Angly, "Taxes Save the Bootlegger," *Forum* 92 (November 1934), 274–275.

13. Walter Davenport, "What'll You Have?" *Collier's* 42 (December 23, 1933), 13.

14. "Liquor: Old Controversy over What Is Whisky Is Revived," *Newsweek* 2 (December 30, 1933), 7–8.

15. Angly, "Taxes Save the Bootlegger," 274.
16. "Liquor: Bootlegger in Demand to Satisfy Excessive Thirst," *Newsweek* 2 (December 23, 1933), 7–8.
17. "Young Old Liquor," *Business Week*, April 7, 1934, 18.
18. "Attempts to Accelerate Aging of Liquor," *Scientific American* 150 (June 1934), 319.
19. "To Cut Liquor Tax," *Business Week*, August 4, 1934, 9.
20. E.M. Sheehan, "The Marketing of California Wines," *California Grape Grower* 15, no. 6 (June 1934): 3; "Report by Burke H. Critchfield to the Wine Institute, June 1935," Appendix II in Critchfield, *The California Wine Industry during the Depression*, 53–54.
21. Amerine, *The University of California and the State's Wine Industry*, 14–15.
22. Gallo, *The E. & J. Gallo Winery*, 18–19.
23. Veach, *Kentucky Bourbon Whiskey*, 81–85.
24. Pinney, *A History of Wine in America*, 26; Teiser and Harroun, *Winemaking in California*, 178–179; Teiser and Harroun, "The Volstead Act, Rebirth, and Boom," 57–58, 60–61; Okrent, *Last Call*, 177–178.
25. Cinotto, *Italian American Table*, 38.
26. Teiser and Harroun, "The Volstead Act, Rebirth and Boom," 56–57.
27. Pinney, *A History of American Wine*, 26–27. Though industry folklore has it that California vineyardists ripped out their precious old growths or grafted them over to the inferior varieties, *Fortune* reported that vineyardists destroyed only 2 percent of the pre-Prohibition acreage; "The Great Wine Boom," *Fortune* 23 (May 1941), 122.
28. Fromm, *Marketing California Wine and Brandy*, 4–5.
29. Haller, "Bootleggers and Businessmen," 143–145.
30. Jo Chamberlin, "Repeal Has Its Headaches," *Review of Reviews* 91, no. 3 (March 1935), 42, 76.
31. "Liquor: Audit of Beverages Swallowed and Taxes Paid," *Newsweek* 3 (April 14, 1934), 7.
32. "Repeal: A Year Ends," *Newsweek* 4 (December 8, 1934), 3–4.
33. Chamberlin, "Repeal Has Its Headaches," 41.
34. Chamberlin, "Repeal Has Its Headaches," 41.
35. Chamberlin, "Repeal Has Its Headaches," 40–42, 76.
36. Amerine, *The University of California and the State's Wine Industry*, 16–17; quoted material in Sheehan, "The Marketing of California Wines," 3.
37. For more on how industrial, processed foods have conditioned the American palate and sensory perceptions of taste, see Bentley, *Inventing Baby Food*; De La Peña, *Empty Pleasures*; Fitzgerald and Petrick, "In Good Taste," 392–404.
38. Lender and Martin, *Drinking in America*, 146–147.
39. Hooker, *Food and Drink in America*, 305.
40. Warburton, *The Economic Results of Prohibition*, 260; Levine and Reinarman, "From Prohibition to Regulation," 467–468; Hooker, *Food and Drink in America*, 303. These figures are based on per capita consumption of the drinking age population (15+).

41. Mendelson, *From Demon to Darling*, 50.
42. Okrent, *Last Call*, 249–251; Baron, *Brewed in America*, 314; Ogle, *Ambitious Brew*, 183–184; Mittelman, *Brewing Battles*, 89.
43. Cinotto, *Italian American Table*, 130, 190.
44. The consumption figures come from the report by Wickersham Commission, appointed by President Herbert Hoover to study crime and law enforcement, especially with respect to Prohibition. Pinney, *A History of Wine in America*, 20–21.
45. Teiser and Harroun, "The Volstead Act, Rebirth, and Boom," 50–51; Okrent, *Last Call*, 176.
46. Ware, *Greenwich Village, 1920–1930*, 60; and Young, *My Old New York Neighborhoods*, 14; both quoted in Cinotto, *Italian American Table*, 191.
47. Lanza, *California Grape Products and Other Wine Enterprises*, 70.
48. Okrent, *Last Call*, 245; Angle, *Bloody Williamson*.
49. "Prohibition: Woodcock and Grapemen," *Time* 16 (October 20, 1930), 16.
50. Okrent, *Last Call*, 258.
51. Barr, *Drink*, 170–171; Ostrander, *The Prohibition Movement in California, 1848–1933*, 178–179.
52. Lerner, *Dry Manhattan*, 107.
53. Perelli-Minetti, *A Life in Wine Making*, 59–60; Baccigaluppi, *California Grape Products and Other Wine Enterprises*, 92–93.
54. Adams, *Wines of America*, 25. A suit filed in the United States District Court, San Francisco, against the makers of Vino Sano Grape Brick found them not guilty of violating the National Prohibition Act.
55. Baccigaluppi, *California Grape Products*, 95; Pinney, *A History of Wine in America*, 24–25.
56. Adams, *Revitalizing the California Wine Industry*, 30–31; Adams, *The Wines of America*, 26; Ostrander, *The Prohibition Movement in California*, 179–180; Pinney, *A History of Wine in America*, 27–29; Teiser and Harroun, "The Volstead Act, Rebirth, and Boom," 62–63.
57. Baccigaluppi, *California Grape Products*, 87; Mendelson, *From Demon to Darling*, 65–66; for more on the illegal channels opened by sacramental wine, see Okrent, *Last Call*, 184, 187–190.
58. H.F. Stoll, Jr., "What the Younger Generation Thinks about Wine," *California Grape Grower* 15 (August 1934), 20–21.
59. Adams, *Revitalizing the California Wine Industry*, 7; Cinotto, *Italian American Table*, 191.
60. Levenstein, *Revolution at the Table*, 168.
61. Jessica McLachlin, "Merchandising Wine in Southern California's Oldest Restaurant," *American Restaurant Magazine* 26 (November 1942), 32, 62–63.
62. Dighe, "A Taste for Temperance," 1–32.
63. Walter Davenport, "What'll You Have?" *Collier's* 42 (December 23, 1933), 48; quoted material from Okrent, *Last Call*, 214–215.
64. "Liquor Comes of Age," *Business Week*, December 4, 1937, 17.
65. Letter from Paul Garrett to Marvin H. McIntyre, secretary to the president, March 31, 1938, Box 1, Official File 369: Wines, Franklin D. Roosevelt

Papers as President (FDRPP); letter from Henry Burr, president, American Temperance-Wine League, to Stephen Early, secretary to the president, April 20, 1936, Box 1, Official File 369: Wines, FDRPP.

66. Joseph H. Choate, Jr., "Choate Urges Shift to Wines," *New York Times*, January 26, 1936, enclosed with letter from Paul Garrett to M.H. McIntyre, secretary to the president, February 28, 1926, Box 1, Official File 369: Wines, FDRPP.

67. Powers, "Women and Public Drinking, 1890–1920," 46–52; Duis, *The Saloon*, 96.

68. Murdock, *Domesticating Drink*, 55–58.

69. McClellan, *Lady Lushes*, 68–72; Murdock, *Domesticating Drink*, 88–89, 95, 101–105, 110; Margaret Culkin Banning, "Lit Ladies," *Harper's Magazine* 160 (January 1930), 161–169; Eudora Richardson, "Drinking Mothers," *Outlook and Independent* 158 (June 10, 1931), 174–175.

70. For more on the WONPR, see Rose, *American Women and the Repeal of Prohibition*; Murdock, *Domesticating Drink*, 137–158; Neumann, "The End of Gender Solidarity," 31–51; Kyvig, "Women Against Prohibition," 465–482; Kyvig, *Repealing National Prohibition*, 118–127, 160–161, 169–170.

71. Tugwell, "Wine, Women, and the New Deal," 2–3.

72. Tugwell, "Wine, Women, and the New Deal," 1–2.

73. Comments by Gerald Early in Burns, dir., *Jazz*, episode 2, "The Gift," 2007.

74. Dinerstein, *Swinging the Machine*, 22.

75. Heap, *Slumming*, chap. 5, quoted at 190–191; Mumford, *Interzones*, chap. 8; Baldwin, *Chicago's New Negroes*, 12–13, 25–26; Chauncey, *Gay New York*, 327–328.

76. Ogren, *The Jazz Revolution*; Peretti, *Jazz in American Culture*.

77. Tugwell, "Wine, Women, and the New Deal," 1–2.

78. Tugwell, "Wine, Women, and the New Deal," 2–5.

79. Rexford Tugwell, "The Liquor Trade," December 3, 1933, 2, Box 56, Folder: "Drafts of Newspaper Column United Features, 1934," Box 56, RTC.

80. Currell, *The March of Spare Time*.

81. Stuart Chase, quoted in Currell, *The March of Spare Time*, 20.

82. Dinerstein, *Swinging the Machine*, 29–41.

83. Tugwell, "Women, Wine, and the New Deal," 1, 3.

84. Tugwell, "The Liquor Trade," 2.

85. Addams, *The Spirit of Youth and the City Streets*; Cavallo, *Muscles and Morals*.

86. Rexford Tugwell, "The Methodists Are Offended," 1934, 1–3, Box 56, RTC.

87. Letter from Eleanor Roosevelt to Rexford Tugwell, May 3, 1934, Box 56, RTC.

88. Handwritten note on the back of Tugwell, "The Methodists Are Offended," 4.

89. Cook, *Eleanor Roosevelt: The Defining Years*, 53.

90. Letter from Paul Garrett to President Roosevelt, May 22, 1936, Box 1, Official File 369: Wines, FDRPP.

91. Tugwell, "Wine, Women, and the New Deal," 1.
92. Tugwell, "Wine, Women, and the New Deal," 1.
93. Whitaker, *Bacchus Behave!*, 4–7.
94. Frank Schoonmaker, "New Decalogues of Drinking," *Saturday Literary Review* 253 (November 3, 1934), 260; "Alma Whitaker, Retired Times Columnist, Dies," *Los Angeles Times*, November 24, 1956, B1.
95. Whitaker, *Bacchus Behave!*, 7–8.
96. Whitaker, *Bacchus Behave!*, 4–7.
97. Whitaker, *Bacchus Behave!*, 3, 5–6, 63.
98. Seldes, *The Future of Drinking*, 87, 88, 161, 165, 167, 170.
99. Strauss, *Setting the Table for Julia Child*, 46–49, 56, chaps. 3–4. Even by the most liberal estimates, national membership in gourmet dining societies numbered around fifteen hundred in 1949; see Strauss, 128.
100. Lisa McGirr argues that the post-repeal liquor laws represented the "more permissive norms of a business and professional middle class" in *War on Alcohol*, 248.
101. Mendelson, *From Demon to Darling*, 4.
102. Peyser, *The Law and the California Wine Industry*, 15–16.
103. Lerner, *Dry Manhattan*, chap. 1.
104. Pegram, *Battling Demon Rum*, 186.
105. Mendelson, *From Demon to Darling*, 99.
106. Frendreis and Tatalovich, "A Hundred Miles of Dry," 302–319. For more on the relationship between evangelicalism and dry liquor laws, see McShane, "Class, Christ, and Cocktails."
107. Kerr, "The Rebirth of Brewing and Distilling in the United States in 1933," 5, 7–10. Mendelson, *From Demon to Darling*, 101–117.
108. Mendelson, *From Demon to Darling*, 104–106, 109–10.
109. Kay, "Balance-Sheet of Repeal," 20.
110. Barr, *Drink*, 187–88; for an extended analysis of the Rockefeller Report, see Levine, "The Birth of American Alcohol Control," 63–115, typescript, 14–21.
111. Henderson, *A New Deal in Liquor*, 13, 179–180; Mendelson, *From Demon to Darling*, 97. Henderson thought the federal government needed to tax spirits at a much higher rate, and he advocated additional measures to discourage the consumption of spirits: a "relatively low tax" on fortified wines under 20 percent to encourage their use as a cocktail substitute and a low federal tax (and no state taxes) on whiskey that the distillery had diluted to 12 percent.
112. Barr, *Drink*, 187–188; Levine, "The Birth of American Alcohol Control," 18; quoted passages from "Lest We Try to Drink Ourselves into Law-Abiding Prosperity," *American City* 48 (November 1933), 36.
113. Phillips, *Alcohol*, 299.
114. H. Phelps Gates, "Dry Revolt Around the Corner," *Christian Science Monitor*, June 17, 1936, 8; Edwin A. Brown, "Liquor and the Profit System," *Christian Century* 50 (December 27, 1933), 1642.
115. Mendelson, *From Demon to Darling*, 98.
116. Kerr, "The Rebirth of Brewing and Distilling," 7.

117. Harry G. Levine also sees alcohol controls after repeal as "far more pervasive, intrusive, and effective" than some historians have acknowledged; Levine, "The Birth of American Alcohol Control," 22–23.

118. Anthony M. Turano, "The Comedy of Repeal," *American Mercury* 39 (October 1936), 169.

119. "An Era Ends," *Newsweek* 2 (December 9, 1933), n.p. For more on the ways the American state has enlisted the private sector to gather information about citizens and document their behavior, see Lauer and Lipartito, eds., *Surveillance Capitalism in America*.

120. Thompson and Genosko, *Punched Drunk*, 14; Phillips, *Alcohol*, 283. The names of customers suspected of abusing alcohol were put on an interdiction list that prohibited them from buying alcohol and drinking in bars. For a fascinating analysis of how the LCBOs and the police used the interdiction list to control Indians, vagrants, sexually promiscuous women, mixed-race couples, and rowdy working-class men, see Thompson and Genosko, *Punched Drunk*, 19–21, 158–162; and Valverde, "A Postcolonial Women's Law?," 566–588.

121. Thompson and Genosko, *Punched Drunk*, 16–17; Heron, *Booze*, 280.

122. Thompson and Genosko, *Punched Drunk*, 147

123. Turano, "The Comedy of Repeal," 169; Murphy, "Bootlegging Mothers and Drinking Daughters," 174–194.

124. Turano, "The Comedy of Repeal," 170.

125. "State Control Loses," *Business Week*, January 19, 1935, 9.

126. Mendelson, *From Demon to Darling*, 103–104. Craig Heron similarly described the government stores in Canada as "coldly austere places, more like banks than retail stores"; Heron, *Booze*, 279.

127. For excellent studies of the saloon, see Duis, *The Saloon*; Rosenzweig, *Eight Hours for What We Will*; Powers, *Faces Along the Bar*.

128. "An Era Ends," *Newsweek* 2 (December 9, 1933), n.p.; C. H. Baldwin, "Solo Buying—No Treating," letter to the Editor, *The Rotarian* 44 (April 1934), 36.

129. "Liquor Returns—Under Control," *Business Week*, December 9, 1933, 5–6.

130. Turano, "The Comedy of Repeal," 171–172.

131. "Liquor Selling—Where—How?," *American City* 50 (May 1935), 93.

132. Turano, "The Comedy of Repeal," 171; "Liquor Selling—Where—How?," 93.

133. Jennifer Le Zotte, "Seeing Straight: Policing Sexualities in 1930s Manhattan Nightclubs," 135–136.

134. Turano, "The Comedy of Repeal," 168–73.

135. Peyser, *The Law and the California Wine Industry*, 15–16.

136. Campbell, "Managing the Marginal," 109.

137. Heron, *Booze*, 282, 294.

138. Thompson and Genosko, *Punched Drunk*, 151–153; Malleck, *Try to Control Yourself*, 69.

139. Turano, "The Comedy of Repeal," 170.

140. "Taverns in Chicago: Summary of Investigation of the Juvenile Protective Association from May 28, 1936 to September 1, 1936," 1–11, UBIF file–1937,

Box 356, BP. The practice of hiring women to work as drink solicitors increased in the 1940s and 1950s. For more on B-girls, see Littauer, *Bad Girls*, chap. 2.

141. Blahut, "Raising the Bar," 214–216.

142. Lauer and Lipartito, "Introduction: Surveillance Under Capitalism," 14.

143. Le Zotte, "Seeing Straight," 135.

144. Chauncey, *Gay New York*, 334–339; Heap, *Slumming*, 89–96. For more on repeal's impact on lesbian communities in the 1930s, see Kennedy and Davis, *Boots of Leather, Slippers of Gold*, 30–38.

145. H. L. Mencken, "A Year of Legal Liquor," *The Nation* 139 (December 12, 1934), 666.

146. Will Irwin, "The Resurrection of Mr. Volstead," *Scribner's Magazine* 105 (February 1939), 14; Dobyns, *The Amazing Story of Repeal*, 403–404.

147. Turano, "The Comedy of Repeal," 168–173.

148. Mrs. John S. Sheppard, "Address by Mrs. John S. Sheppard to Federation of Liquor Dealers of New York," March 9, 1937, 2–3, UBIF file, Box 354, BP.

149. For more on the tied-house saloon, see Pegram, *Battling Demon Rum*, 94–97; Timberlake, *Prohibition and the Progressive Movement*, 104–105; Duis, *The Saloon*, 24–28; Kerr, *Organized for Prohibition*, 23–24.

150. Kerr, "The Rebirth of Brewing and Distilling," 6; Joseph H. Choate, Jr., "Choate Urges Shift to Wines," *New York Times*, January 26, 1936, enclosed with letter from Paul Garrett to M. H. McIntyre, secretary to the president, February 28, 1926, Box 1, Official File 369: Wines, FDRPP. Eager to head off negative publicity, the national shippers backed the Federal Alcohol Administration's proposed restrictions on giveaways in 1936; "Disapproval Brews," *Business Week*, January 18, 1936, 31.

151. Kay, "Balance-Sheet of Repeal," 20.

152. "Editorial: Five Years of Repeal," *Christian Century* 60 (December 14, 1938), 1533.

153. Erenberg, "From New York to Middletown," 761–778.

154. Rorabaugh, "Drinking in the 'Thin Man' Films, 1934–1947," 51–68.

155. Irwin, "The Resurrection of Mr. Volstead," 14.

156. Bernays, *Propaganda;* with an introduction by Miller, 54; Ewen, *PR!*, 162–163.

157. Ewen, *PR!*, 163.

158. Tye, *The Father of Spin*, 52.

159. Bernays, *Propaganda*, 73.

160. Edward L. Bernays, "Recommendations for Public Relations Activities to Protect and Expand the Brewing Industry of the United States: Facts and Figures on Which Our Recommendations Are Based," volume II, 1936, 45–50, Box 351, BP.

161. Bernays, *Propaganda*, 37–38; Tye, *The Father of Spin*, 92–97; Ewen, *PR!*, 12–13.

162. Tye, *The Father of Spin*, 101.

163. Bernays, "Recommendations for Public Relations Activities," 47.

164. Bernays, "Recommendations for Public Relations Activities," 62, 69–70.

165. Bernays, "Recommendations for Public Relations Activities," 69–70.
166. Bernays, "Recommendations for Public Relations Activities," 62.
167. Bernays, "Recommendations for Public Relations Activities," 52, 54–55, 59, 62, 65, 72–73.
168. "Memorandum to Mr. S. J. Quinn from D. E. Heckman," 1–2.
169. "Memorandum to Mr. S. J. Quinn from D. E. Heckman," 1–2.
170. Okrent, *Last Call*, 42–46; Davis, *Jews and Booze*, 120–130; Timberlake, *Prohibition and the Progressive Movement*, 120–121; Sullivan, "Lee Levy and 'Black Cock Vigor Gin.'"

3. FERMENTED BEVERAGES AND THE GOSPEL OF MODERATION

1. Strauss, *Setting the Table for Julia Child*, 115–117.
2. "Wine Tasters Test Talents on Cheese," *New York Times*, November 10, 1936, 27.
3. Mendelson, *From Demon to Darling*, 14–16.
4. Hannickel, *Empire of Vines*, 119–120.
5. Marshall Wilder, quoted in Hannickel, *Empire of Vines*, 119.
6. Cinotto, *Soft Soil, Black Grapes*, 19, 25–26.
7. Sbarboro, "Wine as Remedy for the Evil of Intemperance," 1–2, 15–16.
8. Sbarboro, *The Fight for True Temperance*, 3–4.
9. Cinotto, *Soft Soil, Black Grapes*, 174; Sbarboro, *The Fight for True Temperance*, 22.
10. Sbarboro, *The Fight for True Temperance*, 23–24.
11. Davis, "The Contradictions of 'Civilizing' Consumption"; Regan-Lefebvre, *Imperial Wine*.
12. Sbarboro, *Temperance vs. Prohibition*.
13. Sbarboro, *Temperance vs. Prohibition*, 17.
14. Sbarboro, *Temperance vs. Prohibition*, 13.
15. Ostrander, *The Prohibition Movement in California, 1848–1933*, 135–139.
16. Rossi, *Italian-Swiss Colony and the Wine Industry*, 41–43, 51–55.
17. Adams, *Revitalizing the California Wine Industry*, 1–26 (quoted at 26), passim.
18. Adams, *Revitalizing the California Wine Industry*, 6.
19. Marchand, *Advertising the American Dream*; Laird, *Advertising Progress*; Lears, *Fables of Abundance*, 160–161, 203–206.
20. Talbot, "The Myth of Whiteness in Classical Sculpture"; Anagnostu, "Forget the Past, Remember the Ancestors!," 25–71.
21. Seldes, *The Future of Drinking*, 78, 134, 140.
22. Schoonmaker and Marvel, *The Complete Wine Book*, 12–14.
23. Teiser and Harroun, "The Volstead Act, Rebirth, and Boom," 70.
24. Teiser and Harroun, "The Volstead Act, Rebirth, and Boom," 70; Pinney, *A History of Wine in America*, 96–98.
25. Pinney, *A History of Wine in America*, 98–99.
26. Howard, "Selling Wine to the French," 197–224; Leon Douarche, "The World Viticultural Crisis," translated by H. F. Stoll Jr., *Wines and Vines* 20 (April 1939), 6–7.

27. Phillips, *Alcohol*, 287.
28. Bittner, *Whites and Reds*, chap. 4.
29. Griffith, "Bacchus Among the Blackshirts," 394–415, quoted at 395, 401, 402.
30. Adams, *California Wine Industry Affairs*, 23–26, 47.
31. "Inaugural Dinner of the Society of Medical Friends of Wine," February 24, 1939, St. Francis Yacht Club, San Francisco, San Francisco Ephemera Collection, California Historical Society, San Francisco.
32. Nasaw, *The Chief*, 433–434.
33. Hearst quoted in Clark, *Deliver Us from Evil*, 196–197.
34. Nasaw, *The Chief*, 441–445.
35. Clark, *Deliver Us from Evil*, 197.
36. Frank, *Buy American*, 56–78.
37. "The Problem of the Wine Producers Association," radio talk by Judge Marion De Vries, *California Grape Grower* 5 (December 1933), 6.
38. Pinney, *A History of Wine in America*, 41–42.
39. Robert D. Rossi, "Post-Repeal Wine Consumption," *Wines and Vines* 16 (January 1935), 3; Pinney, *A History of Wine in America*, 57.
40. Gomberg, *Analytical Perspectives on the California Wine Industry*, 9.
41. Pinney, *A History of Wine in America*, 57–58.
42. Rossi, "Post-Repeal Wine Consumption," 3.
43. Pinney, *A History of Wine in America*, 42.
44. Horowitz, *Kosher USA*, 135–137, 161.
45. Lapsley, *Bottled Poetry*, 5.
46. Gomberg, *Analytical Perspectives on the California Wine Industry*, 9.
47. Editorial in the *New York American* and other Hearst newspapers, quoted in *Wine Institute, Confidential Bulletin to Members* 4 (March 25, 1935), 6.
48. Hearst editorial, quoted in *Wine Institute, Confidential Bulletin to Members* 2 (February 19, 1935), 4.
49. *Wine Institute: Confidential Bulletin to Members* 12 (August 31, 1935).
50. Harry A. Caddow, "The Wine Industry Unites," *California Journal of Development* 25 (September 1935), 22.
51. Sackman, *Orange Empire*, 34–39.
52. *Wine Institute: Confidential Bulletin to Members* 5 (April 16, 1935), 5–6.
53. *Wine Institute: Confidential Bulletin to Members* 10 (June 29, 1935), 2–3.
54. *Wine Institute: Confidential Bulletin to Members* 6 (May 7, 1935), 5.
55. *Wine Institute: Confidential Bulletin to Members* 14 (August 14, 1935).
56. "American Wines for the American People," *Wines and Vines* 18 (April 1937), 23.
57. "Wine Stirreth Itself," *Business Week*, April 6, 1935, 14–15.
58. Pinney, *A History of Wine in America*, 56.
59. "Wine Publicity and Advertising," *California Grape Grower* 15 (April 1934), 18–19.
60. Woeste, *The Farmer's Benevolent Trust*.
61. C. C. Teague, "Sane Marketing Can Turn Farm Surpluses into Profits," *Printers' Ink* 161 (December 15, 1932), 36–37, 40; C. C. Thorpe, "One Way

Back to Agricultural Health," *Banking* 26 (January 1933), 31, 62; "More Advertising, More Sales, and Higher Prices," *Printed Salesmanship* 60 (January 1933), 363–363; "Co-operative Marketing Proves Its Dollar Value," *Printers' Ink* 162 (February 9, 1933), 44.

62. H.F. Stoll Jr., "Merchandising Wines: Increasing Dry Wine Consumption," *Wines and Vines* 16 (November 1935): 8–9.

63. H.F. Stoll Jr., "Advertising Sweet Wines," *Wines and Vines* 17 (June 1936), 20.

64. "An Educational Wine Campaign," *Wines and Vines* 16 (November 1935), 18.

65. Harry Caddow, "A New Era in Wine Advertising," *California Grape Grower* 15 (January 1934), 22–23; for more on Adams's role in writing Wine Institute press releases, journal articles and publicity, see Adams, *Revitalizing the California Wine Industry*, 57.

66. Rossi, *Italian-Swiss Colony and the Wine Industry*, 80–81.

67. Martini, *The Martinis*, 43.

68. Sackman, *Orange Empire*, 94–95.

69. Adams, *Revitalizing the California Wine Industry*, 64.

70. Adams, *Revitalizing the California Wine Industry*, 74–75.

71. Lapsley, *Bottled Poetry*, 4.

72. Pinney, *A History of American Wine*, 61.

73. Adams, *Revitalizing the California Wine Industry*, 64–67, 70–71.

74. Woeste, *The Farmer's Benevolent Trust*.

75. Teague, "Sane Marketing Can Turn Farm Surpluses into Profits," 37, 40.

76. Olson, *The Logic of Collective Action*, 51.

77. Adams, *Revitalizing the California Wine Industry*, 84.

78. Peyser, *The Law and the California Wine Industry*, 11.

79. Peyser, *The Law and the California Wine Industry*, 10–11; Jefferson Peyser, "On the Legal Side," talk before the 28th Annual Membership Meeting of the Wine Institute, San Francisco, CA, May 29, 1962, reprinted in Peyser, *The Law and the California Wine Industry*, app. 1.

80. "Popularizing California Wines," *Wines and Vines* 19 (March 1938), 18.

81. "Wine Industry Acts," *Business Week*, September 3, 1934, 26.

82. Carl Wente, "Economics of Grape Growing in California, 1918–1942," remarks at Livermore Wine Week Dinner, October 24, 1962, reprinted in Burke Critchfield, *California Wine Industry during the Depression*, 61–62.

83. Critchfield, *California Wine Industry during the Depression*, 48.

84. Woeste, *The Farmer's Benevolent Trust*. By the fall of 1938, vintners representing nearly 90 percent of the industry by volume had voted to launch a three-year Wine for America advertising campaign. See H.A. Caddow, "Advertising California Wines," *Wines and Vines* 19 (November 1938), 3.

85. "California Wine Industry Launches $2,000,000 Advertising Program," *Business Week*, December 15, 1938, 28, 53.

86. W.S. Alexander, "Future of the Wine Industry," address at the Wine Institute meeting in Los Angeles, CA, September 13, 1938, reprinted in *Wines and Vines* 19 (October 1938), 5, 22–23. The Wine Institute's press releases touting Alexander's favorable remarks were quoted in "California Wine Indus-

try Launches $2,000,000 Advertising Program," *Business Week*, December 15, 1938, 28, 53.

87. "The 'Wine for America' Drive, Excerpts from an Address by John Boettiger," *Wines and Vines* 20 (June 1939), 6.

88. For more on the moderation campaigns of Canadian brewers, see Bellamy, *Brewed in the North*, 167, 182–185.

89. Pegram, *Battling Demon Rum*, 92, 98.

90. Kerr, *Organized for Prohibition*, 27–28.

91. *Western Brewer* 1 (August 15, 1875), 13; quoted in Mittelman, *Brewing Battles*, 43.

92. Quoted in Mittelman, *Brewing Battles*, 44.

93. Kerr, *Organized for Prohibition*, 21.

94. Pegram, *Battling Demon Rum*, 98–99.

95. Quoted in Pegram, *Battling Demon Rum*, 99.

96. Kerr, *Organized for Prohibition*, 27–28, 34, 177, 183–184; Kerr, "The American Brewing Industry, 1865–1920," 186–191.

97. Stack, "Local and Regional Breweries in America's Brewing Industry," 442–443, 457–459.

98. Kerr, *Organized for Prohibition*, 174–184.

99. Joseph R. Dill, "Unhappy Days for the Brewer," *Christian Century* 54 (June 30, 1937), 834.

100. "Beer Bust," *Business Week*, April 4, 1936, 14; "Brewers Split on Promotion Plan," *Business Week*, October 31, 1936, 31–32; "Alcoholic Defense," *Business Week*, February 1, 1941, 24.

101. "To Battle for Beer," *Business Week*, April 24, 1937, 23–24. In a private meeting with one of Bernays's associates, August Busch confirmed that *Business Week* correctly reported BII's criticisms of the Bernays plan; see "Report of A.M. East on Visit to St. Louis," UBIF file—July 1937, Box 355, BP.

102. "Sorry—We Cannot Endorse Proposed Foundation," *Brewers Journal* 75 (December 15, 1936), 24; "Revise Licensing Laws Immediately," *Brewers Journal* 75 (December 15, 1936), 22–23.

103. Stack, "Local and Regional Breweries in America's Brewing Industry," 459–462; Stack, "Liquid Bread," 289–291; Stack, "A Concise History of America's Brewing Industry."

104. Stack, "Liquid Bread," 194–197.

105. Stack, "Liquid Bread," 236–237, 241, 243, 247; Blocker, *American Temperance Movements*, 137.

106. "Beer in Transition," *Business Week*, April 19, 1941, 59.

107. "Beer's Burden," *Business Week*, August 17, 1935, 16; "Beer with a Collar," *Business Week*, January 4, 1936, 18.

108. "Beer—Just Beer," *Business Week*, April 13, 1935, 22; "Disapproval Brews," *Business Week*, January 18, 1936, 31; "Brewery 'Czar' Held Necessity; Discipline Lax," *World-Telegram*, May 11, 1936, UBIF File 1938, Box 356, BP.

109. For an example of such candid acknowledgements of the tavern problem, see William Piel, "An Advertising and Educational Program," speech presented at the 61st Annual Convention of the USBA in Chicago, October 20, 1936, UBIF pamphlet, 1936, UBIF file, Box 352, BP.

110. "United Brewers Industrial Foundation: The Following Firms Have Signed Subscription Agreement Up to June 1, 1937," UBIF File July 1937, Box 355, BP.

111. Stack, "Liquid Bread," 261–262.

112. Remarks by Sol Abrams, "Convention Action Establishing the Foundation," 33–34, excerpts from Proceedings of Morning Session of 61st Annual Convention of the USBA, October 21, 1936, UBIF pamphlet, 1936, UBIF file, Box 352, BP.

113. *American Brewer* editorial, July 1937, in "Editorial Abstracts," UBIF file—July 1937, Box 356, BP.

114. Joseph Shaplen, "Brewing Industry Under Own Code," *New York Times*, October 29, 1937, 15.

115. Edward L. Bernays, "Summary of News Clippings Received in September," *Reports for the Month of September, 1937: United Brewers Industrial Foundation*, September 28, 1937, Box 351, BP; Edward L. Bernays, "Foundation Speaker Scheduled at Civic Meetings, Etc.," *Reports for the Month of September, 1937: United Brewers Industrial Foundation*, September 28, 1937, Box 351, BP; Edward L. Bernays, "Summary of Total News Clippings Received by UBIF," *Report of Public Relations Activities for Month of October, 1937*, Box 351, BP.

116. *Brewers' Journal*, June 15, 1937, quoted in Dobyns, *The Amazing Story of Repeal*, 420–421.

117. "Against Prohibition No. 3," trade card advertisement, c. 1883, Online Collection, Detroit Historical Society.

118. Marten, "No Beer for Babies," 44.

119. UBIF advertisement in *Presenting United Brewers Industrial Foundation* New York: United Brewers Industrial Foundation, c. 1937), Box 353, BP.

120. Eloise Davison, *Beer in the American Home* (New York: United Brewers Industrial Foundation, 1937), 1–2, UBIF file—1937, Box 356, BP, 2.

121. Davison, *Beer in the American Home*, 24–27.

122. Davison, *Beer in the American Home*, 1–2.

123. Memo, August 31, 1937 UBIF file, September 1937, Box 353, BP; Edward L. Bernays, *Report of Activities of the United Brewers Industrial Foundation to the Directors*, June 23, 1937, 5, Box 355, BP; Hugh Harley, letter re: "900 Merchandising Managers of Department Stores," June 29, 1937, Box 355, BP.

124. "Abstracts from Letters: Press," August 31, 1937, Box 355, BP.

125. Joseph R. Dill, "Unhappy Days for the Brewer," *Christian Century* 54 (June 30, 1937), 833.

126. Charles Ferguson, "Home Is Where the Quart Is," *Christian Century* 55 (October 26, 1938), 1293.

127. "Beer's Virtues for Cooking Extolled by Brewers' Group," *Washington Post*, September 2, 1937, 11.

128. Editorial, May 19, 1937 in "Editorial Abstracts," May 1937, 2, Box 354, BP.

129. Letter from Louis Glaser, Inc. to UBIF, "Abstracts from Letters: Advertising," August 24, 1937, Box 355, BP.

130. "Beer Code or U.S. Permits?," *Business Week*, November 6, 1937, 50; "Brewers Are Urged to Stop Saying Beer Is a Soft Drink," *Christian Science Monitor*, October 27, 1937, 10.

131. Laforge, "Misplaced Priorities," 233–249; "Where Propaganda Failed," *Christian Science Monitor*, January 29, 1938, 18; Pennock, *Advertising Sin and Sickness*, 39.

132. Remarks by William Reydel, transcript of conference meeting with Bernays and UBIF members, c. August 1938, 44–45, Box 356, BP.

133. Speech of Edward L. Bernays at Advertising Conference held in the Waldorf-Astoria on Tuesday, July 12, 1938, 4, Box 356, BP; "The Brewers' Code of Practice," 1937, Box 351, BP.

134. "Wait, Mister! You're aiming at the wrong duck!," UBIF ad, 1938, Box 356, BP; "This symbol means a lot to lovers of good beer!," UBIF ad, 1938, Box 356, BP; "When you drink Beer in a tavern . . . choose your tavern," UBIF ad, 1938, Box 356, BP.

135. UBIF press release, c. October 1938, Box 356, BP.

136. Letter from Edward L. Bernays to Herbert J. Charles, chairman UBIF, October 27, 1937, Box 356, BP.

137. Adams, *Revitalizing the California Wine Industry*, 97.

138. "Memorandum to Mr. S. J. Quinn from D. E. Heckman," February 1936, Box 352, BP.

139. Ferguson, "Home Is Where the Quart Is," 1292–1994.

4. SPIRITOUS BEVERAGES AND THE MUDDLED MEANINGS OF MODERATION

1. Lender and Martin, *Drinking in America*, 68–74.

2. For excellent representations of the "slippery slope" argument in prohibitionist propaganda, see Nathaniel Currier, *The Drunkard's Progress*, lithograph, Currier and Ives, 1846; Frank Beard, *The Downward Path*, cartoon, c. 1890s, Temperance and Prohibition website, Ohio State University, https://prohibition.osu.edu/anti-saloon-league/dry-propaganda/dry-arguments/downward-path.

3. Courtwright, *Forces of Habit;* Herzberg, *Happy Pills in America;* Herzberg, *White Market Drugs;* Richert, *Strange Trips;* Schivelbusch, *Tastes of Paradise*.

4. Veach, *Kentucky Bourbon Whiskey*, 45–47; Berenstein, "Who's Afraid of the Whiskey Trust."

5. Clark, "A Liquid Spirit," 191–203, 216; Veach, *Kentucky Bourbon Whiskey*, 74–76.

6. Clark, "A Liquid Spirit," 215–218, 234–235.

7. Quoted in Clark, "A Liquid Spirit," 272.

8. High and Coppin, "Wiley and the Whiskey Industry," 286–309; Carson, *The Social History of Bourbon*, 170–171; Berenstein, "Who's Afraid of the Whiskey Trust?"

9. Quoted in Clark, "A Liquid Spirit," 278.

10. Clark, "A Liquid Spirit," 279–281.

11. Kerr, *Organized for Prohibition*, 161–164.

12. For more on the origins of the moderation campaign, see Marrus, *Samuel Bronfman*, 196–201; Faith, *The Bronfmans*, 105–106; Robinson, "The Luxury of Moderate Use," 109–139.

13. Marrus, *Samuel Bronfman*, 215, 226–31.

14. Regan and Regan, *The Book of Bourbon*, 78.

15. Frank R. Schwengel, "Opening Address to National Wholesale Liquor Dealers Association," September 25, 1934, Box 216, Series III, Seagram Museum Collection (SMC).

16. Grimes, *Straight Up or on the Rocks*, 109; Faith, *The Bronfmans*, 92–93, 95–97; Marrus, *Samuel Bronfman*, 195.

17. "Hiram Walker Digs In," *Fortune* 19 (March 1939), 96.

18. "Liquor Comes of Age," *Business Week*, December 4, 1937, 17.

19. "Name, Schenley; Age, Three," *Fortune* 13 (May 1936), 159.

20. Marrus, *Samuel Bronfman*, 189. British firms owned just over 70 percent of worldwide stocks and Canadian firms owned just over 20 percent.

21. Advertising tear sheet, "We of Seagram Recognize"; advertising tear sheet, "When Good Fellows Get Together," 1936, Box 109, Series III, SMC.

22. Marchand, *Creating the Corporate Soul*, 202–48.

23. Marrus, *Samuel Bronfman*, 197; Philip Siekman, "The Bronfmans: An Instinct for Dynasty (Part I)," *Fortune* 74 (November 1966) 206, 210.

24. House of Seagram, *Moderation: The Story of a Point of View*, c.1980, Box 85, Series III, SMC.

25. "We who make whiskey suggest: SAY 'NO' When It's One Drink Too Many," May 1936 moderation ad, Box 109, SMC.

26. For more on the changing understandings of alcoholism, see Rotskoff, *Love on the Rocks;* Tracy and Acker, eds., *Altering American Consciousness;* McClellan, *Lady Lushes;* Roizen, "The American Discovery of Alcoholism, 1933–1939"; Tracy, *Alcoholism in America*.

27. "We Don't Want Bread Money," March 1937 ad in Seagram, *Moderation*, Box 85, SMC.

28. Martin, *Devil of the Domestic Sphere;* Parsons, *Manhood Lost;* Pegram, *Battling Demon Rum*.

29. Rotskoff, *Love on the Rocks*, 81.

30. "We Don't Want Bread Money" ad.

31. Rotskoff, *Love on the Rocks*, 83–84.

32. Levine, "American Culture and the Great Depression," 206–230.

33. *"Pay Your Bills First,"* February 1938 ad in Seagram, *Moderation*, Box 85, SMC.

34. "We who make whiskey say: "DRINKING and DRIVING DO NOT MIX," August 1937 ad in Seagram, *Moderation*, Box 85, SMC.

35. "You Can't Call Back a Careless Bullet," November 1955 ad in Seagram, *Moderation*, Box 85, SMC.

36. "You're a Hero . . . To Your Son," June 1938 ad in Seagram, *Moderation*, Box 85, SMC.

37. For more on the food industry's cooptation of health reformers' concerns, see Belasco, *Appetite for Change*.

38. Frank R. Schwengel, "The Threat of Prohibition," March 31, 1942, Box 216, Series III, SMC.
39. Charles Ferguson, "Home Is Where the Quart Is," *Christian Century* 55 (October 26, 1938), 1293.
40. "We who make whiskey say: 'DRINK MODERATELY," October 1934 ad in Seagram, *Moderation*, Box 85, SMC.
41. Calvert ad, September 20, 1934, Box 86, Series III, SMC.
42. Calvert ad, *World Telegram*, April 15, 1937, Box 86, Series III, SMC.
43. Calvert ad, October 11, 1934, Box 86, Series III, SMC.
44. "We who make whiskey say: 'DRINK MODERATELY.'"
45. "We who make whiskey say: 'DRINK MODERATELY.'"
46. "We who make whiskey suggest: SAY 'NO.'"
47. Calvert ad, November 8, 1934, Box 86, Series III, SMC.
48. Seagram's 7 Crown ad, November 1946, Box OV 149, SMC.
49. Calvert ad, September 20, 1934, Box 86, Series III, SMC.
50. "We who make whiskey suggest: SAY 'NO.'"
51. Calvert ads, 1938–1939, Box 86, SMC.
52. "We Who Make Whiskey Suggest: 'SAY "NO" When It's One Drink Too Many," May 1936 moderation ad, Box 109, SMC.
53. Parsons, "Risky Business," 283–307, esp. 287.
54. "When GOOD FELLOWS Get Together . . .," October 1936 moderation ad, Box 109, SMC.
55. Calvert ads, 1938–1939, Box 86, SMC.
56. *The Story of Seagram's Seven Crown* (New York: Seagram Distillers-Corp., 1972), n.p., Box 281, Series IV, SMC.
57. Lears, *Fables of Abundance*, 161–168, 174–176, 179–183.
58. For examples of advertisements directed at adolescent girls that incorporated tips on healthy habits, see Jacobson, *Raising Consumers*, 133–140.
59. Seagram's Seven Crown Blended Whiskeys ad, c. 1936–38, in *Let's Go!* (New York: Seagram Distillers-Corp., 1937), n.p., Box 208, Series III, SMC.
60. Pennock, *Advertising Sin and Sickness*, 38–40; Veach, *Kentucky Bourbon Whiskey*, 92.
61. *Story of Seagram's Seven Crown*.
62. "Name, Schenley; Age, Three," *Fortune* 13 (May 1936), 162.
63. De la Peña, *Empty Pleasures*.
64. Advertisement for Bromo-Seltzer, *Esquire* 9 (June 1938), 110.
65. Parsons, "Risky Business," 283–307, quoted at 284.
66. Rotskoff, *Love on the Rocks*, 24.
67. Herzberg, *Happy Pills in America*, 48–72 (quoted at 68).
68. Calvert ad, *World Telegram*, April 15, 1937, Box 86, SMC.
69. Calvert Blended and Bottled in Bond Whiskeys ad, 1935, Box 108, Series III, SMC.
70. Calvert's Protective Blending ads, c. 1940, Box 86, SMC.
71. Apple, *Vitamania*, 13–31; Biltekoff, *Eating Right in America*, 46–54.
72. Lieberman, "Selling Sex Toys," 393–433; Maines, "Socially Camouflaged Technologies," 3–11.
73. Adams, *The Wines of America*, 25.

74. On homemade beer during Prohibition, see Okrent, *Last Call*, 250–251.
75. House of Seagram, *Moderation*.
76. Mac Shoub Consultants Ltée, "The Seagram Moderation Campaign: Review and Assessment," March 6, 1980, 12, Box 8, SCP.
77. "Name, Schenley; Age, Three," 162, 164.
78. Rydell, *World of Fairs*, 118, 112; Rydell, *All the World's a Fair*.
79. Mauro, *Twilight at the World of Tomorrow*, xx, 20, 27, 48, 50–51, 57.
80. Mauro, *Twilight at the World of Tomorrow*, 60–61 (quoted at 60).
81. Letter from L.K. Herzog (director of exhibits) to C. Healy (Hiram Walker), July 2, 1937, 1–2, Box 477, Folder 21, New York World's Fair, 1939–1940 Collection (NYWF).
82. Letter from Norman Baxter to Maurice Mermey (director of exhibits and concessions), September 13, 1938, Box 475, Folder 7, NYWF.
83. Letter from M.V. Little to A.D. O'Connor, May 9, 1940, Box 475, Folder 5, NYWF.
84. Cotter, *The 1939–1940 New York World's Fair*, 45–53; Applebaum, ed. *The New York World's Fair 1939/1940*, 66–78.
85. Letter from Lewis Rosenstiel to Grover Whalen, June 2, 1937, 1–2, Box 477, Folder 5, NYWF.
86. Exhibit Agreement between New York World's Fair and Distilled Spirits Exhibit, Inc., December 28, 1937, Box 475, Folder 8, NYWF.
87. Preliminary List of Initial Subscribers, Distilled Spirits Exhibit, Inc., December 21, 1937, Box 475, Folder 6, NYWF. The initial subscribers also included Baltimore Pure Rye Distilling, Bernheim Distilling, J.A. Dougherty's Sons, Felton & Son, Golden-Rossell Co., Hamburger Distillery, Hunter Pure Rye Distillery, Labrot & Graham, Laird & Co, Lehigh Warehouse & Transportation, F.C. Linde, Louisville Public Warehouse, Philip Blum & Co, Penfield Distilling Co., Schenley, Security Warehouse, Shewan-Jones, Siegfried Loewnthal, Waken & McLaughlin, and Wilson Distilling.
88. Frank Schwengel, "Suggestions for Educational Exhibit Distilled Spirits Industry," c. 1937, 1–3, Box 475, Folder 8, NYWF.
89. Letter from chairman of creative committee (National Distillers Products stationary) to General Frank Schwengel, September 12, 1938, 1–4, Box 475, Folder 7, NYWF.
90. Applebaum, ed., *The New York World's Fair, 1939/1940*, 71.
91. Press release, Distilled Spirits Exhibit, 1–4, c. 1939, Box 475, Folder 6, NYWF.
92. For more on the Whiskey Ring and the Whiskey Trust, see Carson, *The Social History of Bourbon*, 114–136; Mitenbuler, *Bourbon Empire*, 111–116, 122–127; Berenstein, "Who's Afraid of the Whiskey Trust"; Veach, *Kentucky Bourbon Whiskey*, 64–69.
93. Press release, Distilled Spirits Exhibit, 1–4, c. 1939, Box 475, Folder 6, NYWF.
94. Memo from Maurice Mermey to Administrative Assistant Holmes, February 27, 1939, Box 475, Folder 6, NYWF; telegram from Frank Schwengel to Grover Whalen (president NYWF), March 21, 1939, Box 475, Folder 6,

NYWF; telegram from Grover Whalen to Frank Schwengel, March 24, 1939, Box 475, Folder 6, NYWF.

95. Memo from E.F. Roosevelt (Acting Director of Foreign Government Participation) to Administrative Assistant Holmes Re: Distilled Spirits Exhibit, March 3, 1939, Box 475, Folder 6, NYWF.

96. Ballantine Three Ring Inn Beverage List, Box 1552, Folder 8, NYWF; Ballantine's A La Carte Menu, Box 1552, Folder 8, NYWF; Ballantine Three Ring Inn, operated by The Brass Rail Menu, Beverage List, 1940, Box 1552, Folder 8, NYWF; Schlitz Palm Garden Restaurant Wine and Cocktail List, Box 1557, Folder 5, NYWF.

97. Morabito, "A Food Tour of the 1939 World's Fair."

98. Letter from Schuyler Patterson to W. Earle Andrews, June 15, 1936, Box 474, Folder 3, NYWF.

99. Letter from Ralph Sabbatine to Grover Whalen, December 17, 1937, Box 585, Folder 10, NYWF; Ralph Sabbatino, Application for Concession, December 21, 1937, Box 585, Folder 10, NYWF; Dreier Hotel Management Corporation, Application for Concession, n.d., Box 585, Folder 10, NYWF.

5. BEER GOES TO WAR

1. Henthorn, *From Submarines to Suburbs.*
2. "Morale Is a Lot of *Little* Things," advertising proof sheet, September 11, 1944, USBF, Box 1, J. Walter Thompson Company Archives, Domestic Advertising Collection (DAC).
3. L.J. Pratt, "Slight Progress by Drys Presents Danger," *American Brewer* 75 (March 1942), 19.
4. Brewers had access to tin for the crowns on beer bottles and for the canned beer shipped to troops overseas. Glass bottles were used for domestic beer.
5. For a discussion of how the Anti-Saloon League exploited rising anti-German sentiment to smear brewers in World War I, see Timberlake, *Prohibition and the Progressive Movement*, 179.
6. Dower, *War without Mercy.*
7. Ronnenberg, "The American Brewing Industry Since 1920," 201–202; Courtwright, *Forces of Habit*, 156. The notion that after Repeal the federal government did not become involved in alcohol questions because of its "regard for healthy liquor revenues and fear of reviving the wet-dry wars" is advanced by Lender, "The Historian and Repeal," 187.
8. Rubin, "The Wet War," 251.
9. "From the Editor's Work Bench," *American Brewer* 75 (March 1942), 11.
10. "Rising Dry Tide," *Newsweek* 25 (May 17, 1945), 64.
11. Bentley, *Eating for Victory;* Trentmann and Just, eds., *Food and Conflict in Europe in the Age of the Two World Wars;* Rappaport, *A Thirst for Empire*, chap. 9; Biltekoff, *Eating Right in America*, chap. 3; Helstosky, *Garlic and Oil*. See special issue of *Food, Culture and Society* 10 (Summer 2007), esp. Veit, "'We Were a Soft People'," 167–190; and Mouré and Schwartz, "On Vit Mal," 261–296.

12. Tate, *Cigarette Wars*.
13. Veit, "'We Were a Soft People'," 167–190.
14. "Drys' Drive against Liquor for Armed Forces Seen as Second Wartime Wedge for Prohibition," *Newsweek* 19 (May 11, 1942), 60.
15. State legislatures in Colorado, Iowa, Maine, and Minnesota had petitioned Congress to pass the Sheppard bill in 1941; see "Dry Scare Raised," *Business Week*, June 7, 1941, 42.
16. Letter from Hannah Ericcson to Senator Lee O'Daniel (petitions attached), Petitions, Box 253, Records of the US Senate, 78th Congress, Committee on Military Affairs (SEN).
17. Letter to Hon. Benjamin Jarret, April 26, 1941, petitions attached, Box 351, Records of the US House of Representatives, 77th Congress, Bills and Resolutions in the House (HR).
18. Letter from Mrs. Charles G. Lindner, Secretary of the Women's Missionary Society of the Highland United Presbyterian Church of New Castle, Pennsylvania, to Congressman Graham, February 21, 1942, Box 352, HR.
19. "Petition to Congress: ALCOHOL—Hitler's Best Friend, America's Worst Enemy," 1943, Petitions 2, Box 255, SEN.
20. Petition supporting Sheppard Bill, address to Rep. J. Parnell Thomas, Box 351, HR.
21. Kladstrup and Kladstrup, *Wine and War*, 86.
22. Jos. Dubin, "The Ghost Returns," *Modern Brewery Age* 27 (January 1942), 10.
23. "Flood of Wet Petitions to Deluge Congress," *Modern Brewery Age* 30 (August 1943), 32.
24. Letter from Neil Deighan, chairman of the National Council of State Liquor Dealers' Associations in Camden, NJ, May 21, 1941, Various Subjects, Box 352, HR.
25. "Drys Defeated in First Encounter to Enact Wartime Prohibition," *Modern Brewery Age* 28 (November 1942), 15–18.
26. As noted in chap. 1, 3.2 percent beer (measured in alcohol by weight) is equivalent to 4.0 percent beer (measured in alcohol by volume)—a lighter lager than pre-Prohibition Budweiser, which averaged 4.5 to 4.7 percent alcohol by volume..
27. Tate, *Cigarette Wars*, 72.
28. "Drys Defeated in First Encounter," 15–18.
29. Temperance groups in Canada used similar maternalist rhetoric to protest drinking by "our boys" in the army during World War I. See Cook, "Wet Canteens and Worrying Mothers," 311–330.
30. "Drys Drive against Liquor for Armed Forces Seen as Second Wartime Wedge for Prohibition" *Newsweek* 19 (May 11, 1942), 60.
31. Dubin, "The Ghost Returns," 10.
32. Wylie, *Generation of Vipers*, 203.
33. Pennock, *Advertising Sin and Sickness*, 22.
34. "Beer's Bottlenecks," *Business Week*, May 24, 1942, 19–20.
35. "Embattled Beer," *Business Week*, November 24, 1945, 44.

36. "Beer's Bottlenecks," 19; "Demand for Beer Rising as Breweries Anticipate 10% Drop in Sales," *Business Week*, August 13, 1943, 74; "3.2 Beer Again?" *Business Week*, August 7, 1943, 28.
37. "Brewers' Malt Cut," *Business Week*, March 6, 1943, 30.
38. Kerr, *Organized for Prohibition*, 32; Kerr, "The American Brewing Industry," 189.
39. Kerr, *Organized for Prohibition*, 27–28, 34, 177, 183–184; Kerr, "The American Brewing Industry," 186–191.
40. Jack Van Norden, "Prohibition Is Returning," *American Mercury* 56 (March 1943), 273–280.
41. The artists included Douglass Crockwell, Mead Schaeffer, Lucille Corcos, Stevan Dohanos, Fletcher Martin, Marianne Appel, and Julien Binford.
42. Joe Marsh, "Light Words are 'Grave' Words," No. 88 of a series, placed in newspapers the week of May 22, 1944 (Brewing Industry Foundation, 1944), USBF, Box 1, DAC.
43. Joe Marsh, "From Where I Sit," No. 67 of a series, placed in *South Dakota State Forum* September 10, 1943 (Brewing Industry Foundation, 1943), USBF, Box 1, DAC.
44. Joe Marsh, "From Where I Sit," No. 49 of a series, placed in newspapers during the weeks of September 28, 1942 and October 5, 1942 (Brewing Industry Foundation, 1943), USBF, Box 1, DAC.
45. Joe Marsh, "From Where I Sit," No. 46 of a series (Brewing Industry Foundation, 1942), USBF, Box 1, DAC.
46. Weiner, "Consumer Culture and Participatory Democracy," 117.
47. Joe Marsh, "From Where I Sit," No. 46.
48. Bentley, *Eating for Victory*, 37.
49. Joe Marsh, "From Where I Sit," No. 115 of a series (Brewing Industry Foundation, 1945), USBF, Box 2, DAC.
50. "Morale Is a Lot of *Little* Things," advertising proof sheet, June 1942, USBF, Box 1, DAC.
51. "Morale Is a Lot of *Little* Things," advertising proof sheets, June 1942, August 1942, May 1943, December 1943, USBF, Box 1, DAC.
52. Howard, *Brides, Inc.*, 168.
53. Quoted in Fox, *Madison Avenue Goes to War*, 37.
54. Blum, *V Was for Victory*, 100.
55. Rhonda Metraux, "Popular Beliefs about the Relationship between Specific Foods and Morale," (December 12, 1942), 1–11, Reports: General Folder, 1942, Committee on Food Habits Papers (CFH).
56. "The Relationship between Food Habits and Problems of Wartime Emergency Feeding" (Washington, DC: Committee on Food Habits), May 1942, 4, Reports: General File, 1942, CFH; see also Bentley, *Eating for Victory*, 64–65.
57. *Report on the Morale Building Value of Specific Foods in the American Diet*, 9, Reports: General File, 1942, CFH.
58. *Report on the Morale Building Value of Specific Foods*, 9–10, 13.
59. Margaret Mead, "Making the Food Communique Make Sense to the Average Housewife" (August 7, 1942): 1–4, Reports: General Folder, 1942, CFH.

60. Quoted in Bentley, *Eating for Victory*, 4.

61. Joe Marsh, "From Where I Sit," No. 79 of a series (Brewing Industry Foundation, 1944), USBF, Box 1, DAC.

62. Confidential memo from Margaret Mead, Executive Secretary, to the Executive Members of the Committee on Food Habits, October 10, 1942, 2, Projects Folder, 1941–44, CFH.

63. "Morale Is a Lot of *Little* Things," advertising proof sheet, October 20, 1944, USBF, Box 1, DAC.

64. "Morale Is a Lot of *Little* Things," advertising proof sheets, June 1944, September 11, 1944, October 20, 1944, USBF, Box 1, DAC.

65. Weiner, "Consumer Culture and Participatory Democracy," 113.

66. Westbrook, "Fighting for the American Family," 195–221; McGovern, *Sold America*, 327–328, 334–353, 363 (quoted at 341).

67. Joe Marsh, "From Where I Sit," No. 79 of a Series (Brewing Industry Foundation: 1944), USBF, Box 1, DAC.

68. Joe Marsh, "From Where I Sit," No. 76 of a Series (Brewing Industry Foundation: 1944), USBF, Box 1, DAC.

69. Joe Marsh, "From Where I Sit: One Less Tramp in Our Town," No. 98 of a Series (Brewing Industry Foundation: 1944), USBF, Box 1, DAC.

70. Quoted in Rubin, "The Wet War," 243.

71. Rubin, "The Wet War," 248–249. Eighty-five percent of American servicemen polled by the British Institute of Public Opinion described themselves as wet.

72. Weiner, "Consumer Culture and Participatory Democracy," 124.

73. Joe Marsh, "From Where I Sit," No. 48 of a Series (Brewing Industry Foundation: 1942), USBF, Box 1, DAC; Joe Marsh, "From Where I Sit," No. 70 of a Series, October 1, 1943, *South Dakota State Forum* (Brewing Industry Foundation, 1943), USBF, Box 1, DAC.

74. Joe Marsh, "From Where I Sit: Jeb Wilkins Loses the Wanderlust," September 1945 (United States Brewers' Foundation, 1945), USBF, Box 2, DAC.

75. Joe Marsh, "From Where I Sit: Thad Phibbs' Formula for Fun," No. 93 of a Series, week of September 4, 1944 (Brewing Industry Foundation, 1944), USBF, Box 1, DAC.

76. Advertisement, "Uncle from the West," *American Legion* (March 1946); advertisement, "Grandmother Hangs the Mistletoe," (1946), USBF, Box 2, DAC.

77. Advertisement, "Roof Raising," *Time* 45 (April 16, 1945), 47; advertisement, "Western Barbeque," *United States News* 18 (February 16, 1945); advertisement, "Boston 'Pops' Concert," *Time* 45 (May 14, 1945), 47, USBF, Box 2, DAC.

78. Graebner, *The Age of Doubt*, 60–61.

79. Westbrook, "Fighting for the American Family," 202–204.

80. Bentley, *Eating for Victory*, 62–63.

81. Advertisement, "Western Barbeque."

82. Joe Marsh, "From Where I Sit: Definition of a Great Man," *Successful Farming*, February 1945 (USBF: 1945), USBF, Box 1, DAC; Joe Marsh, "From Where I Sit: What Makes 'A Real American Town?'" No. 85 of a Series, week of May 8, 1944 (Brewing Industry Foundation, 1944), USBF, Box 1, DAC.

83. Advertisement, *Life*, March 9, 1942, USBF, Box 1, DAC.

84. Joe Marsh, "From Where I Sit: Recipe for a Perfect Marriage," No. 92 of a Series (Brewing Industry Foundation: 1944), USBF, Box 1, DAC.

85. For more on the ideologies and cultural practices that reimagined the early twentieth-century middle-class home as a site of pleasure, emotional satisfaction, and mutual understanding, see Jacobson, *Raising Consumers*, esp. chap. 5; Mintz and Kellogg, *Domestic Revolutions*, 107–132; Fass, *The Damned and the Beautiful*, 89–118; May, *Great Expectations;* Marsh, *Suburban Lives;* May, "Myths and Realities of the American Family," 549.

86. Corzine, "Right at Home," 849–850.

87. Bentley, *Eating for Victory*, chap. 2; Biltekoff, *Eating Right in America*, 64–79.

88. Joe Marsh, "From Where I Sit: Herb's Got a Great Little Wife," *Successful Farming*, October 1945 (United States Brewers' Foundation: 1945), USBF, Box 1, DAC.

89. Joe Marsh, "From Where I Sit: Keeping American Homes Intact," No. 95 of a Series, week of September 18, 1944 (Brewing Industry Foundation, 1944), USBF, Box 1, DAC.

90. Samuel, *Pledging Allegiance*.

91. "The Relationship between Food Habits and Problems of Wartime Emergency Feeding," 1–4.

92. Erenberg, "Swing Goes to War," 144–165; May, "Making the American Consensus," 71–102.

93. Joe Marsh, "From Where I Sit: Trouble Often Starts at Home," No. 96 of a Series, week of September 25, 1944 (Brewing Industry Foundation: 1944), USBF, Box 1, DAC.

94. Joe Marsh, "From Where I Sit," No. 75 of a Series, week of February 13, 1944 (Brewing Industry Foundation, 1944), USBF, Box 1, DAC.

95. Joe Marsh, "From Where I Sit: What Made Our Invasion a Success?" No. 89 of a Series, week of August 7, 1944 (Brewing Industry Foundation, 1944), USBF, Box 1, DAC.

96. For more on state food controls and government propaganda during World War I, see Veit, *Modern Food, Moral Food;* Goldstein, *Creating Consumers*, 46–60; Hayden-Smith, *Sowing the Seeds of Victory*.

97. Bentley, *Eating for Victory*.

98. "Resolution for War Time Prohibition," adopted February 13, 1942, Box 352, HR.

99. Letter to Congress, signed by nearly one hundred citizens, undated, Box 354, HR. Brewers used 2,209,200 pounds of rationed sugar each year, according to the War Food Administration. Though substantial, this volume was considerably less than dry estimates of 144,877,697 pounds of sugar used by brewers annually; "Nailing the Lies of the Drys," *American Brewer* 78 (July 1945), 17.

100. Quoted in Glover, *Brewing for Victory*, 17.

101. R. V. Siebel, P. J. F. Weber, and Elsie Singruen, "Brewing is an Essential Food Industry: Brewery Products for the Farmer," *Modern Brewery Age* 27 (April 1942), 16.

102. The brewing trade press occasionally touted the health benefits of beer as a "liquid food," but this argument was not featured in the major public relations campaigns during World War II. Siebel, Weber, and Singruen, "Brewing is an Essential Food Industry," 16.

103. R. V. Siebel, P. J. F. Wever, and Elsie Singruen, "Brewers' Yeast Can Help Win the War," *Modern Brewery Age* 27 (March 1942), 12.

104. "And the Greatest of These Is Yeast," *American Brewer* 75 (February 1942), 38–39.

105. Glover, *Brewing for Victory*, 9. The Canadian brewers made similarly bold claims about beer's nutritional value until the government banned all alcohol advertising in 1942; thereafter the Canadian brewers attempted to burnish their industry's reputation for "wholesomeness" and "patriotism" by publishing impartial nutritional advice that bolstered the government's broader wartime nutrition campaign. See Bellamy, *Brewed in the North*, 200–204.

106. Neuhaus, *Manly Meals and Mom's Home Cooking*, 111–112.

107. Levenstein, *Paradox of Plenty*, 65.

108. "Committee on Nutrition in Industry: Report Presented to Board," March 5, 1943, Committee on Nutrition of Industrial Workers Folder, 1942–45, FNB.

109. Quoted in Levenstein, *Paradox of Plenty*, 22.

110. Russell M. Wilder, MD, PhD, "Vitamin Fortification of Foods as Viewed by the Physician," paper read at the Institute of Food Technologists, Pittsburgh, PA, June 16, 1941, 7–11, Chairman Wilder Folder, FNB.

111. "Foods under Wartime Emergency Conditions," 1, Committee on Wartime Diet Folder, 1942–45, FNB; "Major Activities and Accomplishments of the Food and Nutrition Board during the months December 1942–January 1943," p. b, Activities Reports Folder, 1942–64, FNB.

112. Siebel, Weber, and Singruen, "Brewers' Yeast Can Help Win the War," 12.

113. R. V. Siebel, P. J. F. Weber, and Elsie Singruen, "Brewers' Yeast in Industrial Nutrition," *Modern Brewery Age* 28 (September 1942), 26.

114. Siebel, Weber, and Singruen, "Brewers' Yeast in Industrial Nutrition," 27. For more on how views of women's manual dexterity influenced attitudes toward women workers, see Campbell, "Women in Combat," 303–304.

115. Siebel, Weber, and Singruen, "Brewers' Yeast in Industrial Nutrition," 28.

116. Wilder, "Vitamin Fortification of Foods," 8.

117. Letter from Glenville Giddings, MD, and John Haldi, PhD, to Paul McNutt, Director, Office of Defense Health and Welfare Services, August 1, 1942, Committee on the Nutrition of Industrial Workers Folder, 1942–45, FNB.

118. R. V. Siebel, P. J. F. Weber, and Elsie Singruen, "Brewing Is an Essential Food Industry: Better Food Through Better Feeding with Brewers' Yeast," *Modern Brewery Age* 27 (May 1942), 15.

119. Vernon, *Hunger*, esp. chap. 4; Biltekoff, *Eating Right in America*, 45, 49–54, 79.

120. Vita-Min-Go Game, 1942, Oregon Secretary of State (website), accessed October 17, 2022, https://sos.oregon.gov/archives/exhibits/ww2/Pages/services-nutrition.aspx.

121. *Report on the Morale Building Value of Specific Foods in the American Diet*, 2.

122. Neuhaus, *Manly Meals and Mom's Home Cooking*, 110–112, 142–144.

123. R. V. Siebel, P. J. F. Weber, and Elsie Singruen, "Brewers' Yeast: A Victory Food," *Modern Brewery Age* 28 (August 1942), 18–19.

124. Siebel, Weber, and Singruen, "Brewers' Yeast in Industrial Nutrition," 28, 69.

125. R. V. Siebel, P. J. F. Weber, and Elsie Singruen, "Brewers' Yeast Supplements Wartime Diets," *Modern Brewery Age* 29 (May 1943), 25.

126. Siebel, Weber, and Singruen, "Brewers' Yeast in Industrial Nutrition" 72; Siebel, Weber, and Singruen, "Brewers' Yeast Supplements Wartime Diets," 25.

127. Jane Holt, "Brewers' Yeast to Fortify Food," *New York Times Magazine*, December 5, 1943, 30; Jane Holt, "Brewers' Yeast," *New York Times Magazine*, February 25, 1945, 26.

128. "Brewers' Yeast Comes to the Rescue in Food Rationing," *Modern Brewery Age* 28 (December 1942), 22–23.

129. "Stress Value of Brewers' Yeast, Spent Grains at Regional Meets," *Modern Brewery Age* 32 (July 1944), 29–30.

130. "Army Opens New Food Research 'Lab,'" *Modern Brewery Age* 31 (February 1944), 36.

131. Capt. S. G. Dunlop, "Dried Yeast in Army Rations," *Modern Brewery Age* 33 (March 1945), 24; "More Brewers' Yeast Goes to War," *Modern Brewery Age* 33 (May 1945), 109.

132. "Minutes of Executive Session," Committee on Food Habits, April 15–16, 1944, CFH.

133. "Brewers' Yeast OK'd for Army Rations," *Modern Brewery Age* 32 (December 1944), 51–52; Dunlop, "Dried Yeast in Army Rations," 108. To minimize demand for scarce equipment, *Modern Brewery Age* encouraged brewers to centralize production of yeast by dedicating one or two central plants in each region to drying yeast. See "Brewers Pledge More Yeast for Nation's Food Program," *Modern Brewery Age* 30 (October 1943), 13. Two of the four companies that eventually won military contracts—St. Louis Brewers' Yeast Corporation and Yeast Products Company—were consortiums of regional brewers located in the Midwest and the New York/New Jersey area. See "More Brewers' Yeast Goes to War," 40, 108–109. The military awarded the first contracts to Haffenreffer & Co. of Boston, and to Anheuser-Busch, which had started their yeast program during Prohibition. See "First Brewers' Yeasts Pass Tests for Front Line Rations," *Modern Brewery Age* 33 (February 1945), 26.

134. Hernon and Ganey, *Under the Influence*, 132–133.

135. "Embattled Beer," 42.

136. "3.2 Beer Again?," 27–29; Walter Alwyn-Schmidt, "The Outlook for 1946," *American Brewer* 78 (December 1945), 20.

137. "3.2 Beer Again?," 28.

138. "Embattled Beer," 42.

139. Pennock, *Advertising Sin and Sickness*, 21–24.

6. WHISKEY, WEAPONS, AND THE WARTIME STATE

1. "Patriotic Distillers," *Time* 38 (October 13, 1941), 91–92.
2. "Ebbing Liquor," *Newsweek* 22 (July 26, 1943), 40, 42.
3. "Forced Drought," *Newsweek* 22 (November 15, 1943), 44, 46, 49.
4. Bentley, *Eating for Victory*; Cohen, *A Consumers' Republic*, chap. 2; Jacobs, "'How About Some Meat?,'" 910–941; Jacobs, *Pocketbook Politics*, chap. 5; Deutsch, *Building a Housewife's Paradise*, chap. 6.
5. Lender, "The Historian and Repeal," 187.
6. Collingham, *Taste of War*.
7. Some historians have linked repeal to the formation of the New Deal state and shown how the New Deal aided the reconstruction of alcoholic beverage industries, but few carry that analysis beyond the 1930s; see Pinney, *A History of Wine in America*; Mittleman, *Brewing Battles*. Major synthetic treatments of the New Deal ignore the connections between alcohol and the New Deal after repeal became law; see Kennedy, *Freedom from Fear*; and Brinkley, *The End of Reform*. For more on the wartime politics of alcohol consumption, see Rubin, "The Wet War," 235–258.
8. "More Moonshine?," *Business Week*, November 20, 1943, 84, 86, 89.
9. "Liquor Enlists," *Newsweek* 19 (January 19, 1942), 43.
10. "Why Distillers Plan Voluntary Rationing," *Barron's*, November 22, 1942, 12; M. M. Lebensburger, "Liquor Business," *Printers' Ink* 202 (January 1, 1943), 12.
11. Expenditures on alcoholic beverages come from Economic Research Services, USDA, "Table 4—Alcoholic Beverages: Total Expenditures." Nondurable consumer expenditures calculated from "Personal Consumption Expenditures, Nondurable Goods for United States (Q06087USQ027NNBR)." Inflation rates calculated from MeasuringWorth.com.
12. Brinkley, *Washington Goes to War*, 226.
13. Leo Goldberg and Nate Kallett, "Don't Be an Avoidable War Casualty," *Wine and Liquor Retailer* 10 (April 1943), 36; Old St. Croix Rum advertisement, *Wine and Liquor Retailer* 10 (February 1944), 28–29; Lawton Mackall, "Calm, Cool Collecting," *Esquire* 20 (August 193), 149.
14. Lawton Mackall, "Schnozzles' Radar," *Esquire* 20 (September 1943), 93; Lawton Mackall, "Discretion Does It," *Esquire* 19 (May 1943), 108.
15. Mackall, "Calm, Cool Collecting," 149; David Wondrich, "The Mint Julep's Brandy Roots," May 6, 2017, DailyBeast.com.
16. Grimes, *Straight Up or on the Rocks*, 108; "No Flowing Bowl?," *New York Times*, November 14, 1943, E2. Rum consumption rose from 4.5 million gallons in 1941 to 17.3 million gallons in 1944; "End of Drought?," *Business Week*, June 2, 1945, 22.
17. Application of Walter P. Powers, Chicago, Illinois, for the Determination of Maximum Price for the Sale of Cohasset Liquor 60 Proof, March 23, 1943, 1–5, Box 3860, Office of Price Administration [Price Department, Food Price Division, Grocery Products Branch, Beverage Section], General Correspondence Files, 1942–1946, PI-95 386, RG 188, NARA (OPAPD).
18. "Why Distillers Plan Voluntary Rationing," 12.

19. Sydney B. Self, "Distillers Prepare for Drought," Barron's, November 22, 1943, 5.
20. Walter Davenport, "The Rum Racket Returns," Collier's 110 (November 28, 1942), 78.
21. For more on how French consumers in Vichy France distinguished between honorable and dishonorable black market activities, see Mouré, Marché Noir.
22. "Calls 'Dry' Inroads Major Liquor Peril," New York Times, February 4, 1944, 21; "Liquor Men Decry Black Markets," New York Times, April 15, 1944, 23.
23. Transcript of Treasury Department staff meeting, December 14, 1942, 2–3, Henry Morgenthau Diary 683, 134–135, Henry Morgenthau Diaries, World War II Era, HMD.
24. "A Little Liquor," Business Week, September 11, 1943, 80, 82–83; "How States Ration Whisky," Business Week, November 20, 1943, 80; "Bottoms Up," Business Week, June 26, 1943, 80–81.
25. "Forced Drought," 44, 46, 49.
26. "A Little Liquor," 83.
27. J. F. Burns, untitled paper, c. December 1943, 2–3, 5, Liquor Correspondence State—OPA Cooperation, Box 1172, Enforcement Department, Food Enforcement Division, Agricultural Commodities Enforcement Branch, Records Relating to Commodity Programs, 1943–1946, OPAED; memo for Mr. Sullivan, November 19, 1943, 2, Henry Morgenthau Diary 678, 273, HMD; letter from Steward Berkshire to New York District Supervisor, November 13, 1943, 1, Henry Morgenthau Diary 679, 274, HMD.
28. "Bootleggers Sell Standard Liquors," New York Times, November 12, 1943, 23.
29. "Forced Drought," 44, 46, 49.
30. Transcript of Joint Session of OPA and Open License State Alcoholic Beverage Control Commissioners, Morrison Hotel, Chicago, IL, December 10, 1943, 17, Box 1172, Liquor Correspondence State—OPA Cooperation File, OPAED.
31. Transcript of Joint Session of OPA and Open License State Alcoholic Beverage Control Commissioners, 15; memorandum from Livingston Hall to Chief Price Enforcement Attorneys in Massachusetts, Connecticut, and Rhode Island, September 27, 1943, 1, Box 1172, Liquor General File, OPAED.
32. "Liquor Tightening at Year-End Seen," New York Times, November 8, 1944, 29; James E. Powers, "Liquor Men Revive Rum 'Tie-In' Racket," New York Times, January 21, 1945, 33; "Increase in Whisky Supply Before Holidays Expected," New York Times, November 28, 1943, 1; "Liquor Tie-in Sales Stir State Action," New York Times, December 20, 1944, 32.
33. "Liquor," c. September 1944, 2, Box 1172, Liquor General Correspondence File, OPAED; Pinney, A History of American Wine, 128–129.
34. Rockoff, Drastic Measures, 147; Deutsch, Building a Housewife's Paradise, 170.
35. Institute for Motivational Research, "A Motivational Research Study on the Sales and Advertising Problems of Old Cabin Still," June 1956, 76, Ameri-

can Consumer Culture: Market Research and American Business, 1935–1965, Adam Matthew Digital, online (ACC).
36. Rockoff, "Can Price Controls Work?," 134.
37. "Liquor," 2, OPAED.
38. "Battle for Alcohol," Business Week, February 5, 1944, 17, 19–21.
39. "Cut Out Your Pouring Brands!" Wine and Liquor Retailer 10 (May 1943), 26–27.
40. "Whisky by Stamp," Business Week, November 20, 1943, 79; Self, "Distillers Prepare for Drought," 5.
41. "Whisky by Stamp," 79.
42. "Whisky Hoarding Charged by SLA," New York Times, December 16, 1943, 1; "F.D.R. May Rule on Respite," Spirits 11 (January 1944), 9.
43. "Whither Whisky?," Business Week, April 24, 1943, 32, 34; US Congress, Senate, Investigation of the Alcoholic-Beverage Industry—Partial Report No. 2 of Subcommittee of Committee on the Judiciary, 78th Congress, 2nd sess., August 7, 1944, 4; Self, "Distillers Prepare for Drought," 5.
44. Investigation of the Alcoholic-Beverage Industry, 6.
45. "Argentine Oasis," Business Week, March 4, 1944, 118; "Whisky Battle," Business Week, June 9, 1945, 20–21.
46. Self, "Distillers Prepare for Drought," 5.
47. Frank R. Schwengel, "Address before the National Alcoholic Beverage Control Association," September 13–14, 1944, Chicago, IL, 3, Box 216, Seagram Museum Collection (SMC).
48. "Whisky by Stamp," 80; Self, "Distillers Prepare for Drought," 5.
49. "Liquor: Creeping Prohibition," 80.
50. "Liquor," 1, OPAED.
51. Letter from John K. Galbraith to Congressman Andrew J. May, April 23, 1943, 3, Box 1172, Liquor General Correspondence File, OPAED.
52. Memo to Editors, Publishers, and Commentators from Henry Morgenthau, Jr., December 27, 1943, 2, Henry Morgenthau Diary 687, 12, HMD.
53. Letter from Prentiss M. Brown to Donald M. Nelson, c. March 1943, Box 15, Price—Alcohol and Liquor File, OPAPB; memo from Donald Wallace, James P. Cavin, and Ernest G. Even to Prentiss Brown, re: "Problem of the reduced flow of distilled spirits to Michigan and other Monopoly States," March 27, 1943, 1–4, Box 15, Price—Alcohol and Liquor File, OPABP.
54. Transcript of Joint Session of OPA and Open License State Alcoholic Beverage Control Commissioners, 20, 29.
55. Charles Grutzner, "Liquor Shortage Raises Specter of Bootlegger," New York Times, November 21, 1943, E10.
56. Emerson, Young Lawyer for the New Deal, 201, 246.
57. "Liquor Men Vexed by Black Market," New York Times, October 10, 1943, S9.
58. Blum, From the Morgenthau Diaries, 108–110, 117.
59. Transcript of staff meeting, December 13, 1943, 13, Henry Morgenthau Diary 683, 109, HMD; transcript of staff meeting, December 23, 1943, 4–5,

Henry Morgenthau Diary 686, 179–180, HMD. Morgenthau raised the specter of Prohibition at nearly every Treasury Department staff meeting on the liquor question in December 1943.

60. Transcript of staff meeting, December 23, 1943, 2–4, 177–179, HMD.

61. Memo to Editors, Publishers and Commentators from Morgenthau, 1.

62. Indiana Senator Frederick Van Nuys initially chaired the subcommittee, but Pat McCarran assumed his place when Van Nuys died in January 1944.

63. Transcript of conversation between Senator Walter George and Henry Morgenthau, November 18, 1943, Henry Morgenthau Diary 678, 164–165, HMD.

64. Transcript of staff meeting, December 14, 1943, 2, Henry Morgenthau Diary 683, 134, HMD.

65. Letter from Charles S. Porritt to Prentiss M. Brown, March 31, 1945, 1–2, Box 3860, OPAPD.

66. "Morgenthau for 4-Year Liquor Step," *New York Times*, November 19, 1943, 22.

67. "WPB Opposes Liquor 'Holiday,'" *New York Times*, December 29, 1943, 28.

68. Transcript of Treasury Department staff meeting, December 14, 1943, 11–12, Henry Morgenthau Diary 684, HMD.

69. Transcript of Treasury Department staff meeting, December 21, 1943, 12, Henry Morgenthau Diary 686, HMD.

70. Comments by Alex Elson, transcript of Joint Session of OPA and Open License State Alcoholic Beverage Control Commissioners, 25.

71. "WFA Passes Buck: Cold-Shoulders Allocation Plan," *Spirits* 11 (September 1944), 9.

72. Memo from James Gruener to Harry Jones and Harold Epstein, July 17, 1938, 2, Box 1172, Liquor General Correspondence File, OPAED; transcript of Treasury Department staff meeting, December 21, 1943, 15.

73. Memo from Gruener to Jones and Epstein, 1; letter from M. A. Gants to E. G. Even, April 3, 1943, Box 3860, OPAPD.

74. Howard Hirsch, untitled analysis of liquor enforcement, July 1, 1943, 2, attached to memo from Gruener to Jones and Epstein.

75. Memo from Gruener to Jones and Epstein, 2–3.

76. Letter from Charles S. Porritt to Prentiss M. Brown, March 31, 1945, 2–3, Box 3860, OPAPD.

77. "Statement by Administrator Chester Bowles," meeting of Alcoholic Beverage Control Commissioners and members of the Office of Price Administration, Morrison Hotel, Chicago, IL, December 10, 1943, 2–3, Box 1172, Liquor Correspondence State—OPA Cooperation File, OPAED.

78. Memo from Wallace, Cavin, and Even to Brown, 1–4; "Statement by Administrator Chester Bowles," 2–3.

79. Transcripts of Treasury Department staff meetings on December 23, 1943, 4–5, and December 21, 1943, 15–16.

80. Memo from Wallace, Cavin, and Even to Brown, 3; letter from Charles S. Porritt to Prentiss M. Brown, March 31, 1945, 2, Box 3860, OPAPD.

81. Letter from Galbraith to May, 3.
82. Letter from Galbraith to May, 3; "Liquor: OPA Orders Price Rollback," *Newsweek* 22 (August 23, 1943), 68–71; "Little Liquor," 80, 82–83; "Whisky by Stamp," 81–82; "Liquor Controlled," *Business Week*, January 8, 1944, 84–85.
83. Minutes of Liquor Control Conference, March 17, 1944, 1–34, Box 2004, File 597.201, WPB.
84. Memo from Harry W. Jones to Robert Trenkamp, April 28, 1943, 1–2, Box 1172, Liquor File, OPAED; memo from Harold Epstein to Harry W. Jones, April 23, 1943, 3, Box 1172, Liquor File, OPAED.
85. "Liquor Control," Treasury Department staff meeting, February 1, 1944, 2, Henry Morgenthau Diary 699, 5, HMD; Minutes of Liquor Control Conference, 3.
86. Memo from Jones to Trenkamp, 1–2; memo from Epstein to Jones, 1–3; memo from Harry W. Jones, Harold Epstein to All Regional Enforcement Attorneys and All Chief Food Enforcement Attorneys, September 11, 1943, 1, Box 1172, Liquor General Correspondence File, OPAED.
87. "Liquor," 3–4, OPAED.
88. Memo from Byron C. Sharpe to Alex Elson, March 14, 1944, 12, Box 1175, Monthly Reports by Field Offices, 1944–1945, OPAED.
89. "Liquor," 1, OPAED.
90. Memo from Stanley Jewell to John A. Garfinkel, February 11, 1944, 2, Box 1172, Liquor General Correspondence File, OPAED; memorandum from Livingston Hall to Chief Enforcement Attorneys in Massachusetts, Connecticut, and Rhode Island, September 27, 1943, 1, Box 1172, Liquor General File, OPAED; transcript of Joint Session of OPA And Open License State Alcoholic Beverage Control Commissioners, 18; "Liquor," 5, OPAED.
91. The military worked with state liquor authorities and the United States Brewers' Foundation to ensure that taverns and bars observed closing times and upheld regulations against selling to intoxicated patrons. For more on the military's crackdown on profiteering in the liquor trade, see Hiltner, *Taking Leave, Taking Liberties*, 172–174. For more on the military's more pragmatic response to sex workers (relative to its rigid stance in World War I), see Burnham, *Bad Habits*, 188–190; Bailey and Farber, *The First Strange Place*, chap. 3; Hegarty, "Patriot or Prostitutes?," 112–136.
92. "Don't Let Your Customers Hoard!" *Wine and Liquor Retailer* 10 (June 1943), 24–25.
93. "Smash the Profiteer of He'll Smash You," *Seagram Spotlight* (November 1943), 16–17, Hagley Museum and Library, Wilmington, DE.
94. "Distillers to War on Black Market," *New York Times*, December 1, 1943, 30.
95. "Distillers Ration It," *Business Week*, May 13, 1944, 79; Clark Gavin, "Retail Rationing," *Spirits* 11 (June 1944), 8.
96. Wilson, *Destructive Creation*, 92–94.
97. *Volunteer for Victory*, 4, 6, 16, 24, 27–28.
98. Lawton Mackall, "Cocktails for Hitler," *Esquire* 17 (June 1942), 93, 105 (quoted at 93); "Whisky Shortage: Nation Drinks What It Can as Favorite Spirit Grows Scarce," *Life* 15 (December 13, 1943), 35–39; Lawton Mackall,

"J. Barleycorn Draftee," *Esquire* 17 (April 1942), 79, 178. Science magazines also highlighted the distillers' role in building the nation's arsenal for democracy; see, for example: Philip Harkins, "From Whiskey to Explosives: Condensed from The Elks Magazine," *Science Digest* 114 (November 1943), 54–57; "How Alcohol Handles a Thousand War Jobs," *Popular Science* 145 (August 1944), 129; "Speeding up Alcohol Production," *Science Digest* 14 (July 1943), 74.

99. Cohen, *A Consumers' Republic*, 75.

100. Leff, "The Politics of Sacrifice," 1298.

101. Letter from Rev. Edwin Field to Senator R. Owen Brewster, March 21, 1944, in Henry Morgenthau Diary 720, 60, HMD.

102. George A. Mooney, "Ask Output Holiday for the Distillers," *New York Times*, May 16, 1943, S7 ("political 'dynamite'"); "Distillers Cool to Liquor 'Holiday,'" *New York Times*, December 5, 1943, 50; "Liquor Production Held Urgent Need," *New York Times*, April 19, 1944, 24; "14 States Favor Liquor 'Holiday,'" *New York Times*, April 20, 1944, 13.

103. Letter from Donald M. Nelson to Senator Patrick McCarran, May 10, 1944, Box 2004, File 597.2002, WPB; John F. O'Connell to Senator Pat McCarran, March 16, 1944, 1, New York State Liquor Authority Release, New York Public Library; "14 States Favor Liquor 'Holiday,'" *Tavern News*, May 1, 1944, 1; National Alcoholic Beverage Control Association petition, April 19, 1944, in Henry Morgenthau Diary 730, 23, HMD; "Liquor Production Held Urgent Need," 24.

104. "Henkel Calls for Liquor 'Holiday,' Blames U.S. for Black Market," *New York Times*, April 26, 1944, 21.

105. Howard Schievley, "Whiskey Shortage Made Unnecessary by U.S. Fiat," *Tavern News*, May 1, 1944, 1, 9, 11. The high wartime consumer demand in the United States for whiskey substitutes propelled Mexico's tequila exports from 21,621 liters in 1940 to 4.5 million liters in 1944. The American interest in tequila, however, flagged when the whiskey shortages had abated. By 1948, exports of Mexican tequila had plummeted to only 8,800 liters; Gaytán, *Tequila!*, 65.

106. Mitenbuler, *Bourbon Empire*, 217.

107. Ernest Dichter, "A Psychological Research Study on the Sales and Advertising Problems of Schenley Reserve," May 1953, 13, 51, ACC.

108. Charles E. Egan, "WPB Ready to Ease Ban on Beverages," *New York Times*, March 18, 1944, 15.

109. Abe Marco, "Public to Blame for the 'Run' on Whiskey," *Tavern Weekly News*, December 6, 1943, 6.

110. Schievley, "Whiskey Shortage Made Unnecessary," 1, 9, 11.

111. Gavin, "The Respite Issue," *Spirits* 11 (April 1944), 8.

112. State liquor administrators also referenced Canada's liquor "holiday" to pressure the War Production Board to grant US distillers a respite from war production; "Liquor Production Held Urgent Need," 24. The Canadian government insisted that their "holiday" had allowed Canadian distillers to produce only "minute" quantities; C. P. Trussell, "Release of Whisky Urged by Van Nuys," *New York Times*, December 11, 1943, 28.

113. "Henkel Calls for Liquor 'Holiday,'" 21.

114. Minutes of Liquor Control Conference, 28–29.

115. Delano, "Making Up for War," 33–68; Peiss, "Making Faces," 343–344, 349–352; Peiss, *Hope in a Jar*, chap. 5; Carter, *The Red Menace*, chap. 6.

116. Schievley, "Whiskey Shortage Made Unnecessary," 1, 9, 11.

117. G&W Five Star Blended Whiskey advertisement, *Wine and Liquor Retailer* 10 (November 1943), 7.

118. United States Senate Report of Proceedings Hearing Held Before Subcommittee of the Committee on the Judiciary, S. Res. 206, Part IV, vol. 1, May 4, 1944, Washington DC, 963–964, Box 1660, File 531.1102, WPB.

119. United States Senate Report of Proceedings Hearing . . . Before Subcommittee of the Committee on the Judiciary, 947.

120. "Whisky Reserves Soar as Sugar Rationing Starts," *Christian Century* 59 (April 29, 1942), 547.

121. "Alcohol Shortage May Solve Prohibition Problem," *Science Digest* 13 (January 1943), 17.

122. Mary Hornaday, "Intimate Message: Washington," *Christian Science Monitor*, January 28, 1942, 13.

123. James E. Powers, "McCarran Presses a Liquor 'Holiday,'" *New York Times*, March 12, 1944, 1.

124. *Investigation of the Alcoholic-Beverage Industry*, 2–3.

125. *Investigation of the Alcoholic-Beverage Industry*, 1–8, esp. 3–4; "Liquor: Unnecessary Drought?" *Time* 44 (August 14, 1944); "Stranglehold on Drinks," *Commonweal* 40 (September 1, 1944), 460.

126. Orville Schupp Oral History, interviewed by Thomas H. Syvertsen, February 13, 1985, Tape 90, Side 2, Archives & Special Collections, University of Louisville, Kentucky.

127. Gavin, "WPB's Decision," *Spirits* 11 (October 1943), 8; "Battle for Alcohol," 17, 19–21; letter from Marvin Jones to Donald Nelson, January 26, 1944, Box 1660, File 597.1102, WPB; letter from Marvin Jones to Donald Nelson, December 13, 1943, 1–2, Box 1660, File 531.1102, WPB; memo from Walter F. Whitman re: Meeting on Beverage Alcohol in Secretary Morgenthau's Office, March 21, 1944, Box 2004, File 597.201, WPB.

128. Polenberg, *War and Society*, 227, 229.

129. Finlay, *Growing American Rubber*, 193–194; "Battle for Alcohol," 17, 19–21; United States Senate Report of Proceedings Hearing . . . Before Subcommittee of the Committee on the Judiciary, 939, 942, 944–945. For more on the process of producing synthetic rubber and smokeless gunpowder from industrial alcohol, see Purcell, "Bourbon to Bullets," 61–87.

130. "Drink Is on F.D.R.," *Business Week*, July 8, 1944, 16–17; "WPB Paves Way for More Whisky by August Holiday on War Alcohol," *New York Times*, June 21, 1944, 1.

131. "Drink Is on F.D.R.," 16–17. *Proof*, the Seagram employee newsletter, likened the temporary respite from war production to deserved R&R for "untiring" production soldiers: "After serving in the Armed Services for more than two years just as surely as if they had been . . . drilling every day with the best G.I. Joe extant, the distillers have been given a well-deserved 'furlough'!"; "31

Days Furlough Given Distillery G.I.'s" *Proof* 4 (July 31, 1944), 2, Archives and Special Collections, University of Louisville, KY.

132. Judge Marvin Jones Oral History Interview, conducted by Jerry N. Hess, April 20, 1970, transcript, 144–45, Harry S. Truman Library and Museum, www.trumanlibrary.gov.

133. "Distillers Get War Alky Furlough," *Business Week*, June 24, 1944, 17.

134. Memo from Walter F. Whitman re: Meeting on Beverage Alcohol in Secretary Morgenthau's Office.

135. "Drink Is on F.D.R.," 16.

136. "Drink Is on F.D.R.," 16–17; "Distillers Get War Alky Furlough," 17.

137. "Full Bottles Anyway," *Rochester Democrat and Chronicle*, January 4, 1945, reprinted in *Allied News Letter*, February 16, 1945, 4. For more on the reconversion to civilian production, see Lingeman, *Don't You Know There's a War On?*, 263–266; Casdorph, *Let the Good Times Roll*, 166, 179, 199–200; Blum, *V Was for Victory*, 129–130.

138. "All Depends on War: Quick German Fall Would Hasten Resumption," *Spirits* 11 (September 1944), 40.

139. Lawton Mackall, "Respite for Thirsts," *Esquire* 22 (October 1944), 108.

140. John W. Crimmins Oral History, interviewed by Thomas H. Syvertsen, December 4, 1984, Archives & Special Collections, University of Louisville, Kentucky.

141. C.L. Chapin, "Some Personal Comments," *Repeal Review* 12 (June 1947), 7, box 291, Series IV, SMC.

142. Casdorph, *Let the Good Times Roll*, 255.

143. Bentley, "Reading Food Riots," 181.

144. Rubin, "The Wet War."

145. United States Senate Report of Proceedings Hearing ... Before Subcommittee of the Committee on the Judiciary, 964.

146. Historical Tax Rates," Alcohol and Tobacco Trade and Tax Bureau, US Department of the Treasury, www.ttb.gov/tax-audit/historical-tax-rates.

147. Westbrook, "Fighting for the American Family," 194–221; Fox, *Madison Avenue Goes to War*; Leff, "The Politics of Sacrifice," 1298; Henthorn, *From Submarines to Suburbs*; McGovern, *Sold American*, 327–332, 353, 361.

148. "Whisky Hoarding is Charged by SLA," *New York Times*, December 16, 1943, 1.

149. Brinkley, *The End of Reform*, 170.

150. Jacobs, "How About Some Meat?"

151. Cohen, *A Consumers' Republic*.

7. WINE AND CULINARY INNOVATION ON THE KITCHEN FRONT

1. Mills, *Cooking on a Ration*, ix; Edgar J. Driscoll, Jr., "Marjorie Mills, at 86; Was Herald Columnist," *Boston Herald*, http://www.themeaderfamily.org/Library/Marjorie%20(Meader)%20Burns%20Mills_0511.pdf.

2. Rappaport, *A Thirst for Empire*, chap. 9; Weiner, "Consumer Culture and Participatory Democracy," 117.

3. Cresta Blanca, Petri, and Roma wines sponsored radio programs.

4. Pinney, *A History of Wine in America*, 118, 126, 129. Pinney notes that the loss of French and Italian imports was not that large, as Americans imported about 4 million gallons annually. Wine imports slowed dramatically in 1942, but in 1943 imports from Portugal and Spain matched the prewar level of French and Italian imports and then surpassed that level in 1944.

5. "How to Popularize American Wines," *Wines and Vines* 22 (January 1941), 8.

6. Mrs. J. Molera, "American Wines for American Hotels," *Restaurant Management* 48 (March 1941), 34–35.

7. Yan, "Of Hamburger and Social Space"; Watson, "China's Big Mac Attack," 70–79; Caldwell, "Domesticating the French Fry," 180–196.

8. For more on food rationing and wartime propaganda to promote compliance with food controls, see Bentley, *Eating for Victory*; Biltekoff, *Eating Right in America*; Collingham, *Taste of War*; Rappaport, *A Thirst for Empire*, chap. 9; Veit, *Modern Food, Moral Food*. For more on war and food deprivation, see Goldman and Filtzer, eds., *Hunger and War*; Collingham, *Taste of War*; Cwiertka, *Cuisine, Colonialism and Cold War*; Davis, *Home Fires Burning*; Helstosky, *Garlic and Oil*; Trentmann and Just, eds., *Food and Conflict in Europe in the Age of the Two World Wars*; Seikaly, "A Nutritional Economy," 37–58; Nordstrom, ed., *The Provisions of War*.

9. James L. Williston, "Bullish Budgets for Wines," *Advertising and Selling* 35 (May 1942), 48b.

10. "Wine Makes Food Taste Better," *Wines and Vines* 23 (January 1942), 14.

11. Herman Wente, "Your Part in the Wine Selling Drive," *Wines and Vines* 20 (June 1939), 4.

12. Adams, *Revitalizing the California Wine Industry*, 79–81.

13. "California Wine Advertising Campaign is Launched," *Wines and Vines* 20 (May 1939), 5–6. New York's fair planners worked hard to recruit California's largest wineries and the Wine Institute as exhibitors, but could not deliver what winemakers in California and New York wanted most: the opportunity to offer visitors samples and submit their wines to a juried competition. In the absence of such opportunities, California's wineries concluded that exhibiting in New York was not worth the expense. For a sampling of the correspondence, see: letter from Leslie S. Baker to Edwin N. Davis (Agricultural Experiment Station, NY), January 24, 1939, Box 476, Folder 13, NYWF; memo from Truman Weller to W.F.L. Tuttle, April 3, 1940, 1–2, Box 478, Folder 4, NYWF; letter from Edwin N. Davis to Leslie Baker (director of exhibits), January 27, 1938, Box 473, Folder 13, NYWF; memo from Truman Weller to Director of Exhibits, March 13, 1940, Box 476, Folder 13, NYWF; memo from E.F.C. Parker to A.C. Martin, re: Wine Industry, February 24, 1940, Box 473, Folder 12, NYWF.

14. "California Wine Advertising Campaign is Launched," 5–6.

15. "Wine Tie-ins Attract Fairgoers," *Wines and Vines* 21 (August 1940), 12–13. For more on changing attitudes toward industrial foods, see Bentley, *Inventing Baby Food*; Shapiro, *Something from the Oven*; Shapiro, *Perfection Salad*; Petrick, "Purity as Life," 37–64.

16. For a more extensive discussion of the controversies surrounding American winemakers' use of European place names, see Pinney, *History of Wine in America*, 45–46, 119–125; Mendelson, *From Demon to Darling*, 140–143.

17. "Vintners Say Queensbury Rules for Wine-Bibbing Are All Off," *Sales Management* 47 (December 1, 1940), 70.

18. "Vintners Say Queensbury Rules for Wine-Bibbing Are All Off," 70.

19. John Perry and Alfred H. Sinks, "Wine-Making Goes American," *Nation's Business* 29 (October 1941), 71.

20. "Wine Service 'Freedom,'" *Wines and Vines* 22 (April 1941), 14.

21. Gladys Selverne, "Wine Is in Vogue and in Harper's Bazaar, Too!," *American Wine Merchant* 2 (April 1942), 30–31.

22. *The Wine Cook Book*, 5.

23. Lawton Mackall, "Freedom of Taste," *Esquire* 22 (September 1944), 103–104.

24. Dorothy Rankin, "Is Mrs. Housewife Responsible for Increased Wine Sales?," *Wines and Vines* 23 (January 1942), 11.

25. Johnston and Baumann, "Democracy versus Distinction," 173.

26. Jeanne Owen, "A New American Acquisition—Our Own 'Vin Ordinaire,'" *House Beautiful* 84 (April 1, 1942), 86.

27. WAB ad, Mrs. Edgar Rice Burroughs, 1939, author's collection; WAB ad, Margaret Bourke-White, 1939, author's collection.

28. For more on the use of celebrity endorsers, see Peiss, *Hope in a Jar*, 126, 137–140; Scanlon, *Inarticulate Longings*, 131–132, 192–194, 209–214, 216–220; Segrave, *Endorsements in Advertising*. The Wine Advisory Board ads referred to the wives of famous men by their husband's first and last names, erasing the careers and independent identities of these endorsers. Ouida Bergère (aka Mrs. Basil Rathbone) was an actress and author; Frances Leonard Nash (aka Mrs. Ogden Nash) was a philanthropist; and Florence Gilbert (aka Mrs. Edgar Rice Burroughs) was a silent film actress.

29. WAB ad, Mrs. Edgar Rice Burroughs, 1939; "The March of Wine: The United Effort of the Wine Industry is Bringing Great Gains," reprint of lecture by J. Walter Thompson, *Wines and Vines* 20 (November 1939), 18.

30. WAB ad, Mrs. Basil Rathbone, 1939, author's collection.

31. Bushman, *The Refinement of America*; Grier, *Culture and Comfort*; Kasson, *Rudeness and Civility*.

32. Breazeale, "In Spite of Women," 1–22; Ehrenreich, *The Hearts of Men*, chap. 4.

33. "Wine and Athletes," *Wines and Vines* 21 (June 1940), 15.

34. Levenstein, *Paradox of Plenty*, 46, 127, 142.

35. Levenstein, *Paradox of Plenty*, 45.

36. "Dick's Table Talks with Harold P. Bock," *Restaurant Management* 38 (January 1936), 62.

37. "Dick's Table Talks with Otto J. Baumgarten," *Restaurant Management* 37 (December 1935), 365.

38. "Sale of Liquor at Childs Increases Food Revenue," *American Restaurant Magazine* 20 (September 1937), 48.

39. Hutchinson, "California Wine Industry," Tables 9.1, 9.12, 398, 430.

40. Molera, "American Wines for American Hotels," 34–35.
41. Haley, *Turning the Tables*, 105, 193.
42. Frederick Anderson, "Wining and Dining," *Restaurant Management* 38 (May 1936), 374.
43. "Wine Wins High Place with Patrons," *American Restaurant Magazine* 28 (December 1944), 84.
44. Bert Dale, "Building Beverage Business," *Restaurant Management* 69 (September 1951), 28.
45. H. A. Caddow, "How Much Wine Per Diner: A Basic Factor in Hotel and Restaurant Wine-Selling," *Wines and Vines* 22 (November 1941), 12.
46. Wine Advisory Board ad, *American Restaurant Magazine* 26 (November 1942), 55; Wine Advisory Board ad, *American Restaurant Magazine* 22 (May 1939), 60; Wine Advisory Board ad, *Restaurant Management* 54 (June 1944), 46.
47. Caddow, "How Much Wine Per Diner," 12.
48. Levenstein, *Paradox of Plenty*, 207, 220.
49. Levenstein, *Paradox of Plenty*, 216; Zlotnick, "Domesticating Imperialism," 51–68.
50. Levenstein, *Revolution at the Table*, 207; Gabaccia, *We Are What We Eat*, 120–121.
51. Russek, "Appetites without Prejudice," 40.
52. Strauss, *Setting the Table for Julia Child*, 72–73, 136, 146–147.
53. Hillis, *New York, Fair or No Fair*, 101.
54. "Petri Sells 'Ideas' on New National Hook-up Radio Show," *Wines and Vines* 24 (May 1942), 16.
55. Williston, "Bullish Budgets for Wines," 52; "Wine Boost," *Business Week*, January 16, 1943, 49.
56. Lapsley, *Bottled Poetry*, 114–115.
57. Lapsley, *Bottled Poetry*, 100. According to Lapsley, the California's total wine supply was reduced by one third, with dessert wines falling from 72 million gallons in 1941 to 37 million gallons in 1942.
58. "Vintner's Gloom," *Business Week*, September 19, 1942, 48; "Wine, Too, Goes to War: Its Men, Its Machines, and Its Products," *American Wine Merchant* 2 (April 1943), 22–23.
59. "U.S. Consumption of Wine by States," *Wines and Vines* 26 (August 1945), 35; Alfred Hiller, "Consumption Trend and Defense Program," *Wines and Vines* 22 (February 1941), 12.
60. "Dry Year Ahead," *Business Week*, January 1, 1944, 32.
61. Advertisement, *Life* 14 (January 4, 1943), 31.
62. H. A. Caddow, "Ninth Annual Wine Conference: War and the Wine Industry," *Wines and Vines* 23 (May 1942), 15; "Wine, Too, Goes to War," 22–23.
63. "Wine Is Way," *Business Week*, February 28, 1942, 20; "How Wine is Sold in the U.S.," *American Wine Merchant* 4 (November 1945), 26–27. According to the *American Wine Merchant*, in 1945 package stores sold 40 million gallons of wine; food stores sold 14 million gallons (about 19 percent of all bottled wine sales); state stores and drug stores each sold 8 million gallons, and other stores (department, cigar stores) sold 2 million gallons.

64. "Wine Is Way," 20; Eric Strutt, "Wine and Food," *Wines and Vines* 23 (January 1942), 9.
65. Bentley, *Eating for Victory*, chap. 2; Neuhaus, *Manly Meals and Mom's Home Cooking*, 142–147; Biltekoff, *Eating Right in America*, 54–78.
66. Ladies' Home Journal, *WINS Wartime Homemaking Manual*.
67. *Victory Meat Extenders*.
68. Elias, *Food on the Page*, 83; Neuhaus, *Manly Meals and Mom's Home Cooking*, 104–105. For more on *Gourmet*'s response to wartime food rationing, see Strauss, *Setting the Stage for Julia Child*, 152–154.
69. *The Original Picayune Creole Cook Book*.
70. Cora, Rose, and Bob Brown, *The Wine Cook Book*, book jacket.
71. Hatch, *The American Wine Cook Book*, 3–4.
72. Taylor, *Economy for Epicures*.
73. Mills, *Cooking on a Ration*.
74. See, for example, Mary Grosvenor Ellsworth, "Spirited Cooking," *House Beautiful* 81 (November 1939), 65, 103.
75. *Hostess Book of Favorite Wine Recipes*, 8. For more on women defense workers and their "double day" during World War II, see Anderson, *Wartime Women*; Kessler-Harris, *Out to Work*, chap. 10; Dumenil, *American Working Women in World War II*.
76. For more on government propaganda that encouraged American civilians to do their bit for the war effort, see Samuel, *Pledging Allegiance*; Bentley, *Eating for Victory*; Duis, "No Time for Privacy," 17–45; Bird and Rubenstein, *Design for Victory*.
77. *Hostess Book of Favorite Wine Recipes*, 1, 23.
78. WAB ad, *Life* 16 (January 17, 1944), 11.
79. Mary Frost Mabon, "A Big Difference with a Little Wine," *Wines and Vines* 23 (January 1942), 10.
80. For more on the history of enslaved cookery and soul food, see Opie, *Hog and Hominy*; Deetz, *Bound to the Fire*; Harris, *High on the Hog*.
81. Bentley, *Eating for Victory*, 36, 91–99; Pryzybylek, "'No Attempt at Concealment,'" 405–408; Elvins, "Lady Smugglers and Lynx-Eyed Customs Agents," 506–510.
82. Bentley, *Eating for Victory*, 99.
83. "Wine changes war dishes into 'food for kings,'" WAB ad, 1943, author's collection.
84. WAB ad, *Wines and Vines* 25 (May 1944), 4.
85. Bentley, *Eating for Victory*, 64, 66.
86. Bentley, *Eating for Victory*, 91.
87. Fisher, *How to Cook a Wolf*, 6, 9, 103, 113–114, 164–165.
88. A mock-up of the Fisher ad, which circulated in mass magazines, appeared in a larger ad I found in *Wine and Liquor Retailer* 12 (September 1945), 32.
89. Elias, *Food on the Page*, 89.
90. Bégin, *Taste of the Nation*, 46–51.
91. Elias, *Food on the Page*, 97; Breazeale, "In Spite of Women," 6.
92. Elias, *Food on the Page*, 74.

93. Elias, *Food on the Page*, 90.
94. Isles Brody, "What Cooks with Wine," *Esquire* 18 (October 1942), 89, 114.
95. Breazeale, "In Spite of Women"; for more on how mainstream men's lifestyle magazines covertly courted queer consumers, see Bengry, "Courting the Pink Pound," 122–148.
96. Isles Brody, "Man in the Kitchenette," *Esquire* 18 (July 1942), 86, 139–140.
97. Elias, *Food on the Page*, 97.
98. *Christmas in Connecticut*, 14:56–15:10. Peaches Grenadine are often poached in a sugar syrup mixed with Grenadine and rosé or pink champagne.
99. Brody, "What Cooks with Wine," 89, 114.
100. Advertisement, *Life* 14 (March 29, 1943), 67.
101. "The Wine Industry—and War!" *Wines and Vines* 22 (December 1941), 7.
102. Neuhaus, *Manly Meals and Mom's Home Cooking*, 142–147.
103. Advertisement, *Life* 15 (October 11, 1943), 91.
104. Maude Bruce Stewart, "Your Culinary Customers," *Wine and Liquor Retailer* 10 (August 1943), 40.
105. Stewart, "Your Culinary Customers," 40; "There's Gravy in Cooking with Wine," *Wine and Liquor Retailer* 11 (October 1944), 41–42.
106. "Are Women Here to Stay?" *Wine and Liquor Retailer* 10 (October 1943), 49.
107. "Are Women Here to Stay?" 49; "Selling by Recipe," *Wine and Liquor Retailer* 10 (February 1944), B.
108. "Heaven for Housewives," *Wine and Liquor Retailer* 11 (February 1944), 58–59, 62.
109. Eugene A. Conklin, "Showmanship in Merchandising," *American Wine Merchant* 4 (November 1945), 17, 48.
110. "Profile of a Wine Merchant with a Wine Wagon," *American Wine Merchant* 4 (December 1945), 37, 45.
111. "Are Women Here to Stay?" 48–49.
112. For more on the ideals of the virtuous yeoman farmers, see Smith, *Virgin Land*; Adams, "Natural Virtue," 695–712.
113. Cella, *The Cella Family in the California Wine Industry*, 15.
114. "The Great Wine Boom," *Fortune* 23 (May 1941), 126; Pinney, *A History of Wine in America*, 66–67.
115. "California Invasion," *Time* 41 (February 8, 1943), 73–74.
116. Pinney, *History of Wine in America*, 128.
117. Pinney, *History of Wine in America*, 128–129; Lapsley, *Bottled Poetry*, 102–103.
118. "Editorial," *American Wine Merchant* 2 (April 1943), 7; "The Big Wine Deal," *Fortune* 28 (September 1943), 125, 256.
119. Adams, *Revitalizing the California Wine Industry*, 124.
120. *The Wine Industry: Wine Handbook Series—No. 1*, 21.
121. Adams, *Revitalizing the California Wine Industry*, 87; "Questions on Wine Handbook No. 2, The Wine Study Course," Wine Advisory Board, April

9, 1962, San Francisco Ephemera Collection, San Francisco Public Library (SFEC); "Questions on Wine Handbook No. 1, The Wine Study Course," Wine Advisory Board, April 8, 1962, SFEC.

122. *The Wine Industry: Wine Handbook Series –No. 1*, 27.

123. *The Wine Industry: Wine Handbook Series –No. 1*, 27.

124. "College of Wine Knowledge," *American Wine Merchant* 4 (November 1945), 18, 49; Mary Dee Carlton, "The Feminine Touch," *American Wine Merchant* 3 (Summer 1944), 21, 46–47.

125. "Wine Dictionary for Brides," *House Beautiful* 85 (May 1943), 74.

126. Lapsley, *Bottled Poetry*, 114.

127. "Editorial: Abolish the Word 'Fortified,'" *Wines and Vines* 21 (April 1940), 3, 30. In 1933, the Federal Alcohol Control Administration required wine labels and advertisements for wines above 17 percent to use the word "fortified," but the Wine Institute successfully lobbied the Federal Alcohol Administration (the successor agency) to abandon "fortified" as a regulatory term in 1938.

128. The concept of "set and setting," advanced by psychedelic drug therapy researchers in the 1960s, illuminates this phenomenon. Pollan, *How to Change Your Mind*, 6, 14; Courtwright, *The Age of Addiction*, 186.

129. Letter from H. A. Caddow, Wine Institute, to Idwal Jones, September 29, 1942, Box 1, Wine Institute Correspondence with Idwal Jones, Bancroft Library, University of California, Berkeley, CA.

130. Orville Prescott, "Books of the Times," *New York Times*, September 4, 1942, 21.

131. Institute for Motivational Research, Inc., "Cresta Blanca Work-in-Progress Report," 3, c. 1952, ACC.

132. Blake Ehrlich, "From Our Own Vines: A Heady $600 Million," *Newsweek* 48 (October 29, 1956), 90, 92.

133. "Dry Years Ahead," *Business Week*, January 1, 1944, 31–32; "Wine Sales Rise," *Wine and Liquor Retailer* 10 (February 1944), 26. Improved wine quality resulted in part from price control policies that allowed wineries to charge more for longer-aged wines.

134. Peter Greig, "An Importer Looks at the American Market," *Wines and Vines* 26 (June 1945), 25, 33–34.

135. Frank Schoonmaker," The Future of Quality Wine," *Wines and Vines* 26 (December 1945), 21, 37.

136. "1944 in Facts and Figures," *Wines and Vines* 26 (April 1945), 41.

137. "U.S. Consumption of Wine by States," *Wines and Vines* 26 (August 1945), 26, 34; J. B. Cella, "Our Common Fate," *Wines and Vines* 25 (December 1944), 25, 46.

138. "Regulations Hamper Consumption," *Wines and Vines* 26 (November 1945), 27, 35.

139. "What Retailers Think of the Wine Market," *Wines and Vines* 25 (September 1944), 20–21, 30–33.

140. "Regulations Hamper Consumption," *Wines and Vines* 26 (November 1945), 37.

141. "Merchandising Wine with Food," *Wines and Vines* 23 (January 1942), 8.

142. Horace O. Lanza, "Light Sweet Wine," *Wines and Vines* 26 (December 1945), 29. Lanza imagined light sweet wines as wines with a sugar content of 3 to 5 grams per 100cc as opposed to red wines with a sugar content of 0.5 grams per 100cc.

143. Heinz, *California's Napa Valley*, 300.

144. Ray G. Giordano, "Did the Industry Miss the Bus?," *Wines and Vines* 26 (April 1945), 49. In California, grocery store shoppers could fill their own glass jugs from the shopkeeper's wine barrels, but shopkeepers did not always keep barrels tightly sealed and often did not dispose of leftover wine in the barrel until it had gone bad; see Heinz, *California's Napa Valley*, 288–289.

145. Richard Calvert, "Bootlegging of Dry Wines," *Wines and Vines* 23 (May 1942), 7–8.

146. Neuhaus, *Manly Meals and Mom's Home Cooking*, 235–236.

8. RANK PRIVILEGE

1. Ambrose, *Band of Brothers*, 21.
2. Sergeant John McLeod, "The Heavyweight," *Yank*, September 21. 1945, 4.
3. Enoc P. Waters, "Morale Soars as Pacific Troops Get First Beer," *Chicago Defender*, September 16, 1944, 14.
4. Rubin, "The Wet War,", 235–258.
5. Pyle, *Brave Men*, 102; "News from Home," *Yank*, August 5, 1942, 10, 15; Corporal Margaret Davis, "Houston, Texas," *Yank*, August 3, 1945, 8–9.
6. Quoted in Rutherford, "On Arms and Eggs," 138.
7. De Salcedo, *Combat-Ready Kitchen;* Babic, "Foods of War, and Wars on Food," 160–169; Bruegel, "How the French Learned to Eat Canned Food," 113–130; Cwiertka, *Cuisine, Colonialism, and Cold War*.
8. "Morale Is a Lot of *Little* Things," advertising proof sheet, October 20, 1944, Box 1, United States Brewers' Foundation, DAC.
9. Pyle, *Here Is Your War*, v, viii; Fine, "The 'Pyle Style' of War Reporting," 376.
10. Miller, "From Hoosier Farm Boy to the GIs' Friend," 46.
11. Nichols, ed., *Ernie's War*, 165 (quote); Miller, "From Hoosier Farm Boy to the GIs' Friend," 45, 46; Fine, "The 'Pyle Style' of War Reporting," 377–379.
12. Fine, "The Development of the 'Pyle Style' of War Reporting," 376.
13. Pyle, *Here Is Your War*, 7.
14. Nichols, ed., *Ernie's War*, 84.
15. Fine, "The Development of the 'Pyle Style' of War Reporting," 380–382.
16. Pyle, *Brave Men*, 280.
17. Pyle, *Brave Men*, 473.
18. Nichols, ed., *Ernie's War*, 208.
19. Pyle, *Here Is Your War*, 20–22.
20. Nichols, ed., *Ernie's War*, 186.
21. Nichols, ed., *Ernie's War*, 292–293.
22. Nichols, ed., *Ernie's War*, 389.

23. Nichols, ed., *Ernie's War*, 76.
24. Virden, "Warm Beer and Cold Canons," 86, 87; Cooke, *American Girls, Beer, and Glenn Miller*, 35.
25. Virden, "Warm Beer and Cold Canons," 88–89.
26. Fussell, *Wartime*, 103.
27. Pyle, *Brave Men*, 66.
28. Pyle, *Brave Men*, 124.
29. Pyle, *Brave Men*, 360, 364; Virden, "Warm Beer and Cold Cannons," 84.
30. Pyle, *Brave Men*, 326.
31. Pyle, *Here Is Your War*, 111.
32. Dudziak, "'You didn't see him lying,'" 1–3.
33. Fine, "The 'Pyle Style' of War Reporting," 385.
34. Blum, "The G.I. in the Culture of the Second World War," 51.
35. Pyle, *Brave Men*, 102.
36. Blum, "The G.I. in the Culture of the Second World War," 55–56.
37. Fine, "The 'Pyle Style' of War Reporting," 385.
38. Virden, "Warm Beer and Cold Cannons," 89.
39. Kennett, *G.I.*, Kindle, chap. 5, loc. 1454 of 4847.
40. Virden, "Warm Beer and Cold Cannons," 90.
41. Ellis, *The Sharp End*, 257.
42. Kane, "Paving the Way to a 'Good Understanding,'" 32–33, 44.
43. Michael Adams, quoted in Virden, "Warm Beer and Cold Cannons," 94.
44. Ambrose, *Band of Brothers*, 90.
45. Schrijvers, *The Crash of Ruin*, 168.
46. Kennett, *G.I.*, chap. 10, loc. 3041–3043.
47. Edward B. Toles, "How to Get Drunk in Europe Proves GI Headache," *Chicago Defender*, June 30, 1945, 11. African American journalist Roi Ottley found whiskey priced at $40 a bottle in London; see Huddle, ed., *Roi Ottley's World War II*, 49.
48. Mauldin, *Up Front*, 86–88, 90.
49. Mauldin, *Up Front*, 87.
50. Vaughan-Thomas, *Anzio*, Kindle, loc. 211–213 of 360.
51. Interview of Sergeant Eugene Lester in Motley, *The Invisible Soldier*, 310.
52. Gutierrez, *Patriots from the Barrios*, 91.
53. Kennett, *G.I.*, loc. 3236.
54. Winters, *Beyond Band of Brothers*, 99.
55. Kennett, *G.I.*, loc. 3236.
56. Ellis, *The Sharp End*, 256.
57. Jones, *World War II*, 96–97.
58. Jones, *The Thin Red Line*, Kindle, chap. 2, loc. 1025 of 1789.
59. Sergeant Jud Cook, "Chinese Likker," *Yank*, December 7, 1945, 8.
60. Arnold, "'Your Money Ain't No Good O'er There,'" 107–122, quoted at 109.
61. Cook, "'Tokens of Fritz,'" 211–226; Weingartner, "Trophies of War," 5–67.
62. Jones, *The Thin Red Line*, chap. 6, loc. 1228.
63. Jones, *The Thin Red Line*, chap. 6, loc. 1229.

64. Linderman, *The World within War*, 345.
65. Fussell, *Wartime*, 101.
66. McManus, *The Deadly Brotherhood*, 113.
67. Kennett, *G.I.*, loc. 2222–2226.
68. Jones, *The Thin Red Line*, chap. 6, loc. 1229.
69. McManus, *The Deadly Brotherhood*, 89.
70. Givens, "Liberating the Germans," 33–54.
71. Mauldin, *Up Front*, 90–91.
72. David Webster, quoted in Givens, "Liberating the Germans," 39.
73. Ambrose, *Band of Brothers*, 270–271.
74. Givens, "Liberating the Germans," 50.
75. Linderman, *The World Within War*, 350.
76. Kennett, *G.I.*, loc. 3227. For more on the scope and impact of drunken carousing and sexual assaults by troops, see Hiltner, *Taking Leave, Taking Liberties* and Roberts, *What Soldiers Do*.
77. McManus, *The Deadly Brotherhood*, 91; Fussell, *Wartime*, 102–103.
78. Fussell, *Wartime*, 102–103.
79. Kennett, *G.I.*, loc. 3247–3248.
80. Linderman, *The World within War*, 190, 191.
81. Garcia, "Class and Brass," 686.
82. Linderman, *The World within War*, 199. During the US Civil War, officers' drinking bred resentment among the troops when drunkenness impaired officers' performance. Troops were less troubled by the officers' more abundant alcohol supply perhaps because the troops periodically received whiskey to fortify their strength and morale; see Bever, *At War with King Alcohol*, 54–58.
83. Linderman, *The World within War*, 189.
84. Enoc P. Waters, "Benny Didn't Want to Be Bothered—Until," *Chicago Defender*, March 25, 1944, 7.
85. Cornebise, "American Armed Forces Newspapers in World War II," 214, 217.
86. Letter to *Yank* from Corporal Keith Troxel, "After the Typhoon," *Yank*, December 14, 1945, 19.
87. Letter to *Yank* from Sergeant E.J. Damico, "Officers' Whiskey," March 30, 1945, 18.
88. Cook, "Chinese Likker," 8.
89. Letter to *Yank* from Sergeant L. M, "EM Only," *Yank*, August 17, 1945, 19.
90. Linderman, *The World within War*, 200.
91. Sergeant George Baker, "The Sad Sack: Wide Open Town," *Yank*, March 9, 1945, 16.
92. Sergeant George Baker, "Bottled Booty," *Yank*, November 30, 1945, 14. Troops in the US Civil War similarly complained about officers who rummaged through their care packages and confiscated their liquor; see Bever, *At War with King Alcohol*, 56.
93. Ambrose, introduction to Mauldin, *Up Front*, v, vi, x. Mauldin's perspective resonated so broadly and deeply that a collected volume of his wartime

cartoons maintained its position on the *New York Times* bestseller list for eighteen months after its initial publication in the 1945.

94. Mauldin, *Up Front*, 14–15.
95. Ambrose, "Introduction," Mauldin, viii.
96. Buljung, "From the Foxhole," 55.
97. Mauldin, *Up Front*, 79.
98. Mauldin, *Up Front*, 6.
99. Bill Mauldin cartoon, *Stars and Stripes* (Mediterranean ed.), March 23, 1944, in Mauldin, *Willie and Joe*, ed. DePastino, 369.
100. Mauldin, *Up Front*, 84.
101. Private first class Guy D. Wright, "The Heroes," *Yank*, April 27, 1945, 16–17.
102. Mauldin, *Up Front*, 84.
103. Mauldin, *Up Front*, 88–89.
104. Mauldin, *Up Front*, 84–86. A US Army study conducted shortly after the war, suggested that the military might have reduced the abuse of liquor if the canteens had been permitted to serve wine and beer; Schrijvers, *The Crash of Ruin*, 171.
105. Interview of Major Richard Jennings in Motley, *The Invisible Soldier*, 70; interview of 2nd Lieutenant Albert Evans in Motley, *The Invisible Soldier*, 96.
106. Wynn, *The African American Experience during World War II*, 44–47.
107. Sparrow, "Freedom to Want," 26; Bentley, *Eating for Victory*; Jacobs, *Pocketbook Politics*; Cohen, *A Consumers' Republic*.
108. Sparrow, "Freedom to Want," 26.
109. Delmont, *Half American*, chap. 4, 160–165; Brandt, *Harlem at War*, chap. 10.
110. McGuire, ed., *Taps for a Jim Crow Army*, 166.
111. Morehouse, *Fighting in the Jim Crow Army*, 125.
112. Interview of 2nd Lieutenant Walter Green in Motley, *The Invisible Soldier*, 90.
113. Letter from "A Group of Soldiers" to *Pittsburgh Courier*, February 10, 1943, in McGuire, ed., *Taps for a Jim Crow Army*, 13–15.
114. Interview of Master Sergeant Warren Bryant in Motley, *The Invisible Soldier*, 251.
115. Interview of First Lieutenant Alexander Jefferson in Motley, *The Invisible Soldier*, 218.
116. Wanda Webster, "Army Jim Crow in Texas Assailed," *Chicago Defender*, July 24, 1943, 14.
117. "Race Troops Are Denied Books for Liquor Rations," *Chicago Defender*, January 9, 1943, 3.
118. Cohen, "Jim Crow's Drug War," 55–79; Okrent, *Last Call*, 42–46. For an anti-prohibitionist critique of the sincerity of prohibitionists, see J. M. Gilmore, "Does Prohibition Prohibit?," *North American Review* 201 (March 1915), 463–465.
119. Ward, "'A War for States' Rights,'" 127.

120. Interview of Sergeant Edward Donald in Motley, *The Invisible Soldier*, 162; interview with Lieutenant Lacey Wilson in Motley, *The Invisible Soldier*, 61.

121. Hutchinson, "The Oasis," 40–43. The Army eliminated the alcohol rations for Axis POWs only after Germany surrendered.

122. Wolcott, *Race, Riots, and Roller Coasters*, 45; Cohen, *A Consumers' Republic*.

123. Wolcott, *Race, Riots, and Roller Coasters*, 51; for a small sampling of the literature on the zoot suit riots, see Alvarez, *The Power of the Zoot*; Pagán, *Murder at the Sleepy Lagoon*; Kelley, "The Riddle of the Zoot," chap. 7, in *Race Rebels*, 161–182; Peiss, *Zoot Suit*.

124. "Refused Beer, Wins $100 in Suit," *Chicago Defender*, April 10, 1943, 5; "Refused Beer, Sues Minnesota Tavern for $5,000," *Chicago Defender*, January 29, 1944, 6. In two separate racial discrimination lawsuits, Black men used a new civil rights statute in Minnesota to sue taverns after being refused beer; one jury awarded the plaintiff one hundred dollars in damages; the other jury could not reach a decision.

125. Letter from "A Group of Soldiers," in McGuire, ed., *Taps for a Jim Crow Army*, 13–15.

126. "Democracy So Rare, It Makes News," *Chicago Defender*, March 28, 1942, 1.

127. Memo from "A Negro Soldier" to Reverend D. Adam Clayton Powell Jr., June 2, 1944, in McGuire, ed., *Taps for a Jim Crow Army*, 53–55.

128. Morehouse, *Fighting in the Jim Crow Army*, 109.

129. "FDR Asked to Commute Sentence of Pvt. Levy," *Chicago Defender*, October 23, 1943, 6.

130. Bentley, "Reading Food Riots," 179–194. Bentley notes that the limited availability of highly symbolic foods has often fueled food riots and catalyzed demands for social change.

131. Lawrence LaMarr, "Wreck Stores in Wild L.A. Race Clash," *Chicago Defender*, October 16, 1943, 1; Morehouse, *Fighting in the Jim Crow Army*, 82. LaMarr used the phrase "wreaking havoc" in his report.

132. Earl M. Wright, "West Coast 'Riot' Proves to be Mere Barroom Brawl," *Chicago Defender*, July 10, 1943, 8.

133. Interview of Lieutenant Colonel Henry Peoples in Motley, *The Invisible Soldier*, 230–232.

134. Houston, with Cohn, *Black Warriors*, Kindle, 8, 176.

135. Huddle, ed., *Roi Ottley's World War II*, 77.

136. Huddle, ed., *Roi Ottley's World War II*, 97, 103–104.

137. Smith, *When Jim Crow Met John Bull*, 79–80.

138. Edward B. Toles, "US Jim Crow Invades France, GIs Discover," *Chicago Defender*, June 30, 1945, 1.

139. Brandt, *Harlem at War*, 96–97.

140. In one censored story, Ottley not only discussed the friendly relationships between Black soldiers and British people that netted Black Americans invitations to English "homes, churches, and trade union meetings, but he also

relayed a story about white American soldiers who were so disturbed by seeing Black soldiers converse and hold hands with white English women that one "broke into tears and kept repeating . . ., 'I'm from Georgia an' I jes can't take that!'" See Huddle, ed., *Roi Ottley's World War II*, 97.

141. Perry, *London Is the Place for Me*, 104, 108.

142. Huddle, ed., *Roi Ottley's World War II*, 77.

143. Interview of Staff Sergeant Chest Jones in Motley, *The Invisible Soldier*, 191.

144. Huddle, ed., *Roi Ottley's World War II*, 96.

145. Smith, *When Jim Crow Met John Bull*, 102–103.

146. Huddle, ed., *Roi Ottley's World War II*, 45.

147. Huddle, ed., *Roi Ottley's World War II*, 98.

148. Huddle, ed., *Roi Ottley's World War II*, 98.

149. Huddle, ed., *Roi Ottley's World War II*, 104.

150. Huddle, ed., *Roi Ottley's World War II*, 130; Edward B. Toles, "US Jim Crow Invades France, GIs Discover," *Chicago Defender*, June 30, 1945, 1.

151. Interview of Staff Sergeant Chester Jones in Motley, *The Invisible Soldier*, 191.

152. Billy Rowe, "She Changed Her Mind: Filipino Wanted Only White Yanks in Café," *Pittsburgh Courier*, March 24, 1945, 23.

153. Interview of Lieutenant Christopher Sturkey in Motley, *The Invisible Soldier*, 171-172.

154. Reich, "Food and Drink: Introduction," 278.

155. Delmont, *Half American*, 288.

156. Wolcott, *Race, Riots, and Roller Coasters*, 51–52; Wynn, *The African American Experience during World War II*, 50.

157. Bailey, *An Army Afire*, 194–207.

158. Sparrow, "Freedom to Want," 15–31; Kruse and Tuck, introduction to *Fog of War*, 7; Cohen, *A Consumers' Republic*.

159. Schrijvers, *The Crash of Ruin*, 168–169; US Army Information Branch, *Pocket Guide to the Cities of Southern France*, 8; US Army Information Branch, *Pocket Guide to Italian Cities*, 10.

160. "Vintners Say Queensbury Rules for Wine-Bibbing Are All Off," *Sales Management* 47 (December 1, 1940), 70.

161. Curtis, "Rum and Coca-Cola," 64–70 (quote on p. 64).

162. Bodnar, *The "Good War," in American Memory*, 72.

163. Kennett, *G.I.*, loc. 3665, 3674.

164. Cartoon by Michael Berry, *Collier's*, August 26, 1944, reprinted in *Allied News Letter* 129 (September 8, 1944), 3.

165. John T. Dyson, "A GI's Christmas Plea to Santa Claus," *Pittsburgh Courier*, December 23, 1944, 9.

166. Ambrose, *Band of Brothers*, 90; Schrijvers, *The Crash of Ruin*, 168.

167. Sergeant Mere Miller, "Berlin Today," *Yank*, August 10, 1945, 7.

168. "Franklin Delano Roosevelt, 1882–1945," *Yank*, May 11, 1945, 19.

169. Enoc P. Waters, "Pacific Patter," *Chicago Defender*, February 26, 1944, 11.

EPILOGUE

1. "The National Alcohol Awareness Test" (Ronks, PA: House of Seagram, c. 1984), Box 85, Series III, SMC.
2. Tucker, Hoyland, and Wilcox, "Consumer Response to Seagram's Equivalency Ad Campaign," 837–838.
3. The advocacy group Mothers Against Drunk Driving discussed alcohol equivalency in their publications. "Seagram Dropping Equivalence Ad Campaign," *Market Watch* 9 (January/February 1986), 60, Box 85, Series III, SMC.
4. Tucker, Hoyland, and Wilcox, "Consumer Response to Seagram's Equivalency Ad Campaign," 835.
5. *Brewers Digest*, quoted in Rubin, "The Wet War," 243.
6. "Will the French make WINE DRINKERS of our Soldiers? *American Wine Merchant* 3 (Christmas 1944), 35.
7. Jesse Stechel, "Seagram's 'Weekend,'" *Spirits* 13 (February 1936), 47.
8. House of Seagram advertisement, *Spirits* 13 (February 1936), 5.
9. One of Seagram's moderation campaign ads used the tagline "Pay Your Bills First."
10. Basinger, *The It's a Wonderful Life Book*, 269, 285.
11. James Agee, "Films," *The Nation* 164 (February 15, 1947), 193.
12. Manny Farber, "Mugging Main Street: A Review of *It's a Wonderful Life*," *New Republic*, January 6, 1947, https://newrepublic.com/article/98662/mugging-main-street-review-its-a-wonderful-life.
13. Rotskoff, *Love on the Rocks*, 90–91.
14. Rotskoff, *Love on the Rocks*, 96.
15. Jacobson, "Will It Be Wine or Cocktails?"
16. Corzine, "Right at Home," 860.
17. Pennock, *Advertising Sin and Sickness*, 43–47; Pereira-Alvares, "Make Any Occasion a Special Event."
18. Kate Taylor, "The Dark Reason Liquor Stores Are Considered Essential Businesses," *Business Insider*, April 20, 2020, https://www.businessinsider.com/liquor-stores-essential-businesses-heres-why-2020-4.

Bibliography

ARCHIVES

Adam Matthew Digital, online, American Consumer Culture: Market Research and American Business, 1935–1965
Bancroft Library, University of California, Berkeley
    Wine Institute Correspondence with Idwal Jones
California History Society, San Francisco, California, San Francisco Ephemera Collection
Detroit Historical Society, Online Collection
Franklin D. Roosevelt Presidential Library, Hyde Park, New York
    Franklin D. Roosevelt Papers as President, Official File (FDRPP)
    Henry Morgenthau Diaries, World War II Era (HMD)
    Rexford F. Tugwell Collection (RTC)
Hagley Museum and Library, Wilmington, Delaware
    Seagram Company Papers
    Seagram Museum Collection, Series III, Series IV (SMC)
    Seagram Spotlight
Harry Truman Library and Museum, online
John W. Hartman Center for Sales, Marketing, and Advertising History, Rubenstein Library, Duke University, Durham, NC
    J. Walter Thompson Company Archives, Domestic Advertising Collection (DAC)
Library of Congress, Washington, DC
    Library of Congress Manuscripts Collection, Bernays Papers (BP)
National Archives I, Center for Legislative Archives, Washington, DC
    Records of the US House of Representatives, 77th Congress, Committee on Military Affairs, Petitions and Memorials, HR77A-H12.1 (HR)

Records of the US Senate, 78th Congress, Committee on Military Affairs, Committee Papers of the Committee on Military Affairs and Its Predecessors, SEN78A-J14 (SEN)
National Archives II, College Park, Maryland
　Record Group 179: Records of the War Production Board
　　Policy Documentation Files, 1939–1947, Entry PI-15 1 (WPB)
　Record Group 188: Records of the Office of Price Administration
　　Office of Price Administration, Price Department, Food Price Division, Grocery Products Branch, Beverage Section, General Correspondence Files, 1942–1946, Entry PI-95 386 (OPAPD)
　　Office of the Administrator, Administrative Subject Files of Prentiss Brown, 1943, Entry UD-3 (OPAPB)
　　Office of Price Administration, Enforcement Department, Food Enforcement Division, Agricultural Commodities Enforcement Branch (OPAED)
　　　Records Relating to Commodity Programs, 1943–1946, Entry A1 E150
　　　Monthly Reports by Field Offices, 1944–1945, Entry A1 E151
National Research Council, Washington, DC
　Committee on Food Habits Papers (CFH)
　Food and Nutrition Board Papers (FNB)
New York Public Library Manuscripts and Archives Division, New York City, New York World's Fair, 1939–1940 Collection (NYWF)
San Francisco Public Library, California, San Francisco Ephemera Collection (SFEC)
Temperance and Prohibition website, Ohio State University, https://prohibition.osu.edu/
University of Louisville, Kentucky, Archives and Special Collections
　Distillery Reference Collection
　Joseph E. Seagram and Sons, Inc., *Proof*, vols. 1–12, 1941–1952
　Kentucky Distilling Industry Oral Histories

COOKBOOKS AND DRINKING GUIDEBOOKS

(See also cookbooks listed under "Trade Association Publications, Alcoholic Beverage Industry Advocacy.")

Brown, Cora, Rose Brown, and Bob Brown. *The Wine Cook Book*. Boston: Little, Brown, and Company, 1941.

Carlisle, Donald Thompson, and Elizabeth Dunn. *Wining and Dining with Rhyme and Reason*. New York: Murton, Balch, 1933.

Drex, A. *ABC of Wines, Cocktails, and Liqueurs*. New York: Crown Publishing, 1933.

Drinkwater, Calib. *How to Serve Wine and Beer*. Cleveland: Warkins Publishing, 1933.

Elliott, Virginia. *Quiet Drinking: A Book of Beer, Wines and Cocktails and What to Serve with Them*. New York: Harcourt, Brace, 1933.

Fisher, M. F. K. *How to Cook a Wolf*. New York: North Point Press, 1954.

Gray, James. *After Repeal: What a Host Should Know about Serving Wines and Spirits.* St. Paul, MN: Brown Blodgett, 1933.
Hartman, David. *Wine and Liquor: What, When, and How to Serve.* Washington, DC: Congressional Press, 1933.
Hatch, Ted. *The American Wine Cook Book.* New York: G. P. Putnam's Sons, 1941.
Hillis, Marjorie. *New York, Fair or No Fair: A Guide for the Woman Vacationist.* New York: Simon & Schuster, 1939.
Ladies' Home Journal. *WINS (Women in National Service) Wartime Homemaking Manual.* Philadelphia: Curtis Publishing Co., 1943.
Mills, Majorie. *Cooking on a Ration: Food Is Still Fun.* Boston: Houghton Mifflin, 1943.
The Original Picayune Creole Cook Book, 10th ed. New Orleans: Times-Picayune Publishing Co., 1945.
Owen, Jeanne. *A Wine Lover's Cook Book.* New York: M. Barrows and Company, 1940.
Schoonmaker, Frank, and Tom Marvel. *The Complete Wine Book.* New York: Simon and Schuster, 1934.
Seldes, Gilbert. *The Future of Drinking.* New York: Little, Brown and Company, 1930.
Stoll, Horatio F. *Wine-wise.* San Francisco: H. S. Crocker Press, 1933.
Street, Julian. *Wines: Their Selection, Care, and Service.* New York: Alfred A. Knopf, 1933.
Stringer, Carlton. *Wines: What to Serve, When to Serve.* Scarborough, NY: Canape Parade, 1933.
Taylor, Mary L. R. *Economy for Epicures: A Practical Menu and Recipe Book.* New York: Oxford University Press, 1943.
Victory Meat Extenders: Meat Recipe Book. Chicago: National Live Stock and Meat Board, c. 1941–1945.
Whitaker, Alma. *Bacchus Behave!: The Lost Art of Polite Drinking.* New York: Frederick A. Stokes, 1933.

FILMS, NEWSREELS, NOVELS

Burns, Ken, director. *Jazz.* Episode 2, "The Gift." Boston: PBS Home Video, 2007.
Capra, Frank, director. *It's a Wonderful Life.* Liberty Films, 1946.
Godfrey, Peter, director. *Christmas in Connecticut.* Warner Bros., 1945.
Hobart, Alice Tisdale. *The Cup and the Sword.* New York: Bobbs-Merrill Company, 1942.
Jones, Idwal. *The Vineyard.* Forward by Robert Mondavi. Berkeley: University of California Press, 1997 [1942].
Jones, James. *The Thin Red Line.* In *The World War II Trilogy: From Here to Eternity, The Thin Red Line, and Whistle,* Kindle ed. Open Road Media, 2012.
"Mayor James J. Walker Leads the Great Beer Parade in New York City." Newsreel. CriticalPast Archive. Accessed on July 23, 2022. https://www.youtube.com/watch?v=rXyldRD9WcU.

Wellman, William A., director. *The Public Enemy*. Warner Bros., 1931.
Wilder, Billy, director. *The Lost Weekend*. Paramount Pictures, 1945.
Wyler, William, director. *The Best Years of Our Lives*. Samuel Goldwyn Productions, 1946.

GOVERNMENT DOCUMENTS

Economic Research Services, USDA. "Nominal Food Expenditures, with taxes and tips, from previously published estimates." https://www.ers.usda.gov/data-products/food-expenditure-series/.
National Bureau of Economic Research. "Personal Consumption Expenditures, Nondurable Goods for United States." FRED, Federal Reserve Bank of St. Louis. https://fred.stlouisfed.org/series/Q06087USQ027NNBR, August 20, 2023.
National Institute on Alcohol Abuse and Alcoholism. "Table 1: Apparent Per Capita Ethanol Consumption, United States, 1850–2018 [Gallons of ethanol, based on population age 15 and older prior to 1970 and on population age 14 and older thereafter]." *Surveillance Report*, no. 115. Archived May 20, 2022. https://web.archive.org/web/20220520030414/https://pubs.niaaa.nih.gov/publications/surveillance115/tab1_18.htm.
US Army Information Branch. *Pocket Guide to Italian Cities*. Washington, DC: War Department, 1944.
US Army Information Branch. *Pocket Guide to the Cities of Southern France*. Washington, DC: War Department, 1944.
US Congress, House of Representatives, Committee on Ways and Means. *Modification of the Volstead Act: Hearings before the Committee on Ways and Means*. 72nd Congress, 2nd sess., December 7–14, 1932.
US Congress, Senate, Committee on Manufactures. *Amendment of the Prohibition Act: Hearings before a Subcommittee of the Committee on Manufactures*. 72nd Congress, 1st session, January 8-February 19, 1932.
US Congress, Senate, *Investigation of the Alcoholic Beverage Industry—Partial Report No. 2 of Subcommittee of Committee on the Judiciary*. 78th Congress, 2nd sess., August 7, 1944.

ORAL HISTORIES

Adams, Leon. *California Wine Industry Affairs: Recollections and Opinions*. Interview by Ruth Teiser. Berkeley: Regional Oral History Office, Bancroft Library, University of California, 1990.
———. *Revitalizing the California Wine Industry*. Interview by Ruth Teiser. Berkeley: Regional Oral History Office, Bancroft Library, University of California, 1974.
Amerine, Maynard. *The University of California and the State's Wine Industry*. Interview by Ruth Teiser. Berkeley: Regional Oral History Office, Bancroft Library, University of California, 1971.

Baccigaluppi, Harry. *California Grape Products and Other Wine Enterprises.* Interview by Ruth Teiser. Berkeley: Regional Oral History Office, Bancroft Library, University of California, 1971.

Cella, John B., II. *The Cella Family in the California Wine Industry.* Interview by Ruth Teiser. Berkeley: Regional Oral History Office, Bancroft Library, University of California, 1984.

Crimmins, John W. Oral History. Interview by Thomas H. Syvertsen. Archives & Special Collections, University of Louisville, Kentucky, December 4, 1984.

Critchfield, Burke. *The California Wine Industry during the Depression.* Interview by Ruth Teiser. Berkeley: Regional Oral History Office, Bancroft Library, University of California, 1971.

Dailey, Frank M. Oral History. Interview by Thomas H. Syvertsen. Archives & Special Collections, University of Louisville, Kentucky, November 29, 1984.

Fromm, Alfred. *Marketing California Wine and Brandy.* Interview by Ruth Teiser. Berkeley: Regional Oral History Office, Bancroft Library, University of California, 1984.

Gallo, Ernest. *The E. & J. Gallo Winery.* Interview by Ruth Teiser. Berkeley: Regional Oral History Office, Bancroft Library, University of California, 1995.

Gomberg, Louis. *Analytical Perspectives on the California Wine Industry.* Interview by Ruth Teiser. Berkeley: Regional Oral History Office, Bancroft Library, University of California, 1990.

Jones, Judge Marvin. Oral History. Interview by Jerry N. Hess. Harry S. Truman Library and Museum, April 20, 1970. https://www.trumanlibrary.gov/library/oral-histories/jonesjm2.

Lanza, Horace O. *California Grape Products and Other Wine Enterprises.* Interview by Ruth Teiser. Berkeley: Regional Oral History Office, Bancroft Library, University of California, 1971.

Martini, Louis M. *The Martinis: Wine Making in the Napa Valley.* Interview by Lois C. Stone and Ruth Teiser. Berkeley: Regional Oral History Office, Bancroft Library, University of California, 1973.

Motley, Mary Penick, ed. *The Invisible Soldier: The Experience of the Black Soldier, World War II.* Detroit: Wayne State University Press, 1987.

Perelli-Minetti, Antonio. *A Life in Wine Making.* Interview by Ruth Teiser. Berkeley: Regional Oral History Office, Bancroft Library, University of California, 1975.

Peyser, Jefferson. *The Law and the California Wine Industry.* Interview by Ruth Teiser. Berkeley: Regional Oral History Office, Bancroft Library, University of California, 1974.

Rossi, Edmund A. *Italian Swiss Colony and the Wine Industry.* Interview by Ruth Teiser. Berkeley: Regional Oral History Office, Bancroft Library, University of California, 1971.

Schupp, Orville. Oral History. Interview by Thomas H. Syvertsen., Tape 90, Side 2. Archives & Special Collections, University of Louisville, Kentucky, February 13, 1985.

Wente, Ernest. *Wine Making in the Livermore Valley*. Interview by Ruth Teiser. Berkeley: Regional Oral History Office, Bancroft Library, University of California, 1971.

MEMOIRS, LETTERS, DIARIES

Emerson, Thomas I. *Young Lawyer for the New Deal: An Insider's Memoir of the Roosevelt Years*. Savage, MD: Rowan and Littlefield Publishers, 1991.

Houston, Ivan J., with Gordon Cohn. *Black Warriors: The Buffalo Soldiers of World War II; Memories of the Only Negro Infantry Division to Fight in Europe during World War II*, Kindle ed. Bloomington, IN: Universe, Inc., 2009.

Huddle, Mark A., ed. *Roi Ottley's World War II: The Lost Diary of an African American Journalist*. Lawrence: University Press of Kansas, 2011.

Jones, James. *World War II: A Chronicle of Soldiering*. Chicago: University of Chicago Press, 1975.

Mauldin, Bill. *Up Front*. New York: W. W. Norton & Company, 2000.

———. *Willie and Joe: Back Home*, edited by Todd DePastino. Seattle: Fantagraphics Books, 2011.

McGuire, Phillip, ed. *Taps for a Jim Crow Army: Letters from Black Soldiers in World War II*. Santa Barbara, CA: ABC-Clio, 1983.

Winters, Major Dick. *Beyond Band of Brothers: The War Memoirs of Major Dick Winters*. New York: Dutton Caliber, 2006.

PERIODICALS

Magazines

American City
American Legion
American Mercury
Atlantic Monthly
Banking
Barron's
Business Insider
Business Week
California Journal of Development
Christian Century
Collier's
Commonweal
Congressional Digest
Esquire
Fortune
Forum
Harper's Magazine
House Beautiful
Life
Literary Digest

The Nation
Nation's Business
New Republic
Newsweek
New York Times Magazine
North American Review
Outlook and Independent
Popular Science
Review of Reviews
The Rotarian
Saturday Evening Post
Science Digest
Scientific American
Scribner's Magazine
South Dakota State Forum
Survey Graphic
Time
Yank

Newspapers

Boston Herald
Chicago Daily Tribune
Chicago Defender
Christian Science Monitor
Los Angeles Times
New York American
New York Times
New York World-Telegram
Pittsburgh Courier
Rochester Democrat and Chronicle
San Francisco News
Stars and Stripes
Wall Street Journal
Washington Post

Trade Journals

Advertising and Selling
Allied News Letter
American Brewer
American Restaurant Magazine
American Wine Merchant
Brewers Journal
Brewery Age
California Grape Grower
Modern Brewery Age

Package Store Management
Printed Salesmanship
Printers' Ink
Restaurant Management
Sales Management
Spirits
Successful Farming
Tavern News
Tavern Weekly News
Western Brewers
Wine and Liquor Retailer
Wine Institute, Confidential Bulletin to Members
Wines and Vines

TRADE ASSOCIATION PUBLICATIONS, ALCOHOLIC BEVERAGE INDUSTRY ADVOCACY

Davison, Eloise. *Beer in the American Home.* New York: United Brewers Industrial Foundation, 1937.

Hostess Book of Favorite Wine Recipes: Wartime Edition. San Francisco: Wine Advisory Board, c. 1942.

Sbarboro, Andrea. *The Fight for True Temperance: Practical Thoughts from a Practical Man.* San Francisco, 1908.

———. *Temperance vs. Prohibition: Important Letters and Data from Our American Consuls, the Clergy, and Other Eminent Men.* San Francisco: H. S. Crocker Co., 1909.

———. "Wine as a Remedy for the Evil of Intemperance." Address Delivered at California Fruit Growers' Convention in Hanford, CA, December 4, 1906.

Volunteer for Victory: The Story of How a Great Industry Enlisted for War. New York: Liquor Publications Inc., 1943.

The Wine Cook Book: Fifty-seven Thrifty Home-Tested Recipes for Making Good Food Taste Better. San Francisco: Wine Advisory Board, c. 1940s.

The Wine Industry: Wine Handbook Series—No. 1. San Francisco: Wine Advisory Board, c. 1943.

SECONDARY SOURCES

Adams, Leon D. *The Wines of America.* New York: McGraw-Hill Book Company, 1985.

Adams, William. "Natural Virtue: Symbol and Imagination in the American Farm Crisis." *Georgia Review* 39, no. 4 (Winter 1985): 695–712.

Addams, Jane. *The Spirit of Youth and the City Streets.* New York: Macmillan, 1909.

Allen, Frederick Lewis. *Only Yesterday: An Informal History of the 1920s.* New York: Harper & Row, 1931.

Alvarez, Luis. *The Power of the Zoot: Youth Culture and Resistance in World War II.* Berkeley: University of California Press, 2009.

Ambrose, Stephen. *Band of Brothers: E Company 506th Regiment, 101st Airborne from Normandy to Hitler's Eagle's Nest*, 25th Anniversary ed. New York: Simon & Schuster Paperbacks, 2017.

Anagnostu, Yiorgos. "Forget the Past, Remember the Ancestors! Modernity, 'Whiteness,' American Hellenism, and the Politics of Memory in Early Greek America." *Journal of Modern Greek Studies* 22, no. 1 (May 2004): 25–71.

"Analysis of Six New York Beers." *American Journal of Public Health* 23 (July 1933): 704.

Anderson, Karen. *Wartime Women: Sex Roles, Family Relations, and the Status of Women during World War II*. Westport, CT: Greenwood Press, 1981.

Angle, Paul M. *Bloody Williamson: A Chapter in American Lawlessness*. Urbana: University of Illinois Press, 1992.

Appadurai, Arjun, ed. *The Social Life of Things: Commodities in Cultural Perspective*. New York: Cambridge University Press, 1986.

Apple, Rima D. *Vitamania: Vitamins in American Culture*. New Brunswick, NJ: Rutgers University Press, 1996.

Applebaum, Stanley. *The New York World's Fair 1939/1940 in 155 Photographs by Richard Wurts and Others*. New York: Dover Publications, Inc., 1977.

Arnold, Bruce Makoto. "'Your Money Ain't No Good O'er There': Food as Real and Social Currency in the Pacific Theater of World War II." *Food and Foodways* 25, no. 2 (2017): 107–122.

Asbury, Herbert. *The Great Illusion: An Informal History of Prohibition*. Garden City, NY: Doubleday, 1950.

Babic, Annessa Ann. "Epilogue: Foods of War, and Wars on Food: The American Military Commissary and (Re)shaping the American Diet." *Food and Foodways* 25, no. 2 (2017): 160–169.

Bailey, Beth. *An Army Afire: How the US Army Confronted Its Racial Crisis in the Vietnam Era*. Chapel Hill: University of North Carolina Press, 2023.

Bailey, Beth L., and David Farber. *The First Strange Place: Race and Sex in World War II Hawaii*. Baltimore: Johns Hopkins University Press, 1992.

Baldwin, Davian L. *Chicago's New Negroes: Modernity, The Great Migration, and Black Urban Life*. Chapel Hill: University of North Carolina Press, 2007.

Baron, Stanley. *Brewed in America: A History of Beer and Ale in the United States*. Boston: Little, Brown, and Company, 1962.

Barr, Andrew. *Drink: A Social History of America*. New York: Carroll and Graf Pub., 1999.

Basinger, Jeanine. *The It's a Wonderful Life Book*. New York: Alfred A. Knopf, 1986.

Bégin, Camille. *Taste of the Nation: The New Deal Search for America's Food*. Urbana: University of Illinois Press, 2016.

Belasco, Warren. *Appetite for Change: How the Counterculture Took on the Food Industry*. New York: Pantheon Books, 1989.

Belasco, Warren, and Philip Scranton, eds. *Food Nations: Selling Taste in Consumer Societies*. New York: Routledge, 2001.

Bellamy, Matthew J. *Brewed in the North: A History of Labatt's*. Montreal: McGill-Queen's University Press, 2019.

Bengry, Justin. "Courting the Pink Pound: *Men Only* and the Queer Consumer, 1935–1939." *History Workshop Journal* (Autumn 2009): 122–148.
Bentley, Amy. *Eating for Victory: Food Rationing and the Politics of Domesticity*. Champaign: University of Illinois Press, 1998.
———. *Inventing Baby Food: Taste, Health, and the Industrialization of the American Diet*. Berkeley: University of California Press, 2014.
———. "Reading Food Riots: Scarcity, Abundance and National Identity." In *Food, Drink, and Identity: Cooking, Eating and Drinking in Europe since the Middle Ages*, edited by Peter Scholliers, 179–194. Oxford, UK: Berg, 2001.
Berenstein, Nadia. "Who's Afraid of the Whiskey Trust." NadiaBerenstein.com (blog), October 30, 2015. http://nadiaberenstein.com/blog/2015/10/30/whos-afraid-of-the-whisky-trust.
Bernays, Edward. *Propaganda*. With an introduction by Mark Crispin Miller. New York: IG Publishing, 2005 [1928].
Bever, Megan L. *At War with King Alcohol: Debating Drinking and Masculinity in the Civil War*. Chapel Hill: University of North Carolina Press, 2022.
Biltekoff, Charlotte. *Eating Right in America: The Cultural Politics of Food and Health*. Durham, NC: Duke University Press, 2013.
Bird, William L., and Harry R. Rubenstein. *Design for Victory: World War II Posters on the American Home Front*. New York: Princeton Architectural Press, 1998.
Bittner, Stephen V. *Whites and Reds: A History of Wine in the Land of Tsar and Commissar*. Oxford, UK: Oxford University Press, 2021.
Blocker, Jack S. *American Temperance Movements: Cycles of Reform*. Boston: Twayne Publishers, 1989.
Blum, John M. "The G.I. in the Culture of the Second World War." *Ventures* 8, no. 1 (1968): 51–56.
Blum, John Morton. *From the Morgenthau Diaries: Years of Crisis, 1928–1938*. Boston: Houghton Mifflin Company, 1959.
———. *V Was for Victory: Politics and American Culture during World War II*. New York: Harcourt Brace Jovanovich, 1976.
Bodnar, John. *The "Good War" in American Memory*. Baltimore: Johns Hopkins University Press, 2012.
Bonnie, Richard J., and Charles H. Whitebread II. *The Marijuana Conviction: A History of Marijuana Prohibition in the United States*. New York: Lindesmith Center, 1999.
Brandt, Allan M. *The Cigarette Century: The Rise, Fall, and Deadly Persistence of the Product That Defined America*. New York: Basic Books, 2009.
Brandt, Nat. *Harlem at War: The Black Experience in WWII*. Syracuse, NY: Syracuse University Press, 1996.
Breazeale, Kenon. "In Spite of Women: *Esquire* Magazine and the Construction of the Male Consumer." *Signs* 20, no. 1 (Autumn 1994): 1–22.
Brinkley, Alan. *The End of Reform: New Deal Liberalism in Recession and War*. New York: Vintage Books, 1995.
Brinkley, David. *Washington Goes to War*. New York: Alfred A. Knopf, 1988.

Bruegel, Martin. "How the French Learned to Eat Canned Food, 1809–1930s." In *Food Nations: Selling Taste in Consumer Societies*, edited by Warren Belasco and Philip Scranton, 113–130. New York: Routledge, 2002.

Buljung, Brianna. "From the Foxhole: American Newsmen and the Reporting of World War II." *International Social Science Review* 86, no. 1/2 (2011): 44–64.

Burk, Robert F. *The Corporate State and the Broker State: The du Ponts and American National Politics, 1925–1940*. Cambridge, MA: Harvard University Press, 1990.

Burke, Timothy. *Lifebuoy Men, Lux Women: Commodification, Consumption, and Cleanliness in Modern Zimbabwe*. Durham, NC: Duke University Press, 1996.

Burnham, John C. *Bad Habits: Drinking, Smoking, Taking Drugs, Gambling, Sexual Misbehavior, and Swearing in American History*. New York: New York University Press, 1993.

Bushman, Richard. *The Refinement of America: Persons, Houses, Cities*. New York: Alfred A. Knopf, Inc., 1992.

Calder, Lendol. *Financing the American Dream: A History of Consumer Credit*. Princeton, NJ: Princeton University Press, 1999.

Caldwell, Melissa L. "Domesticating the French Fry: McDonald's and Consumerism in Moscow." In *The Cultural Politics of Food and Eating*, edited by James Watson and Melissa L. Caldwell, 180–196. Malden, MA: Blackwell Publishing, 2005.

Campbell, D'Ann. "Women in Combat: The World War II Experience in the United States, Great Britain, Germany, and the Soviet Union." *Journal of Military History* 57 (April 1993): 301–323.

Campbell, Robert A. "Managing the Marginal: Regulating and Negotiating Decency in Vancouver's Beer Parlours, 1925–1954." *Labour/Le Travail* 44 (Fall 1999): 109–127.

Campos, Isaac. *Home Grown: Marijuana and the Origins of Mexico's War on Drugs*. Chapel Hill: University of North Carolina Press, 2012.

———. "Mexicans and the Origins of Marijuana Prohibition in the United States: A Reassessment." *Social History of Alcohol and Drugs* 32 (2018): 6–37.

Carson, Gerald. *The Social History of Bourbon*. Lexington: University of Kentucky Press, 2010 [1963].

Carter, Ilise S. *The Red Menace: How Lipstick Changed the Face of American History*. Lanham, MD: Prometheus Books, 2021.

Casdorph, Paul D. *Let the Good Times Roll: Life at Home in America during World War II*. New York: Paragon House, 1989.

Cavallo, Dominick. *Muscles and Morals: Organized Playgrounds and Urban Reform, 1880–1920*. Philadelphia: University of Pennsylvania Press, 1981.

Chauncey, George. *Gay New York: Gender, Urban Culture, and the Making of the Gay Male World, 1890–1940*. New York: Basic Books, 1994.

Chrzan, Janet. *Alcohol: Social Drinking in Cultural Context*. New York: Routledge, 2013.

Cinotto, Simone. *The Italian American Table: Food, Family, and Community in New York City*. Urbana: University of Illinois Press, 2013.

———. *Soft Soil, Black Grapes: The Birth of Italian Winemaking in California.* New York: New York University Press, 2012.
Clark, Norman H. *Deliver Us from Evil: An Interpretation of American Prohibition.* New York: W. W. Norton & Co., 1976.
Cohen, Lizabeth. *A Consumers' Republic: The Politics of Mass Consumption in Postwar America.* New York: Alfred A. Knopf, 2003.
Cohen, Michael M. "Jim Crow's Drug War: Race, Coca Cola, and the Southern Origins of Drug Prohibition." *Southern Cultures* 12 (Fall 2006): 55–79.
Collingham, Lizzie. *Taste of War: World War II and the Battle for Food.* New York: Penguin Press, 2012.
Cook, Blanche Wiesen. *Eleanor Roosevelt: The Defining Years, Volume 2, 1933–1938.* New York: Penguin Books, 1999.
Cook, Tim. "'Tokens of Fritz': Canadian Soldiers and the Art of Souveniring in the Great War." *War and Society* 31, no. 3 (October 2012): 211–226.
———. "Wet Canteens and Worrying Mothers: Alcohol, Soldiers, and Temperance Groups in the Great War." *Histoire Sociale/Social History* 35, no. 70 (November 2002): 311–330.
Cooke, James J. *American Girls, Beer, and Glenn Miller: GI Morale in World War II.* Columbia: University of Minnesota Press, 2012.
Cornebise, Alfred E. "American Armed Forces Newspapers in World War II." *American Journalism* 12, no. 3 (1995): 213–224.
Corzine, Nathan Michael. "Right at Home: Freedom and Domesticity in the Language and Imagery of Beer Advertising, 1933–1960." *Journal of Social History* 43, no. 4 (Summer 2010): 843–866.
Cotter, Bill. *The 1939–1940 New York World's Fair: The World of Tomorrow.* San Francisco: Arcadia Publishing, 2009.
Courtwright, David. *The Age of Addiction: How Bad Habits Became Big Business.* Cambridge, MA: Belknap Press of Harvard University Press, 2019.
———. *Dark Paradise: A History of Opiate Addiction in America.* Cambridge, MA: Harvard University Press, 2009.
———. *Forces of Habit: Drugs and the Making of the Modern World.* Cambridge, MA: Harvard University Press, 2001.
Cross, Gary. *An All-Consuming Century: Why Commercialism Won in Modern America.* New York: Columbia University Press, 2002.
Currell, Susan. *The March of Spare Time: The Problem and Promise of Leisure in the Great Depression.* Philadelphia: University of Pennsylvania Press, 2005.
Curtis, Wayne. "Rum and Coca-Cola: The Murky Derivations of a Sweet Drink and a Sassy World War II Song." *American Scholar* 75, no. 3 (Summer 2006): 64–70.
Cwiertka, Katarzyna J. *Cuisine, Colonialism and Cold War: Food in Twentieth-Century Korea.* London: Reaktion Books, 2012.
Davis, Belinda J. *Home Fires Burning: Food, Politics, and Everyday Life in World War I Berlin.* Chapel Hill: University of North Carolina Press, 2000.
Davis, Chelsea. "The Contradictions of 'Civilizing' Consumption: Colonial Wine and Race in Britain's Nineteenth Century Imperial Project." *Global Food History* 10, no. 1 (2024): 28–51.

Davis, Marni. *Jews and Booze: Becoming American in the Age of Prohibition.* New York: New York University Press, 2012.
Deetz, Kelly Fanto. *Bound to the Fire: How Virginia's Enslaved Cooks Helped Invent American Cuisine.* Lexington: University Press of Kentucky, 2017.
DeGrandpre, Richard. *The Cult of Pharmacology: How America Became the World's Most Troubled Drug Culture.* Durham, NC: Duke University Press, 2006.
Delano, Page Dougherty. "Making Up for War: Sexuality and Citizenship in Wartime Culture." *Feminist Studies* 26, no, 1 (Spring 2000): 33–68.
De La Peña, Carolyn. *Empty Pleasures: The Story of Artificial Sweeteners from Saccarin to Splenda.* Chapel Hill: University of North Carolina Press, 2010.
Delmont, Matthew F. *Half American: The Epic Story of African Americans Fighting World War II at Home and Abroad.* New York: Viking, 2022.
Deutsch, Tracey. *Building a Housewife's Paradise: Gender, Politics, and American Grocery Stores in the Twentieth Century.* Chapel Hill: University of North Carolina Press, 2010.
Dighe, Ranjit S. "Pierre S. Du Pont and the Making of an Anti-Prohibition Activist." *Social History of Alcohol and Drugs* 42 (Summer 2010): 97–118.
———. "A Taste for Temperance: How American Beer Got to Be So Bland." *Business History* 58, no. 5 (2016): 752–784.
Dinerstein, Joel. *Swinging the Machine: Modernity, Technology, and African American Culture between the World Wars.* Amherst: University of Massachusetts Press, 2003.
Dobyns, Fletcher. *The Amazing Story of Repeal: An Exposé of the Power of Propaganda.* Chicago: Willett, Clark, and Company, 1940.
Douglas, Ann. *Terrible Honesty: Mongrel Manhattan in the 1920s.* New York: Farrar, Straus, and Giroux, 1995.
Dower, John. *War without Mercy: Race and Power in the Pacific War.* New York: Pantheon, 1987.
Dudziak, Mary. "'You Didn't See Him Lying . . . Beside the Gravel Road in France': Death, Distance, and American War Politics." *Diplomatic History* 42, no. 1 (2018): 1–16.
Duis, Perry R. *The Saloon: Public Drinking in Chicago and Boston, 1880–1920.* Urbana: University of Illinois Press, 1999.
———. "No Time for Privacy: World War II and Chicago's Families." In *The War in American Culture: Society and Consciousness during World War II,* edited by Lewis A. Erenberg and Susan E. Hirsch, 17–45. Chicago: University of Chicago Press, 1996.
Dumenil, Lynn. *American Working Women in World War II: A Brief History with Documents.* Boston: Bedford/St. Martin's, 2010.
Edensor, Tim. "The Social Life of the Senses: Ordering and Disordering the Modern Sensorium." In *A Cultural History of the Senses in the Modern Age,* edited by David Howes, 31–54. London: Bloomsbury Academic, 2014.
Ehrenreich, Barbara. *The Hearts of Men: American Dreams and the Flight from Commitment.* Palatine IL: Anchor Books, 1983.
Elias, Megan. *Food on the Page: Cookbooks and American Culture.* Philadelphia: University of Pennsylvania Press, 2017.

Ellis, John. *The Sharp End: The Fighting Man in World War II*. New York: Charles Scribner's Sons, 1980.

Elvins, Sarah. "Lady Smugglers and Lynx-Eyed Customs Agents: Gender, Morality, and Cross Border Shopping in Detroit and Windsor." *Canadian Historical Review* 101, no. 4 (December 2020): 497–521.

Enstad, Nan. *Cigarettes, Inc.: An Intimate History of Corporate Imperialism*. Chicago: University of Chicago Press, 2018.

———. *Ladies of Labor, Girls of Adventure: Working Women, Popular Culture, and Labor Politics at the Turn of the Twentieth Century*. New York: Columbia University Press, 1999.

Erenberg, Lewis A. "From New York to Middletown: Repeal and the Legitimization of Nightlife in the Great Depression." *American Quarterly* 38, no. 5 (Winter 1986): 761–778.

———. "Swing Goes to War: Glenn Miller and the Popular Music of World War II." In *The War in American Culture: Society and Consciousness during World War II*, edited by Lewis A. Erenberg and Susan E. Hirsh, 144–165. Chicago: University of Chicago Press, 1996.

Ewen, Stuart. *PR! A Social History of Spin*. New York: Basic Books, 1996.

Faith, Nicholas. *The Bronfmans: The Rise and Fall of the House of Seagram*. New York: Thomas Dunne Books, 2006.

Fass, Paula. *The Damned and the Beautiful: American Youth in the 1920s*. New York: Oxford University Press, 1977.

Ferraiolo, Kathleen. "From Killer Weed to Popular Medicine: The Evolution of American Drug Control Policy, 1937–2000." *Journal of Policy History* 19 (2007): 147–179.

Fine, Richard. "The Development of the 'Pyle Style' of War Reporting: French North Africa, 1942–1943." *Media History* 23, no. 3/4 (2017): 377–390.

Finlay, Mark R. *Growing American Rubber: Strategic Plants and the Politics of National Security*. New Brunswick, NJ: Rutgers University Press, 2009.

Fitzgerald Gerald J., and Gabriella M. Petrick. "In Good Taste: Rethinking American History with Our Palates." *Journal of American History* 95 (September 2008): 392–404.

Fosdick Raymond D., and Albert L. Scott. *Toward Liquor Control*, Kindle ed. Alexandria, VA: The Center for Alcohol Policy, 2011.

Fox, Frank W. *Madison Avenue Goes to War: The Strange Military Career of American Advertising, 1941–45*. Provo, UT: Brigham Young University Press, 1975.

Frank, Dana. *Buy American: The Untold Story of Economic Nationalism*. Boston: Beacon Press, 1999.

Frendreis, John, and Raymond Tatalovich. "'A Hundred Miles of Dry': Religion and the Persistence of Prohibition in the U.S. States." *State Politics and Policy Quarterly* 10, no. 3 (Fall 2010): 302–319.

"From the Archives: Control of Liquor Sales Was States' New Job in 1933," *US News and World Report*, January 16, 2020. https://www.usnews.com/news/best-states/articles/2020-01-16/end-of-prohibition-gave-states-a-new-job-regulating-liquor.

Fussell, Paul. *Wartime: Understanding and Behavior in the Second World War.* New York: Oxford University Press, 1989.

Gabaccia, Donna. *We Are What We Eat: Ethnic Food and the Making of Americans.* Cambridge, MA: Harvard University Press, 1998.

Garcia, Daniel Eugene. "Class and Brass: Demobilization, Working Class Politics, and American Foreign Policy between World War and Cold War." *Diplomatic History* 34, no. 4 (September 2010): 681–698.

Gaytán, Marie Sarita. *Tequila! Distilling the Spirit of Mexico.* Stanford, CA: Stanford University Press, 2014.

Givens, Seth A. "Liberating the Germans: The US Army and Looting in Germany during the Second World War." *War in History* 21, no. 1 (January 2014): 33–54.

Glover, Brian. *Brewing for Victory: Brewers, Beer and Pubs in World War II.* Cambridge, UK: The Lutterworth Press, 1988.

Goldman Wendy Z., and Donald A. Filtzer, eds. *Hunger and War: Food Provisioning in the Soviet Union during World War II.* Bloomington: Indiana University Press, 2015.

Goldstein, Carolyn. *Creating Consumers: Home Economists in Twentieth-Century America.* Chapel Hill: University of North Carolina Press, 2012.

Graebner, William. *The Age of Doubt: American Thought and Culture in the 1940s.* Boston: Twayne Publishers, 1991.

Grier, Katherine C. *Culture and Comfort: Parlor Making and Middle-Class Identity, 1850–1930.* Washington, DC: Smithsonian Books, 2010.

Griffith, Brian J. "Bacchus among the Blackshirts: Wine Making, Consumerism and Identity in Fascist Italy, 1919–1937." *Contemporary European History* 29 (2020): 394–415.

———. "(Inter)National Spirits: On the Cultural Politics of the 'Cocktail Craze' in Fascist Italy, 1920s–1930s." In *Drinks in Vogue: Exploring the Changing Worlds of Fashions and Beverages,* edited by David Inglis and Hang Kei Ho, 77–103. New York: Routledge, 2023.

Grimes, William. *Straight Up or On the Rocks: The Story of the American Cocktail.* New York: North Point Press, 2001.

Gusfield, Joseph. "Passage to Play: Rituals of Drinking Time in American Society." In *Constructive Drinking: Perspectives on Drink from Anthropology,* edited by Mary Douglas, 73–90. New York: Routledge, 2003.

Gutierrez, Davie. *Patriots from the Barrios: The Story of Company E, 141st Infantry: The Only All Mexican American Army Unit in World War II.* Yardley, PA: Westholme Publishing, 2018.

Guy, Kolleen. *When Champagne Became French: Wine and the Making of a National Identity.* Baltimore: Johns Hopkins University Press, 2003.

Hacker, Louis M. "If Beer Returns." *Current History* 37 (January 1933): 385–392.

Haley, Andrew. *Turning the Tables: Restaurants and the Rise of the American Middle Class, 1880–1920.* Chapel Hill: University of North Carolina Press, 2011.

Haller, Mark H. "Bootleggers and Businessmen: From City Slums to City Builders." In *Law, Alcohol, and Order: Perspectives on National Prohibition,* edited by David Kyvig, 139–158. Westport, CT: Greenwood Press, 1985.

Hannickel, Erica. *Empire of Vines: Wine Culture in America*. Philadelphia: University of Pennsylvania Press, 2013.

Harris, Jessica B. *High on the Hog: A Culinary Journey from Africa to America*. New York: Bloomsbury USA, 2011.

Hayden-Smith, Rose. *Sowing the Seeds of Victory: American Gardening Programs of World War I*. Jefferson, NC: McFarland & Company, 2014.

Heap, Chad. *Slumming: Sexual and Racial Encounters in American Nightlife, 1885–1940*. Chicago: University of Chicago Press, 2009.

Hegarty, Marilyn E. "Patriot or Prostitute? Sexual Discourses, Print Media, and American Women during World War II." *Journal of Women's History* 10, no. 2 (Summer 1998): 112–136.

Heinz, William. *California's Napa Valley: One Hundred Sixty Years of Wine Making*. San Francisco: Scottwall Associates, 1999.

Helstosky, Carol F. *Garlic and Oil: Food and Politics in Italy*. New York: Berg, 2004.

Henderson, Yandell. *A New Deal in Liquor: A Plea for Dilution*. Garden City, NY: Doubleday, Dornan and Company, 1934.

Henthorn, Cynthia Lee. *From Submarines to Suburbs: Selling a Better America, 1939–1959*. Athens: Ohio University Press, 2006.

Hernon, Peter, and Terry Ganey. *Under the Influence: The Unauthorized Story of the Anheuser-Busch Dynasty*. New York: Simon & Schuster, 1991.

Heron, Craig. *Booze: A Distilled History*. Toronto: Between the Lines, 2003.

Herzberg, David. *Happy Pills in America: From Miltown to Prozac*. Baltimore: Johns Hopkins University Press, 2008.

———. *White Market Drugs: Big Pharma and the Hidden History of Addiction in America*. Chicago: University of Chicago Press, 2020.

High, Jack, and Clayton A. Coppin. "Wiley and the Whiskey Industry: Strategic Behavior in the Passage of the Pure Food Act." *Business History Review* 62, no. 2 (Summer 1988): 286–309.

Hiltner, Aaron. *Taking Leave, Taking Liberties: American Troops on the World War II Home Front*. Chicago: University of Chicago Press, 2020.

Himmelstein, Jerome L. *The Strange Career of Marihuana: Politics and Ideology of Drug Control in America*. Westport, CT: Greenwood Press, 1983.

Hooker, Richard J. *Food and Drink in America: A History*. Indianapolis, IN: Bobbs-Merrill Company, 1981.

Horowitz, Roger. *Kosher USA: How Coke Became Kosher and Other Tales of Modern Food*. New York: Columbia University Press, 2016.

Howard, Sarah. "Selling Wine to the French: Official Attempts to Increase French Wine Consumption, 1931–1936." *Food and Foodways* 12, no. 4 (2004): 197–224.

Howard, Vicki. *Brides, Inc.: American Weddings and the Business of Tradition*. Philadelphia: University of Pennsylvania Press, 2006.

———. *From Main Street to Mall: The Rise and Fall of the American Department Store*. Philadelphia: University of Pennsylvania Press, 2015.

Hutchinson, Daniel. "The Oasis: German POWS at Fort McClellan." *Alabama Heritage* (Summer 2008): 40–52.

Jacobs, Meg. "'How About Some Meat?': The Office of Price Administration, Consumption Politics, and State Building from the Bottom Up, 1941–1946." *Journal of American History* 84 (December 1997): 910–941.

———. *Pocketbook Politics: Economic Citizenship in Twentieth-Century America*. Princeton, NJ: Princeton University Press, 2007.

Jacobson, Lisa. *Raising Consumers: Children and the American Mass Market in the Early Twentieth Century*. New York: Columbia University Press, 2004.

———. "Will It Be Wine or Cocktails? The Quest to Build a Mass Market for California Wine after Prohibition." *Enterprise and Society* 18, no. 2 (June 2017): 360–399.

Johnston, Josée, and Shyon Baumann. "Democracy versus Distinction: A Study of Omnivirousness in Gourmet Food Writing." *American Journal of Sociology* 113, no. 1 (July 2007): 165–204.

Kane, Liam. "Paving the Way to a 'Good Understanding': Recreation and Australian-American Army Cooperation in the South West Pacific Area, 1941–1945." *Australian Journal of American Studies* 37, no. 2 (December 2018): 27–52.

Kasson, John F. *Rudeness and Civility: Manners in Nineteenth-Century Urban America*. New York: Hill and Wang, 1991.

Kay, H. H. "Balance-Sheet of Repeal." *Survey Graphic* 26, no. 1 (January 1937): 20–24.

Kelley, Robin D. G. "The Riddle of the Zoot: Malcolm Little and Black Cultural Politics in World War II." In *Race Rebels: Culture, Politics, and the Black Working Class*, 161–182. New York: Free Press, 1994.

Kennedy, David M. *Freedom from Fear: The American People in Depression and War, 1929–1945*. New York: Oxford University Press, 1999.

Kennedy, Elizabeth Lapovsky, and Madeline D. Davis. *Boots of Leather, Slippers of Gold: The History of a Lesbian Community*, 20th Anniversary ed. New York: Routledge, 2014.

Kennett, Lee. *G.I.: The American Soldier in World War II*, Kindle ed. New York: Charles Scribner's Sons, 2014.

Kerr, K. Austin. "The American Brewing Industry, 1865–1920." In *The Dynamics of the International Brewing Industry Since 1800*, edited by R. G. Wilson and T. R. Gourvish, 176–192. New York: Routledge, 1998.

———. *Organized for Prohibition: A New History of the Anti-Saloon League*. New Haven, CT: Yale University Press, 1985.

———. "The Rebirth of Brewing and Distilling in the United States in 1933: Government Policy and Industry Structure." *Business and Economic History On-Line* 3 (2005): 1–10.

Kessler-Harris, Alice. *Out to Work: A History of Wage-Earning Women in the United States*. New York: Oxford University Press, 1982.

Kladstrup, Don, and Petie Kladstrup. *Wine and War: The French, the Nazis, and the Battle for France's Greatest Treasure*. New York: Broadway Books, 2002.

Kobler, John. *Ardent Spirits: The Rise and Fall of Prohibition*. New York: Putnam, 1973.

Kruse, Kevin M., and Stephen Tuck, eds. *Fog of War: The Second World War and the Civil Rights Movement*. New York: Oxford University Press, 2012.

Kyvig, David. *Repealing National Prohibition*, 2nd ed. Kent, OH: Kent State University Press, 2000.

———. "Women Against Prohibition." *American Quarterly* 28, no. 4 (Autumn 1976): 465–482.

Laird, Pamela. *Advertising Progress: American Business and the Rise of Consumer Marketing*. Baltimore: Johns Hopkins University Press, 1998.

Lapsley, James. *Bottled Poetry: Napa Winemaking from Prohibition to the Modern Era*. Berkeley: University of California Press, 1996.

Larson, Cedric. "The Drinkers Dictionary." *American Speech* 12 (April 1937): 87–92.

Lauer, Josh, and Kenneth Lipartito. "Introduction: Surveillance under Capitalism," In *Surveillance Capitalism in America*, 1–26. Philadelphia: University of Pennsylvania Press, 2021.

———, eds. *Surveillance Capitalism in America*. Philadelphia: University of Pennsylvania Press, 2021.

Lears, Jackson. *Fables of Abundance: A Cultural History of Advertising in America*. New York: Basic Books, 1994.

Leff, Mark H. "The Politics of Sacrifice on the American Home Front in World War II." *Journal of American History* 77, no. 4 (March 1991): 1296–1318.

Lender, Mark Edward. "The Historian and Repeal: A Survey of the Literature and Research Opportunities." In *Law, Alcohol, and Order: Perspectives on National Prohibition*, edited by David Kyvig, 177–206. Westport, CT: Greenwood Press, 1985.

Lender, Mark Edward, and James Kirby Martin. *Drinking in America: A History*, rev. ed. New York: Free Press, 1987.

Lerner, Michael. *Dry Manhattan: Prohibition in New York City*. Cambridge, MA: Harvard University Press, 2007.

Leuchtenberg, William. *The Perils of Prosperity, 1914–1932*, 2nd ed. Chicago: University of Chicago Press, 1993 [1958].

Levenstein, Harvey. *Paradox of Plenty: A Social History of Eating in Modern America*, rev. ed. Berkeley: University of California Press, 2003.

———. *Revolution at the Table: The Transformation of the American Diet*. Berkeley: University of California Press, 2003.

Levine, Harry G. "The Birth of American Alcohol Control: Prohibition, the Power Elite, and the Problem of Lawlessness." *Contemporary Drug Problems* (Spring 1985): 63–115. https://qcpages.qc.cuny.edu/~hlevine/The-Birth-of-American-Alcohol-Control.pdf.

———. "Vocabulary of Drunkenness." *Journal of Studies on Alcohol* 42 (November 1981): 1038–1051.

Levine, Harry G., and Craig Reinarman. "From Prohibition to Regulation: Lessons from Alcohol Policy for Drug Policy." *Milbank Quarterly* 69, no. 3 (1999): 461–494.

Levine, Lawrence. "American Culture and the Great Depression." In *The Unpredictable Past: Exploration in American Cultural History*, 206–230. New York: Oxford University Press, 1993.

———. *Highbrow/Lowbrow: The Emergence of Cultural Hierarchy in America*. Cambridge, MA: Harvard University Press, 1995.

Le Zotte, Jennifer. "Seeing Straight: Policing Sexualities in 1930s Manhattan Nightclubs." In *Surveillance Capitalism in America*, edited by Josh Lauer and Kenneth Lipartito, 118–137. Philadelphia: University of Pennsylvania Press, 2021.

Lieberman, Hallie. "Selling Sex Toys: Marketing and the Meaning of Vibrators in Early Twentieth-Century America." *Enterprise and Society* 17, no. 2 (June 2016): 393–433.

Linderman, Gerald F. *The World within War: America's Combat Experience in World War II*. New York: Free Press, 1997.

Lingeman, Richard R. *Don't You Know There's a War On? The American Home Front, 1941–1945*. New York: G.P. Putnam's Sons, 1970.

Littauer, Amanda H. *Bad Girls: Young Women, Sex, and Rebellion before the Sixties*. Chapel Hill: University of North Carolina Press, 2015.

Lukacs, Paul. *American Vintage: The Rise of American Wine*. New York: Houghton Mifflin, 2000.

Maines, Rachel. "Socially Camouflaged Technologies: The Case of the Electromechanical Vibrator." *IEEE Technology and Society Magazine* 8, no. 2 (July 1989): 3–11.

Malleck, Dan. *Try to Control Yourself: The Regulation of Public Drinking in Post-Prohibition Ontario, 1927–44*. Vancouver: UBC Press, 2012.

Marchand, Roland. *Advertising the American Dream: Making Way for Modernity, 1920–1940*. Berkeley: University of California Press, 1985.

———. *Creating the Corporate Soul: The Rise of Public Relations and Corporate Imagery in American Big Business*. Berkeley: University of California Press, 1998.

Marrus, Michael R. *Samuel Bronfman: The Life and Times of Seagram's Mr. Sam*. Hanover, NH: Brandeis University Press, 1991.

Marsh, Margaret. *Suburban Lives*. New Brunswick, NJ: Rutgers University Press, 1990.

Marten, James. "'No Beer for Babies': The Child Welfare Exhibit," *Chicago History* 33 (Spring 2005): 36–51.

Martin, Scott C. *Devil of the Domestic Sphere: Temperance, Gender, and Middle-Class Ideology, 1800–1860*. DeKalb: Northern Illinois University Press, 2008.

Marx De Salcedo, Anastacia. *Combat-Ready Kitchen: How the U.S. Military Shapes the Way You Eat*. New York: Current, 2015.

Materson, Lisa G. "African American Women, Prohibition, and the 1928 Presidential Election." *Journal of Women's History* 21, no. 1 (Spring 2009): 63–86.

Mauro, James. *Twilight at the World of Tomorrow: Genius, Madness, Murder and the 1939 World's Fair on the Brink of War*. New York: Ballantine Books, 2010.

May, Elaine Tyler. *Great Expectations: Marriage and Divorce in Post-Victorian America*. Chicago: University of Chicago Press, 1980.

———. "Myths and Realities of the American Family." In *A History of Private Life: Riddles of Identity in Modern Times*, vol. 5, edited by Antoine Prost and Gerard Vincent, 539–594. Cambridge, MA: Belknap Press of Harvard University Press, 1991

May, Lary. "Making the American Consensus: The Narrative of Conversion and Subversion in World War II Films." In *The War in American Culture: Society and Consciousness during World War II*, edited by Lewis A. Erenberg and Susan E. Hirsh, 71–102. Chicago: University of Chicago Press, 1996.

McClellan, Michelle L. *Lady Lushes: Gender, Alcoholism, and Medicine in Modern America*. New Brunswick, NJ: Rutgers University Press, 2017.

McCracken, Grant. *Culture and Consumption: New Approaches to the Symbolic Character of Consumer Goods and Activities*. Bloomington: Indiana University Press, 1988.

McGirr, Lisa. *The War on Alcohol: Prohibition and the Rise of the American State*. New York: W. W. Norton & Company, 2016.

McGovern, Charles F. *Sold American: Consumption and Citizenship, 1890–1945*. Chapel Hill: University of North Carolina Press, 2006.

McManus, John C. *The Deadly Brotherhood: The American Combat Soldier in World War II*. New York: Ballantine Books, 1998.

MeasuringWorth.com. "Seven Ways to Compute the Relative Value of a U.S. Dollar Amount: 1790-Present." https://www.measuringworth.com/calculators/uscompare/.

Mendelson, Richard. *From Demon to Darling: A Legal History of Wine in America*. Berkeley: University of California Press, 2009.

Miller, John E. "Ernie Pyle: From Hoosier Farm Boy to the GIs' Friend." *American History* (October 2005): 40.

Mills, Geofrey, and Hugh Rockoff. "Compliance with Price Controls in the United States and the United Kingdom during World War II." *Journal of Economic History* 47 (March 1987): 197–213.

Milov, Sarah. *The Cigarette: A Political History*. Cambridge, MA: Harvard University Press, 2019.

Mintz, Steven, and Susan Kellogg. *Domestic Revolutions: A Social History of American Family Life*. New York: Free Press, 1988.

Mitenbuler, Reid. *Bourbon Empire: The Past and Future of America's Whiskey*. New York: Penguin Books, 2015.

Mitgang, Herbert. *Once Upon a Time in New York: Jimmy Walker, Franklin Roosevelt, and the Last Great Battle of the Jazz Age*. New York: Free Press, 2000.

Mittleman, Amy. *Brewing Battles: A History of American Beer*. New York: Algora Publishing, 2008.

Morehouse, Maggi M. *Fighting in the Jim Crow Army: Black Men and Women Remember World War II*. Lanham, MD: Rowan & Littlefield, 2000.

Mouré, Kenneth. "Capitalism's Black Heart in Wartime France." In *Capitalism's Hidden Worlds*, edited by Kenneth Lipartito and Lisa Jacobson, 139–156. Philadelphia: University of Pennsylvania Press, 2020.

———. *Marché Noir: The Economy of Survival in Second World War France*. New York: Cambridge University Press, 2023.

Mouré, Kenneth, and Paula Schwartz. "On Vit Mal: Food Shortages and Popular Culture in Occupied France, 1940–1944." *Food Culture and Society* 10, no. 2 (2007): 261–295.

Morabito, Greg. "A Food Tour of the 1939 World's Fair." *Eater New York* (blog), June 19, 2012. https://ny.eater.com/2012/6/19/6581073/a-food-tour-of-the-1939-worlds-fair.
Mumford, Kevin. *Interzones: Black/White Sex Districts in Chicago and New York in the Early Twentieth Century.* New York: Columbia University Press, 1997.
Murdock, Catherine Gilbert. *Domesticating Drink: Women, Men, and Alcohol in America, 1870–1940.* Baltimore: Johns Hopkins University Press, 1998.
Murphy, Mary. "Bootlegging Mothers and Drinking Daughters: Gender and Prohibition in Butte, Montana." *American Quarterly* 46 (June 1994): 174–194.
Nasaw, David. *The Chief: The Life of William Randolph Hearst.* New York: Mariner Books, 2001.
Neuhaus, Jessamyn. *Manly Meals and Mom's Home Cooking: Cookbooks and Gender in Modern America.* Baltimore: Johns Hopkins University Press, 2003.
Neumann, Caryn E. "The End of Gender Solidarity: The History of the Women's Organization for National Prohibition Reform in the United States, 1929–1933." *Journal of Women's History* 9 (Summer 1997): 31–51.
Nichols, David ed. *Ernie's War: The Best of Ernie Pyle's World War II Dispatches.* New York: Simon and Schuster, 1987.
Nordstrom, Justin ed. *The Provisions of War: Expanding the Boundaries of Food and Conflict, 1840–1990.* Fayetteville: University of Arkansas Press, 2021.
Ogle, Maureen. *Ambitious Brew: The Story of American Beer.* New York: Harcourt, 2006.
Ogren, Kathy. *The Jazz Revolution: Twenties America and the Meaning of Jazz.* New York: Oxford University Press, 1989.
Okrent, Daniel. *Last Call: The Rise and Fall of Prohibition.* New York: Scribner, 2010.
Olson, Mancur. *The Logic of Collective Action: Public Goods and The Theory of Groups.* Cambridge, MA: Harvard University Press, 1971 [1965].
Opie, Frederick Douglass. *Hog and Hominy: Soul Food from Africa to America.* New York: Columbia University Press, 2008.
Ostrander, Gilman. *The Prohibition Movement in California, 1848–1933.* University of California Publications in History, vol. 57. Berkeley: University of California Press, 1957.
Pagán, Eduardo Obregón. *Murder at the Sleepy Lagoon: Zoot Suits, Race, and Riots in Wartime L.A..* Charlotte: University of North Carolina Press, 2003.
Panunzio, Constantine. "The Foreign Born and Prohibition." *Annals of the American Academy of Political and Social Science* 163 (September 1932): 147–154.
Parsons, Elaine Frantz. *Manhood Lost: Fallen Drunkards and Redeeming Women in the Nineteenth-Century United States.* Baltimore: Johns Hopkins University Press, 2003.
———. "Risky Business: The Uncertain Boundaries of Manhood in the Midwestern Saloon." *Journal of Social History* (Winter 2000): 283–307.
Pauly, Phillip J. "Is Liquor Intoxicating? Scientists, Prohibition, and the Normalization of Drinking." *American Journal of Public Health* 84, no. 2 (February 1994): 305–313.

Pegram, Thomas. *Battling Demon Rum: The Struggle for a Dry America, 1800–1933*. Chicago: Ivan R. Dee, 1998.
Peiss, Kathy. *Hope in a Jar: The Making of America's Beauty Culture*. New York: Metropolitan Books, 1998.
———. "Making Faces: The Cosmetics Industry and the Cultural Construction of Gender, 1890–1930." In *Unequal Sisters: An Inclusive Reader in U.S. Women's History*, 4th ed, edited by Vicki L. Ruiz and Ellen Carol DuBois, 342–362. New York: Routledge, 2008.
———. *Zoot Suit: The Enigmatic Career of an Extreme Style*. Philadelphia: University of Pennsylvania Press, 2011.
Pennock, Pamela E. *Advertising Sin and Sickness: The Politics of Alcohol and Tobacco Marketing, 1950–1990*. DeKalb: Northern Illinois Press, 2007.
Pennock Pamela E., and K. Austin Kerr. "In the Shadow of Prohibition: Domestic American Alcohol Policy Since 1933." *Business History* 47, no. 3 (July 2005): 383–400.
Pereira-Alvarez, Rochelle. "Make Any Occasion a Special Event: Hospitality, Domesticity, and Female Cordial Consumption in Magazine Advertising, 1950–1969." In *Women in Magazines: Research, Representation, Production and Consumption*, edited by Rachel Ritchie, Sue Hawkins, Nicola Phillips, and S. Jay Kleinberg, 81–91. New York: Routledge, 2016.
Peretti, Burton W. *Jazz in American Culture*. Chicago: Ivan R. Dee, 1997.
———. *Nightclub City: Politics and Amusement in Manhattan*. Philadelphia: University of Pennsylvania Press, 2007.
Perry, Kennetta Hammond. *London Is the Place for Me: Black Britons, Citizenship, and the Politics of Race*. New York: Oxford University Press, 2015.
Petrick, Gabriella M. "'Purity as Life': H. J. Heinz, Religious Sentiment, and the Beginning of the Industrial Diet." *History and Technology* 27, no. 1 (March 2011): 37–64
Phillips, Rod. *Alcohol: A History*. Chapel Hill: University of North Carolina Press, 2014.
Pilcher, Jeffrey M. "Imperial Hops: Beer in the Age of Empire." *Global Food History* 10, no. 1 (2024): 52–67.
Pinney, Thomas. *A History of Wine in America: From Prohibition to the Present*. Berkeley: University of California Press, 2005.
Polenberg, Richard. *War and Society: The United States, 1941–1945*, rev. ed. Westport, CT: Greenwood Press, 1980 [1972].
Pollan, Michael. *How to Change Your Mind: What the New Science of Psychedelics Teaches Us about Consciousness, Dying, Addiction, Depression, and Transcendence*. New York: Penguin Press, 2018.
Powers, Madelon. *Faces Along the Bar: Lore and Order in the Workingman's Saloon, 1870–1920*. Chicago: University of Chicago Press, 2004.
———. "Women and Public Drinking, 1890–1920." *History Today* (February 1995): 46–52.
Pryzybylek, Leslie. "'No Attempt at Concealment': Ray Sprigle and Pittsburgh's Black Market Meat Scandal." *Pennsylvania Magazine of History and Biography* 142, no. 3 (October 2018): 405–408.

Purcell, Aaron D. "Bourbon to Bullets: Louisville's Distilling Industry during World War II, 1941–1945." *Register of the Kentucky Historical Society* 96, no. 1 (Winter 1998): 61–87.
Pyle, Ernie. *Here Is Your War: The Story of G.I. Joe*. Lincoln: University of Nebraska Press, 2004.
———. *Brave Men*. Lincoln: University of Nebraska Press, 2001.
Rappaport, Erika. *A Thirst for Empire: How Tea Shaped the Modern World*. Princeton, NJ: Princeton University Press, 2017.
Regan, Gary, and Mardee Haidin Regan. *The Book of Bourbon and Other Fine American Whiskeys*. Shelburne, VT: Chapters Publishing Ltd., 1995.
Regan-Lefebvre, Jennifer. *Imperial Wine: How the British Empire Made Wine's New World*. Oakland: University of California Press, 2022.
Reich, Steven A. "Food and Drink: Introduction." In *The World of Jim Crow America*, vol. 1, edited by Steven A. Reich, 277–278. Santa Barbara: Greenwood Press, 2019.
Reinarman, Craig. "Policing Pleasure: Food, Drugs, and the Politics of Ingestion." *Gastronomica* 7, no. 3 (Summer 2007): 53–61.
Richert, Lucas. *Strange Trips: Science, Culture, and the Regulation of Drugs*. Montreal: McGill Queen's University Press, 2018.
Roberts, Mary Louise. *What Soldiers Do: Sex and the American GI in World War II France*. Chicago: University of Chicago Press, 2013.
Robinson, Daniel J. "'The Luxury of Moderate Use': Seagram and Moderation Advertising, 1934–1955." In *Communicating Canada's Past: Essays in Media History*, edited by Gene Allen and Daniel J. Robinson, 109–139. Toronto: University of Toronto Press, 2009.
Rockoff, Hugh. *America's Economic Way of War: War and the US Economy from the Spanish American War to the Persian Gulf War*. New York: Cambridge University Press, 2012.
———. "Can Price Controls Work?" In *Second Thoughts: Myths and Morals of U.S. Economic History*, edited by Donald McCloskey, 132–135. New York: Oxford University Press, 1993.
———. *Drastic Measures: A History of Wage and Price Controls in the United States*. New York: Cambridge University Press, 1984.
Roizen, Ron. "How Does the Nation's 'Alcohol Problem' Change from Era to Era? Stalking the Social Logic of Problem-Definition Transformations Since Repeal." In *Altering American Consciousness: The History of Alcohol and Drug Use in the United States, 1800–2000*, edited by Sarah Tracy and Caroline Acker, 61–90. Amherst: University of Massachusetts Press, 2004.
Ronnenberg, Herman W. "The American Brewing Industry Since 1920," In *The Dynamics of the International Brewing Industry Since 1800*, edited by R.G. Wilson and T.R. Gourvish, 193–212. New York: Routledge, 1998.
Rorabaugh, W.J. "Drinking in the 'Thin Man' Films, 1934–1947." *Social History of Alcohol and Drugs* 18 (2003): 51–68.
Rose, Kenneth D. *American Women and the Repeal of Prohibition*. New York: New York University Press, 1996.

Rosenzweig, Roy. *Eight Hours for What We Will: Workers and Leisure in an Industrial City, 1870–1920*. Cambridge, UK: Cambridge University Press, 1983.

Rotskoff, Lori. *Love on the Rocks: Men, Women, and Alcohol in Post-World War II America*. Chapel Hill: University of North Carolina Press, 2002.

Rubin, Jay. "The Wet War: American Liquor Control, 1941–1945." In *Alcohol, Reform, and Society: The Liquor Issue in Social Context*, edited by Jack S. Blocker, 235–258. Westport, CT: Greenwood Press, 1979

Russek, Audrey. "Appetites without Prejudice: U.S. Foreign Restaurants and the Globalization of American Food between the Wars." *Food and Foodways* 19, no. 1/2 (2011): 34–55.

Rutherford, Phillip T. "On Arms and Eggs: GI Egg Mania on the Battlefields of World War II." *Food and Foodways* 25, no. 2 (2017): 123–141.

Rydell, Robert. *All the World's a Fair: Visions of Empire at American International Expositions, 1876–1916*. Chicago: University of Chicago Press, 1984.

———. *World of Fairs: The Century-of-Progress Expositions*. Chicago: University of Chicago Press, 1993.

Sackman, Douglas Cazaux. *Orange Empire: California and the Fruits of Eden*. Berkeley: University of California Press, 2005.

Samuel, Lawrence R. *Pledging Allegiance: American Identity and the Bond Drive of World War II*. Washington, DC: Smithsonian Institution, 1997.

Scanlon, Jennifer. *Inarticulate Longings: The Ladies' Home Journal, Gender, and the Promises of Consumer Culture*. New York: Routledge, 1995.

Schivelbusch, Wolfgang. *Tastes of Paradise: A Social History of Spices, Stimulants, and Intoxicants*, translated from the German by David Jacobson. New York: Vintage Books, 1992.

Schrad, Mark Lawrence. *Smashing the Liquor Machine: A Global History of Prohibition*. New York: Oxford University Press, 2021.

Schrijvers, Peter. *The Crash of Ruin: American Combat Soldiers in Europe during World War II*. New York: New York University Press, 1998.

Segrave, Kerry. *Endorsements in Advertising: A Social History*. Jefferson, NC: McFarland & Company, 2005.

Seikaly, Sherene. "A Nutritional Economy: The Calorie, Development, and War in Mandate Palestine." In *Home Fronts: Britain and the Empire at War, 1939–45*, edited by Mark J. Crowley and Sandra Trudgen Dawson, 37–58. Suffolk, UK: Boydell and Brewer, 2017.

Shapiro, Laura. *Perfection Salad: Women and Cooking at the Turn of the Century*. New York: Farrar, Straus & Giroux, 1986.

———. *Something from the Oven: Reinventing Dinner in 1950s America*. New York: Penguin Books, 2005.

Sinclair, Andrew. *Prohibition: The Era of Excess*. Boston: Little Brown, 1962.

Sklar, Lauren Rebecca. "Constructing G.I. Joe Louis: Cultural Solutions to the 'Negro Problem' during World War II." *Journal of American History* 89, no. 3 (December 2002): 958–983.

Smith, Graham. *When Jim Crow Met John Bull: Black American Soldiers in World War II Britain*. London: I. B. Tauris & Co Ltd, 1987.

Smith, Henry Nash. *Virgin Land: The American West as Symbol and Myth.* Vintage Books, 1957.
Sparrow, James T. "Freedom to Want: The Federal Government and Politicized Consumption in World War II." In *Fog of War: The Second World War and the Civil Rights Movement,* edited by Kevin M. Kruse and Stephen Tuck, 15–31. New York: Oxford University Press, 2012.
———. *Warfare State: World War II Americans and the Age of Big Government.* New York: Oxford University Press, 2011.
Spillane, Joseph F. *Cocaine: From Medical Marvel to Modern Menace in the United States, 1884–1920.* Baltimore: Johns Hopkins University Press, 2000.
Stack, Martin. "Local and Regional Breweries in America's Brewing Industry, 1865–1920." *Business History Review* 74, no. 3 (Autumn 2000): 435–463.
Stack, Martin H. "A Concise History of America's Brewing Industry." EH.Net Encyclopedia, edited by Robert Whaples, July 4, 2003. http://eh.net/encyclopedia/a-concise-history-of-americas-brewing-industry/.
Strauss, David. *Setting the Table for Julia Child: Gourmet Dining in America, 1934–1961.* Baltimore: Johns Hopkins University Press, 2011.
Sullivan, Jack. "Lee Levy and 'Black Cock Vigor Gin.'" *Those Pre-Pro-Whiskey Men!* (blog), November 29, 2018. https://pre-prowhiskeymen.blogspot.com/2018/11/lee-levy-and-black-cock-vigor-gin.html.
Talbot, Margaret. "The Myth of Whiteness in Classical Sculpture." *New Yorker,* October 22, 2018. https://www.newyorker.com/magazine/2018/10/29/the-myth-of-whiteness-in-classical-sculpture.
Tate, Cassandra. *Cigarette Wars: The Triumph of "The Little White Slaver."* New York: Oxford University Press, 1999.
Taylor, Kate. "The Dark Reason Liquor Stores Are Considered Essential Businesses." *Business Insider,* April 20, 2020. https://www.businessinsider.com/liquor-stores-essential-businesses-heres-why-2020-4.
Teiser, Ruth, and Catherine Harroun. "The Volstead Act, Rebirth, and Boom." In *The Book of California Wine,* edited by Doris Muscatine, Maynard A. Amerine, and Bob Thompson, 50–81. Berkeley: University of California Press/Sotheby Publications, 1984.
———. *Winemaking in California.* New York: McGraw-Hill Book Company, 1983.
Thompson, Scott, and Gary Genosko. *Punched Drunk: Alcohol, Surveillance, and the LCBO, 1927–1975.* Halifax, NS: Fernwood Publishing, 2009.
Timberlake, James H. *Prohibition and the Progressive Movement, 1900–1920.* New York: Atheneum, 1970.
Tracy, Sarah W. *Alcoholism in America: From Reconstruction to Prohibition.* Baltimore: Johns Hopkins University Press, 2005.
Tracy, Sarah W., and Caroline Jean Acker, eds. *Altering American Consciousness: The History of Alcohol and Drug Use in the United States, 1800–1920.* Amherst: University of Massachusetts Press, 2004.
Trentmann, Frank, and Fleming Just, eds. *Food and Conflict in Europe in the Age of the Two World Wars.* New York: Palgrave Macmillan, 2006.

Tucker, Lauren, Roxanne Hovland, and Gary Wilcox. "Consumer Response to Seagram's Equivalency Ad Campaign on TV." *Journalism Quarterly* 64 (December 1987): 837–838.
Tye, Larry. *The Father of Spin: Edward L. Bernays and the Birth of Public Relations*. New York: Owl Books, 1998.
Tyrrell, Ian. *Woman's World/Woman's Empire: The Woman's Temperance Christian Union in International Perspective, 1880–1930*. Chapel Hill: University of North Carolina Press, 1991.
Valverde, Mariana. "A Postcolonial Women's Law? Domestic Violence and the Ontario Liquor Board's 'Indian List,' 1950–1990." *Feminist Studies* 30, no. 3 (Fall 2004): 566–588.
Vaughan-Thomas, Wynford. *Anzio*, Kindle ed. Arcole Publishing, 2017 [1961].
Veach, Michael. *Kentucky Bourbon Whiskey: An American Heritage*. Lexington: University Press of Kentucky, 2013.
Veit, Helen Zoe. *Modern Food, Moral Food: Self-Control, Science, and the Rise of Modern American Eating in the Early Twentieth Century*. Chapel Hill: University of North Carolina Press, 2013.
———. "'We Were a Soft People': Asceticism, Self-Discipline and American Food Conservation in the First World War." *Food, Culture, and Society* 10, no. 2 (Summer 2007): 167–190.
Vernon, James. *Hunger: A Modern History*. Cambridge, MA: Harvard University Press, 2007.
Virden, Jenel. "Warm Beer and Cold Canons: US Army Chaplains and Alcohol Consumption in World War II." *Journal of American Studies* 48 no. 1 (February 2014): 79–97.
Warburton, Clark. *The Economic Results of Prohibition*. New York: Columbia University Press, 1932.
Ward, Jason Morgan. "'A War for States' Rights': The White Supremacist Vision of Double Victory." In *Fog of War: The Second World War and the Civil Rights Movement*, edited by Kevin M. Kruse and Stephen Tuck, 126–144. New York: Oxford University Press, 2012.
Ware, Caroline. *Greenwich Village, 1920–1930*. New York: Houghton Mifflin Co., 1935.
Watson, James. "China's Big Mac Attack." In *The Cultural Politics of Food and Eating*, edited by James Watson and Melissa L. Caldwell, 70–79. Malden, MA: Blackwell Publishing, 2005.
Watson, James L., and Melissa L. Caldwell, eds. *The Cultural Politics of Food and Eating*. Malden, MA: Blackwell Publishing, 2005.
Weiner, Mark. "Consumer Culture and Participatory Democracy: The Story of Coca-Cola during World War II." *Food and Foodways* 6, no. 2 (1996): 109–129.
Weingartner, James J. "Trophies of War: US Troops and the Mutilation of Japanese War Dead, 1941–1945." *Pacific Historical Review* 61, no. 1 (February 1992): 53–67.
Westbrook, Robert B. "Fighting for the American Family: Private Interests and Political Obligation in World War II." In *The Power of Culture: Critical*

Essays in American History, edited by Richard Wightman Fox and T. J. Jackson Lears, 195–221. Chicago: University of Chicago Press, 1993.

———. *Why We Fought: Forging American Obligations in World War II*. Washington, DC: Smithsonian Books, 2010.

Wilson, Mark R. *Destructive Creation: American Business and the Winning of World War II*. Philadelphia: University of Pennsylvania Press, 2016.

Woeste, Victoria Saker. *The Farmer's Benevolent Trust: Law and Agricultural Cooperation in Industrial America, 1986–1945*. Chapel Hill: University of North Carolina Press, 1998.

Wolcott, Victoria. *Race, Riots, and Roller Coasters: The Struggle over Segregated Recreation in America*. Philadelphia: University of Pennsylvania Press, 2012.

Wondrich, David. "The Mint Julep's Brandy Roots." *Daily Beast*, May 6, 2017. https://www.thedailybeast.com/the-mint-juleps-brandy-roots.

Wylie, Philip. *Generation of Vipers*. Champaign, IL: Dalkey Archive Press, 1996 [1942].

Wynn, Neil A. *The African American Experience during World War II*. Lanham, MD: Rowman & Littlefield Publishers, 2010.

Yan, Yunxiang. "Of Hamburger and Social Space: Consuming McDonald's in Beijing." In *Consumer Revolution in Urban China*, edited by Deborah Davis, 201–225. Berkeley: University of California Press, 2000.

Young, Katherine. *My Old New York Neighborhoods*. New York: Profile Press, 1979.

Zlotnick, Susan. "Domesticating Imperialism: Curry and Cookbooks in Victorian England." *Frontiers: A Journal of Women Studies* 16, no. 2/3 (1996): 51–68.

DISSERTATIONS, THESES, CONFERENCE PAPERS

Blahut, Adam. "Raising the Bar: Consumption, Gender, and the Birth of a New Public Drinking Culture." PhD dissertation, University of New Mexico, Albuquerque, 2014

Clark, Sierra Burnett. "A Liquid Spirit: Materiality and Meaning in the Making of Quality American Whiskey." PhD dissertation, New York University, 2014.

Hutchinson, Ralph Burton. "California Wine Industry." PhD dissertation, University of California, Los Angeles, 1969.

Laforge, Robert G. "Misplaced Priorities: A History of Federal Alcohol Regulation and Public Health Policy." PhD dissertation, Johns Hopkins University, 1987.

McShane, Charles Clifton. "Class, Christ, and Cocktails: The Clash of Business Boosterism and Southern Baptism in Charlotte, North Carolina, 1965–1980." MA thesis, University of North Carolina at Charlotte, 2011.

Roizen, Ronald. "The American Discovery of Alcoholism, 1933–1939." PhD dissertation, University of California, Berkeley, 1991.

Stack, Martin. "Liquid Bread: An Examination of the American Brewing Industry, 1865–1940." PhD dissertation, University of Notre Dame, 1998.

Index

2.75 percent beer, 20, 23, 27–288
3.2 percent beer: arguments favoring legalization of, 23–24, 27–31; compared to 2.75 percent beer, 23, 27–28; limited availability in PX stores, 238; military personnel's attitudes toward, 245–246, 276–277; relative potency of, 312n26; testing of alcohol content, 37, 294n100. *See also* United States military, alcoholic beverage policies

Abrams, Sol, 98
Adams, Leon, 75, 78–79, 89, 90–91, 93; development of wine study correspondence course, 229–231; publicity work for Wine Institute, 82–83, 89, 205
Adams, Michael, 246
Addams, Jane, 57
advertising of alcoholic beverages: cooptation of temperance rhetoric, 106, 113–115, 116–117; criticisms of, 71–72, 102, 123; inculcating new habits of responsible drinking, 118–119; regulations barring health claims, 209, 212; regulation of, 63, 64, 102, 123; spending on, 204; veiled drug references in, 128. *See also* Calvert whiskey; Schenley Distillers; Seagram Company; United States Brewers' Foundation; Wine Advisory Board
African Americans. *See* Black American military personnel; Black American officers; Black Americans
Agee, James, 280
alcoholic beverage regulations: California's liberal wine policies, 88, 232, 332n144; disorderly conduct laws, 67; dry states, 60; federal government regulations, 62; flaws in federalist approach to liquor control, 177–178, 182; licensing fees, 96; local option provisions, 60–61, 62; new modes of consumer surveillance, 63–64, 67; monopoly states, 61, 63, 64, 177–178, 182; open states, 61, 63, 177–178; principle of dilution, 62, 67, 299n111; regulation of 3.2 percent beer, 36–39; regulation of on-premises sales in restaurants and hotels, 61–62; regulation of taverns and bars, 64–66, 67, 68; rejection of federal monopoly, 64; three-tier distribution system, 61, 96; wide variations in, 60, 233
alcoholic beverages: changing patterns of consumption, 42, 48–53, 84–85; cultural reinvention of, 1–2, 3, 4, 5, 6, 12, 106–107, 202–203, 234–235; limits of alcohol's cultural reinvention, 274–275, 277, 283–284; public relations value of alcohol revenues, 98, 136, 150–151, 188; spending on during World War II, 175; taxation of, 3, 15–16, 47, 62, 84, 85–86, 88, 183, 198,

367

alcoholic beverages *(continued)*
232; World War II's impact on alcohol's cultural reinvention, 8, 9, 144, 169–170, 236, 276–277, 283–284; World War II's impact on veterans' preferences in, 268–269, 270*fig*
Alcoholics Anonymous, 62, 268
alcoholism, 3, 82, 113, 115, 268, 280; representation in film of, 277–278, 282
Alcohol Tax Unit, 102, 123, 183, 186–187
Alexander, Wilford S., 92–93, 102
Allen, Frederick Lewis, 2
Allied Liquor Industries, 188
Ambrose, Stephen, 246
American Brewers' Association (ABA), 95, 103
American Federation of Labor (AFL), 20, 31, 83, 102, 146
American Legion, 146
American Pomological Society, 76
American Society for the Promotion of Temperance (ASPT), 105–106
American Temperance-Wine League, 53
Amerine, Maynard, 44
Anderson, Frederick, 213
Angly, Edward, 43
Anheuser-Busch, 34, 49, 94, 95–96, 97, 128, 168
anti-drunk driving messages, 106, 116, 275, 282
anti-prohibitionists, 5, 15–17, 19–21, 99, 100*fig*, 146–147. *See also* repeal of Prohibition; Volstead Act, proposals to modify
Anti-Saloon League, 27, 37, 38, 61, 145, 293n80
Anzio, 241, 247
Asher, Adolph, 72
Association Against the Prohibition Amendment (AAPA), 19, 20
Astor, Vincent, 20

Babcock, Myles, 253
Baker, George, 255, 272
Ballantine's Scotch, 110, 137
Ballantine Three Ring Inn, 136–137
Bank of America, 80, 91, 92
Baptists, 2
Barkley, Alben, 22
bars: gay and lesbian, 2, 67; regulation of, 64–65, 66; restrictions on women, 66. *See also* taverns
Bass, Benny, 209
Bassenak, Felix, 226

Baxter, Kenneth, 177
Baxter, Norman, 133
beer: alcohol content during Prohibition of, 23; as beverage of moderation and conviviality, 31–33, 93–94, 282; changing consumer preferences for, 52; as cooking aid, 99, 101, 102; as emblem of American national identity and pluralistic values, 144–145, 158–159, 160–161, 169–170, 276; as emblem of whiteness and small town virtue, 156, 158, 280; as "liquid bread" or "liquid food," 9, 95–96, 98–99, 100*fig*, 162; and marital success, 159; as morale booster, 151, 154, 155, 156, 159–160; "near beer," 48–49; "needle beer," 49; popular demands to relegalize during Prohibition, 15–17, 22; representation in film of, 281; sales of, 169
Beer and Wine Revenue Act (1933), 18; provisions of, 34, 36–37; prohibitionists' criticisms of, 293n80.
beer cookery, 99, 101–102
beer gardens, 5, 32–33, 35, 42, 55, 56–57, 66, 138
Beer Institute, 274
beer parades, 15–17, 39
beer parlors, 35, 66
Bentley, Amy, 158
Berchtesgaden, 251
Bergère, Ouida, 327n28
Bernays, Edward, 69–70, 78–79, 94; assessment of brewers' public relations problems, 42, 70–72; public relations campaign for United Brewers Industrial Foundation, 98–99, 101–103
Best Years of Our Lives, The, 280–282
Big Four distillers: acquisition of California wineries, 175, 180, 228, 229; Department of Justice antitrust investigation of, 180
binge drinking, 32
Bingham, Hiram, 18
Bishop, William Henry, 78
Black American military personnel, 11; alliances with the Black press and clergy, 263, 272; civil disobedience and protests by, 260, 266, 272; lawsuits against tavern owners, 262–263, 336n124; racial discrimination off base against, 259–268; racial discrimination on base against, 259–261, 268; reception by Europeans of, 264–265, 336n140; role in postwar civil rights movement of,

267; violent resistance by, 263–264, 266–267; yearnings for decent whiskey, 269.
Black American officers: civil disobedience by, 263, 264; officers' mess of, 261; racial discrimination against, 259, 260
Black Americans, 2, 15, 55–56; culinary traditions, 219, 221; heightened wartime expectations of fair treatment, 259–260; opposition to Prohibition, 15, 19; protests against segregated leisure, 262–263, 267, 268; winemaking by, 85.
Black and Tan clubs, 2
Black & White Whisky, 254
Black Cock Vigor Gin, 72
Blanton, Thomas, 24
Blatz Brewing Company, 34, 96
Blum, John, 182, 245
Boettiger, John, 93
bootlegging: during Prohibition, 47, 52, 110, 293n76; after Prohibition, 43, 47, 61; during World War II, 171, 177, 178, 182, 234
Borah, William, 24
Boudreau, Frank G., 165
Bourke-White, Margaret, 208, 238
Bowles, Chester, 184, 185, 197
Boyle, Hal, 241
Bradley, Omar, 239, 244
Brewers' Board of Trade, 138
brewers' yeast, 10, 49, 128, 162–168, 163fig, 165fig, 217, 317n133
brewing industry: conflicts within, 94–98, 103–104; courtship of women consumers by, 6, 159, 283; classification as "essential" wartime industry, 9, 143, 148, 163fig, 169; divisions over post-repeal tavern regulations, 97–98, 103; involvement in regulating taverns, 103, 322n91; opposition to and support for saloon regulation, 34, 94, 96, 149; packaged beer market, 96–97, 104; Prohibition's impact on, 45, 48–49, 52; public relations problems of, 68, 70–72; public relations strategy of, 98–101, 149, 162, 164–166, 169; use and avoidance of "liquid food" argument, 162, 316n102; regulatory advantages accrued by national shippers, 34; violations of tavern regulations, 68, 97, 103.
Brewing Industry, Inc. (BII), 95–96, 103, 305n101
Brinkley, Alan, 200

Brinkley, David, 175
Brody, Isles, 225, 226
Bronfman, Samuel, 47, 110, 112, 130
Browne Vintners, 47
Brown-Forman Distillers, 45, 134
Bryant, Warren, 261
Budweiser, 23, 168
Burnham, John, 3
Burroughs, Edgar Rice, 209, 327n28
Busch, August A., 23–24, 34–35, 35, 95, 305n101
Buy American campaigns, 83–88, 87fig, 213

Cabot, Richard C., 30
Caddow, Harry, 89, 214, 231
California brandy, 175, 217
California Department of Agriculture, 10, 91
California Department of Public Health, 81
California Fruit Growers, 77
California Marketing Order, 91–92, 304n84
California raisin industry, 88, 90, 92, 232
California wine industry, 7, 10; before Prohibition, 78; Central Valley grape and wine producers, 45–46, 80, 90–92, 205; collaboration with allied industries, 205–206; conflicts within, 80, 89–92; courtship of women consumers by, 6, 89, 207–209, 217; contributions to war effort, 217; impact of whiskey shortages on, 216, 227; Napa Valley winemakers, 45, 216, 231; participation in wine competitions, 275, 326n13; Prohibition's impact on, 43, 44–46, 50–51; resistance to cooperative advertising, 88–89, 91; support for protective tariffs, 84; World War II's impact on wine production and wine quality, 216–217, 234, 328n57; World War II's impact on wine sales, 216, 232–235, 326n4, 328n63; use of European place names by, 206. See also Wine Advisory Board; Wine Institute
California wines, reputation of, 43, 175, 196–197, 229, 231–232, 234, 269, 270fig, 332n144
Caligrapo grape concentrate, 50
calvados, 249, 252, 258
Calvert whiskey, advertising of, 118, 119, 120, 121, 126, 127fig, 128, 129fig, 172fig
Camp Barkeley, 260–261, 263
Camp Clifford, 260

370 | INDEX

Canada: beer parlours in, 66–67; Canadian drinking habits, 130; distilling companies, 110; liquor holidays in, 191, 323n112; liquor smuggling during Prohibition, 47, 64; nutritional claims by brewers in, 316n105; regulation of alcoholic beverages in, 64, 300n120, 300n126; response to Prohibition's repeal, 41; temperance groups in, 312n29.
Capra, Frank, 278, 279–280
Carrillo, Alex, 248–249
Cathay distillers, 254
Catholic Church, 51
Central Winery, 229
Chapin, C. L., 147
Chase, Stuart, 57
Chase, William Sheafe, 36
Chauncey, George, 4, 67
Child's restaurant, 212
Choate, Joseph, 47, 53, 68
Christmas in Connecticut, 225–226
Chrysler, Walter, 15
cigarette advertising, 103
Cobb, Ty, 208, 209, 211*fig*
Coca Cola Company, 166, 202
cocktails: critics of Prohibition-era cocktail culture, 18, 26, 29, 31–32, 33, 80, 293n72; popularity of, 2, 212–213, 215, 283; wartime adaptations of classic recipes, 175, 176*fig*, 177
cognac, 258
Committee on Food and Nutrition, 164, 165, 168
Committee on Food Habits, 153, 154, 160, 166
Committee on Nutrition of Industrial Workers, 166
Conference of Alcoholic Beverage Industries (CABI), 177
Conn, Donlad D., 51
cookbooks, 201–202, 220; beer focused, 99, 101–102; wine focused, 205, 207, 218–219, 223–224
cooperative advertising, 88–89, 91–92
Corzine, Nathan, 159
COVID-19, 284
Creole recipes, 219
Crimmins, John, 197
Cullen-Harrison Act. *See* Beer and Wine Revenue Act
cultures of drink, creation of, 6–7, 53–60, 73–74, 137–138, 228–232, 274–275
culture wars, 2, 4–5, 276

Curtis, Wayne, 268
Cutty Sark, 110

Damico, E. J., 254
Davis, Marni, 72
Davison, Eloise, 99, 101
D-Day, 195–196, 199
Democratic National Convention (1932), 22
Democratic Party, 21, 22, 36, 39, 199
De Palma, Ralph, 209
Department of Justice, Anti-trust Division, 187
Derry, Fred, 281–282
De Vries, Marion, 25, 26, 35, 84
Dewey, Bradley, 195
Dinerstein, Joel, 55
distilled spirits: blamed for drinking problems and social decay, 31, 33, 75, 105; changing consumer preferences for, 52
distilled spirits industry: ban on women in liquor ads, 6, 283; consolidation of during World War II, 197; contributions to war effort and cultivation of patriotic reputation, 188–189, 189*fig*, 277; evasion of price controls, 179–180; government investigations of, 183–184, 191, 194, 196–197, 200; industrial alcohol production during World War II, 171, 188–189, 194, 195, 196, 199; Prohibition's impact on, 43, 45, 52; proposal to regulate as a public utility, 200; public relations problems of, 177, 179, 180, 188, 197, 200, 277, 283; regulation of whiskey labeling, 107–109; resistance to regulations, 69; rivalries within, 107–109, 123, 130; role in exacerbating whiskey shortages, 178, 181; support for liquor furlough, 183, 189–190, 195; support for saloon regulation, 109; wartime acquisition of wineries and distilleries, 175, 179, 180, 194, 228, 229
Distilled Spirits Institute, 69, 123, 283; exhibit at New York World's Fair, 106, 133, 134–135, 136
Dixon, Thomas, 72
domestic hospitality, role of alcoholic beverages in, 58–59, 208–209, 210*fig*, 211*fig*, 221, 222*fig*, 226, 232
Double Victory, 259
drinking as a right, 21, 150, 155, 160, 174, 284; right to "decent whiskey," 186, 190–192, 194, 199–200, 253–254, 272

drinking cultures: Anglo-American, 71; immigrant, 31, 35, 40; European wine-drinking cultures, 25–26, 32–33, 77, 79, 85; German beer-drinking cultures, 32–33; Italian American, 76, 278, 279; working class, 31
drinking guidebooks, 41, 58–60
drinking reformers, 3, 5, 6, 26, 31–35, 41–42, 53–60, 75–80, 215
Dunford, Edward B., 293n80
du Pont family (Irénée, Lammot, Pierre), 20

Earle, Jack, 228
Early, Gerald, 55
Early Fruit Co., 229
Edgewater Beach Hotel, 213
Eighteenth Amendment, 2, 17, 19, 22, 23, 26, 27, 82, 95, 145
Eisenhower, Dwight D., 251, 266
Elson, Alex, 184
Emerson, Thomas, 182
Esquire, 125, 209, 224–225, 226
evangelical Protestant churches, prohibitionist lobbying by, 8, 61, 145–146

Federal Alcohol Administration (FAA), 9, 92, 102–103, 123, 331n127
Federal Alcohol Control Administration (FACA), 43–44, 47, 53, 68, 331n127
Federal Council of Churches of Christ, 58
Federal Farm Board, 51
Federal Writers' Project *America Eats* series, 224
Ferguson, Charles, 104
Field, Edwin, 190
Field, Marshall, 20
films, 73, 86, 115, 160, 192; representations of alcoholic beverages in, 225–226, 277–282; representations of problem drinking in, 277–278, 279, 282
Fine, Richard, 244
Fisher, M. F. K., 223–224
Fitzgerald, F. Scott, 55
Fontaine, Lynn, 208
food and drink columnists, 175, 189, 197, 201, 207–208, 213, 225, 226
food-drug divide, 9–10, 99, 133–134
Food Fights for Freedom campaign, 10, 151, 161, 166, 217, 220
Food Will Win the War campaign, 161
Fort McClellan, 262
Fosdick, Raymond, 62–63
Four Freedoms, 158
Four Roses Bourbon, 269

France: reception of Black troops in, 265, 266; soldiers' wine ration, 258; wine drinking customs, 5, 9, 25, 26, 32, 77, 289n30; wine industry in 1930s, 41; wine promotion in 1930s, 81–82
Frankfort Distillers, 45, 134
Franklin, Benjamin, 24
Freedom from Want, 158, 168, 169
Freeman Field, 263
Freud, Sigmund, 69
Fromm, Alfred, 46
Fruit Industries, Inc., 51

Gailbraith, John, 186
Gallo, Ernest, 44–45, 89
G & W Five Star Blended Whiskey, 192, 193*fig*
Garrett, Paul, 51, 53, 58
Gavin, Clark, 191
General Federation of Women's Clubs, 194
George, Walter, 183
George Lonz Winery, 50
German Americans, 15, 50, 97–98, 101
German army: alcohol looted and requisitioned by, 238, 242, 251, 255, 256*fig*,
German POWs, 262
Germany: alcohol during Allied occupation, 251, 269; beer gardens in, 5, 32–33; reception of Black troops in, 265
Giannini, A. P., 80
Gilbert, Florence, 327n28
gin, 52, 72, 174, 175, 196–197
GIs: alcoholic beverage preferences of, 169, 277; antiprohibitionist attitudes of, 155–156, 169; drinking by, 239–245, 247, 252; Ernie Pyle's portrait of, 239–245, 252; representation in beer advertising, 141, 142*fig*, 150, 154, 155, 160, 239, 240*fig*, 243. *See also* Black American military personnel; white enlisted men
Glenmore Distillery Company, 45, 134
Goering, Hermann, 251
Golden Gate International Exposition (1939–1940), cooking demonstrations at, 205–206
Gompers, Samuel, 20, 31
gourmet dining societies, 215, 299n99
Gourmet magazine, 215, 218, 219, 224–225
Grape Growers' League of California, 25, 26

grapes: Alicante Bouschet, 45–46; scuppernong, 51, 85; Thompson Seedless, 90; varieties used in home winemaking, 45–46, 79, 85
Great Britain, 41, 162, 215; colonial wine industries, 78; enlisted men's patronage of pubs in, 244; officers' mess in London, 243–244; promotion of brewers' yeast in, 162–163; reception of Black troops in, 264, 265, 266, 336n140; soldiers' liquor ration in, 258; whiskey prices and whiskey black markets in, 186, 191, 247
Great Depression, 3, 4; calls for protective wine tariffs during, 84; impact on alcohol sales, 42, 44; impact on global wine industry, 81–82; public relations campaigns during, 111, 131–133. *See also* Buy American campaigns
Greek Americans, 26
Green, Walter, 260
Greenwich Village, 49
Greig, Peter, 232
Griffith, D. W., 72

Haley, Andrew, 213
Hammett, Dashiell, 69
Hannickel, Erica, 76
Hatch, Harry, 47
Hatch, Ted, 219
Haworth, Mary, 159
Hearst, William Randolph, 46, 83
Hearst newspapers, 85–86
Heatter, Gabriel, 208
Heckman, Dayton E., 71–72
Henderson, Leon, 194
Henderson, Yandell, 25–26, 27–33, 39–40, 67
Henkel, Paul, 190, 191–192
Herzberg, David, 126
Herzog, Laurence, 132–133
heterosociability, 56, 60, 67
Hillis, Marjorie, 215
Hiram Walker, 47, 110, 133, 123, 180, 181, 229. *See also* Big Four distillers
Hitchcock, Gilbert, 22
Hitler, Adolph, 146, 251
Hobart, Alice Tisdale, 231
Hogarth, William, 105
Holt, Jane, 167
home economists: role as wine educators, 207, 208; role in promoting beer, 99, 101; role in promoting brewers' yeast, 166, 167; role in promoting wine cookery, 205, 206, 220–221

home winemaking: during Prohibition, 26–27, 45–46, 47, 49–51, 78, 84; after Prohibition, 85, 86, 202, 216
Hoover, Herbert, 51
Horne, Lena, 269
Hutton, E. F., 15

Imperial Scotch, 250, 251
industrial alcohol, 45, 171, 191–192, 195
International Brewery Workers' Union, 146
intoxication: euphemisms and coded language for, 24, 50, 120, 128; legal definitions of, 18, 22–23; scientific and medical understandings of, 25–31, 39–40, 122
Italian Americans, 15, 26, 49–50, 89, 278, 279; winemakers, 49–50, 76–78, 85
Italian-Swiss Colony winery, 26, 78, 229
Italy: enlisted men's encounters with alcoholic beverages in, 242, 243, 247, 248, 248fig; reception of Black troops in, 264; wine drinking customs in, 5, 9, 26, 46, 77–78; wine promotion in Fascist Italy, 81, 82, 293n72
It's a Wonderful Life, 278–280

jazz, 55–56, 279, 280
Jazz Age, 8, 18, 53, 55–56
Jefferson, Alexander, 261
Jefferson, Thomas, 74–75
Jennings, Richard, 262
Jewish Americans, 21, 35, 51, 72
Jim Crow, 259, 260, 264–266
Jones, Chester, 265, 266–267
Jones, Idwal, 231
Jones, James, 249, 250, 251
Jones, Marvin, 196
Jones Act, 83
J. Walter Thompson, 149, 150, 204, 208, 209

Keiss, Mary Jane, 227
Kennett, Lee, 246, 269
Kentucky, dry counties in, 61, 182
Knox, Frank, 146
K-ration, 249
Krauskopf, Joseph, 35
Ku Klux Klan, 37, 50

labor unions, 15, 29, 146. *See also* American Federation of Labor
Lane, Elizabeth, 225–226
Lanza, Horace, 50, 234

INDEX | 373

Lee, John Clifford Hodges, 266
Lee, Martha, 206
Leff, Mark, 190
leisure: critiques of mass recreation and nightlife, 55–57; ideals of, 56–57, 58
Lerner, Michael, 22
Lester, Eugene, 248
Levenstein, Harvey, 52
Levy, Alton, 263
Levy, Lee, 72
Lewis, Joe, 71
Lewis, Meade "Lux," 279
Lincoln Air Base, 263
Linderman, Gerald, 252
Liquor Control Board of Ontario, 64
Liquor Dealer's Association, 146, 190
liquor furloughs/holidays, 10–11, 173, 183, 186, 189–190, 324n131; advocacy by allied industries for, 190–192; government reluctance to grant, 194–196; impact on sales of other alcoholic beverages, 196–197; rationale for granting, 196, 199, 200
liquor stores: consumer retribution against, 187, 197; impact of liquor furlough on, 196–197; monitoring and prosecution of price control violations by, 187–188; promotion of wine by, 226–228, 229; racial discrimination by, 263–264; responses to whiskey shortages of, 178–179. *See also* alcoholic beverage regulations; state liquor stores
Little, Lawson, 208
local option elections, 68, 70–71, 72, 144, 145, 148, 149, 217, 276.
Longworth, Nicholas, 75–76, 93
Lord & Thomas, 131
Lost Weekend, The, 277–278
Louis, Joe, 71
Lusk, Graham, 25

Mabon, Mary Frost, 207, 220
MacGregor, Clifford, 98
Mackall, Lawton, 175, 189, 197, 207–208
Madeira, 76
Manischewitz, 85
Mardikian, George, 205
Marrus, Michael, 112
Marshall, George C., 254
Martini, Louis M., 89
Marvel, Tom, 80
masculinity: beer drinking and new visions of, 141, 145, 158; and constructions of the virtuous whiskey drinker, 106,

115–116, 121, 122–123, 125–126, 127fig; efforts to preserve homosocial world of male drinking, 60, 66–67; and gourmet culture, 224–225; and holding one's liquor, 121, 125–126; and sherry drinking, 209, 211fig; and war souvenirs-for-alcohol trade, 250; and wine cookery, 225–226; and wine drinking, 207–208
Matfaldi-Simon, 180
Mauldin, Bill, 247, 251, 258, 272, 334n93; cartoons by, 255, 256fig, 257fig, 258
Mauro, James, 132
McCarran, Pat, 183, 321n62
McCarran Committee, 183–184, 194, 196–197, 200
McCay, Clive, 167
McCurley, Lansing, 209
McDill Field, 261
McGirr, Lisa, 3, 37
McGovern, Charles, 155
McLachlin, Jessica, 52
Mead, Margaret, 154, 168
Médecins amis du vin, 81
Mencken, H. L., 66, 67–68
Methodists, 2, 57–58, 196
Mexican-American Company E, 247–248
middlebrow culture, 111, 208
Milland, Ray, 277
Miller, Max, 227
Miller Brewing Company, 49
Mills, Marjorie, 201–202, 220, 223
model license leagues, 109
moderation: alcoholic beverage industry's resistance to, 74, 103; conceptions of, 5, 6, 7–8, 73, 105–106; changing meanings of "true temperance," 20–21, 76, 77, 83; consumer resistance to, 74; gospel of beer, 93–94; gospel of wine, 74–80, 86; heterosociability as protector of, 56, 60, 67; muddled meanings of, 107, 119–121, 122–130, 133. *See also* women drinkers
moderation leagues, 19
Molera, J., 213
Molly Pitcher Clubs, 20
Montana liquor laws, 64
moonshine, 47
Morgenthau, Henry, 110, 190, 192; desire to make repeal work, 11, 173–174, 182–183, 321n59; response to whiskey black markets, 181, 182–184, 185, 187
Morris, Art, 227
Morton Sabin, Pauline, 20

Mosely, George, 122
Mothers Against Drunk Driving, 338n3

Naples, Italy, 242, 243, 247
Nash, Frances Leonard, 327n28
Nash, Odgen, 209, 327n28
National Council of State Liquor Dealers' Association, 146
National Distillers, 45, 134, 229. *See also* Big Four distillers
National Liquor Dealers' Association, 94
Native Americans, 2
Nazis, 146, 238
Nelson, Donald, 192, 194, 195, 196, 198
neoprohibitionism, 275
New Dealers, 84; as advocates of drinking reform, 53, 55–58, 92–93
New Deal liberalism, 10–11, 198–200
Newell-Emmett, 103
New York State Liquor Authority (NYSLA), 180, 191, 200
New York wine industry, 50, 51
New York World's Fair (1939–1940), 131–138, 205; alcoholic beverages sold at, 136–138; beer pavilions and restaurants at, 136–138; Distilled Spirits Institute exhibit at, 133–136; failure to recruit wine industry exhibitors, 326n13
Norton, Mary, 31
nutrition science, 30, 144, 164–168

O'Connell, John, 180, 191, 200
O'Connor, John J., 37
O'Connor Bill, 22
Office of Price Administration (OPA), 200; criticisms of liquor retailers' forced tie-in sales, 179; policy debates over response to whiskey black markets, 10, 181–182, 184–186, 198; response to prohibitionists, 194; role in policing liquor price control violations, 187–188.
Office of War Information, 150
Ohio wine industry, 50, 233
Okrent, Daniel, 46
Old Grand Dad, 254
Omar Khayyam restaurant, 205
Oran, Algeria, 242
Osborn, Frederick H., 260
Osborne, Oliver T., 29
Otis & Lee liquor store, 227
Ottley, Roi, 264, 265, 266
Owen, Jeanne, 208

Pabst Brewing Company, 34, 49, 94, 95, 96
package stores. *See* state liquor stores
Parrish, Homer, 281–282
Parsons, Elaine Frantz, 125
Paul, Albert, 89
Pauly, Philip, 39
Pennsylvania Liquor Board, 230
Peoples, Henry, 264
Petri Wine Co., 229
Peyser, Jefferson, 91–92
Philippines: reception of Black troops in, 267
Piel, William, 97
pleasure: as key to wartime morale, 148, 153–154; defense of, 18, 30, 32–35, 39–40; nutrition-centered cooking as enemy of, 223–225; politics of, 40, 99, 104, 239, 253, 268, 272–273, 284; valorization of gastronomic pleasure, 219–220, 222*fig*, 223–226; white racial anxieties about, 30, 31, 224
pleasure revolution, 6, 8, 11–12, 224, 225, 268
Port Moresby, Papua New Guinea, 246
Prendergast and Davies, 47
price controls: impact on wine quality, 216–217; rationale for, 172–173, 185–186; evasions of, 179
Progressive Era, 57, 78, 99, 122, 148
Prohibition (1920–1933): changing alcohol preferences during, 48–52; heavy drinking during, 31–32; impact on working class, 19–20, 29; in popular memory, 3; jury nullification of, 50; Ku Klux Klan vigilantism during, 50; more restrictive than other countries, 18; poisoned alcohol, 20, 290n12; sacramental wine market, 51, 84; urban nightlife during, 56; violations of, 2, 56. *See also* bootlegging; cocktails; home winemaking; Prohibition's legacies; Volstead Act
Prohibition Bureau, 27
prohibitionists, 1–2, 33, 94, 96; analysis of causes of problem drinking, 113, 115, 116, 119; continuing political influence after repeal, 57–58, 61, 63–66, 68, 101–102, 104, 276; criticisms of alcoholic beverage industry after repeal, 68–69, 101–102, 104; demands to halt wartime whiskey production, 194; maternalist rhetoric of, 145–148; nativism of, 40, 72, 76, 78; opposition to legalizing beer and light wines, 24,

29, 30–31, 35–36, 37–38; opposition to liquor furlough, 190; post-repeal regulations proposed by, 63; racism of, 71–72, 261–262; women prohibitionists, 6, 37–38, 54, 217; support for bans on alcohol advertising, 169–170; support for exemptions in Volstead Act, 26, 49; support for alcohol prohibitions during World War II, 8, 138, 142–143, 145–148, 149–150, 155, 217, 272; support for prohibition as food conservation measure, 143, 144, 145, 161–162. *See also* Anti-Saloon League; Woman's Christian Temperance Union
Prohibition Party, 162
Prohibition's legacies: economic and reputational impact on alcoholic beverage industry, 42–48; historiography of, 3; impact on restaurants and dining, 52; impact on sensory perceptions of taste, 42, 48–49, 51–53, 84; impact on wine quality, 46
public drinking, 42, 64–67, 71–72
Pure Food and Drug Act, 107–109
Pyle, Ernie, 239–245, 246

Quartermaster Corps, 168

Rankin, Dorothy, 208
Rathbone, Basil, 208, 327b28
Reconstruction Finance Corporation, 92
Reinarman, Craig, 9
Renault & Sons, 86, 87fig
Repeal Associates, 147
repeal of Prohibition, 85, 137, 145, 173, 196, 271–272, 275–276; assessments of repeal's successes and failures in 1930s, 67–72; campaign for, 3, 17, 19–21, 22, 62, 79, 83, 199; conservatism of, 4–5, 53–54, 68–69, 276, 300n117; as a defining generational event, 270–272; economic arguments for, 21, 290n22; historiography of, 39–40, 143, 173, 198; international responses to, 41; scientists' and physicians' contributions to, 39–40
Republican Party, 20, 21, 36
restaurants: Armenian American, 204; bottled beer regulations, 22, 34–35; dominance of cocktails in, 212–213, 215; imported wines on menu, 212–214; Italian American, 49, 52; Prohibition's impact on, 52; regulation of on-premises alcohol sales, 61, 65; efforts to popularize wine drinking in, 137, 203, 204, 205, 212–214; promotion of American wines in, 137, 213
Reydel, William, 103
Richardson, Eudora, 54
Richardson, William, 109
Rockefeller Jr., John D., 62
Rockefeller Report (*Toward Liquor Control*), 39, 62–63
Rockwell, Norman, 149, 151, 156, 158, 208, 280
Roma Winery, 228–229
Roosevelt, Eleanor, 58
Roosevelt, Franklin Delano, 11, 36, 58, 182, 196; *Yank* magazine tribute to, 271–272
Roosevelt Administration: support for drinking reform, 41–42, 53–58; support for liquor furlough, 196, 199
Rosemond, Nacho, 249
Rosenstiel, Lewis, 47, 111, 130, 134, 277
Rossi, Edmund A., 26, 33, 78
Rossi, Pietro Carlo, 76
Rossi, Robert, 78, 85
Rotskoff, Lori, 115
Rubin, Jay, 143
rum, 138, 175, 177, 196–197
Ruppert, Jacob, 27–28, 95, 97, 98
Rush, Benjamin, 75
Russek, Audrey, 215
Rydell, Robert, 131

Sabath, Adolph, 21
Sad Sack comic strip, 255
saloons: culture of, 125; post-repeal efforts to banish, 61, 64–65, 66, 68, 138; tied-house, 68, 96–97; women's presence in, 54. *See also* brewing industry
Sbarboro, Andrea, 76–78, 93
Schaefer, Rudolph, 97
Schenley Distillers, 111, 132, 134; advertising by, 123, 130–131; operations during Prohibition, 45, 47, 110; deteriorating quality of wartime whiskey, 191; and New York World's Fair, 132, 134; wartime acquisitions of distilleries and wineries, 180, 229. *See also* Big Four distillers
Schenley Reserve Black Label, 191
Schlitz Brewing Company, 34, 49, 95, 96, 97, 98
Schlitz Palm Garden, 136–137
Schoonmaker, Frank, 80, 232

Schupp, Orville, 195
Schwengel, Frank, 117, 134, 136, 192
Scotch, 110, 250, 251
Scott, Albert, 62–63
Scribner, Charles, 20
Seagram Company: acquisition of California wineries, 229; equivalency campaign (1984–1985), 119, 274–275; guidance to liquor retailers, 180, 188; moderation campaign, 106, 107, 110–113, 114*fig*, 115–117, 118–119, 120–121, 128, 130, 131, 277–278; New York World's Fair exhibit proposed by, 134, 136; promotion of *The Lost Weekend*, 277; response to liquor furlough, 324n131. *See also* Big Four distillers; Calvert whiskey
Seagram's 7 Crown Whiskey, 119–120, 122–125, 124*fig*
Seagram's VO Whiskey, 254
Seldes, Gilbert, 59–60, 79–80
Selfridge Field, 261
Setrakian, Arpaxat, 92
Sheppard, Morris, 17, 145
Sheppard bill (S860), 145–147
Shoub, Mac, 130
Smith, Robert Layton, 79
Society of Medical Friends of Wine, 82–83
Society of Restaurateurs, 190
Soviet Union, wine promotion in, 81, 82
Stafford, William, 33
Stars and Stripes, 253, 254, 255, 256*fig*, 257*fig*
state liquor administrators, 181, 187
state liquor stores, 64, 65*fig*, 177–178, 261. *See also* liquor stores
Steinbeck, John, 208, 212
Stella beer, 245
Stephenson, Al, 281–282
Stimson, Henry, 143, 146
Stitzel Distillers, 45
Stoll Jr., H.F., 52, 88–89
Sturkey, Christopher, 267
Sunkist Growers, 89
Sun-Maid Raisin Company, 88
Sutter's Gold, 86
synthetic rubber program, 171, 188, 195–196, 199, 217

Taft, Howard, 108
taste, consumers' sensory perceptions of: impact of Prohibition on, 42, 48–49, 51–53, 84; distillers' efforts to retrain, 7, 106, 117–118; California winemakers' efforts to retrain and adapt to, 7, 214, 230–231, 234
Tavern Leagues, 190
taverns: criticisms of, 68, 71–72; cultivation of respectable image, 66; racial discrimination by, 263. *See also* alcoholic beverage regulations; brewing industry
Taylor, Mary, 219–220, 223
temperance movements and societies, 9, 75, 77, 105–106, 117
tequila, 175, 323n105
Thin Man, The, 69
Toles, Edward, 247
Tom Collins, 249
Torrio, John, 47
Touhig, D.T., 212
Treasury Department, 10, 102, 171; efforts to eradicate illicit distilling, 182; initial reluctance to police liquor markets, 181; proposed punitive actions to end whiskey shortage, 180, 183–184, 186, 198
Truman, Harry S., 22
Tugwell, Rexford, 41–42, 55, 56–58, 63
Turano, Anthony, 66, 68
Twenty-First Amendment, 3, 17, 41, 42–43, 58, 60, 63, 173
Tye, Larry, 69

United Brewers Industrial Foundation (UBIF): collaboration with allied trades, 101; courtship of women consumers, 98–99, 101; criticisms of public relations campaign, 101–104; public relations campaign of, 97–98, 99, 101; tavern regulation work, 103
United States Brewers Association (USBA), 69–70, 93, 94–95, 97, 98, 149
United States Brewers' Foundation (USBF): appeals to rural voters, 149–151; "Beer Belongs" campaign, 156, 157*fig*, 280; courtship of women consumers, 159; end of collective advertising campaign, 283; Home Life in American campaign, 158; Joe Marsh column, 149–151, 154, 155, 156, 158–160; "Morale Is a Lot of Little Things" campaign, 141, 142*fig*, 151, 152*fig*, 154; role in regulating taverns, 322n91
United States Committee on Public Information, 69
United States Department of Agriculture, 41, 166

United States military: basic training, 236; censorship of journalists by, 241, 265; reforms in treatment of Black troops, 267–268; policies sanctioning racial discrimination off base, 260, 263, 263, 266; meat allocated to, 221; racial conflict in, 238, 259-268; racial segregation in, 11, 160, 237-238, 259-261; pocket guides to European cities, 268; provisioning of cigarettes, 144, 147, 236, 252; requisitioning of raisin grapes by, 202, 216, 234; treatment of German POWs, 262; use of brewers' yeast in rations by, 168, 169

United States military, alcoholic beverage policies: 3.2 percent beer in PX stores, 11, 146–147, 236, 238, 242, 245–246, 252, 262; alcohol allotted to officers, 11, 237, 243; edicts against looting, 251; efforts to curb drunkenness, 252; failure to minimize excessive drinking, 245, 252, 258; influence of prohibitionists' on, 236, 242, 246, 258; more restrictive than other countries, 236, 258; opposition to banning 3.2 percent beer, 146–147, 182; public statements on soldiers' sobriety, 150, 243; role in combatting profiteering in liquor trade, 187–188, 322n91;

United States Supreme Court, 22, 27

US Navy Seabees, 237*fig*

Van Nuys, Frederick, 321n62
Vargas, Albert, 225
Veit, Helen Zoe, 30, 144
Vine-Glo grape concentrate, 51
Vino Sano Grape Brick, 50, 297n54
Virginia Dare wine, 51
vitamin B, 10, 164, 166,
V-J Day, 197, 271*fig*
Volstead Act, 54; definition of "intoxicating" in, 17–18, 27; medicinal whiskey exemption, 45, 47; Section 29 (fermented fruit juice clause), 26–27, 45–46, 49, 51
Volstead Act, proposals to modify, 15–17, 18, 19, 21, 79, 83; bills legalizing beer and wine, 21–22; Congressional hearings on (1932–1933), 17–18, 21–35, 39, 122, 275; defense of beer as nonintoxicating, 23–24, 27–31; defense of wine as nonintoxicating, 24–27; opponents of, 24, 30–31, 35–36

Walker, Jimmy, 15
Wallace, Henry, 164

Ware, Caroline, 49
War Food Administration (WFA), 181, 184, 194–195, 196
War Production Board (WPB), 153, 181, 192, 194, 195, 198
Warren, Earl, 92
Webb-Kenyon Act, 94
Webster, David, 251
Weiner, Mark, 150–151
Welcome, Ann, 206
Wente, Ernest, 295n8
Wente, Herman, 204–205
Whalen, Grover, 132, 136
Wheeler, Wayne, 27
whiskey: aging shortcuts, 44; high status of, 10, 177, 186, 253–254, 269, 277, 283; hoarding of, 177; low quality after Prohibition, 43, 110, 118; low quality during World War II, 175, 190–191; as marker of class respectability, 107, 116, 123, 126, 283; as marker of whiteness and white privilege, 112, 253, 261, 269; as masculine drink, 6, 112, 133, 192, 194, 250, 253, 263, 283; as scapegoat for problem drinking, 7, 23, 33–34; representation in film of, 278, 281; value as barter currency on battlefront, 250
whiskey black markets: bootlegging rings and liquor traffickers, 178, 185; impact on whiskey prices, 174, 333n47; policy debates over, 171–174, 181–186; wholesalers' involvement in, 178, 179; retailers' evasions of price controls, 179
whiskey industry. *See* distilled spirits industry
Whiskey Ring, 136
whiskey shortages during World War II: causes of, 171, 174–175, 177–178; GIs' interest in news about, 238; proposed solutions to, 183–184; public complaints about, 10, 171, 178–179, 180, 181, 182; Senate Judiciary investigation of, 183, 191. *See also* McCarran Committee
Whiskey Trust, 135–136
whiskey types: blended, 52, 108, 110, 121–126, 124*fig*, 127*fig*, 128, 129*fig*, 191, 196; competing claims about whiskey purity, 108–109, 122, 123; rectified, 108–109; straights, 108–109, 110–111, 123. *See also* Scotch
Whitaker, Alma, 59
White, Wilbur, 24

white enlisted men: cigarette consumption by, 242; drinking 3.2 percent beer by, 236, 237fig, 242, 245–246, 247, 254, 271fig, 276–277; drinking during Civil War by, 334n82, 334n92; encounters with alcoholic beverages in the European theater, 242, 243, 246–249, 269–270; encounters with alcoholic beverages in the Pacific theater, 249–251, 254; excessive drinking by, 237, 249, 252; experience of alcohol scarcity, 243, 244, 249; gripe letters by, 253–254; illicit alcohol made and consumed by, 238, 246, 247, 249, 251–252, 258; alcohol looting by, 251; participation in war souvenirs-for-whiskey trade, 249–250; protests against segregation, 267; racist treatment of Black military personnel, 262, 265–267, 337n140; resentment of inequitable access to alcoholic beverages, 241, 250, 252–258, 259, 270, 272; satirical cartoons by, 255–258; use of alcohol to structure time, 250–251; yearnings for beer, 238, 241, 245; yearnings for whiskey, 238, 272. *See also* GIs

white officers: alcohol supplied in officers' mess, 237, 243–244; drinking during the Civil War by, 334n82; greater access to alcohol, 241, 253, 254; racist treatment of Black military personnel, 261, 265, 266; as targets of enlisted men's resentment, 253, 254, 255, 257fig, 258

Wilder, Marshall, 76
Wilder, Russell M., 164, 166
Wiley, Anna Kelton, 292n56.
Wiley, Harvey, 109, 292n56.
Willebrandt, Mabel Walker, 51
Wilson, Edmund, 24
Wilson, Robert E., 253–254
Wilson, Woodrow, 22, 31, 58
wine: advice on serving, 59–60; and American identity, 86–88, 87fig, 203, 206–207, 213–215, 278; athletes' consumption of, 208–209; as a beverage of moderation and conviviality, 31–33, 208–209, 210fig, 211fig; changing consumer preferences for, 48–53, 84–85; as a condiment, 214, 220; as a cooking aid, 202–204, 218–221, 222fig, 223–228, 230, 276, 283; as a food, 25–26, 86; gospel of wine, 75, 76, 77–78, 91, 93; low quality of, 43, 44–45, 234, 295n8, 296n27; as a marker of respectability and whiteness, 59, 60, 79, 208–209, 210fig, 211fig, 280, 283; as a mealtime beverage, 10, 26, 29, 31, 58, 77–78, 216, 220; as a morale booster, 217, 226; obstacles to achieving mass market success, 6, 202–203, 212–214; protective tariffs on, 84, 212; representation in films of, 278, 279; sales of, 84, 216, 232–234, 276, 277, 283. *See also* home winemaking; restaurants; wine types

Wine Advisory Board (WAB): collective advertising campaign, 208–209, 210fig, 211fig, 222fig, 226, 283; courtship of women consumers, 208–209, 210fig, 220–221; creation of, 204; efforts to demystify wine, 203, 206–207, 232, 268; merchandising materials, 204, 205, 230; promotion of wine cookery, 207, 220, 221, 222fig, 223, 224, 226, 227; training for restaurants, waitstaff, 214; use of celebrity endorsers, 208–209, 210fig, 211fig; *Wine Cook Book,* 205, 207

Wine and Food Society, 60, 73, 212
wine bricks, 50, 128
wine connoisseurs, representations of, 73, 80, 206–207, 212, 219, 225
Wine Drive for America, 92, 204, 205, 206
wine-halls, 56, 57
Wine Institute, 52, 69, 75, 78, 80–81, 205, 274; Buy California campaigns of, 86–88; collaboration with allied industries, 86; cultivation of wine industry's agrarian mystique, 91–92, 228–232; efforts to demystify wine, 206–207, 232; formation of, 80; lobbying to permit wine sales in grocery stores, 233; objections to use of term "fortified," 331n127; promotion of wine quality standards, 81; relationship with food writers and novelists, 226, 231; support for cooperative advertising, 91–92; wine study correspondence course, 229–231

wine nomenclature, 229–231; opposition to use of term "fortified," 230–231, 331n127

Wine Temple, 205–206
wine types: American vintners' use of European place names, 206; appetizer and dessert wines, 84, 90, 207–208, 233; fortified wines, 25, 84, 90, 230, 231; light wines, defined, 24–25; light

sweet wines, 234, 332n142; table wines, 84, 90, 216, 230, 231, 233, 234
Winters, Dick, 249, 251
Woll, Matthew, 29, 31
Woman's Christian Temperance Union, 8, 37, 57, 77, 145
women drinkers: advice on hospitality, 58–59; ads targeting, 283; anxieties about, 66–67, 71; as bargoers and bartenders, 66–67, 71, 279; courtship by liquor stores, 227–228; as guardians of responsible drinking, 5, 6, 42, 53–55, 58–59; during Prohibition, 2, 54; negative depictions of, 54, 59–60; in nineteenth century, 54
Women's National Democratic Club, 41–42, 55
Women's Organization for National Prohibition Reform (WONPR), 20–21, 55
World War I, 27, 28, 36, 69; food conservation campaigns during, 144, 161; prohibition campaign during, 8, 143, 147–148

World War II, 3, 4; calls for consumer sacrifice during, 141, 153–154; and civil rights activism, 259–260, 262–263, 267, 268, 272–273; conservation of scarce resources during, 148; image as the "good war," 244–245; impact on preferences in alcoholic beverages, 268–269, 270*fig*; morale management during, 8–9, 141, 153; official propaganda, 259; shortages of food and other goods, 10, 138, 174, 201; resurgence of prohibitionism during, 8, 138, 142–143, 145–148, 149–150; wartime food crusades, 10, 151, 161–162, 164, 166, 201–202, 203–204, 217–218, 220, 221
Wylie, Philip, 147
Wynne, Shirley, 43

Yank, 249, 253, 254, 255, 269, 271–272
Young, Katherine, 49

Zoot Suit Riots, 262
Zwillman, Abner, 47

CALIFORNIA STUDIES IN FOOD AND CULTURE

Darra Goldstein, Editor

1. *Dangerous Tastes: The Story of Spices*, by Andrew Dalby
2. *Eating Right in the Renaissance*, by Ken Albala
3. *Food Politics: How the Food Industry Influences Nutrition and Health*, by Marion Nestle
4. *Camembert: A National Myth*, by Pierre Boisard
5. *Safe Food: The Politics of Food Safety*, by Marion Nestle
6. *Eating Apes*, by Dale Peterson
7. *Revolution at the Table: The Transformation of the American Diet*, by Harvey Levenstein
8. *Paradox of Plenty: A Social History of Eating in Modern America*, by Harvey Levenstein
9. *Encarnación's Kitchen: Mexican Recipes from Nineteenth-Century California: Selections from Encarnación Pinedo's* El cocinero español, by Encarnación Pinedo, edited and translated by Dan Strehl, with an essay by Victor Valle
10. *Zinfandel: A History of a Grape and Its Wine*, by Charles L. Sullivan, with a foreword by Paul Draper
11. *Tsukiji: The Fish Market at the Center of the World*, by Theodore C. Bestor
12. *Born Again Bodies: Flesh and Spirit in American Christianity*, by R. Marie Griffith
13. *Our Overweight Children: What Parents, Schools, and Communities Can Do to Control the Fatness Epidemic*, by Sharron Dalton
14. *The Art of Cooking: The First Modern Cookery Book*, by the Eminent Maestro Martino of Como, edited and with an introduction by Luigi Ballerini, translated and annotated by Jeremy Parzen, and with fifty modernized recipes by Stefania Barzini
15. *The Queen of Fats: Why Omega-3s Were Removed from the Western Diet and What We Can Do to Replace Them*, by Susan Allport
16. *Meals to Come: A History of the Future of Food*, by Warren Belasco
17. *The Spice Route: A History*, by John Keay
18. *Medieval Cuisine of the Islamic World: A Concise History with 174 Recipes*, by Lilia Zaouali, translated by M. B. DeBevoise, with a foreword by Charles Perry
19. *Arranging the Meal: A History of Table Service in France*, by Jean-Louis Flandrin, translated by Julie E. Johnson, with Sylvie and Antonio Roder; with a foreword to the English-language edition by Beatrice Fink
20. *The Taste of Place: A Cultural Journey into Terroir*, by Amy B. Trubek
21. *Food: The History of Taste*, edited by Paul Freedman
22. *M. F. K. Fisher among the Pots and Pans: Celebrating Her Kitchens*, by Joan Reardon, with a foreword by Amanda Hesser
23. *Cooking: The Quintessential Art*, by Hervé This and Pierre Gagnaire, translated by M. B. DeBevoise
24. *Perfection Salad: Women and Cooking at the Turn of the Century*, by Laura Shapiro
25. *Of Sugar and Snow: A History of Ice Cream Making*, by Jeri Quinzio

26. *Encyclopedia of Pasta*, by Oretta Zanini De Vita, translated by Maureen B. Fant, with a foreword by Carol Field
27. *Tastes and Temptations: Food and Art in Renaissance Italy*, by John Varriano
28. *Free for All: Fixing School Food in America*, by Janet Poppendieck
29. *Breaking Bread: Recipes and Stories from Immigrant Kitchens*, by Lynne Christy Anderson, with a foreword by Corby Kummer
30. *Culinary Ephemera: An Illustrated History*, by William Woys Weaver
31. *Eating Mud Crabs in Kandahar: Stories of Food during Wartime by the World's Leading Correspondents*, edited by Matt McAllester
32. *Weighing In: Obesity, Food Justice, and the Limits of Capitalism*, by Julie Guthman
33. *Why Calories Count: From Science to Politics*, by Marion Nestle and Malden Nesheim
34. *Curried Cultures: Globalization, Food, and South Asia*, edited by Krishnendu Ray and Tulasi Srinivas
35. *The Cookbook Library: Four Centuries of the Cooks, Writers, and Recipes That Made the Modern Cookbook*, by Anne Willan, with Mark Cherniavsky and Kyri Claflin
36. *Coffee Life in Japan*, by Merry White
37. *American Tuna: The Rise and Fall of an Improbable Food*, by Andrew F. Smith
38. *A Feast of Weeds: A Literary Guide to Foraging and Cooking Wild Edible Plants*, by Luigi Ballerini, translated by Gianpiero W. Doebler, with recipes by Ada De Santis and illustrations by Giuliano Della Casa
39. *The Philosophy of Food*, by David M. Kaplan
40. *Beyond Hummus and Falafel: Social and Political Aspects of Palestinian Food in Israel*, by Liora Gvion, translated by David Wesley and Elana Wesley
41. *The Life of Cheese: Crafting Food and Value in America*, by Heather Paxson
42. *Popes, Peasants, and Shepherds: Recipes and Lore from Rome and Lazio*, by Oretta Zanini De Vita, translated by Maureen B. Fant, foreword by Ernesto Di Renzo
43. *Cuisine and Empire: Cooking in World History*, by Rachel Laudan
44. *Inside the California Food Revolution: Thirty Years That Changed Our Culinary Consciousness*, by Joyce Goldstein, with Dore Brown
45. *Cumin, Camels, and Caravans: A Spice Odyssey*, by Gary Paul Nabhan
46. *Balancing on a Planet: The Future of Food and Agriculture*, by David A. Cleveland
47. *The Darjeeling Distinction: Labor and Justice on Fair-Trade Tea Plantations in India*, by Sarah Besky
48. *How the Other Half Ate: A History of Working-Class Meals at the Turn of the Century*, by Katherine Leonard Turner
49. *The Untold History of Ramen: How Political Crisis in Japan Spawned a Global Food Craze*, by George Solt
50. *Word of Mouth: What We Talk About When We Talk About Food*, by Priscilla Parkhurst Ferguson
51. *Inventing Baby Food: Taste, Health, and the Industrialization of the American Diet*, by Amy Bentley

52. *Secrets from the Greek Kitchen: Cooking, Skill, and Everyday Life on an Aegean Island,* by David E. Sutton
53. *Breadlines Knee-Deep in Wheat: Food Assistance in the Great Depression,* by Janet Poppendieck
54. *Tasting French Terroir: The History of an Idea,* by Thomas Parker
55. *Becoming Salmon: Aquaculture and the Domestication of a Fish,* by Marianne Elisabeth Lien
56. *Divided Spirits: Tequila, Mezcal, and the Politics of Production,* by Sarah Bowen
57. *The Weight of Obesity: Hunger and Global Health in Postwar Guatemala,* by Emily Yates-Doerr
58. *Dangerous Digestion: The Politics of American Dietary Advice,* by E. Melanie DuPuis
59. *A Taste of Power: Food and American Identities,* by Katharina Vester
60. *More Than Just Food: Food Justice and Community Change,* by Garrett M. Broad
61. *Hoptopia: A World of Agriculture and Beer in Oregon's Willamette Valley,* by Peter A. Kopp
62. *A Geography of Digestion: Biotechnology and the Kellogg Cereal Enterprise,* by Nicholas Bauch
63. *Bitter and Sweet: Food, Meaning, and Modernity in Rural China,* by Ellen Oxfeld
64. *A History of Cookbooks: From Kitchen to Page over Seven Centuries,* by Henry Notaker
65. *Reinventing the Wheel: Milk, Microbes, and the Fight for Real Cheese,* by Bronwen Percival and Francis Percival
66. *Making Modern Meals: How Americans Cook Today,* by Amy B. Trubek
67. *Food and Power: A Culinary Ethnography of Israel,* by Nir Avieli
68. *Canned: The Rise and Fall of Consumer Confidence in the American Food Industry,* by Anna Zeide
69. *Meat Planet: Artificial Flesh and the Future of Food,* by Benjamin Aldes Wurgaft
70. *The Labor of Lunch: Why We Need Real Food and Real Jobs in American Public Schools,* by Jennifer E. Gaddis
71. *Feeding the Crisis: Care and Abandonment in America's Food Safety Net,* by Maggie Dickinson
72. *Sameness in Diversity: Food and Globalization in Modern America,* by Laresh Jayasanker
73. *The Fruits of Empire: Art, Food, and the Politics of Race in the Age of American Expansion,* by Shana Klein
74. *Let's Ask Marion: What You Need to Know about the Politics of Food, Nutrition, and Health,* by Marion Nestle, in conversation with Kerry Trueman
75. *The Scarcity Slot: Excavating Histories of Food Security in Ghana,* by Amanda L. Logan
76. *Gastropolitics and the Specter of Race: Stories of Capital, Culture, and Coloniality in Peru,* by María Elena García
77. *The Kingdom of Rye: A Brief History of Russian Food,* by Darra Goldstein
78. *Slow Cooked: An Unexpected Life in Food Politics,* by Marion Nestle

79. *Yerba Mate: The Drink That Shaped a Nation*, by Julia J. S. Sarreal
80. *Wonder Foods: The Science and Commerce of Nutrition*, by Lisa Haushofer
81. *Ways of Eating: Exploring Food through History and Culture*, by Benjamin A. Wurgaft and Merry I. White
82. *From Label to Table: Regulating Food in America in the Information Age*, by Xaq Frohlich
83. *Intoxicating Pleasures: The Reinvention of Wine, Beer, and Whiskey after Prohibition*, by Lisa Jacobson

Founded in 1893,
UNIVERSITY OF CALIFORNIA PRESS
publishes bold, progressive books and journals
on topics in the arts, humanities, social sciences,
and natural sciences—with a focus on social
justice issues—that inspire thought and action
among readers worldwide.

The UC PRESS FOUNDATION
raises funds to uphold the press's vital role
as an independent, nonprofit publisher, and
receives philanthropic support from a wide
range of individuals and institutions—and from
committed readers like you. To learn more, visit
ucpress.edu/supportus.

www.ingramcontent.com/pod-product-compliance
Lightning Source LLC
Chambersburg PA
CBHW021333230426
43666CB00006B/284